MASTERING
ADOBE
ILLUSTRATOR®

MASTERING
ADOBE
ILLUSTRATOR®

MACINTOSH® **3.0** VERSION

BUSINESS ONE IRWIN
Desktop Publishing Library

Homewood, IL 60430

Deke McClelland

Sponsoring editor: Susan Glinert Stevens, Ph.D.
Project editor: Becky Dodson
Production manager: Ann Cassady
Printer: R. R. Donnelley & Sons Company

Library of Congress Cataloging-in-Publication Data

McClelland, Deke, 1962–
    Mastering Adobe Illustrator, Macintosh 3.0 version / Deke McClelland.
        p.   cm.
    Includes index.
    ISBN 1–55623–442–2
    1. Desktop publishing. 2. Adobe illustrator (Computer program)
3. Macintosh (Computer)—Programming. 4. Computer Graphics.
I. Title.
Z286.D47M3753   1991
686.2′2544536—dc20   90–19544

Printed in the United States of America

3 4 5 6 7 8 9 0 DO 7 6 5 4 3 2 1

Acknowledgements

Thank you to the following people
for helping in the creation of this book:

Bill Gladstone, Susan Glinert, Craig Danuloff

R.D., S.R., J.G., A.E., and J.M.

Kathi Townes of TechArts for copy editing

Tom Midgley and Susan Janow for imagesetting

Russell McDougal for photography

LaVon Collins, Paul Towner, and Kathy Mandle for product

John Brand, Tony Kulesa, and Jerry for technical support

Elizabeth Pheasant for the index and marriage

Mom, Dad, Denise, and Dan for everything else

Contents

Chapter 7:
Reshaping Existing Paths 205

Chapter 8:
Creating and Editing Type 259

Chapter 12:
Transforming and Duplicating Objects   409

Mastering
Adobe
Illustrator

When it was first released in 1987, Adobe Illustrator was a graphic arts tool without equal. Unlike anything that had come before it, Illustrator applied the power of the personal computer to the full range of artistic expression: suddenly technical illustrations, logotypes, business graphics, fine art, product illustrations, and countless other forms could be created on an affordable computer system with uncompromisingly professional results.

1

Illustrator was unique and powerful because it removed the artificial constraints that had previously plagued affordable computer-graphics tools—the trade-offs between power, precision, and performance. With its Bézier curve drawing model, its fantastic range of manipulative tools, and its ability to produce truly professional-quality output, Adobe Illustrator provided an incredible tool to anyone with the need or desire to produce high-quality artwork.

That was then; this is two versions later. With Illustrator 3.0, Adobe is again turning heads. New path-editing tools, charting capabilities, enhanced keyboard control, 24-bit monitor compatibility, and a vast array of powerful type-handling features have been added to the capabilities provided in the original program. Illustrator 3.0 allows users who have been taking advantage of previous versions of the software to expand their capabilities and allows new users to benefit from the success and experience of a powerful industry leader.

About this book

With the power of Adobe Illustrator 3.0 comes responsibility. Although the package adheres strictly to all the friendly interface guidelines required of a Macintosh application and is basically straightforward and easy to use, you will get the full benefit of this software only if you *master* it. This means becoming familiar with the drawing model on which Illustrator is based; understanding the tools, commands, and dialog box options that Illustrator provides; and gaining hands-on experience by completing a wide variety of quick but informative exercises. *Mastering Adobe Illustrator* is dedicated to the relentless, exhaustive delivery of this knowledge!

In the chapters that follow, you will find each of the concepts, features, and functions of Illustrator described completely, including functional descriptions required by novices, advice aimed at intermediate users, and advanced discussions demanded by power-users. Throughout, *Mastering Adobe Illustrator* adopts the viewpoint of the user. In addition to objective, technical details, Illustrator's strengths and weaknesses are considered, what to avoid and what to rely on. In every manner possible, this book captures the insights born from years of artistic and computing experience, with the hope that *Mastering Adobe Illustrator* will become your personal Illustrator 3.0 trainer, providing both bookwise details *and* street-smart tips and tricks.

Conventions

This book employs the following conventions to make it easier for you to understand Adobe Illustrator 3.0 and to glean useful information without slogging through a lot of words:

 The *keyboard equivalent icon* calls out commands, options, and other features that can be accessed from the keyboard, allowing you to increase your speed and devote your mouse hand to the more important task of drawing.

The *power tips icon* calls out tips. Not press-this-key-to-get-this tips, but real, honest-to-goodness thoughtful tips that will improve your drawing capability by leaps and bounds. If you didn't think it was possible to do something with Illustrator, we'll show you how.

We don't like everything about Adobe Illustrator, and the *gripe icon* allows us to share our complaints. Sometimes, our gripes come in the form of warnings or advice; sometimes, we're just plain upset. And for those of you who have access to more than one drawing program, we'll let you know if that other program does a better job.

Chapter summaries

Mastering Adobe Illustrator is composed of 15 chapters, two appendices, and an index. The following is a summarization of their contents:

- **Chapter 1** looks at the concepts behind graphic creation in programs like Adobe Illustrator. In this discussion we provide a brief history of the development of computer graphics on the Apple Macintosh using applications like MacPaint, MacDraw, and Adobe Illustrator 1.1.

- **Chapter 2** opens with a glossary of basic Macintosh terminology, followed by a comprehensive tour of the Illustrator toolbox and menu commands. This chapter is designed to familiarize you with the software in case you want to begin using Illustrator 3.0 immediately. If you are an experienced Macintosh user, you will probably be able to begin creating graphics after a brief survey of this chapter. If you are new to Macintosh or to this type of graphics application, this chapter will provide a thorough introduction to your new tools.

- **Chapter 3** discusses how to create a new illustration or open an existing illustration in Illustrator, including how to introduce, use, and change tracing templates. We take a brief tour through Illustrator's on-screen environment, including view sizes and page setup. We also introduce the PREFERENCES dialog box, Illustrator's central control station. The chapter finishes by addressing the topics of saving your illustration and quitting the application.

- **Chapter 4** uses a conceptual tutorial to focus on the strategy used to draw complex graphics in Illustrator. Here, the creation of a sample illustration is approached from an entirely theoretical vantage; no specific commands or tools are discussed. Instead, this chapter addresses the thought process required to solve electronic drawing problems. This chapter will be beneficial to both the novice and the experienced graphic creator.

- **Chapter 5** examines how to draw geometric and free-form images from scratch using the rectangle and oval tools, the freehand tool, and the all-powerful pen tool. Here's everything you ever wanted to know about point and path theory, but were afraid to ask.

- **Chapter 6** looks at tracing bitmapped and scanned images. If you can't draw, you can trace using the autotrace tool. And if you own or are thinking of purchasing Adobe Streamline, this is the only book in existence that describes how to use it.

- **Chapter 7** focuses on the manipulation of existing lines and shapes. Everything in Illustrator can be molded and reshaped to your heart's desire. We look first at moving points and segments and measuring distances. We next turn our attention to three new tools for adding, subtracting, and converting points. Finally, you will learn all there is to know about Bézier control handles.

- **Chapter 8** is a chapter that should excite familiar and new users alike. This is where we get down to Illustrator's new text features, most of which are too good to believe. We explain how to create type on a point, in a path, and on a path. Want to import type? No problem. Want to wrap it around a graphic? That's easy, too. Want to convert it to a path and manipulate it until it doesn't even look like text any more? Check out Chapter 8.

- **Chapter 9** is about fills. The chapter starts out easy, but then we turn on the steam with exhaustive discussions of tile patterns, clipping paths, and compound paths. These last items, completely new to Illustrator 3.0, allow you to cut holes in objects so you can see the doily through the doughnut.

- **Chapter 10** is about the other side of the painting coin—strokes. Everything's here: line weights, line caps, dash patterns, dash pattern with line caps, dash patterns and line caps with line weights layered on each other . . . well, you get the idea. We even show you how to add arrowheads to the ends of lines.

- **Chapter 11** colorizes your artwork. This chapter includes information on using the Pantone Colors library, as well as a theoretical introduction to the issues of color as they relate to working with computer-generated art and four-color process printing.

- **Chapter 12** dwells on transformations and duplications. You will learn how to create a precision drawing environment using rulers and guides. Next we discuss the four transformation tools, with which you can scale, flip, rotate, and slant any graphic object or text block. The last half of the chapter covers duplication, layering, and blending.

- **Chapter 13** discovers the six new graphing tools. Here's charts as you've never seen them before, as only a true drawing program can make them. We demonstrate how to create bar graphs, percentage charts, pie graphs, line graphs, area charts, and scatter graphs, all by entering a few values into Illustrator's GRAPH DATA window, complete with spreadsheet and import options. You can also create *pictographs*, which feature images stretched to various heights.

- **Chapter 14** looks at the importing and exporting of graphic images. Illustrator supports the popular Encapsulated PostScript format used by most scanning software, drawing programs, and desktop publishing software available for the Macintosh computer. In the end, we peruse Adobe's straightforward DrawOver utility, which converts PICT images to illustrations.

- **Chapter 15** focuses on printing your illustrations. This chapter also examines all issues related to the creation and use of color separations generated by the Adobe Separator utility.

- **Appendix A** describes how to install Adobe Illustrator on your hard drive, just in case you need some help getting started. Even if you're already up and running, you may want to check out our detailed description of the Adobe Type Manager.

Each chapter contains practical tips and advice designed to increase your user potential. In addition, we provide essential warnings to minimize unforeseen problems and aggravation. From cover to cover, *Mastering Adobe Illustrator, Macintosh Version 3.0* is designed to provide you with all the information that you will need to get the most out of this powerful application.

Drawing on the Macintosh

The first image of Macintosh computer that many users saw was a seemingly handwritten "Hello" scrawled across a tiny black-and-white screen. From this image alone, it was immediately apparent that the Mac was unlike everything computing had been before. Sure, the computer was a new shape, sort of a miniature arcade game, but that wasn't the giveaway. The scribbled "Hello" signaled something much more important.

Gone was the monotonous computer lettering that was a constant reminder of a computer's robotic nature. In its place was a free-form word, written at an angle in letters three inches high and looking distinctly friendly. The image on the screen, we'd later learn, was from a new piece of software called MacPaint.

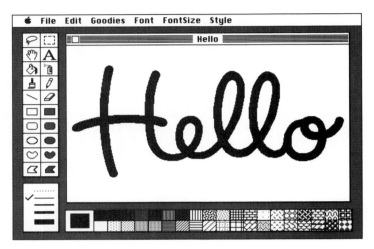

Figure 1.01: The debut of the friendly Macintosh computer.

MacPaint was as much of a revolution in applications software as the Macintosh itself was in hardware and the System/Finder was in operating systems. MacPaint was probably as responsible for Mac's early success as were these other items. Looking back, it is easy to pinpoint MacPaint as a real turning point for personal computer graphics. All the promise held in that handwritten "Hello" unfolded as MacPaint became a familiar tool. Gone were the box like constrictions and programming tedium that had previously epitomized personal computer graphics. Instead, a diverse set of familiar drawing tools, such as the pencil, paintbrush, and spraypaint can were now *on-screen* drawing tools, adapted for computer use with an amazing similarity to their real-world counterparts.

The advent of MacPaint was important for two reasons. First, skilled artists were quickly able to produce tremendous works using MacPaint. The diversity of MacPaint's tools proved enough for the production of thousands of images that soon turned up in publications, art exhibits, and on clip-art disks and computer screens everywhere. The second important result of MacPaint was the effect the program had on "the rest of us," the non-artist masses who had never dreamed of lifting brush to canvas or stroking pen to paper in anything more elaborate than a telephone doodle. To this group, MacPaint provided freedom to try, forgiveness to correct, and tools to empower. Just as word processors had encouraged the writing process, MacPaint encouraged graphic creation and placed it within the grasp of everyone.

While the inevitable wish list for additional MacPaint features grew, the more important limitation had already become apparent: its low-resolution bitmapped nature—which was in large part responsible for its power—was a limiting factor on the printed page. Many images require fluid curves, and MacPaint's stair-stepped approximations inhibited this new brand of computer art from establishing itself in the many areas where quality was the paramount concern.

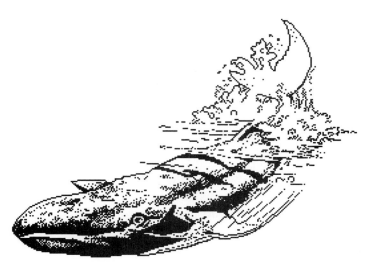

Figure 1.02: Soon after its introduction, MacPaint became synonymous with low-resolution graphics.

This limitation became more pronounced with the introduction of the LaserWriter. With the PostScript language built inside, this toner-based laser printer was actually capable of printing Macintosh-created words and pictures at 300 dots per inch—four times the resolution of the computer's screen. The stair-steps that appeared on the screen were re-placed with nearly perfect curves. The catch, however, was that only Post-

Script-compatible typefaces and mathematically defined graphics could utilize the full resolution of PostScript printers. Alas, MacPaint was still MacPaint, cemented at the 72-dot-per-inch resolution of the software.

MacDraw, on the other hand, suddenly moved from its role as a technically oriented specialty application to the center stage of Macintosh graphics. This is because MacDraw took advantage of the full resolution of the LaserWriter. MacDraw's limitation—a limited set of tools useful for creating rather boxy images—was overlooked in favor of its sharp, smooth output. Computer graphics could now match the clarity of traditional graphics, but they were limited in their expressive range.

Figure 1.03: MacDraw took advantage of the LaserWriter's high resolution, but its output was typically stylized and simplistic.

As the abilities of the PostScript interpreter inside the LaserWriter became better understood, users began to search for an application powerful enough to drive its precise laser-printing engine. Held against this potential, MacPaint was seen as the toy its critics had always proclaimed it to be. Even MacDraw, utilizing only the most basic of PostScript's capabilities, was inadequate. It wasn't until Adobe released Illustrator and, later, Aldus released FreeHand, that the power of PostScript began to be tapped.

These new programs offered the resolution capabilities of MacDraw combined with drawing freedoms similar to MacPaint. Precise lines and shapes could be drawn in any weight, turning and curving limitlessly. Enclosed areas could be filled with any screen density or pattern that could be defined in the PostScript language. Not only were the vast quantity of PostScript typefaces useful for traditional writing tasks, but type itself became an object that could be manipulated to produce any graphic effect.

Figure 1.04: The new breed of PostScript drawing applications offered artistic freedom and high-resolution output.

By providing users with the ability to utilize the full power of the PostScript language, programs like Adobe Illustrator have shattered the distinction between computer art and traditional art. In the areas of graphic illustration, technical illustration, and for many other graphic forms, art finally enjoys the power of the personal computer.

Figure 1.05: The field of graphic arts now enjoys the full power of the personal computer.

Terms, Tools, Menus, and Shortcuts

As a Macintosh application, Adobe Illustrator very closely follows the Macintosh interface. Your proficiency with Illustrator thus depends on how well you use your mouse and keyboard to interact with a collection of menus, tools, and dialog boxes. This chapter is an introduction to these fundamental aspects of Illustrator.

Each Illustrator tool and menu command, as well as many associated dialog boxes, will be discussed. After reading this chapter, you will have a good understanding of the range of capabilities provided by Adobe Illustrator. More experienced users—especially those familiar with previous versions of Illustrator such as 1.1 or 88—may find this information sufficient to allow them to begin their own experimentations with Illustrator 3.0. Less experienced users may find these summaries a bit overwhelming. In either case, remember that this is only a brief tour; the remainder of this book will provide all the details required to master the range of possibilities suggested in this chapter.

Before touring the menus and tools, however, we will take a moment to define the terms used throughout this book in describing the basic Macintosh interface. Terms like *select*, *choose*, *options*, and so on are defined here to remove ambiguity and to facilitate your learning experience. Because most of these terms are not universally defined, we recommend that even experienced Macintosh users review this section before going on to the other chapters of the book.

We will assume that you know how to perform a few functions required for the fundamental operation of your Macintosh. These include turning on your computer, inserting a disk, and copying files. You must also be familiar with the meaning of the terms *mouse*, *monitor*, *window*, *icon*, *cursor*, and *desktop*. If you are unfamiliar with these functions or terms, please consult your Macintosh operation manual.

Basic terminology

The terms defined in the following pages are ones with which you are probably familiar in a general sense. However, in the context of this book, they represent unique concepts that are applicable to operating a Macintosh computer. While they might have different or alternative meanings elsewhere, our use of these words will be confined to the definitions contained in this chapter. Other terminology specifically applicable to using Adobe Illustrator will be introduced in later chapters. Whether defined in this chapter or later, all vocabulary words will appear in *italic type*.

Mouse operations

We will first review mouse operations. To *click* the mouse is to press the mouse button and immediately *release*. To *drag* is to press and hold down the mouse button, move your mouse to a new location, and release. To *double-click* is to press and release the mouse button twice in rapid succession. Each of these operations is demonstrated in Figure 2.01.

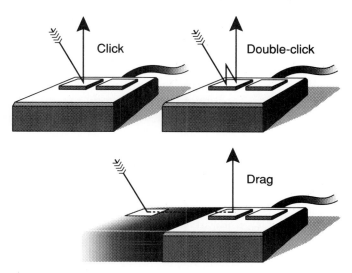

Figure 2.01: The three fundamental mouse operations.

Menus

Commands are organized into groups of related commands called *menus*. Each menu is assigned a name, which appears along the top of your screen in the *menu bar*. To *choose* a command is to pick it from a menu by clicking and holding your mouse button down on the menu name, then dragging down the list of commands. When the command you wish to choose is *highlighted*—displayed with white letters against a black background—release your mouse button.

Like other Macintosh applications, Illustrator offers four kinds of menu commands:

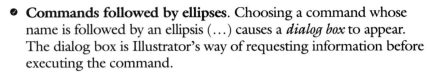

- **Commands followed by ellipses**. Choosing a command whose name is followed by an ellipsis (...) causes a *dialog box* to appear. The dialog box is Illustrator's way of requesting information before executing the command.

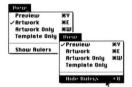

- **Pop-up menu commands**. As soon as these commands are highlighted, a second menu pops up either to the right or to the left of the command (depending upon the amount of space available on your screen). This second menu, called a *hierarchical pop-up menu*, contains a list of *options* that you may choose much in the same way you choose a menu command. Drag onto the pop-up menu, then drag up or down the menu until the desired option is highlighted, and finally release the mouse button. If the entire pop-up menu is not visible, it will scroll as you drag toward its top or bottom.

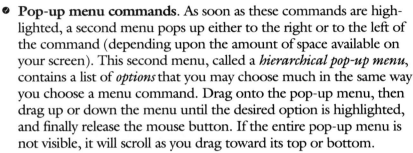
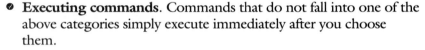

- **Toggling command options**. These are commands that turn on and off a particular Illustrator function. In some cases, these commands display a check mark in front of the command name when the feature is turned on. In other cases, the name of the command itself changes to reflect its new purpose.

- **Executing commands**. Commands that do not fall into one of the above categories simply execute immediately after you choose them.

Many menu commands may be chosen by simultaneously pressing two or more keys on your keyboard. Such a key sequence is called a *keyboard equivalent*. In most cases, the keyboard equivalent for a command is listed to the right of the command in its menu. Throughout this book, we will list any applicable keyboard equivalents in parentheses each time a menu command is introduced. The cloverleaf symbol (⌘) represents the COMMAND key, the switch symbol (⌥) represents the OPTION key, and the up arrow (⇧) represents the SHIFT key.

Dialog boxes

A *dialog box* can present information to you, request information from you, or both. In most cases, dialog boxes appear in response either to a command that you have chosen or to some action that you have taken. When a dialog box requests information, it does so by presenting you with options, similar in function to those offered in hierarchical pop-up menus.

Four kinds of options are found in dialog boxes:

Artwork board
- ○ Tile imageable areas
- ○ Tile full pages
- ◉ Single full page

Ruler units
- ○ Centimeters
- ○ Inches
- ◉ Picas/Points

● **Radio buttons**. Within a group of options among which you may select only one, small round buttons appear before each option name. These are called *radio buttons*. To *select* or *deselect* a radio button option, click on the round button itself or on the name of the option following the button. Only one radio button option in a set may be selected at a time: selecting any one will deselect all others. A set of radio buttons are usually physically adjacent. Several sets of radio buttons may appear in a single dialog box, but only one from each set may be selected at any one time. A radio button indicates that an option is selected when the button is filled black and deselected when the button is empty.

▤ Preferences ▤
- ☒ Snap to point
- ☐ Transform tiles
- ☒ Scale line weight
- ☒ Preview patterns
- ☐ Show placed images
- ☐ Split long paths

● **Check boxes**. Within a group of options among which you may select any number of alternatives, small square buttons appear before each option name. These are called *check boxes*. To *select* or *deselect* a check box, click on the square before the option name or directly on the option name itself. If that option was previously deselected, it will become selected; if it was selected, the option will become de-selected. Multiple check boxes within a set may be selected or deselected. A check box indicates that an option is selected when an × is displayed and is deselected when the box is empty.

Cyan:	0	%
Magenta:	0	%
Yellow:	0	%
Black:	0	%

● **Option boxes**. Options for which you must enter data are called *option boxes*. Most option boxes contain default data when the dialog box first appears. When this default data is selected (highlighted with white characters on a black background), you can enter new values from the keyboard and the default data will be replaced. To *select* a value in an option box, double-click on a newly entered value or drag over the current value.

In a dialog box that contains several option boxes, you can move from one option box to the next by pressing the TAB key.

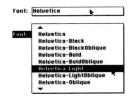

● **Pop-up menus**. Options that are presented as *pop-up menus* display only the current option setting when the dialog box first appears. To view the list of alternatives for such options, the current option (or an icon in some cases) must be selected by pressing and holding down the mouse button on top of it. This will "pop up" a menu displaying the available options. An option is selected from the pop-up menu by dragging up or down the listing and releasing the mouse button when the name of the desired alternative is highlighted. If an option in a pop-up menu is followed by an ellipsis (...), choosing it will bring up yet another dialog box, which contains additional options.

Once you have finished entering, selecting, and choosing options, you may exit a dialog box by clicking on buttons. The most common buttons are the OK and CANCEL buttons. Buttons may also serve as commands when they are placed within dialog boxes, where they are used to initiate an action or bring up another dialog box.

Dialog boxes that do not request information are known as *alert boxes*, since their purpose is to alert you to some fact. Some alert boxes warn you of the consequences of the action you are about to take and allow you to abort that action. Others inform you of some event that has already happened, allowing you only to acknowledge that you are aware of the event.

You will sometimes discover that an option, command, or menu is *dimmed*. Dimming an item indicates that it has no effect on a certain situation. Dimmed items cannot be chosen or selected.

Typographic conventions

Occasionally, this book will instruct you to press a key while performing a mouse operation. When not represented by symbols (⌘, ⇧, ⌥)—as in the case of keyboard equivalents—keys are listed in small caps (COMMAND, SHIFT, OPTION). Menus (FILE, EDIT), commands (SAVE, OPEN...), buttons (APPLY, CANCEL), and dialog box names (PREFERENCES, TYPE STYLE) are also listed in small caps to set them apart from standard text. Option names are set apart with quotation marks, whether they appear in pop-up menus ("Helvetica," "Justified") or in dialog boxes ("Snap to point," "Magenta").

The toolbox

The following are brief descriptions of the *tools* offered by Adobe Illustrator 3.0 to create and manipulate the lines, shapes, and text that will make up your Illustrator documents. These are provided simply as a taste of the possibilities that exist. More thorough descriptions are presented in the following chapters.

A tool is chosen from the *toolbox*, or *palette*, by clicking on it. The chosen tool will become highlighted. A positive feature of the Illustrator toolbox is that it is entirely independent of an Illustrator drawing window. Therefore, if you reduce a drawing window, the toolbox remains unchanged so that all tools are visible and easily accessible. You may move the toolbox by dragging at its title bar, or hide the toolbox by clicking in its close box. To redisplay the toolbox, choose the Show toolbox command from the Window menu. One toolbox serves, and is positioned in front of, any and all open Illustrator windows.

The toolbox contains 16 tool *slots*. The tools that appear in these slots when you first launch Illustrator are called the *default tools*. But Illustrator offers also 23 *alternate tools* that are initially hidden. For example, of the three arrow tools available, only one arrow tool is displayed in the top slot at any one time. To display an alternate tool, click and hold your mouse button down on the tool icon. All alternates for that tool will display to the right of the slot, as shown in Figure 2.02. Select the desired alternate tool as you would a command by dragging, highlighting the tool, and releasing your mouse button.

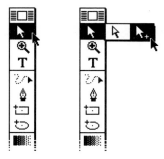

Figure 2.02: Drag at a slot to choose an alternate tool.

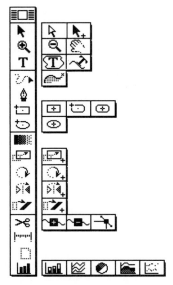

Figure 2.03: The toolbox with all default and alternate tools displayed.

The default tool and all alternates for each slot in the toolbox are displayed in Figure 2.03 and are described in the following text:

The arrow tool slot

The *arrow tool* (also called the *selection tool*) is the tool most commonly used in Adobe Illustrator. It is used to select, move, and duplicate existing objects in your illustration. The arrow tool may be used as follows:

- Click on a point, segment, group, or text block to select it and deselect the previous selection.

- Press OPTION and click a point or segment to select an entire path.

- Press SHIFT and click an object to add it to the current selection.

- Drag on an empty portion of the screen to create a *marquee*. All objects surrounded by the marquee will become selected.

- Drag a selected object to move the current selection.

- Drag a selected object and press OPTION before completing the drag to clone the current selection.

The two other tools that may appear in this slot are the *direct-selection tool*, which appears as a hollow arrow, and the *object-selection tool*, which appears as an arrow with a plus sign. The direct-selection tool allows you to select individual points and segments inside a grouped object, a compound path, or a path which is joined with type. You may also edit the shape of a text block and flow large amounts of text into multiple columns using this tool.

The object-selection tool selects an entire path, just as if you had OPTION-clicked on the path with the arrow tool.

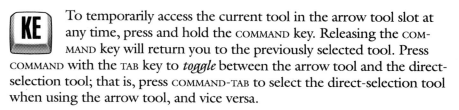

To temporarily access the current tool in the arrow tool slot at any time, press and hold the COMMAND key. Releasing the COMMAND key will return you to the previously selected tool. Press COMMAND with the TAB key to *toggle* between the arrow tool and the direct-selection tool; that is, press COMMAND-TAB to select the direct-selection tool when using the arrow tool, and vice versa.

Pressing OPTION and clicking on the arrow tool slot in the toolbox brings up the MOVE dialog box (just as if you had chosen the MOVE... command from the EDIT menu).

The zoom tool slot

The *zoom tool*, which appears as a magnifying glass with an inset plus sign, is used to expand or contract the *view size* of the current illustration. The image itself is not affected by this tool. Rather, it allows you to zoom in on a detail or zoom out to take in the big picture. The zoom tool may be used as follows:

- Click anywhere in the drawing area to expand a portion of your illustration to twice its previous level of magnification.

- Press OPTION and click anywhere in the drawing area to contract a portion of your illustration to half its previous level of magnification.

- Drag to expand the illustration and then scroll it inside the window (as if using the hand tool). OPTION-drag to contract, then scroll.

The two other tools for this slot are the *zoom-out tool*, which appears with an inset minus sign, and the *hand tool* (also called the *grabber hand*). The zoom-out tool contracts the view size of the current illustration just as if you had OPTION-clicked with the standard zoom tool.

The hand tool is used to *scroll* the illustration; that is, move it with respect to the Illustrator window boundaries. Dragging with the hand tool scrolls the illustration in 48-pixel increments.

 To temporarily access the zoom tool at any time, press and hold the COMMAND key with the SPACEBAR. Releasing both keys will return you to the previously selected tool. Press COMMAND-OPTION-SPACEBAR to access the zoom-out tool. And, except when editing text, press the SPACEBAR by itself to display the hand tool.

Double-clicking the zoom tool icon in the toolbox is another way to expand your illustration to twice its previous magnification level. Likewise, OPTION-double-clicking the zoom tool icon or double-clicking the zoom-out tool icon contracts the illustration. Double-clicking the hand tool icon contracts the current illustration to the *fit-in-window* view size, so the entire drawing area can be seen in the window (as if you had chosen FIT IN WINDOW from the VIEW menu). OPTION-double-clicking the hand tool icon changes the view size to 100% (as if you had chosen ACTUAL SIZE).

The type tool slot

T The *type tool* has been enhanced in Illustrator 3.0. Rather than displaying a text-entry dialog box, the type tool now lets you add and edit existing text directly on the page. The type tool may be used as follows:

- Click outside an existing text block to position an *alignment point*. Text entered from the keyboard will align to this point.
- Drag outside an existing text block to draw a *column*. Text entered from the keyboard will appear inside this column.
- Click on existing closed path or OPTION-click open path to create *area type*. Text entered from the keyboard will appear inside the path.
- Click on existing oprn path or OPTION-click closed path to create *path type*. Text entered from the keyboard will follow along the path.
- Click inside an existing text block to position the blinking *insertion marker*. Text entered from the keyboard will begin at the marker.
- Drag inside an existing text block to select multiple characters of type. Selected text appears highlighted, and may be formatted or replaced by entering new text from the keyboard.
- Double-click inside an existing text block to select a word of type.
- Triple-click inside an existing text block to select a paragraph.

The two other tools for this slot are the *area-type tool*, which appears as a letter inside a shape, and the *path-type tool*, which appears as a letter on a curve. The area-type tool allows you to set type inside an existing free-form path. The path-type tool joins the *baseline* of a block of type to an existing free-form path to create text on a curve. Each tool is operated by clicking on the desired path and entering text from the keyboard.

Press the CONTROL key to temporarily access the type tool when the area-type tool or path-type tool is selected. If your keyboard does not provide a CONTROL key, press the Z key instead.

Regardless of the tool used to create it, a block of type may be edited with any of the three type tools.

The freehand tool slot

The *freehand tool*, which appears as a small arrowhead drawing a dotted line, is used to draw free-form paths. Illustrator automatically determines the placement and identity of the points required to define a free-form path. The freehand tool may be used as follows:

- Drag on an empty portion of the screen to create a free-form path.

- Press COMMAND while dragging with the tool to erase portions of the path you have just drawn.

- Drag from either end of an existing open path to extend the length of the path.

- Drag from one end of an existing open path to the other end of the same path to close the path.

- Drag from the end of one existing open path to the end of a different open path to join the two paths into one.

- Press OPTION and drag from the end of an existing open path to ensure that the point from which you drag is a corner point.

Press the CONTROL key to temporarily access the freehand tool when the pen tool (the tool in the slot below the freehand tool slot) is selected. If your keyboard does not provide a CONTROL key, press the Z key instead.

The only alternate tool for this slot is the *autotrace tool*, which appears as an × above a small hill of dots. This tool is used to convert imported *bitmaps* into smooth object-oriented graphics by tracing the outline of an image with a closed path. The autotrace tool may be used as follows:

- Click within six pixels of an imported bitmap to create a single closed path that traces the outline of the image.

- Drag from one point near a bitmap to another point near the same bitmap to trace only that portion of the image that lies between the click and release points.

- Drag from either end of an existing open path near a bitmap to extend the length of the path.

- Press OPTION and drag from the end of an existing open path to ensure that the point from which you drag is a corner point.

You may also extend an existing open path with the autotrace tool in the same way described for the freehand tool, provided that the existing path follows the outline of an imported bitmap.

The pen tool slot

 The *pen tool* is used to draw a path as a series of individual points. Typically, you click or drag to establish the first point in a path. As you click or drag to create a second point, Illustrator draws a *segment* joining the two points. Another segment joins the second point to the third, the third to the fourth, and so on. Drawing with the pen tool is more laborious than drawing with either the freehand or autotrace tools, but it tends to be more accurate as well. The pen tool may be used as follows:

- Click on an empty portion of the screen to create a *corner point*.

- Press SHIFT and click to constrain the segment to an angle that is a multiple of 45°.

- Drag on an empty portion of the screen to create a *smooth point* with two symmetrical *Bézier control handles*.

- Click on an existing smooth endpoint to change it to a corner point with only one Bézier control handle.

- Press OPTION and drag from an existing smooth endpoint to change it to a *cusp*, a corner point with two independent control handles.

Press the CONTROL key to temporarily access the pen tool when the freehand tool is selected. If your keyboard does not provide a CONTROL key, press the Z key instead.

No other tool may appear in the pen tool slot.

The rectangle tool slot

 The *rectangle tool* is used to create a grouped rectangle with a center point. The rectangle tool may be used as follows:

- Drag to draw a rectangle from corner to opposite corner.

- Press OPTION and drag to draw a rectangle from center point to corner.

- Press SHIFT and drag or SHIFT-OPTION-drag to draw a perfect square.

- Click to display a dialog box requesting you to enter the dimensions and corner radius of the prospective rectangle. The click point becomes the upper left corner of the shape.

- Press OPTION and click to display a dialog box requesting you to enter the dimensions and corner radius of the prospective rectangle. The click point becomes the center of the shape.

 The three alternate tools for this slot are the *centered-rectangle tool*, the *rounded-rectangle tool*, and the *centered-rounded-rectangle tool*. (The two centered tools are distinguished with inset plus signs.) The centered-rectangle tool draws a rectangle from center point to corner, as if you had OPTION-dragged with the standard rectangle tool.

 Both rounded-rectangle tools are used to create rectangles with rounded corners. The standard rounded-rectangle tool draws from corner to corner; the centered-rounded-rectangle tool draws from center point to corner.

Pressing OPTION and clicking or OPTION-dragging with either of the centered-rectangle tools draws a rectangle from corner to corner.

The oval tool slot

The *oval tool* is used to create a grouped ellipse with a center point. The oval tool may be used as follows:

- Drag to draw an ellipse from the middle of one arc to the middle of the opposite arc.

- Press OPTION and drag to draw an ellipse from center point to arc.

- Press SHIFT and drag or SHIFT-OPTION-drag to draw a perfect circle.

- Click to display a dialog box requesting you to enter the dimensions of the prospective ellipse. The click point becomes the middle of the upper left arc of the shape.

- Press OPTION and click to display a dialog box requesting you to enter the dimensions of the prospective ellipse. The click point becomes the center of the shape.

The other tool for this slot is the *centered-oval tool*, distinguished with an inset plus sign. The centered-oval tool draws an ellipse from center point to arc, as if you had OPTION-dragged with the standard oval tool.

Pressing OPTION and clicking or OPTION-dragging with the centered-oval tool draws an ellipse from arc to arc.

The blend tool slot

The *blend tool* is used to create intermediate form, fill, and stroke manipulations between two selected open paths or between two selected closed paths with similar numbers of points. To use the blend tool, select one or more points in each of the two paths. Click twice, once on a selected point in each path, to bring up the BLEND dialog box. Enter the number of steps desired and press the RETURN key. Illustrator then creates the intermediary number of steps as instructed.

No other tool may appear in the blend tool slot.

The scale tool slot

The *scale tool* is used to reduce or enlarge one or more selected objects in your illustration. An object is resized with respect to a single point, called a *scale origin*. The scale tool may be used as follows:

- Click to establish the scale origin. In a separate mouse operation, drag toward the scale origin to reduce the selected object.

- Click to establish the scale origin, then drag away from the scale origin to enlarge the selected object.

- Click to establish the scale origin, then SHIFT-drag to resize the selected object proportionally.

- Click to establish the scale origin, then OPTION-drag to simultaneously resize and clone the selected object.

- Press OPTION and click to display a dialog box requesting you to enter the percentage by which you want to reduce or enlarge the selected object.

The other tool for this slot is the *scale-dialog tool*, which is distinguished by a plus sign in its lower right corner. The scale-dialog tool displays the SCALE dialog box, just as if you had OPTION-clicked with the standard scale tool.

Press OPTION to use the scale-dialog tool like the standard scale tool.

The rotate tool slot

The *rotate tool* is used to rotate one or more selected objects in your illustration around a single point, called a *rotation origin*. The rotate tool may be used as follows:

- Click to establish the rotation origin. In a separate mouse operation, drag around the origin to rotate the selected object.

- Click to establish the rotation origin, then SHIFT-drag to rotate the selected object by any angle that is a multiple of 45°.

- Click to establish the rotation origin, then OPTION-drag to simultaneously rotate and clone the selected object.

- Press OPTION and click to display a dialog box requesting you to enter the angle by which you want to rotate the selected object.

The other tool for this slot is the *rotate-dialog tool*, which is distinguished by a plus sign in its lower right corner. The rotate-dialog tool displays the ROTATE dialog box, just as if you had OPTION-clicked with the standard rotate tool.

Press OPTION to use the rotate-dialog tool like the standard rotate tool.

The reflect tool slot

The *reflect tool* is used to flip one or more selected objects in your illustration around a *reflection axis*, which may be oriented horizontally, vertically, or at some angle. The reflect tool may be used as follows:

- Click to secure one end of the reflection axis. In a separate mouse operation, click or drag to determine the location of the other end of the axis, about which Illustrator flips the selected object.

- Click to secure one end of the reflection axis, then SHIFT-click to constrain the angle of the axis to any angle that is a multiple of 45°.

- Click to secure one end of the reflection axis, then OPTION-click or OPTION-drag to simultaneously flip and clone the selected object.

- Press OPTION and click to display a dialog box requesting you to enter the orientation of the reflection axis about which you want to flip the selected object.

The other tool for this slot is the *reflect-dialog tool*, which is distinguished by a plus sign in its lower right corner. The reflect-dialog tool displays the REFLECT dialog box, just as if you had OPTION-clicked with the standard reflect tool.

Press OPTION to use the reflect-dialog tool like the standard reflect tool.

The shear tool slot

The *shear tool* is used to slant (or *skew*) one or more selected objects in your illustration. An object is skewed with respect to a single point, called a *shearing origin*. The shear tool may be used as follows:

- Click to establish the shearing origin. In a separate mouse operation, drag with respect to the origin to skew the selected object.

- Click to establish the shearing origin, then SHIFT-drag to constrain the angle of the skew to any angle that is a multiple of 45°.

- Click to establish the shearing origin, then OPTION-drag to simultaneously skew and clone the selected object.

- Press OPTION and click to display a dialog box requesting you to enter the angle by which you want to skew the selected object and the angle of the *shearing axis*.

The other tool for this slot is the *shear-dialog tool,* which is distinguished by a plus sign in its lower right corner. The shear-dialog tool displays the SHEAR dialog box, just as if you had OPTION-clicked with the standard shear tool.

Press OPTION to use the shear-dialog tool like the standard shear tool.

The scissors tool slot

The *scissors tool* is used to split segments and to add points to a path. Illustrator automatically determines the identity of the points based on the form of the path. The scissors tool may be used as follows:

- Click on a segment to insert two endpoints, splitting the segment. This technique can be used to open a closed path or to divide an open path into two open paths.

- Click on a point to convert the point into two endpoints, thus opening a closed path or dividing an open path into two open paths.

- Press OPTION and click on a segment to add a single point to the path without splitting it.

The three alternate tools for this slot are the *add-point tool*, which appears as a curve running through a reversed plus sign, the *delete-point tool*, which appears as a curve with a reversed minus sign, and the *convert-point tool*, which looks like a corner point flanked by Bézier control handles. The add-point tool inserts a point into a path segment, just as if you had OPTION-clicked with the scissors tool. Conversely, clicking with the delete-point tool deletes a point. The delete-point tool does not break the path, as happens when you delete a selected point by pressing the DELETE key. Instead, a new segment connects the two points neighboring the deleted point.

The convert-point tool is used to convert corner points to smooth points, and smooth points to cusps and corner points. The convert-point tool may be used as follows:

- Click on a smooth point to convert it to a corner point with no Bézier control handle.

- Drag one of the Bézier control handles of a smooth point to move it independently of the other Bézier control handle, thus converting the smooth point to a cusp.

- Drag from a corner point to convert it to a smooth point with two symmetrical Bézier control handles.

KE Press the CONTROL key to temporarily access the convert-point tool when any tool from the arrow tool slot is selected. If your keyboard does not provide a CONTROL key, press the Z key instead. When any other tool is selected, press COMMAND-CONTROL to access the convert-point tool. (Pressing COMMAND-Z also works, but this may also have the effect of choosing the UNDO command.)

The measure tool slot

The *measure tool* is used to measure the distance and direction between two points. To use the measure tool, click twice, once at each of two different screen locations. The MEASURE dialog box will display, listing the distance and angle between the two clicks, as well as the horizontal and vertical components of the measure. Make note of this information and press RETURN to close the dialog.

To make precise moves, first measure the distance that you want to move an object with the measure tool. Close the MEASURE dialog box and choose the MOVE... command from the EDIT menu. The information from the MEASURE dialog now displays in the MOVE dialog box. Simply press RETURN to complete the move.

No other tool may appear in the measure tool slot.

The page tool slot

The *page tool* is used to position of the current page size within the 18-inch-by-18-inch drawing area. To use the page tool, first choose FIT IN WINDOW from the VIEW menu. Then click or drag with the page tool to position the lower left corner of the page size or tile boundary.

No other tool may appear in the page tool slot.

The bar-graph tool slot

The *bar-graph tool* automatically generates a standard bar chart (also known as a *cluster bar chart* or a *grouped column chart*) from a spreadsheet of numbers. The bar-graph tool may be used as follows:

- Drag to draw the rectangular boundary for the chart from corner to corner.

- Press OPTION and drag to draw the rectangular boundary for the chart from center to corner.

- Press SHIFT and drag or SHIFT-OPTION-drag to draw a square boundary.

- Click to display a dialog box requesting you to enter the dimensions of the prospective chart boundary. The click point becomes the upper left corner of the chart.

- Press OPTION and click to display a dialog box requesting you to enter the dimensions of the prospective chart boundary. The click point becomes the center of the chart.

After you determine the size of the chart, Illustrator displays the GRAPH DATA window. Here you may enter or import data into a typical spreadsheet matrix made up of rows and columns. Press the ENTER key to instruct Illustrator to process the data and generate the chart.

Five alternate charting tools are available for this slot. They include, in order of appearance, the *stacked-bar-graph tool,* the *line-graph tool,* the *pie-graph tool,* the *area-graph tool,* and the *scatter-graph tool.* Each tool generates a different variety of chart from data entered or imported into the GRAPH DATA window.

The stacked-bar-graph tool stacks related values for different *series* (columns of data in the spreadsheet) one upon another, rather than positioning them side by side, as in a standard bar chart. When each row of values adds up to 100%, a stacked bar chart is called a *percentage chart.*

The line-graph tool maps your data as points on an XY-coordinate grid. Generally speaking, the X axis represents time and the Y axis displays the values. Straight segments connect points in a single series (column in spreadsheet), clearly displaying rising and falling values.

The pie-graph tool gives each series (row in spreadsheet) of data its own pie, so that values in a series can be compared to the series as a whole. Percentages, rather than specific values, are represented.

The area-graph tool generates what amounts to a filled-in line graph. Each series (column in spreadsheet) is stacked upon the previous one to avoid overlapping, emphasizing the total performance of all series over time.

The scatter-graph tool maps *paired data* on an XY-coordinate grid. The first series (column in spreadsheet) of data produces Y-axis values, the second series produces X-axis values. Each point is therefore the intersection of the two values in a single row of data.

Resetting the toolbox

The default tools that appear in the toolbox when you first run Illustrator represent the most commonly used tools. However, as you work on an illustration, you will no doubt select various alternate tools, changing the composition of the toolbox. To reset the toolbox to its original 16 default tools at any time, simply choose the RESET TOOLBOX command from the WINDOW menu.

You may also reset a single slot to display its default tool by pressing SHIFT and double-clicking the desired slot. To quickly reset the entire toolbox, press both SHIFT and COMMAND and double-click any slot.

Menus and commands

The following are brief descriptions of the menus and commands offered by Adobe Illustrator 3.0. Again, these descriptions are provided simply as brief introductions to the commands. More thorough descriptions are presented throughout later chapters. Keyboard equivalents are listed in parentheses when applicable.

The Apple (🍎) menu

The APPLE menu behaves exactly as it does within all other Macintosh applications and at the Finder. You have access to all desk accessories currently available to your System file. When operating under MultiFinder, your APPLE menu also contains a list of other currently running applications. Choosing any one of these applications will bring it forward as the active program and send Illustrator to the background. Return to Illustrator by choosing the Adobe Illustrator 3.0 icon (🖋) from the list of running applications in the APPLE menu or by clicking in the upper right corner of your Macintosh screen until the Illustrator toolbox reappears. (The toolbox is always hidden when Illustrator runs in the background.)

ABOUT ADOBE ILLUSTRATOR... Choose this command to display the same startup screen that is displayed when launching the program. This time, however, the screen displays the amount of free RAM (*random access memory*) that remains unused by the application. Click anywhere on the startup screen to close it.

The File menu

As in most Macintosh applications, the Adobe Illustrator FILE menu controls broad document-level activities, including the opening, closing, printing, and saving of illustrations. Additionally, the FILE menu controls the importation of text and graphic images and the exportation of EPS (*Encapsulated PostScript*) files.

NEW... (⌘-N) brings up the PLEASE OPEN TEMPLATE dialog box, which allows you to choose a bitmap tracing template saved in the MacPaint or PICT format, create a new file without a template, or cancel the creation of a new file.

Open... (⌘-O) brings up the PLEASE OPEN ILLUSTRATION OR TEMPLATE dialog box, which allows you to open any available Illustrator 1.1, 88, or 3.0 file, open a bitmap tracing template saved in the MacPaint or PICT format, or cancel the open operation. By pressing the OPTION key when choosing OPEN... (⌘-⌥-O) you may add, change, or discard the template for an existing illustration.

Place Art... brings up the PLEASE OPEN EPS FILE dialog box, which allows you to place an Encapsulated PostScript document into an illustration or cancel the place operation. Illustrator 1.1, 88, and 3.0 files that were not saved as EPS documents may also be placed, although they will not preview correctly.

Import Text... appears in place of the PLACE ART... command when you activate a text block using one of the type tools. When chosen, this command brings up the PLEASE OPEN DOCUMENT dialog box, which allows you to import a text document. Microsoft Word 4.0, RTF (Rich Text Format), MacWrite II, WriteNow 2.2, and straight text files are all supported.

Close closes the current illustration, but does not quit the Illustrator application. If any changes have been made to a document before it is closed, a SAVE CHANGES dialog box will appear, allowing you to save your changes, confirm the loss of your changes, or cancel the close operation.

Save (⌘-S) updates the disk file of your current document to include all changes made since it was last saved. If the current document already has a name, you are given no opportunity to confirm the save or to change the location or name of the file. If the current document is "Untitled art" followed by a number, the SAVE ILLUSTRATION dialog box will appear, allowing you the opportunity to enter a name for the document and to determine on which drive and in which folder you would like to save your file. You may also indicate that a new Illustrator file should include a Macintosh or IBM Encapsulated PostScript screen representation for importation into a page-layout program such as Aldus PageMaker or QuarkXPress. The SAVE command will be dimmed if no changes have been made to the current document since it was last saved.

Save As... brings up the SAVE ILLUSTRATION dialog box, which allows you to change the name or location of the file you are saving. You may also add a Macintosh or IBM EPS screen representation to an existing Illustrator file.

Page Setup… brings up Apple's standard LaserWriter Page Setup dialog box, provided that you have selected a PostScript-compatible printer with your Chooser desk accessory. The dialog box allows you to specify the size and orientation of your electronic page and the percentage enlargement or reduction of the illustration when printed. Other options have little effect in Illustrator.

Print… (⌘-P) brings up Apple's standard LaserWriter Print dialog box, provided that you have selected a PostScript-compatible printer with your Chooser desk accessory. The dialog box allows you to specify which pages you wish to print, the number of copies, and the paper source.

Quit (⌘-Q) exits the Illustrator application, closing all open illustrations and returning control to the Macintosh Finder (or possibly to some other application if you are running under MultiFinder). A Save changes dialog box will appear for every illustration that has unsaved changes. If an illustration is untitled, the Save illustration dialog will appear, prompting you to name the file.

The Edit menu

Most of the commands in the Edit menu will be familiar to you if you have worked in other Macintosh applications. These commands control the duplication of objects via the Macintosh Clipboard, common layering manipulations, and so on. Two Edit commands—Paste In Front and Paste In Back—are unique to Illustrator, although they conform to the Edit menu tradition of working directly with the Clipboard.

Undo (⌘-Z) steps backward through the last immediate operation performed in Illustrator. As an operation is undone, all effects relating to that operation are also undone; the file returns to the exact state in which it existed prior to the operation. To help you keep track of what those operations were, the Undo command lists the command it will undo if chosen, such as Undo Move. The Undo command will be dimmed if the last operation cannot be undone, such as selecting an element or even a random on-screen click. Immediately after undoing an operation, the Undo command becomes a Redo command, allowing you to reimplement an undone operation.

Cut (⌘-X) deletes one or more selected objects from your illustration and stores them in the Macintosh Clipboard, replacing the Clipboard's previous contents. If no object is selected, the Cut command is dimmed.

COPY (⌘-C) makes a copy of one or more selected objects in your illustration and stores them in the Macintosh Clipboard, replacing the Clipboard's previous contents. If no object is selected, the COPY command is dimmed.

PASTE (⌘-V) makes a copy of the items in the Macintosh Clipboard and places them inside the current illustration. If the Clipboard is empty, the PASTE command is dimmed.

CLEAR (DELETE, BACKSPACE, or CLEAR) deletes one or more selected objects from your illustration, but does so without placing them in the Clipboard or disturbing the Clipboard's contents. The objects can be brought back immediately by choosing UNDO CLEAR; otherwise, they are lost for good. If no object is selected, the CLEAR command is dimmed.

SELECT ALL (⌘-A) selects every element—including all points—within the drawing area of the current document. The only exception to this occurs if a text block has been activated with one of the type tools, in which case choosing SELECT ALL highlights all text in the current *story* (one or more linked text blocks).

PASTE IN FRONT (⌘-F) pastes the contents of the Clipboard in front of any and all selected objects at the exact location from which the Clipboard contents were cut or copied. If nothing is selected, the newly pasted objects become the frontmost objects in the Illustrator drawing area. This command is dimmed if the Clipboard is empty.

PASTE IN BACK (⌘-B) pastes the contents of the Clipboard in back of any and all selected objects at the exact location from which the Clipboard contents were cut or copied. If nothing is selected, the newly pasted objects become the rearmost objects in the Illustrator drawing area. This command is dimmed if the Clipboard is empty.

BRING TO FRONT (⌘-=, COMMAND-EQUAL) moves any and all selected objects in front of all other objects in the Illustrator drawing area. Although this command appears to act somewhat like a combined CUT-and-PASTE IN FRONT command, the Clipboard is not affected. If no object is selected, the BRING TO FRONT command is dimmed.

SEND TO BACK (⌘--, COMMAND-HYPHEN) moves any and all selected objects in back of all other objects in the Illustrator drawing area. Again, the contents of the Clipboard are not affected. If no object is selected, the SEND TO BACK command is dimmed.

MOVE... displays the MOVE dialog box, which allows you to move any and all selected objects a specified distance in a specified direction. This dialog box may also be accessed by OPTION-clicking the arrow tool slot in the toolbox. If no object is selected, the MOVE... command is dimmed.

PREFERENCES... (⌘-K) brings up the PREFERENCES dialog box, in which several basic attributes affecting the on-screen drawing environment are specified. The PREFERENCES dialog box allows you to control how points snap together, the display and transformation of patterns and placed artwork, the scaling of line weights, whether long paths are broken into smaller paths, the angle of the constraint axis, the corner radius of simple rectangles, the movement equivalent of cursor keystrokes, the sensitivity of the freehand and autotrace tools, the manner in which artwork is printed, the unit of measure, the degree to which keystrokes affect text formatting, and the on-screen color display.

The Arrange menu

Arrange	
Transform Again	⌘D
Group	⌘G
Ungroup	⌘U
Join...	⌘J
Average...	⌘L
Lock	⌘1
Unlock All	⌘2
Hide	⌘3
Show All	⌘4
Make Guide	⌘5
Release All Guides	⌘6
Set Cropmarks	
Release Cropmarks	

Commands in the ARRANGE menu affect relationships between selected objects. Most commands—such as TRANSFORM AGAIN, GROUP, and JOIN...—are drawing standards that have been included in Adobe Illustrator since its initial release. The commands at the bottom of the menu, those which control guides and crop marks, are new to Illustrator 3.0.

TRANSFORM AGAIN (⌘-D) repeats the transformation just performed on the current selection, including any cloning. TRANSFORM AGAIN is particularly useful for experimenting with slight transformations; you can nudge the transformation along until the object meets your exact requirement. This command is dimmed if a transformation was not the most recently performed operation.

GROUP (⌘-G) combines all currently selected elements into a single object. A single path may be grouped so that it cannot be reshaped with the standard arrow tool. Grouping one or more points or segments in a single path groups the entire path. Multiple groups may also be grouped as a single object. The GROUP command changes the layering order of selected objects, bringing them forward to just behind the frontmost object in the group. Grouping is the final step in creating a *clipping path* (masking object). A single element in a group may be selected and adjusted using the direct-selection tool without ungrouping. If no object is selected, the GROUP command is dimmed.

UNGROUP (⌘-U) separates a selected group into its original elements. Many images are created as groups. These include geometric shapes (rectangles and ovals), blends, and graphs. Ungrouping these objects allows you to edit them with the arrow tool; however, it may also prevent you from editing the object in different ways. For example, if you ungroup a graph, you may no longer edit it using commands from the GRAPH menu. If no object is selected, the UNGROUP command is dimmed.

JOIN… (⌘-J) is used to join two selected endpoints, thereby joining two open paths or closing a single open path. If one selected endpoint is directly in front of the other, the JOIN… command brings up the JOIN dialog box, which allows you to select the identity (corner or smooth) of the resulting single point. If the two selected endpoints exist at separate locations, a straight segment is drawn between them. If no object is selected, the JOIN… command is dimmed.

AVERAGE… (⌘-L) repositions multiple selected elements according to the vertical and horizontal averages of their current locations. Choosing this command brings up the AVERAGE dialog box, which allows you to specify repositioning along a horizontal axis, a vertical axis, or at a single average location. This command is most frequently applied in preparation for using the JOIN… command. If no object is selected, the AVERAGE… command is dimmed.

LOCK (⌘-1) locks any and all selected objects so that they may not be selected or manipulated in any manner. Locking one or more points or segments in a single path locks the entire path. Pressing the OPTION key when choosing the LOCK command locks all objects that are *not* currently selected.

UNLOCK ALL (⌘-2) unlocks *all* locked objects in the current Illustrator file. A single locked object may not be unlocked independently of other locked objects in the same file.

HIDE (⌘-3) hides any and all selected objects so that they are not visible on screen, nor may they be selected or manipulated in any manner. Hiding one or more points or segments in a single path hides the entire path. An object will neither print nor preview when it is hidden. Pressing the OPTION key when choosing the HIDE command hides all objects that are *not* currently selected. Hiding is not saved: hidden objects therefore reappear the next time the current file is opened.

Show All (⌘-4) displays *all* hidden objects in the current Illustrator file. A single hidden object may not be displayed independently of other hidden objects in the same file.

Make Guide (⌘-5) converts any and all selected objects into a *guide*; that is, a non-printing image used to align objects in the drawing area. Guides appear with dotted outlines in the artwork mode. Since they do not print, they do not appear in the preview mode and they may not be stroked or filled. Converting one or more points or segments in a single path converts the entire path. Guides may not be selected or manipulated in the normal fashion. If no object is selected, the **Make Guide** command is dimmed.

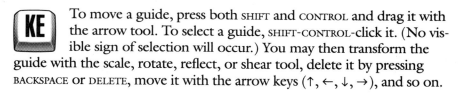 To move a guide, press both SHIFT and CONTROL and drag it with the arrow tool. To select a guide, SHIFT-CONTROL-click it. (No visible sign of selection will occur.) You may then transform the guide with the scale, rotate, reflect, or shear tool, delete it by pressing BACKSPACE or DELETE, move it with the arrow keys (↑, ←, ↓, →), and so on.

Release All Guides (⌘-6) converts *all* guides back into editable, printing objects. This includes *ruler guides* dragged out from the horizontal or vertical ruler.

 To convert a single guide into an editable object, press SHIFT and CONTROL and double-click the guide. This same technique may also be used to convert ruler guides.

Set Cropmarks converts a selected rectangle into *crop marks*, printing guides that indicate the boundaries of the final printed trimmed page. If the "Single full page" option is selected in the PREFERENCES dialog box, the **Set Cropmarks** command creates crop marks around the page size. Crop marks always have a 0.5-point line weight, regardless of the fill and stroke of the original rectangle. They may not be selected or manipulated. Only one set of crop marks may appear in an illustration, so choosing **Set Cropmarks** always deletes any previous crop marks. This command is dimmed when no rectangle is selected and the "Tile imageable areas" or "Tile full page" option is selected in the PREFERENCES dialog box.

Release Cropmarks converts any crop marks back into a rectangle. This command is useful primarily when you want to alter the crop marks: choose **Release Cropmarks**, resize and move the rectangle, and choose **Set Cropmarks** to convert them back.

The View menu

The VIEW menu contains commands that affect how you see elements in the drawing area. The first five commands control the display mode. The next two commands alter the view size. The last commands control the display of movement-tracking rulers and unpainted items.

PREVIEW ILLUSTRATION (⌘-Y) previews an illustration, displaying all objects as they will appear when printed, complete with strokes, fills, patterns, colors, and so on. Guides and tracing templates neither display in the preview mode nor print. No element in the current document may be created or manipulated while the *preview mode* is active (indicated by a check mark in front of the command).

ARTWORK & TEMPLATE (⌘-E) displays most objects in the current document with transparent fills and black, hairline strokes. The only exception is type, which is filled black and not stroked. Guides display as dotted lines. A grayed version of the bitmapped tracing template is also visible, provided that a template exists in the current document. Elements may be created and manipulated while the *artwork-&-template mode* is active (indicated by a check mark in front of the command).

ARTWORK ONLY (⌘-W) displays most objects in the current document with transparent fills and black, hairline strokes. The only exception is type, which is filled black and not stroked. Guides display as dotted lines. However, if a bitmapped tracing template exists in the current document, it is not shown. Elements may be created and manipulated while the *artwork mode* is active (indicated by a check mark in front of the command).

TEMPLATE ONLY displays only the bitmapped tracing template exactly as it would appear in MacPaint or a similar painting program, provided that a template exists in the current document. No portion of the current illustration is visible, nor may an element be created or manipulated while the *template mode* is active (indicated by a check mark in front of the command).

PREVIEW SELECTION (⌘-⌥-Y) previews any and all selected objects. Objects that are not selected disappear. Unlike the preview mode, you may move and reshape objects when previewing a selection. Generally, however, this display mode is most useful for previewing a detail of an drawing, a less time-consuming operation than previewing an entire illustration.

ACTUAL SIZE (⌘-H) changes the view of the current document to a full-size representation. This view size displays all objects in an illustration at the size at which they will print. The size of your screen determines how much of the document may be seen at a time. The actual view size may also be accessed by OPTION-double-clicking the hand tool icon.

FIT IN WINDOW (⌘-M) changes the view size of the current document so that the entire 18-inch-by-18-inch drawing area is visible on your screen. The exact size at which your illustration is displayed varies, depending on the size of your monitor. The fit-in-window view size may also be accessed by double-clicking the hand tool icon.

SHOW/HIDE RULERS (⌘-R) toggles the display of horizontal and vertical rulers on the bottom and right sides of the current Illustrator window. Rulers display in the current unit of measure specified in the PREFERENCES dialog box.

HIDE/SHOW UNPAINTED OBJECTS toggles the display of objects that are neither stroked nor filled. This command functions only in the artwork mode.

The Paint menu

Commands in the PAINT menu are used to specify the strokes and fills of objects in your illustration. Special tile patterns and colors may be created using the commands in this menu. You may also combine objects into *compound paths*, so that one path cuts a hole through another.

STYLE... (⌘-I) brings up the PAINT STYLE dialog box, which allows you to specify the fill and stroke of one or more selected objects. Fill attributes include tint, color, and pattern. Stroke attributes include all those applicable to fill as well as line weight, line cap, line join, miter limit, and dash pattern. You may also change the *flatness* of an object if a document will not print due to a "limitcheck" error. Select the "Mask" option to indicate that an object should act as a *clipping path*, which masks elements in front of it and grouped with it. Select the "Reversed" option to make the frontmost objects in a compound path transparent, cutting holes in the rearmost object.

PATTERN... brings up the PATTERN dialog box, which is used to define, name, and organize *tile patterns*. The selected pattern appears in the bottom, right corner. To define a new pattern, select a rectangle with a collection of pattern elements in front of it, choose the PATTERN... command, and click the NEW button. Patterns defined in this way may then be used in the stroke or fill of an object via the PAINT STYLE dialog box. If no object is selected and no tile patterns currently exist in any open illustration, the PATTERN... command is dimmed.

CUSTOM COLOR... brings up the CUSTOM COLOR dialog box, which is used to define, name, and organize *custom colors*. The selected color appears in the bottom right corner, either in color or as a black-and-white composite, depending upon the color capabilities of your monitor. Generally, this dialog box is used to define colors as a combination of cyan (light blue-green), magenta (purplish red), yellow, and black tints. Colors defined in the CUSTOM COLOR dialog box may then be used in the stroke or fill of an object via the PAINT STYLE dialog box.

MAKE COMPOUND (⌘-⌥-G) combines two or more selected objects into a single *compound path*, in which the foremost objects cut holes in the fill of the rearmost object. You may determine which objects cut holes and which do not by selecting individual objects with the direct-selection tool and using the "Reverse" option in the PAINT STYLE dialog box. Objects from different groups may not be combined with the MAKE COMPOUND command. If no object is selected, this command is dimmed.

RELEASE COMPOUND (⌘-⌥-U) separates a compound path into its original objects. The "Reverse" option in the PAINT STYLE dialog box becomes dimmed, and all objects become opaque. If no object is selected, the RELEASE COMPOUND command is dimmed.

The Type menu

For years, Adobe Illustrator has been criticized for its poor text handling, and deservedly so. Text blocks were limited to 255 characters and different type specifications could not be combined in a single block. But now all that has been changed. In fact, with version 3.0, Illustrator has advanced from one of the worst programs for creating type to one of the best. Perhaps no other software provides such a wide variety of text formatting capabilities.

Type	
Style...	⌘T
Font	▶
Size	▶
Leading	▶
Alignment	▶
Spacing Options...	⌘⇧O
Tracking...	⌘⇧K
Link	⌘⇧G
Unlink	⌘⇧U
Make Text Wrap	
Release Text Wrap	
Create Outlines	

STYLE… (⌘-T) brings up the TYPE STYLE dialog box, in which you may alter the font, type size, leading, tracking, vertical shift, and horizontal scaling of the currently selected type or, if no text is selected, the next text entry. If a text block is selected with the arrow tool, the new formatting specifications affect the entire block. If type is highlighted with one of the type tools, the formatting affects only the highlighted text. The TYPE STYLE dialog box also controls paragraph formatting, including alignment, indentation, hanging punctuation, vertical paragraph spacing, as well as horizontal word spacing and letter spacing.

FONT displays a pop-up menu filled with the names of *fonts* (typefaces) you have used since first launching Illustrator as well as those contained in the Adobe Illustrator Startup file. To access fonts that are not listed, choose the "Other…" option (or press ⌘-⇧-F) to bring up the FONT dialog box, which offers access to every font available to your System. A check mark next to a font name indicates the typeface of the selected characters. If the selected text is set in more than one typeface, no check mark will display.

Typefaces are always listed individually in the FONT pop-up menu—"Helvetica-Regular," "Helvetica-Oblique," "Helvetica-Bold"—so that a single large family like Helvetica can fill an entire screen. Ironically, Adobe distributes a utility called Type Reunion that groups fonts by family, but it is incompatible with Illustrator 3.0.

SIZE displays a pop-up menu of type-size options (measured in points). These options represent the most common sizes, but any size between 0.1 and 1296 points is permitted. To access an uncommon size, choose the "Other…" option (or press ⌘-⇧-S) to bring up the TYPE SIZE dialog box. Enter a size and leading value and press RETURN. A check mark next to an option indicates the type size of the selected characters. If the selected text is set in more than one type size, no check mark will display.

Type size can be adjusted from the keyboard by the amount specified in the TYPE PREFERENCES dialog box (accessed by way of the PREFERENCES… command). Press COMMAND-SHIFT-< to decrease the type size, press COMMAND-SHIFT-> to make selected letters larger.

LEADING displays a pop-up menu of *leading* options (the amount of space between lines of type, measured in points). These options represent the most common leadings, but any size between 0.1 and 1296 points is permitted. To access an uncommon leading, choose the "Other…"

option (or press ⌘-⇧-S) to bring up the TᲠᲺᲠ SᲉᴢᲠ dialog box. Enter a size and leading value and press ᲩᲩᲬ᳊Ჩ᳈. A check mark next to an option indicates the leading value of the selected characters. If the selected text is not uniformly leaded, no check mark will display.

Leading can be adjusted from the keyboard by the amount specified in the TᲠᲺᲠ PᲩᲠ᳈ᲠᲩᲠ᳆᳈ᲠᲽ dialog box. Press ᴡᲺ᳈Ᲊᴡ᳆-↑ to decrease the amount of space between lines of type, press ᴡᲺ᳈Ᲊᴡ᳆-↓ to increase the leading.

AᲴᲉᲰ᳆ᲽᲠ᳆᳈ displays a pop-up menu of alignment options for one or more selected paragraphs. Your choices are "Left" (⌘-⇧-L), "Centered" (⌘-⇧-C), "Right" (⌘-⇧-R), and "Justified" (⌘-⇧-J). A check mark next to an option indicates the alignment of the selected characters. If the selected paragraphs are aligned differently, no check mark will display.

S᳄ᲠᲉᲰ᳈ O᳄᳆Ᲊᴡ᳈᳆… (⌘-⇧-O) brings up the S᳄ᲠᲉᲰ᳈ O᳄᳆Ᲊᴡ᳈᳆ dialog box, which controls the amount of horizontal space between letters and words in a selected paragraph. Both word spacing and letter spacing are measured in percentages of the width of a space character in the current type size and font.

TᲩᲠᲽᲳᲉ᳈Ჰ… (⌘-⇧-K) brings up the TᲩᲠᲽᲳᲉ᳈Ჰ dialog box, which allows you to tighten or loosen the amount of spacing between multiple characters of type. *Tracking* is like letter spacing, except that it is measured differently, in increments of $\frac{1}{1000}$ of an *em space* (a space as wide as the current type size—for example, a 12-point em space is 12 points wide). Negative values squeeze letters closer together, positive values spread them apart.

The Type menu:
- Style... ⌘T
- Font ▸
- Size ▸
- Leading ▸
- Alignment ▸
- Spacing Options... ⌘⇧O
- Kern... ⌘⇧K
- Link ⌘⇧G
- Unlink ⌘⇧U
- Make Text Wrap
- Release Text Wrap
- Create Outlines

KᲠᲩ᳈… (⌘-⇧-K) appears in place of the TᲩᲠᲽᲳᲉ᳈Ჰ… command when you click between two characters with one of the type tools, rather than highlighting one or more letters. Choosing this command brings up the KᲠᲩ᳈Ᲊ᳈Ჰ dialog box, which allows you to tighten or loosen the amount of spacing between two particular characters of type. Like tracking, *kerning* is measured in increments of $\frac{1}{1000}$ em space. Negative values squeeze the pair of letters closer together, positive values spread them apart.

Both tracking and kerning can be adjusted from the keyboard by the distance specified in the TᲠᲺᲠ PᲩᲠ᳈ᲠᲩᲠ᳆᳈ᲠᲽ dialog box. Press ᴡᲺ᳈Ᲊᴡ᳆-← to squeeze letters together, press ᴡᲺ᳈Ᲊᴡ᳆-→ to spread them apart. To squeeze or spread selected letters by five times the distance set in the TᲠᲺᲠ PᲩᲠ᳈ᲠᲩᲠ᳆᳈ᲠᲽ dialog, press ᲳᴡᲽᲽᲠ᳆᳈-ᴡᲺ᳈Ᲊᴡ᳆-← or ᲳᴡᲽᲽᲠ᳆᳈-ᴡᲺ᳈Ᲊᴡ᳆-→.

Link (⌘-⇧-G) is used to link columns of text. If you enter or import more text than will fit into a single column drawn with the type tool, a small plus sign will display in the bottom, right corner of the column rectangle. To *flow* the type into additional columns, select both the overfull column and one or more paths (which can be any shape or size, open or closed) and choose the Link command. Paths from different groups may not be combined with the Link command. If no object is selected, this command is dimmed.

Unlink (⌘-⇧-U) separates linked text blocks as well as the type they contain. All paths contain the same type they did before, but now each text block is separate; changing the shape of a path with the direct-selection tool will not cause text to flow from one text block to another. If no object is selected, the Unlink command is dimmed.

Make Text Wrap forces type to flow around the boundary of a graphic image. To wrap text, position the paths that make up the graphic image in front of the text you wish to wrap. Select text and graphics and choose the Make Text Wrap command. All selected objects are combined into a single *wrapped image*.

To change the amount of gutter (called *standoff*) between text and graphics, rewrap the text around an unpainted path that matches the basic outline of the graphic image. Then reshape the path to conform to the graphic image in a more desirable manner.

Release Text Wrap separates a selected wrapped image into its original text and graphic objects. Type will pass behind the paths that make up the graphic just as they did prior to choosing the Make Text Wrap command.

Create Outlines converts a block of text selected with the arrow tool into a collection of editable paths. For example, the letter A would be converted into a path that forms the outline of the letter A. This command is most useful for converting large type that you intend to use to create logos and other textual effects. The selected type must be set in a Type 1 font, which includes any typeface marketed by Adobe, Linotype, Bitstream, and many other major distributors. Note that this command functions only if Adobe Type Manager 2.0 (included with Illustrator 3.0) has been copied to your System folder and is currently running.

The Window menu

The commands in the WINDOW menu control the display of the Clipboard and toolbox. They also allow you to juggle multiple illustrations as well as multiple views of a single illustration.

SHOW/HIDE CLIPBOARD toggles the display of the CLIPBOARD window, which shows the current contents of the Macintosh Clipboard. Click the close box or choose HIDE CLIPBOARD to close the CLIPBOARD window.

 The CLIPBOARD window almost never accurately displays objects cut or copied from Illustrator. Rather than displaying the element, the phrase "1 objects" may appear. In such a case, you must execute the PASTE command to view the Clipboard contents.

HIDE/SHOW TOOLBOX toggles the display of the Illustrator toolbox (described earlier in this chapter). The toolbox is independent of the current document.

RESET TOOLBOX resets the Illustrator toolbox to its default collection of tools. All alternate tools are replaced.

NEW WINDOW displays a new view of the current window. Each new window that you create may utilize a different display mode and view size. However, each window of the current document will continuously update as you create and manipulate objects, thus slowing the drawing process. After creating a new window, if you choose the ARTWORK & TEMPLATE command from the VIEW menu for one window and choose the PREVIEW command for the other window, you may then draw in the first window and preview your results in the second, effectively allowing you to draw in the preview mode.

Below these is the name of each open illustration. The name of the current illustration is preceded by a check mark. Selecting any file name command will bring that window to the forefront of your screen.

The Graph menu

Like the TYPE menu, the GRAPH menu is a new addition to the Illustrator 3.0 menu bar. The commands in this menu control the manipulation of charts created with the graphing tools available from the bar-graph tool slot. Although the placement of this menu is a little flawed (*no* menu should appear to the right of the WINDOW menu), there is a certain symmetry to the fact that the last menu corresponds to the last tool slot.

GRAPH STYLE... (⌘-⇧-⌥-S) brings up the GRAPH STYLE dialog box, which allows you to change the graph type used to represent a selected graph or series. For example, if you changed a bar chart to a line chart, the data would remain the same, only the way in which it was represented would change. You may also select from various graph attributes, some of which are unique to the selected graph type and some of which are applicable to any selected chart. The "Axis" options determine the positioning of the Y axis, the size of tick marks, and the location of labels.

GRAPH DATA... (⌘-⇧-⌥-D) displays the same GRAPH DATA dialog box that appears after you click or drag with one of the graphing tools. Here you may enter, import, and edit data associated with the selected chart, transpose rows and columns in the spreadsheet, switch the X and Y axes, adjust the number of significant digits in decimals, and change the width of columns in the spreadsheet matrix. If no object is selected, the GRAPH DATA... command is dimmed.

USE COLUMN DESIGN... (⌘-⇧-⌥-C) allows you to select from a library of *graph designs*, created using the DEFINE GRAPH DESIGN... command, which will appear as columns in a cluster or stacked bar chart. You may also specify whether the design is scaled to represent different values, repeated, or stretched in a predetermined area. For example, if the design were a drawing of a hammer, you might create it so that the handle stretched to represent large values, but that the base and head of the hammer remain constant in size. If no design has yet been defined, the USE COLUMN DESIGN... command is dimmed.

USE MARKER DESIGN... (⌘-⇧-⌥-M) allows you to select from a library of graph designs, created using the DEFINE GRAPH DESIGN... command, which will appear as markers in a line or scatter chart. If no design has yet been defined, the USE MARKER DESIGN... command is dimmed.

DEFINE GRAPH DESIGN... (⌘-⇧-⌥-G) brings up the DESIGN dialog box, used to define, name, and organize graph designs. The selected design appears in the bottom right corner of the dialog box. To define a new design, select a rectangle with a collection of design elements in front of it, choose the DEFINE GRAPH DESIGN... command, and click the NEW button. Designs defined in this way may then be applied as columns in bar charts, using the USE COLUMN DESIGN... command, or as markers in line or scatter charts, using the USE MARKER DESIGN... command. If no object is selected, the DEFINE GRAPH DESIGN... command is dimmed.

Shortcuts

As with any drawing program, most interaction with Adobe Illustrator must be performed using your mouse. However, a number of commands, options, and other operations can also be executed by way of the keyboard or via keyboard and mouse combinations. The charts in this section contain all keyboard equivalents applicable to Illustrator, categorized by function. The following is a list of commonly accepted Apple keyboard symbols used throughout our charts:

⌘	COMMAND (cloverleaf) or APPLE (⍟) key
⇧	SHIFT key
⌥	OPTION key
⌃	CONTROL key (Mac Plus users substitute Z key)
⇥	TAB key
↩	RETURN key
⤻	ENTER key
⌫	DELETE or BACKSPACE key
▦	precedes characters that must be accessed from keypad
▦⌀	CLEAR key
▬	SPACEBAR
↑	UP CURSOR ARROW key
←	LEFT CURSOR ARROW key
↓	DOWN CURSOR ARROW key
→	RIGHT CURSOR ARROW key

We also make use of the following mouse symbols:

▸	mouse click
▸▸	double-click
▸▸▸	triple-click
┄▸	mouse drag

In each keyboard equivalent, keyboard symbols are separated by hyphens. This indicates that you should simultaneously press all keys displayed. For example, the keyboard equivalent for the Select All command is ⌘-A. This means that you should press both the command key and the A key *at the same time* to perform the Select All command.

Mouse actions are a little more difficult. If one or more key symbols precede a mouse symbol, you should press the key(s), perform the mouse operation, and then release the key(s). For example, the shorthand for selecting multiple objects is ⇧-▶. This means to press shift, click the object, and release the shift key; the shift key is held down throughout the completion of the mouse operation. On the other hand, if the key symbol appears *after* the mouse symbol, you are instructed to begin performing the mouse operation, *then* press the key, release the mouse button, and then release the key. To constrain the movement of one or more selected objects in a perpendicular direction, for example, you should perform the operation ▒▶-⇧, which means to begin dragging the selected object before pressing the shift key. When you are pleased with the new positioning, release the mouse button and then release the shift key.

The keyboard equivalents lists start on the following page.

Menu commands

The following list shows how to access most of the menu commands included in Adobe Illustrator 3.0 using keystrokes and simple mouse operations. All commands that are not listed cannot be accessed from the keyboard and must be chosen from a menu.

Command or option	Keystroke and/or mouse action
Actual Size	⌘-H or ⌥-👆👆 hand tool icon in toolbox
Average…	⌘-L
Artwork & Template	⌘-E
Artwork Only	⌘-W
Bring To Front	⌘-= (COMMAND-EQUAL)
Centered (Alignment pop-up)	⌘-⇧-C
Clear	⌫ or ⌨✐
Close	👆 close box in illustration title bar
Copy	⌘-C
Cut	⌘-X
Define Graph Design…	⌘-⇧-⌥-G
Fit In Window	⌘-M or 👆👆 hand tool icon in toolbox
Graph Data…	⌘-⇧-⌥-D
Graph Style…	⌘-⇧-⌥-S
Group	⌘-G
Hide	⌘-3
Hide Rulers	⌘-R
Hide Toolbox	👆 close box in toolbox title bar
Join…	⌘-J
Justified (Alignment pop-up)	⌘-⇧-J
Kern…	⌘-⇧-K
Left (Alignment pop-up)	⌘-⇧-L
Link	⌘-⇧-G
Lock	⌘-1
Make Compound	⌘-⌥-G
Make Guide	⌘-5
Move…	⌥-👆 arrow tool slot in toolbox
New…	⌘-N
New… (with no template)	⌘-⌥-N

Command or option	Keystroke and/or mouse action
Open…	⌘-O
Open… (with new template)	⌘-⌥-O
Other… (Font pop-up)	⌘-⇧-F
Other… (Size or Leading)	⌘-⇧-S
Paste	⌘-V
Paste In Back	⌘-B
Paste In Front	⌘-F
Preferences…	⌘-K
Preview Illustration	⌘-Y
Preview Selection	⌘-⌥-Y
Print…	⌘-P
Quit	⌘-Q
Redo [Operation]	⌘-Z
Release Compound	⌘-⌥-U
Release Guides (all)	⌘-6
Release Guides (single)	⇧-⌃-▶▶ guide in drawing area
Reset Toolbox (all slots)	⌘-⇧-▶▶ any slot in toolbox
Reset Toolbox (single slot)	⇧-▶▶ specific slot in toolbox
Right (Alignment pop-up)	⌘-⇧-R
Save	⌘-S
Select All	⌘-A
Send To Back	⌘-– (COMMAND-HYPHEN)
Show All	⌘-4
Show Rulers	⌘-R
Spacing Options…	⌘-⇧-O
Style (Paint menu)	⌘-I
Style (Type menu)	⌘-T
Transform Again	⌘-D
Tracking…	⌘-⇧-K
Undo [Operation]	⌘-Z
Ungroup	⌘-U
Unlink	⌘-⇧-U
Unlock All	⌘-2
Use Column Design…	⌘-⇧-⌥-C
Use Marker Design…	⌘-⇧-⌥-M

Tools

This list shows how to access many of the Adobe Illustrator tools. In most cases, a tool may be accessed only for as long as a key is pressed. Releasing the key returns you to the previously selected tool. Such equivalents are distinguished by the symbol ⚓, to indicate that the key must be held down. All tools that are not listed cannot be accessed from the keyboard and must be selected normally.

Tool	Keystroke
Current tool in arrow slot	⚓ ⌘
Arrow	⌘-➔ when direct-selection tool is selected
Direct-selection	⌘-➔ when arrow tool is selected
Object-selection	⚓⌥ when arrow tool is selected
Zoom	⚓ ⌘-␣
Zoom-out	⚓ ⌘-⌥-␣ or ⚓⌥ when zoom tool is selected
Hand	⚓ ␣
Type	⚓⌃ when area-type tool or path-type tool is selected
Area-type	⚓ on closed path or ⌥-⚓ on open path with type tool
Path-type	⚓ on open path or ⌥-⚓ on closed path with type tool
Freehand	⚓⌃ when pen tool is selected
Pen	⚓⌃ when freehand tool is selected
Centered-rectangle	⚓⌥ when rectangle tool is selected
Centered-rounded-rectangle	⚓⌥ when rounded-rectangle tool is selected
Centered-oval	⚓⌥ when oval tool is selected
Scale-dialog	⚓⌥ when scale tool is selected
Rotate-dialog	⚓⌥ when rotate tool is selected
Reflect-dialog	⚓⌥ when reflect tool is selected
Shear-dialog	⚓⌥ when shear tool is selected
Add-point	⚓⌥ when scissors tool is selected
Convert-point	⚓⌘-⌃ or ⚓⌃ when arrow tool is selected

Creating and manipulating type

This list explains how to create, select, flow, and reposition type using tools available from the arrow tool and type tool slots.

Type manipulation	Keystroke and/or mouse action
Create type at origin point	↑ with type tool, enter text
Create type in column	···↑ with type tool, enter text
Create type inside path	↑ on path with type tool or area-type tool, enter text
Create type on path	↑ on path with path-type tool, enter text
Insert type in text block	↑ in block with any type tool, enter text
Select type in text block	···↑ in block with any type tool
Select word	↑↑ in block with any type tool
Select paragraph	↑↑↑ in block with any type tool
Delete type in text block	···↑ in block with any type tool, ⌫ or ▭⌮
Delete word	↑↑ in block with any type tool, ⌫ or ▭⌮
Delete paragraph	↑↑↑ in block with any type tool, ⌫ or ▭⌮
Replace type in text block	···↑ in block with any type tool, enter text
Replace word	↑↑ in block with any type tool, enter text
Replace paragraph	↑↑↑ in block with any type tool, enter text
Flow text into new column	↖-···↑ column with direct-selection tool
Flow text into new path	↖-···↑ path with direct-selection tool
Move text along path	···↑ I-beam with arrow tool
Flip direction of text on path	↑↑ I-beam with arrow tool

Formatting type

Although all text created in Adobe Illustrator must be entered from the keyboard, much of the formatting must be accomplished by choosing a command and applying various options. The handful of formatting functions that can be accessed from the keyboard are included in the list below. All keyboard formatting controls except alignment rely on increments set in the TYPE PREFERENCES dialog box. Text must first be selected with the arrow or type tool before formatting can be applied.

Formatting function	Keystroke
Increase type size	⌘-⇧-<
Decrease type size	⌘-⇧->
Increase leading	⌥-↓
Decrease leading	⌥-↑
Kern together by increment	⌥-←
Kern apart by increment	⌥-→
Kern together by 5× increment	⌘-⌥-←
Kern apart by 5× increment	⌘-⌥-→
Increase tracking	⌥-→
Decrease tracking	⌥-←
Increase track by 5× increment	⌘-⌥-→
Decrease track by 5× increment	⌘-⌥-←
Increase vertical shift	⇧-⌥-↓
Decrease vertical shift	⇧-⌥-↑
Hyphenate word	⌘-⇧-— (COMMAND-SHIFT-HYPHEN)
Center-align paragraph	⌘-C
Justify paragraph	⌘-J
Left-align paragraph	⌘-L
Right-align paragraph	⌘-R

Using dialog boxes

Keyboard equivalents can also be used to select options and activate buttons inside dialog boxes. Most of the keystrokes listed below work inside all dialog boxes. The only exception in the NONE button, which is available only in the PLEASE OPEN TEMPLATE dialog box.

Dialog box function	Keystroke
Advanced to next option box	➔|
Cancel button	⌘-. (COMMAND-PERIOD)
None button	⌘-N
OK button	↵ or ⤜
Select contents of option box	⌘-A
Delete contents of option box	⌘-A, ⌫

Entering graph data

The GRAPH DATA dialog box is operated differently than any other dialog box in Adobe Illustrator. It allows additional and alternate keyboard equivalents, as listed below.

Dialog box function	Keystroke
Select cell data	↖ in cell
Select multiple cells	⸱⸱⸱↖ over cells
Clear multiple cells	⸱⸱⸱↖ over cells, ⌨⬗
Return character in cell data	| (vertical line character, SHIFT-BACKSLASH)
Use numerical value as label	" (straight quote marks) around number
Move one cell right	➔| or →
Move one cell left	←
Move one cell up	↑
Move one cell down	↵ or ↓
Change width of cell	⸱⸱⸱↖ column handle
OK button	⤜
Cancel change to cell data	⌘-Z
Cancel all changes	↖ close box, ↖ DON'T SAVE button

Creating and reshaping objects

The items below describe ways to create and edit various common elements in Adobe Illustrator. All of these items require the use of a mouse in one way or another. Many require use of the keyboard as well.

Drawing operation	Keystroke and/or mouse operation
Circle, draw from arc	⇧-⌖ with oval tool
Circle, draw from center	⇧-⌥-⌖ with oval tool
Circle, adjust curvature	⌖ Bézier control handle with direct-selection tool
Close open path	⌖ around points with arrow tool, ⌘-J
Corner point, create	⌖ with pen tool
Corner point, add handle	⌖, ⌥-⌖ same point with pen tool
Corner pt., make smooth	⌖ point with convert-point tool
Curved line, draw	⌖, ⌖ separate locations with pen tool
Curved segment, adjust	⌖ Bézier control handle or segment with arrow tool
Cusp point, create	⌖, ⌥-⌖ same point with pen tool
Delete point, break path	⌖ point with arrow tool, ⌫
Delete point, do not break	⌖ point with delete-point tool
Ellipse, draw from arc	⌖ with oval tool
Ellipse, draw from center	⌥-⌖ with oval tool
Ellipse, adjust curvature	⌖ BCH with direct-selection tool
Extend open path	⌖ endpoint with pen, freehand, or autotrace tool
Insert point in path	⌥-⌖ segment with scissors tool
Insert two endpoints in path	⌖ segment with scissors tool
Join two endpoints into one	⌖ around points with arrow tool, ⌘-L, ↵, ⌘-J, ↵
Join two endpoints with line	⌖ around points with arrow tool, ⌘-J
Open closed path	⌖ point or segment with arrow tool, ⌫; or ⌖ point or segment with scissors tool
Perpendicular line, draw	⌖, ⇧-⌖ separate locations with pen tool

Drawing operation	Keystroke and/or mouse operation
Rectangle, draw from corner	⋯↖ with rectangle tool
Rectangle, draw from center	✍-⋯↖ with rectangle tool
Rounded rect., from corner	⋯↖ with rounded-rectangle tool
Rounded rect., from center	✍-⋯↖ with rounded-rectangle tool
Rounded rect., adjust corner	⋯↖ Bézier control handle with direct-selection tool
Rounded square, from corner	⇧-⋯↖ with rounded-rectangle tool
Rounded square, from center	⇧-✍-⋯↖ with rounded-rectangle tool
Rounded sqr., adjust corner	⋯↖ Bézier control handle with direct-selection tool
Select grouped path	↖ point or segment with arrow tool
Select ungrouped path	✍-↖ point or segment with arrow tool
Select single path in group	✍-↖ point or segment with direct-selection tool
Select point	↖ point with arrow tool
Select point in group	↖ point with direct-selection tool
Select multiple points	⋯↖ around points or ↖ one, ⇧-↖ another with arrow or direct-selection tool
Select segment	↖ segment with arrow tool
Select segment in group	↖ segment with direct-selection tool
Smooth point, create	⋯↖ with pen tool
Smooth point, delete handle	⋯↖, ✍-↖ same point with pen tool
Smooth pt., make corner	↖ point with convert-point tool
Smooth pt., make cusp	⋯↖ Bézier control handle with convert-point tool
Split point into endpoints	↖ point with scissors tool
Square, draw from corner	⇧-⋯↖ with rectangle tool
Square, draw from center	⇧-✍-⋯↖ with rectangle tool
Straight line, draw	↖, ↖ separate locations with pen tool

Manipulating objects

Manipulating elements in Adobe Illustrator also requires some use of a mouse as well as occasional keystrokes. The following are the most common transformations and duplications.

Manipulation	Keystroke and/or mouse operation
Clone entire object	⌥-⌖ object with arrow tool
Clone partial object	⌖-⌥ object with arrow tool
Move object	⌖ object with arrow tool
Move object perpendicularly	⌖-⇧ object with arrow tool
Move by specified increment	↑, ←, ↓, or →
Reflect selected object	⤢, ⤢ separate locations with reflect tool
Reflect object horizontally	⤢, ⇧-⤢ to left or right with reflect tool
Reflect object vertically	⤢, ⇧-⤢ above or below with reflect tool
Reflect and clone object	⤢, ⌥-⤢ with reflect tool
Reflect and duplicate object	⤢, ⌥-⤢ with reflect tool, ⌘-D
Rotate selected object	⤢, ⌖ separate locations with rotate tool
Rotate object multiple of 45°	⤢, ⇧-⌖ with rotate tool
Rotate and clone object	⤢, ⌥-⌖ with rotate tool
Rotate and duplicate object	⤢, ⌥-⌖ with rotate tool, ⌘-D
Scale selected object	⤢, ⌖ separate locations with scale tool
Scale object horizontally	⤢, ⇧-⌖ to left or right with scale tool
Scale object proportionally	⤢, ⇧-⌖ diagonally with scale tool
Scale object vertically	⤢, ⇧-⌖ above or below with scale tool
Scale and clone object	⤢, ⌥-⌖ with scale tool
Scale and duplicate object	⤢, ⌥-⌖ with scale tool, ⌘-D
Slant selected object	⤢, ⌖ separate locations with shear tool
Slant object horizontally	⤢, ⇧-⌖ to left or right with shear tool
Slant object vertically	⤢, ⇧-⌖ above or below with shear tool
Slant and clone object	⤢, ⌥-⌖ with shear tool
Slant and duplicate object	⤢, ⌥-⌖ with shear tool, ⌘-D

A Brief Tour
of Adobe
Illustrator 3.0

Now that we have defined the terms we will use to discuss Adobe Illustrator 3.0 and have taken a look at the tools and menus of the application, it is time to start using Illustrator. This chapter will introduce the most basic activities you will perform when using Illustrator: starting the application, creating new files, opening existing files, altering the view size of your drawing area, previewing your drawing, saving files, closing files, and quitting Illustrator.

Starting Illustrator

After you have installed Adobe Illustrator and its related utilities and documents as described in Appendix A, *Installing Illustrator*, you must *launch* the application before you can begin drawing. Illustrator may be launched in any of the following ways:

- **Double-click the Illustrator application icon**. The Illustrator application icon is shown with an Illustrator document in Figure 3.01 as it appears inside a folder at the Finder level. You may double-click the icon to launch the program, or select the icon by clicking on it and choose the OPEN command from the Finder FILE menu.

- **Double-click an Illustrator 3.0 document**. Figure 3.01 displays a typical Illustrator 3.0 file, also called an *illustration*. Double-clicking on this file will launch Illustrator and immediately open the file. Alternatively, you may select the file and choose OPEN from the Finder FILE menu.

 To open multiple illustrations at once, press SHIFT and click on each of the files you want to open. Then press the OPTION key and double-click on any one of the selected files.

- **Use a launching utility**. If you own a launching utility such as OnCue, Desktop, or MasterJuggler, you may launch Illustrator by choosing it as a command from a menu of application names. Using a macro program like QuicKeys or Tempo, you may launch Illustrator by pressing a sequence of keys, such as COMMAND-CONTROL-I.

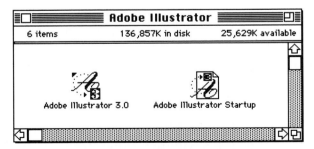

Figure 3.01: The Illustrator application (left) with an illustration file (right) as they appear at the Finder level.

If you are launching Illustrator for the first time (assuming no one has previously launched this copy of the application), you will be presented with the PLEASE PERSONALIZE dialog box shown in Figure 3.02. Here, you must personalize your copy of Illustrator by entering the appropriate information into the "Name" and "Organization" option boxes. (It is not necessary to enter an organization in order to run the application.)

Figure 3.02: The Please personalize dialog box appears the first time you launch Adobe Illustrator.

Each time you launch Illustrator, the startup screen shown in Figure 3.03 will appear, displaying the name and organization that you entered into the PLEASE PERSONALIZE dialog box. The startup screen is provided simply as an introduction, to let you know that you are in fact running the Illustrator application. It will automatically disappear after a few seconds. Incidentally, if you ever wish to see the startup screen again, you may select ABOUT ADOBE ILLUSTRATOR... from the APPLE (⬤) menu. This screen features an extra line of text listing the amount of free space that currently remains available in the portion of your computer's RAM allocated to Adobe Illustrator (known as *application RAM*). To prevent system errors that may crash your machine and result in the loss of time and data, at least 300K of application RAM should remain unused at all times while using Adobe Illustrator.

Figure 3.03: The Adobe Illustrator 3.0 startup screen, which lists copyright, memory, and personalized user information.

After Illustrator finishes launching and the startup screen disappears, you will find yourself at the *Illustrator desktop*. Unless you are running under MultiFinder, the desktop is empty except for the menu bar at the top of the screen. For the present, most of Illustrator's menus are dimmed. The only exceptions are the following:

- **New**..., which allows you to create a new illustration with or without a bitmapped tracing template.

- **Open**..., which allows you to open an existing illustration or create a new illustration, with or without a bitmapped tracing template.

- **Preferences**..., which allows you to adjust settings that control the performance of various tools and commands.

- **Quit**, which exits the Illustrator desktop and returns you to the Macintosh Finder (or previous application if running under MultiFinder).

All of these options are discussed in this chapter.

Creating a
new illustration

A new illustration is created by choosing the NEW… command under the FILE menu (⌘-N). Choosing NEW… displays the PLEASE OPEN TEMPLATE dialog box, shown in Figure 3.04.

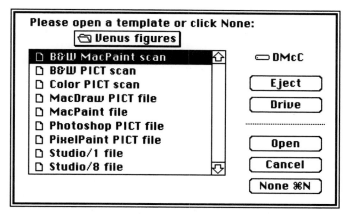

Figure 3.04: The Please open template dialog box allows you to select a bitmapped tracing template.

This dialog box allows you to select a bitmapped *tracing template* to aid in the creation your new illustration, create a new illustration without a template, or cancel the document creation process entirely. If you intend to use a tracing template for your illustration (as discussed on the next page), select a template document from the *scrolling file list* and click the OPEN button or press the RETURN key, or double-click on the template file name.

As in most Macintosh dialog boxes of this type, you can quickly locate a specific file by entering the first few letters in its name. The first file in alphabetical order whose name begins with these letters will be selected. (Any typing performed in the PLEASE OPEN TEMPLATE dialog does not appear on screen.) You may also press ↑ or ↓ to move up and down the scrolling file list.

If the file that you wish to open is on a disk or hard drive volume other than the one containing your Illustrator application, use the DRIVE and EJECT buttons to move between available drives and remove disks so that other disks may be inserted. Double-clicking a folder name in the scrolling file list will open that folder and display the files it contains. Drag down on the *folder bar* above the scrolling file list to close a folder and display the contents of the drive or folder in which the previous folder resides.

 Press the TAB key to activate the DRIVE button. Press COMMAND-SHIFT-1 to eject a disk from the upper (or only) floppy drive, press COMMAND-SHIFT-2 to eject a disk from the lower drive. Press COMMAND-↓ to open the selected folder, press COMMAND-↑ to close the current folder. Press COMMAND-PERIOD to cancel.

Clicking on the NONE button (⌘-N) instructs Illustrator to create a new illustration without a template. (You may always add a template later if you so desire.) Clicking on the CANCEL button directs the application to cancel the creation of the new document.

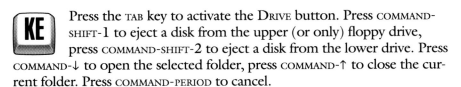 Press COMMAND-OPTION-N to bypass the PLEASE OPEN TEMPLATE dialog box and create a new document without a tracing template. An untitled illustration window will immediately display.

After opening a tracing template or clicking the NONE button, Illustrator creates a new document. An untitled *illustration window* and the Illustrator toolbox will appear. If you drag on a menu name, you will find that most of the commands are no longer dimmed.

Using tracing templates

To aid in the creation of high-resolution artwork, you may open a MacPaint or PICT-format file to use as a *tracing template*. The template appears in the background of your painting so that you can trace it using one of Illustrator's drawing tools. In many cases, it is easier to begin an illustration by tracing an existing image than by drawing the illustration from scratch. This is true even when the template is inexact or is only a partial representation of the graphic you wish to create, because Illustrator's powerful tools allow you to easily edit the image after you have traced it.

Any document saved in either the *MacPaint format* or the *PICT format* can be a tracing template. MacPaint-format documents may originate not only from MacPaint itself but also from other popular painting programs like DeskPaint, SuperPaint, PixelPaint, and Studio/1, as well as from scanning applications like ThunderWare. The MacPaint format is one of the most widely supported graphics formats for the Macintosh computer. Unfortunately, it is also the most limited. MacPaint files are exclusively *monochrome* (black and white—no colors or gray values), no larger than 8 inches by 10 inches, vertically oriented, and always bit-mapped at a resolution of 72 dots per inch. (See Chapter 1, *Drawing on the Macintosh.*

The PICT (QuickDraw picture) format, on the other hand, provides much more flexibility. The PICT format is most commonly associated with moderately powerful drawing applications such as MacDraw, Canvas, and MacDraft. But, in fact, PICT goes much farther. It is the original file-swapping format developed by Apple for the purpose of transferring both bitmapped and object-oriented pictures from one graphics application to another. PICT can accommodate any size graphic, resolutions exceeding 300 dots per inch, and over 16 million colors. For this reason, many scanning and image-editing applications, such as ImageStudio, PixelPaint, Studio/32, and PhotoShop, support this format. Sadly, Illustrator only marginally supports the PICT format. Object-oriented graphics are converted to bitmaps. Regardless of the resolution of the PICT image, Illustrator displays the file at 72 dot per inch. And although you may open color PICT files, Illustrator converts them to black and white. Light colors are changed to white, dark colors are changed to black. Typically, the result is a highly polarized graphic in which details become hard to trace or are completely obscured.

 When working from a color tracing template, convert the scan to black and white in your scanning or image-editing software before opening it in Illustrator.

Figure 3.05 on the next page demonstrates how a typical color scan appears when opened directly in Illustrator and when converted to black and white prior to being opened in Illustrator.

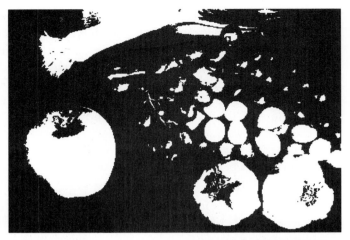

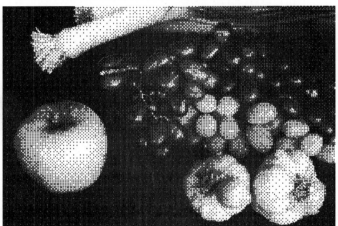

Figure 3.05: A color template converted to black and white by Illustrator (top) provides less detail than one that is converted to black and white in an image-editing software and then opened in Illustrator (bottom).

Whether the tracing template is a MacPaint or PICT file, Illustrator places it in the background of an illustration. A template image is generally displayed on screen in a uniform gray tone, as shown in Figure 3.06, so you may easily distinguish it from the illustration itself. No more than one template may exist within a single illustration at any one time. Also, a tracing template may not be moved, transformed, or duplicated; in fact, it cannot be manipulated in any manner. The placement of a template within the Illustrator window corresponds directly to the image's placement within the software from which it originates. To manipulate a template, you must perform the manipulation in the original application prior to introducing the template into an Illustrator file. Once in Illustrator, a template is not considered to be an integral part of an illustration. A template will neither preview nor print. In Illustrator, a template is useful for tracing, and nothing more.

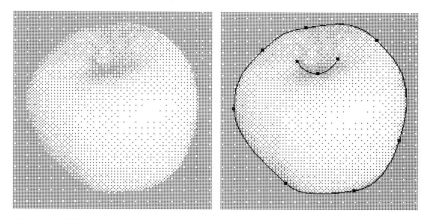

Figure 3.06: A tracing template appears grayed in the background of an Illustrator window to distinguish it from the lines and shapes used to trace it (right).

Kinds of tracing templates

The best way to think of a tracing template is in terms of its purpose, which may fall into one of three broad categories:

- **Scans** are electronic images of photographs, prints, or drawings. Black-and-white scans are commonly saved as MacPaint documents. Oversized or color scans may use the PICT format. Scans, especially when taken from photographs, offer exceptionally accurate tracing backgrounds. They are useful for detail work, such as schematic drawings, medical illustrations, and other situations where accuracy is paramount. They are also useful for people who wish to draw, but do not consider themselves very skilled in drawing. Scans can be the perfect bridge between an amateur effort and a professional product.

- **Sketches** are deeply embedded in the artistic tradition. If you were creating an oil painting, for example, you might make several sketches before deciding how the finished piece should look. After arriving at a satisfactory design, you would pencil it onto the canvas. Only after finalizing the sketch would you begin laying down the oils. Like oil paint, Illustrator is ill-suited to sketching. Sketches are best created in a painting application like MacPaint, DeskPaint, or SuperPaint. Painting programs provide an environment conducive to spontaneity, allowing you to scribble, erase, and create much like the pencil you use in sketching—quickly and freely. Once the final sketch has been completed, you may use it as a template in Illustrator, where the high-resolution, final artwork is created.

- **Drafts** are CAD (*computer-aided design*), schematic, or structured drawings created in MacDraw, MacDraft, Claris CAD, and similar applications. Perhaps the original drawing program did not provide the array of free-form illustration tools and capabilities available in Illustrator 3.0, or you wish to add details which may be coupled with the graphic in a page-layout software like PageMaker or QuarkXPress. Draft templates are typically transported via the PICT format.

The Illustrator desktop

Figure 3.07 on the next page shows the result of choosing NEW... and selecting a bitmapped sketch as the tracing template. This is the same Illustrator desktop that appears immediately after launching the Illustrator application, only now it contains an open *illustration window*. The desktop in Figure 3.07 is labeled, clearly displaying the following items (labeled items appear in bold type):

- **The menu bar** provides access to the nine menus discussed in the *Menus and commands* section of Chapter 2. Drag at a menu name to display a menu; release on a command name to choose a command.

- **The toolbox** includes the 16 default tools and the 23 alternate tools discussed in *The toolbox* section of Chapter 2. Also known as the *palette*, the toolbox includes its own title bar and close box.

Drag the **toolbox title bar** to move the toolbox; click the **toolbox close box** to hide the toolbox.

- **The illustration window** is the large window in the middle of the desktop. A window appears for every open illustration. Like the toolbox, the illustration includes a **window title bar** and a **window close box** for moving and closing the current illustration window. The title bar lists the names of the current illustration and the current tracing template file, separated by a colon (:). If the illustration has not been saved, the name will appear as "Untitled art" followed by a number. The title bar also includes a **window zoom box**, which when clicked enlarges the window to fill the entire screen (although it has no effect on the illustration itself). Click the zoom box again to reduce the window to normal size. Drag the **window size box** in the bottom right corner of the window to manually enlarge or reduce the size of the window.

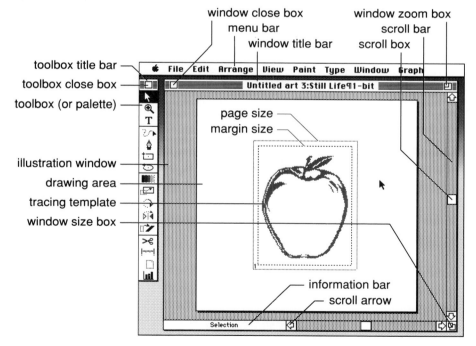

Figure 3.07: The Illustrator desktop, with all parts labeled.

- **The drawing area** is the white 18-inch-by-18-inch square inside the illustration window where objects and type may be created and manipulated. No object may be viewed if it is moved to a location outside the drawing area. The entire drawing area is visible when viewed at the fit-in-window view size (as shown in Figure 3.07). The dotted lines inside the drawing area indicate the **page size**, as specified with the PAGE SETUP... command, and the **margin size**, which defines the area of the page that may be printed (known as the *imageable area*). Objects in the *margin*—the space between the page size and the margin size borders—generally may not be printed. The grayed **tracing template** also appears in the drawing area.

- **The scroll bars** appear along the right and bottom edges of the illustration window, as they do in most Macintosh applications. They allow you to *scroll* the window; that is, move the window with respect to the drawing area. Click a **scroll arrow** to scroll the window 48 pixels. Click in the gray area of a scroll bar to scroll the window 240 pixels. Drag a **scroll box** to manually determine the distance scrolled.

- **The information bar** in the bottom left portion of the illustration window lists the name of the current tool or the current operation.

The cursor

The only desktop item not labeled in Figure 3.07 is the arrow-shaped *cursor*, the most important item in any drawing software. The cursor tracks the movement of your mouse as it relates to the Macintosh screen area. When positioned in any other part of the desktop but the drawing area, the cursor appears as a black arrow. In the drawing area, the cursor changes to reflect the current tool or the current operation. Table 3.01 shows every cursor that may appear in Adobe Illustrator 3.0 and describes the action that it implies.

Table 3.01: Cursors that may appear in the drawing area
and their meanings

selecting objects with arrow tool

selecting objects with object-selection tool

selecting objects with direct-selection tool

selecting whole paths with direct-selection tool (option key pressed)

dragging with any selection tool; freehand, autotrace, or pen tool; rectangle, rounded-rectangle, or oval tool; any transformation tool; the page tool; or any graph tool

cloning (option-dragging) with any selection or transformation tool

snapping to point or guide when dragging with any selection tool; pen tool; rectangle, rounded-rectangle, or oval tool; or any transformation or graph tool; erasing with freehand tool

cloning and snapping with any selection or transformation tool

expanding view size to twice previous magnification

contracting view size to half previous magnification

view size has reached maximum level of expansion or contraction

scrolling illustration window with hand tool

creating text in a column or aligned to a point with type tool

creating text inside a free-form path with area-type tool

fixing text to a free-form path with path-type tool

entering or editing existing type with any type tool

freehand or autotrace cursor prior to operation; pen tool cursor when no path is currently active

pen tool cursor when a path is active; rectangle, rounded-rectangle, or oval tool cursor prior to operation; reshaping a path with scissors, add-point, or delete-point tool; any graph tool prior to operation

Table 3.01: Cursors that may appear in the drawing area
and their meanings (cont.)

⊞	centered-rectangle, centered-rounded-rectangle, or centered-oval tool cursor prior to operation
┼	blend tool, any transformation (scale, rotate, flip, or shear) tool, measure tool, or page tool prior to initial click
┼····	blend tool, any transformation tool, or measure tool after initial click; any transformation-dialog tool prior to operation
↖	reshaping a path with convert-point tool
I	entering text in the Graph Data dialog box
⊞	adjusting column width in the Graph Data dialog box
⌚	waiting patiently for an operation to conclude

Opening an existing file

Existing illustrations can be opened while running Illustrator or directly from the Finder level. Illustrator 3.0 can also open files created in older versions of Illustrator, such as version 1.1 and Adobe Illustrator 88. Both alternatives are discussed in the following sections.

Opening illustrations at the Finder

If Illustrator is not already running, you can simultaneously open the Illustrator 3.0 application and a specific illustration file by double-clicking an illustration file icon at the Finder level. Figure 3.08 shows the various kinds of icons that may be associated with Illustrator documents. Double-clicking any of the files shown in the top row of the figure will launch the Illustrator 3.0 application. The two lower rows of files belong to Illustrator 88 and Illustrator 1.1, respectively. Double-clicking any of these files will launch an older version of Adobe Illustrator, or display the message "Application not found" if the older version of the Adobe Illustrator application does not reside on an available disk or hard drive. Such illustrations must be opened from inside Illustrator 3.0, as described in the next section.

Adobe Illustrator documents
9 items
141,780K in disk
20,706K available
3.0 file
3.0 Mac EPS file
3.0 PC EPS file
88 file
88 Mac EPS file
88 PC EPS file
1.1 file
1.1 Mac EPS file
1.1 PC EPS file

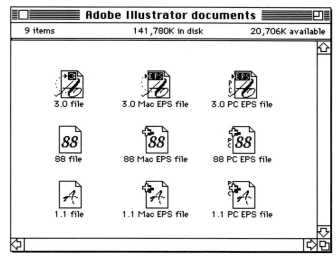

Figure 3.08: The nine types of Illustrator documents viewed by icon at the Finder level.

Figure 3.09 shows the files from Figure 3.08 when viewed by name. Be sure to double-click the small page icon rather than the file name when launching an illustration displayed in this manner.

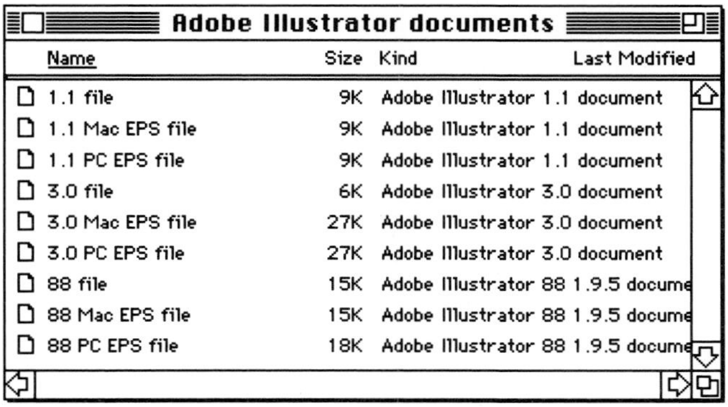

Adobe Illustrator documents
Name
Size
Kind
Last Modified
1.1 file 9K Adobe Illustrator 1.1 document
1.1 Mac EPS file 9K Adobe Illustrator 1.1 document
1.1 PC EPS file 9K Adobe Illustrator 1.1 document
3.0 file 6K Adobe Illustrator 3.0 document
3.0 Mac EPS file 27K Adobe Illustrator 3.0 document
3.0 PC EPS file 27K Adobe Illustrator 3.0 document
88 file 15K Adobe Illustrator 88 1.9.5 docume
88 Mac EPS file 15K Adobe Illustrator 88 1.9.5 docume
88 PC EPS file 18K Adobe Illustrator 88 1.9.5 docume

Figure 3.09: The same illustration files viewed by name at the Finder level.

Opening files inside Illustrator 3.0

To open an existing illustration while inside Illustrator 3.0, choose the OPEN... command from the FILE menu (⌘-O). Figure 3.10 displays the PLEASE OPEN ILLUSTRATION OR TEMPLATE dialog box that appears after choosing this command. To open an Illustrator document, double-click its name in the scrolling file list, or select the file and click the OPEN button or press RETURN. You may open an illustration created in Illustrator 3.0, Illustrator 88, or Illustrator 1.1. You may also open a template document, creating a new document with a tracing template just as if you had chosen the NEW... command and selected a template.

✱ The PLEASE OPEN ILLUSTRATION OR TEMPLATE dialog box makes no distinction between illustration and tracing template documents in its scrolling file list. To avoid confusion, we recommend that you employ a naming scheme. For example, you may append a ¶ symbol (OPTION-7) to the end of MacPaint and PICT file names.

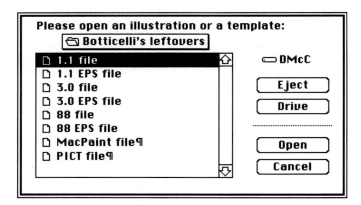

Figure 3.10: The Please open illustration or template dialog box allows you to either an illustration or template file.

The DRIVE and EJECT buttons, folder bar, and keyboard equivalents operate the same way as described for the PLEASE OPEN TEMPLATE dialog box in the *Creating a new illustration* section earlier in this chapter. Click the CANCEL button or press COMMAND-PERIOD to cancel the OPEN... operation.

Swapping tracing templates

Normally, when you open an existing illustration, the tracing template that was used to create the illustration is also opened and displayed in the drawing area. If you prefer to open an illustration with a different template or with no template at all, press the OPTION key while you choose the OPEN... command (⌘-⌥-O). After double-clicking an illustration name in the PLEASE OPEN ILLUSTRATION OR TEMPLATE dialog box, the PLEASE OPEN TEMPLATE dialog will appear. Here you may select a new template, eliminate the template by clicking NONE (⌘-N), or cancel the OPEN... command. In this way, you may add a template to an illustration that originally had none, subtract a template from an existing illustration, or replace one template with another.

You can open multiple files in Adobe Illustrator, provided that sufficient application RAM is available. An opened illustration will display in a window similar to that shown in Figure 3.07.

Working in the illustration window

Once you have opened an illustration or created a new one, it is important to know how to use tools, commands, and scroll bars to move around inside the illustration window. In this section, we discuss how to change the view size, scroll the drawing area inside the window, preview your illustration, and adjust the page size and placement.

Changing the view size

Illustrator provides nine *view sizes*; that is, levels of magnification at which the drawing area may be displayed in the illustration window. Expanded view sizes provide great detail, but allow only small portions of a page to be displayed at a time. Contracted view sizes allow you to look at a larger portion of the drawing area, but may provide insufficient detail for creating and manipulating objects. Because Illustrator makes it easy to quickly changes between various view sizes, you can accurately edit your artwork and still maintain an overall design consistency.

When you first enter a new or existing illustration, the drawing area is displayed at *actual size*. At actual size, the details of your illustration are displayed on screen at the size they will appear when printed. For this reason, actual size generally provides the most natural visual feedback concerning the progress of your artwork. The view size can be changed to actual size at any time by choosing the ACTUAL SIZE command from the VIEW menu (⌘-H).

Figure 3.11: An illustration viewed at actual size.

Another useful view size is *fit-in-window*, which reduces the drawing area so that it can be displayed in the illustration window in its entirety. The actual magnification level required to produce the fit-in-window view size is dependent on the size and resolution of your monitor, a calculation which Illustrator makes automatically. To get the scoop on the big picture, choose FIT IN WINDOW from the VIEW menu (⌘-M).

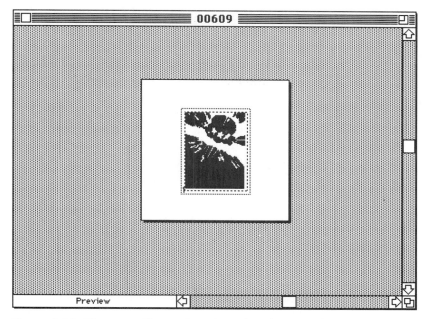

Figure 3.12: The same illustration viewed at fit-in-window size.

In addition to the actual and fit-in-window view sizes, Illustrator provides seven other levels of magnification, each accessed by using the *zoom tool*. When the zoom tool is selected, your cursor becomes a magnifying glass, displaying either a plus sign, a minus sign, or nothing in its center. The magnifying glass with inset plus sign functions as a *zoom-in tool*. Clicking in the drawing area with the zoom-in tool expands your view size to twice its previous level of magnification, thus displaying only half as much of your artwork. The magnifying glass with inset minus sign functions as a *zoom-out tool*. Clicking with the zoom-out tool contracts the view size to half its previous level of magnification, thus displaying twice as much of your artwork. The magnifying glass cursor appears empty when your current view size is at either the maximum (1600%) or minimum (6.25%) level of magnification possible; you may therefore zoom in or out no further. Clicking with the empty zoom tool temporarily displays the hand tool, which allows you to reposition the drawing work area on your screen (as described later in this chapter). Dragging with the zoom-in or zoom-out tool also temporarily accesses the hand tool after performing the desired expansion or contraction.

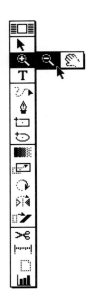

To access the zoom-in tool, select the zoom tool in the toolbox. If the zoom tool is not displayed in the second tool slot, press SHIFT and double-click the slot to reset it. To access the zoom-out tool, select the zoom tool and hold down the OPTION key. Or choose the zoom-out tool by dragging from the zoom tool slot.

To temporarily access the zoom tool when some other tool is selected, press and hold the COMMAND key and SPACEBAR. Releasing both keys will return the cursor to its previous appearance. Press COMMAND-OPTION-SPACEBAR to temporarily access the zoom-out tool.

Scrolling the drawing area inside the illustration window

Since most Macintosh screens are not as large as a full page, most users are not able to see their entire drawing when expanded to actual size or to a higher level of magnification. Therefore, Illustrator provides you with the ability to position your drawing area in reference to your illustration window, a technique known as *scrolling*.

The first method for scrolling the drawing area is to use the two *scroll bars*, which are located at the bottom and right sides of the window. (Refer to Figure 3.07 for their location in respect to the Illustrator desktop.) At both ends of each scroll bar are the *scroll arrows*. Clicking directly on a scroll arrow scrolls the illustration window 48 pixels in that direction. But because the window remains stationary in the Illustrator desktop, the drawing area appears to move in the opposite direction. For example, if you click the *up* scroll arrow, the drawing area and its objects will appear to move *down*. This is because your window into the drawing area has been raised.

To scroll the window more quickly, drag one of the two *scroll boxes* that move back and forth inside the scroll bars. Be sure to drag in small increments; if you drag a scroll bar all the way to one side or the other of a scroll bar, you will scroll completely outside the drawing area.

You may also click within the gray area of a scroll bar. This will cause the drawing area to move 240 pixels (five times the result of clicking a scroll arrow) in one direction or another, depending on where you click in relation to the scroll box. If you click to the right of a scroll box, for example, the window scrolls to the right (so your drawing area appears to move to the left).

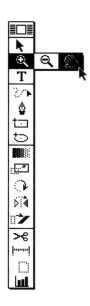

An easier way to move about your drawing area is to use the *hand tool*. You may choose the hand tool by dragging from the zoom tool slot. The hand tool allows you to drag the drawing area in 48-pixel increments with respect to the illustration window. In most situations, dragging with the hand tool is more convenient and more accurate than clicking on the arrows and dragging the boxes of the scroll bars.

KE To temporarily access the hand tool when some other tool is selected, press and hold the SPACEBAR. Releasing the SPACEBAR will return the cursor to its previous appearance. The hand tool may not be accessed from the keyboard when editing text.

Using display modes

Display modes provide another way to control the way you see images in the drawing area. When you first create a new illustration or open an existing one, images do not appear as they will print. Instead, they are displayed as fine black outlines with transparent interiors. Only text displays as solid black, rather than outlined. No colors are shown. Any tracing template appears in the background as grayed.

This display mode is called the *artwork-&-template mode*, because you enter this mode by choosing the ARTWORK & TEMPLATE command from the VIEW menu (⌘-E). Only the objects that make up your artwork and the template may be seen. To its credit, the artwork-&-template mode is very fast. Illustrator doesn't have to spend time displaying complicated visual effects. However, drawing in the artwork-&-template mode may take some getting used to. In Figure 3.13, we have opened a drawing of some flowers. The grayed image is the template, the black outlines represent lines and shapes that make up the illustration. With some imagination and experience, you will become accustomed to drawing in this mode.

Sometimes, the template may obscure the objects that make up your artwork. This is particularly true if you are making changes to an image as you trace it. To hide the template, choose the ARTWORK ONLY command from the VIEW menu (⌘-W). This accesses the *artwork mode*, the only other display mode in which you may create and manipulate type and graphic objects in Adobe Illustrator. You may redisplay the tracing template by choosing ARTWORK & TEMPLATE.

Figure 3.13: An illustration viewed in the artwork-&-template mode.

If you wish to display the tracing template independently of your artwork, access the *template mode* by choosing the Template Only command from the View menu. All artwork and text objects will disappear. Rather than being grayed, the template is displayed in black as demonstrated earlier in this chapter in Figure 3.05. Any colors associated with a template do not appear, even if you are using a color monitor. To continue drawing, choose the Artwork Only or Artwork & Template command.

Previewing an illustration

Illustrator also allows you to *preview* the printed appearance of your illustration by choosing the Preview Illustration command from the View menu (⌘-Y). Figure 3.14 show how our flowers appear in the preview mode. Figure 3.15 shows the flowers when printed. The two are very similar, making the preview mode a useful method for assessing the appearance of your artwork. However, you may not draw in the preview mode. To create and manipulate type and graphic objects, you must return to the artwork mode or the artwork-&-template mode.

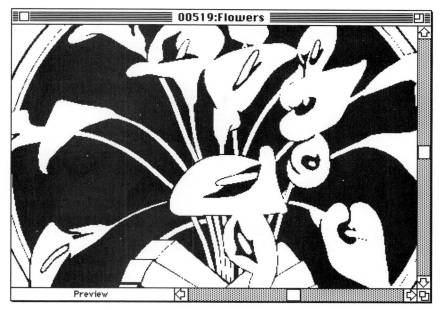

Figure 3.14: An illustration viewed in the preview mode.

Figure 3.15: The same illustration as it appears when printed.

But *why* doesn't Illustrator allow you to draw an image and preview it at the same time like most other applications? The primary reason is impracticality. Most Macintosh applications display images on your screen in a computer language called QuickDraw. When it comes time to print to a LaserWriter or comparable device, the software converts the QuickDraw image to the PostScript printer language. In most cases, this translation is made without any loss of information. Only when images are very complex do problems begin to arise. To avoid these complex printing problems, Illustrator both displays and prints images using the PostScript language. There are many advantages to this scheme: with few exceptions, drawings preview exactly as they will appear when printed, Type 1 fonts can be converted to editable paths in one or two seconds, and complex images may be printed to PostScript output devices with a degree of consistency that puts almost every other Macintosh application to shame. But there is one big disadvantage: You can figure that a drawing takes about the same amount of time to preview on your screen as it does to print. If you were to manipulate a complex illustration in the drawing mode, you would have to wait several seconds between each operation for the screen to refresh!

If, in spite of our warnings, you really prefer to draw in the preview mode, there is a way to fake it. The following steps describe how to set up the illustrator desktop so you can simultaneously manipulate and preview the current illustration:

1. Drag the window size box in the lower, right corner of the illustration window to the left to shrink the window to about half its current width.

2. Choose the New Window command from the Window menu. A new copy of the current illustration appears on your screen.

3. Drag the title bar of the new window to the right side of the screen so that it sits side by side with the original window.

4. Choose the Preview command from the View menu. Also change the view size and scroll the drawing area as desired. Notice that the window on the left side of the screen is unaffected.

5. Click the title bar of the left window to activate it. Draw in the left window. Any object you draw will display in the right window as it will appear when printed.

In Figure 3.16, we have used the NEW WINDOW command to create two windows for our flower drawing. In the left window, we have dragged an object to a new location in the illustration. The right window previews the result. The NEW WINDOW command allows you to create as many alternate views of the current illustration as you desire, each of which may be scrolled independently and may rely on its own view size and display mode.

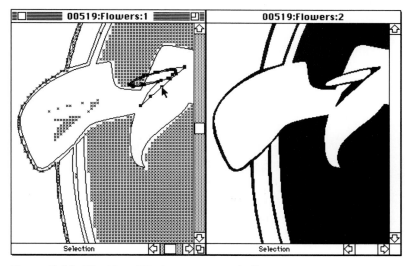

Figure 3.16: The New Window command allows you to simultaneously manipulate and preview an illustration.

By and large, we recommend simply executing an illustration in the artwork-&-template mode without bothering with multiple windows, which tend to be more hassle than they're worth. You may occasionally evaluate changes and check for problems by briefly visiting the preview mode.

To save additional time when previewing a complex illustration, Illustrator allows you to preview only the selected objects in an illustration by choosing the PREVIEW SELECTION command from the VIEW menu (⌘-⌥-Y). Objects that are not selected will not display. For complete information about selecting objects, see the *Selecting elements* section of Chapter 7, *Reshaping Existing Paths*.

Whether instigated using the Preview Illustration or Preview Selection command, you may cancel a screen preview in progress by pressing command-period. The illustration will be returned to the artwork-&-template mode.

Adjusting the page size

Another issue related to your perception of an illustration is *page size*; that is, the size and orientation of the page upon which the final artwork will be printed. The fact that Illustrator 3.0 is being promoted in some marketing niches as the only single-page document-creation program you'll ever need makes this issue even more important. Page size determines the size and positioning of text and graphic objects. Just as Frank Lloyd Wright designed private homes to both compliment and exploit their natural surroundings, you must design your artwork to compliment and exploit the dimensions of a printed page.

Specifying the size and orientation of the dotted page size border in the drawing area is a two-step process. First, choose the Chooser command from the list of desk accessories under the Apple menu. The Chooser desk accessory will appear, as shown in Figure 3.17. One or more *printer drivers* display on the left side of the window. Click on the icon labeled "LaserWriter," which is the driver for all PostScript-compatible printers. This allows you to prepare your illustration to be printed to a PostScript printer even if no such printer is currently hooked up to your Mac. Then click the close box to return to the Illustrator desktop.

 The second step is to choose the Page Setup... command from the File menu. The LaserWriter Page Setup dialog box will appear, as shown in Figure 3.18. You may select from five "Paper" options to determine the page size of the current illustration: "US Letter" (8½ by 11 inches, the default as well as the most common selection), "US Legal" (8½ by 14 inches), "A4 Letter" (a European size measuring 210 by 297 millimeters), "B5 Letter" (also European, 176 by 250 millimeters), and "Tabloid" (11 by 17 inches). If you are using a version of the LaserWriter driver that is older than version 5.2, your LaserWriter Page Setup dialog will not contain a "Tabloid" paper size option. If you are using LaserWriter driver 6.0 (included in the Apple Color folder of the Macintosh

Printing Tools disk for System 6.0.4 and later), you may drag on the "Tabloid" option to display a pop-up menu of other page sizes, including "A3 Tabloid" (European, 296 by 420 millimeters, a little wider and shorter than the American tabloid) and "No. 10 Envelope" (which in Illustrator merely decreases the margin size to about 3⅞ inches by 9⅛ inches inside a standard letter-sized page). This pop-up menu is displayed in Figure 3.18.

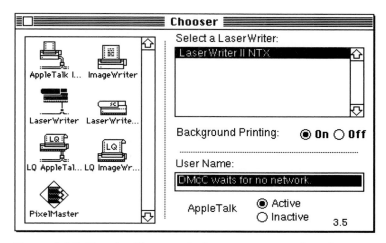

Figure 3.17: Use the Chooser desk accessory to select the LaserWriter printer driver.

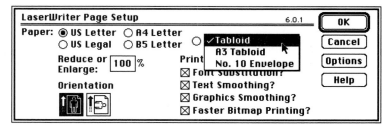

Figure 3.18: Use the LaserWriter Page Setup dialog box to determine page size and orientation.

You specify whether your page is set upright (the portrait setting) or on its side (the landscape setting) by selecting from the tall and wide "Orientation" page icons. Finally, the LASERWRITER PAGE SETUP dialog allows you to specify a scaling percentage by entering a number into the "Reduce or Enlarge" option box. This value alters the size of your printed illustration. Any value under 100% will reduce your illustration; any value over 100% will enlarge your illustration.

The four "Printer Effects" options have no influence over Adobe Illustrator files.

The OPTIONS button brings up the LASERWRITER OPTIONS dialog box, shown in Figure 3.19, which contains the "Larger Printable Area" option. When selected, this option enlarges the dotted *margin size* within the page size boundary in the drawing area. The margin size determines the *imageable area* of a page; that is, the area of the page that may be printed. Images in the *margin* between the margin size and page size boundaries will not print to most PostScript laser printers.

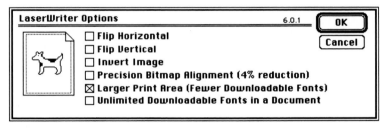

Figure 3.19: Use the LaserWriter Options dialog box to increase the margin size in the drawing area.

As in most dialog boxes, you may escape the LASERWRITER PAGE SETUP dialog box using the OK or CANCEL button. By clicking on the OK button, or pressing the RETURN key, you instruct Illustrator to configure the size and orientation of the page size in the drawing area according to your specifications. If you click CANCEL, your specifications are ignored.

Moving the page size in the drawing area

After specifying the page and margin sizes, you may wish to alter their placement in the drawing area. Page size placement is controlled using the *page tool*, the second-to-last tool in your palette. By clicking inside the drawing area with this tool, you indicate the bottom, left corner of the page size boundary. If you drag with the page tool, Illustrator displays a dotted outline of the page size, allowing you to position it as desired. After releasing your mouse button, Illustrator redraws the page size in its new location.

❋ When adjusting the placement of an illustration on a page, it is typically easier and faster to move the page size with respect to the artwork than to move the artwork inside the page, for the simple reason that you are moving only one element (the page) instead of many text and graphic elements.

Creating a two-page layout

Adobe promotes Illustrator 3.0 as a single-page design program. But it can also accommodate two side-by-side page designs, such as those required for center pages in a newsletter or fold-up flyer. The following steps describe how to display two letter-sized pages in the drawing area:

1. Choose the PREFERENCES... command from the EDIT menu (⌘-K). The PREFERENCES dialog box will appear.

2. Select the "Tile full pages" radio button from the "Artwork board" options to display as many whole pages as will fit in the drawing area. Press RETURN to exit the dialog box.

3. Choose FIT IN WINDOW from the VIEW menu (⌘-M). Notice that the page size in the drawing area remains unchanged. Only one whole page can be displayed in the current position.

4. Select the page tool and drag the page size to the left side of the drawing area, as shown in Figure 3.20 on the next page.

After you release the mouse button, Illustrator will display two pages, side-by-side in the drawing area, as shown in Figure 3.21. Text and graphic objects may be created to extend across both pages.

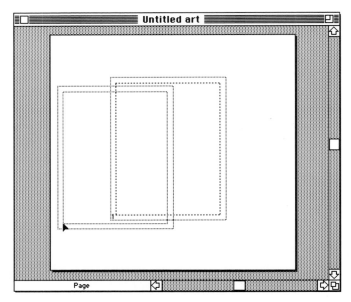

Figure 3.20: Relocating the page size inside the drawing area using the page tool.

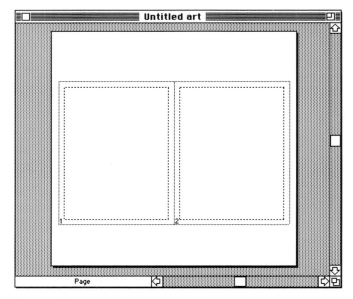

Figure 3.21: The page size moves to accommodate two whole pages in the drawing area.

You may also change the appearance of the page-size boundary to display multiple partial pages (called *tiles*) by choosing the PREFERENCES... command and selecting the "Tile imageable areas" radio button from the "Artwork board" options. Under the current circumstances, selecting this option would cause the drawing area to appear as shown in Figure 3.22. The dotted lines represent the bordering margin-size boundaries, rather than page sizes. In this way, large artwork can be subdivided onto multiple pages for proofing to a laser printer. See Chapter 15, *Printing Your Illustrations*, for more information.

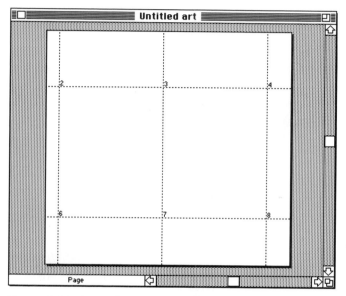

Figure 3.22: Dotted tile lines represent bordering margin size boundaries, allowing you to divide a large drawing onto multiple printed pages.

As well as changing the appearance of the page-size boundary, the PREFERENCES... command allows you to adjust many other settings affecting the performance of Adobe Illustrator 3.0. These settings are discussed in the following section.

Setting preferences

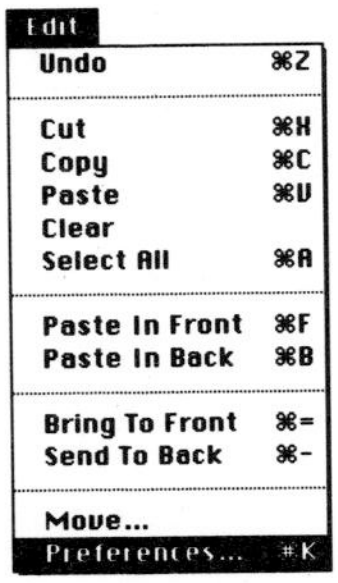

Everyone does not draw alike. For those who draw to a different drummer (in other words, all of us), Illustrator provides the PREFERENCES... command, which allows you to edit a variety of attributes that control the performance of Adobe Illustrator. Choosing PREFERENCES... from the EDIT menu (⌘-K) displays the PREFERENCES dialog box, shown in Figure 3.23. Here you may control the manner in which certain objects in an illustration preview, how elements react to transformations, the distance a selected object is moved when you press an arrow key, the sensitivity of the freehand and autotrace tools, whether dialog boxes display information in points or inches, plus much, much more.

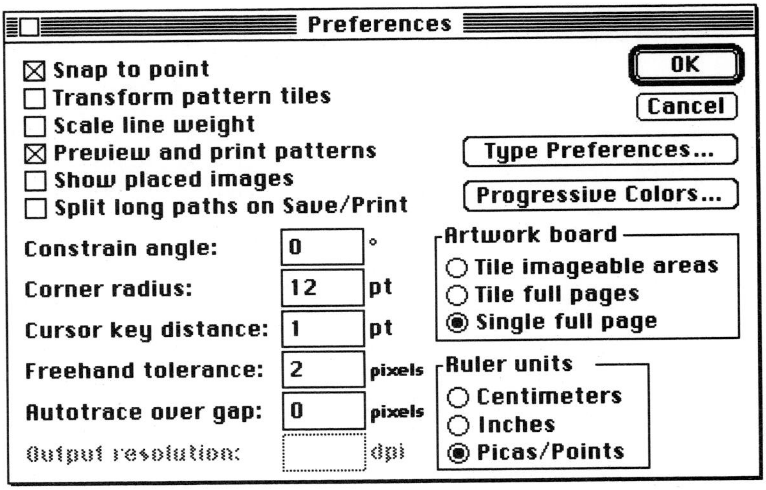

Figure 3.23: The Preferences dialog box allows you to change a variety of settings that affect the performance of Adobe Illustrator 3.0.

The following pages describe each option available in this dialog, plus those available in the related dialog boxes, TYPE PREFERENCES and PROGRESSIVE COLORS. Much of the background required to fully understand these options has not been laid so far in this book. For this reason, each option is covered in greater detail in one or more later chapters.

The options available in the Preferences dialog box are:

- **Snap to point**. This option controls whether a dragged object moves sharply toward a stationary point or guide object when the arrowhead cursor comes within two *pixels* (screen dots) of the point or guide in the drawing area. When a snap occurs, the arrowhead cursor becomes hollow and the phrase "Snap to" appears in the information bar.

- **Transform pattern tiles**. When an object is filled or stroked with a *tile pattern* (as discussed in Chapter 9, *Filling Type and Graphic Objects*), you may determine whether the pattern is *transformed* (moved, scaled, flipped, rotated, or slanted) when the object is transformed, or whether the pattern remains stationary within the object.

- **Scale line weight**. This option determines whether the *line weight* (the thickness of a stroke) of an object is scaled when the object is scaled, or whether the line weight remains constant. This option affects only objects that are scaled proportionally.

- **Preview and print patterns**. This option determines whether tile patterns in the fills and strokes of objects in the drawing area will appear in the preview mode and when printed, or whether they will simply preview and print as gray. When deselected, this option speeds up previewing and printing operations.

- **Show placed images**. When this option is deselected, the PICT preview for an imported EPS image does not display in the artwork and artwork-&-template modes. Rather, the image appears as a rectangular boundary line with intersecting diagonal lines. When selected, a monochrome version of the PICT preview appears inside the rectangular boundary line. Placed EPS images always preview and print. Note that selecting the "Show placed images" option typically slows down the operating speed.

- **Split long paths on Save/Print**. When selected, this option automatically breaks up paths with a large number of points into smaller paths in order to avoid limitcheck errors or other printing problems (as discussed in Chapter 15, *Printing Your Illustrations*). Illustrator determines which paths are split and to what degree based on the value entered into the "Output resolution" option at the bottom of the Preferences dialog. Paths are split whenever you save or print a file.

Do not select the "Split long paths on Save/Print" option unless you are experiencing printing problems. There is no way to automatically reassemble paths that have been split apart; paths must be joined back together manually.

- **Constrain angle**. If you press the SHIFT key while dragging an object, you constrain the direction of its movement to a multiple of 45°; that is, straight up, straight down, left, right, or one of the four diagonal directions. These eight angles make up the *constraint axes*. You may rotate the entire contraint axes by entering a value—measured in degrees—in the "Constrain angle" option box. This value also affects the creation of geometric paths (rectangles and ellipses) and text blocks as well as the performance of transformation tools.

- **Corner radius**. This option allows you to specify the *radius* (the measurement from center point to smooth point on a circle) of the rounded corners of future rectangles drawn with the rounded-rectangle and centered-rounded-rectangle tools. A value of 0 indicates perpendicular corners; larger values make for more rounded rectangles. Radius values are measured in centimeters, inches, or *points* ($1/72$ inch), depending on which radio button is currently selected from the three "Ruler units" options.

- **Cursor key distance**. Illustrator allows you to move any selected object by pressing one of the four arrow keys ($\uparrow$, $\leftarrow$, $\downarrow$, $\rightarrow$). Each keystroke moves the selection the distance entered into this option box, as measured in centimeters, inches, or points, depending on the currently selected "Ruler units" option.

- **Freehand tolerance**. This option controls the sensitivity of both the freehand and autotrace tools. Any value between 0 and 10 is permitted, measured in screen pixels. Lower values make the tools very sensitive, so that—in the case of the freehand tool—the finished path closely matches your cursor movements or—in the case of the autotrace tool—the finished path closely matches the form of the tracing template. Higher values allow both tools to ignore small jags and other imperfections.

- **Autotrace over gap**. Tracing templates frequently contain loose pixels and rough edges; areas where black pixels do not butt up against each other in a consistent manner. However, using this option, you may instruct Illustrator to trace over these gaps. A value of 0 turns the option off, so that the autotrace tool traces rough edges as they appear in the template. A value of 1 allows paths to jump over single-pixel gaps; a value of 2 (the highest value allowed) allows paths to hurdle two-pixel gaps.

- **Output resolution**. This option is dimmed unless the "Splits long paths on Save/Print" check box option is selected. The value in this option should reflect the *resolution* of the final output device (as discussed in Chapter 15, *Printing Your Illustrations*). High resolutions allow more potential for limitcheck errors; therefore, more paths will be broken up and into more pieces. Low resolutions causes fewer paths to be split.

- **Artwork board**. This option determines how the page size and margin size appear in the drawing area. By selecting the "Single full page" radio button, you instruct Illustrator to display one page whose size and orientation correspond to the settings in the LASER-WRITER PAGE SETUP dialog box. "Tile full pages" displays as many whole pages as will fit in the drawing area. "Tile imageable areas" subdivides the drawing area into multiple partial margin sizes. (Both of these options were introduced in the section *Creating a two-page layout* earlier in this chapter.)

- **Ruler units**. This option allows you to select from three units of measurement: "Centimeters," "Inches," and "Picas/Points." (A *pica* is almost exactly equal to ⅙ inch; a *point* is ¹⁄₁₂ pica, or about ¹⁄₇₂ inch.) The selected radio button determines the measurement system used throughout all dialog boxes as well as the horizontal and vertical rulers displayed by choosing the SHOW RULERS command from the VIEW menu (⌘-R).

The PREFERENCES dialog box also includes two buttons used to access related dialog boxes. The first, TYPE PREFERENCES..., displays the TYPE PREFERENCES dialog box shown in Figure 3.24.

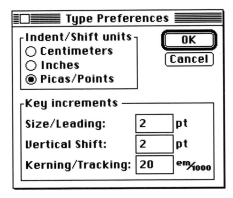

Figure 3.24: The Type Preferences dialog box includes options for altering the increments by which selected type can be formatted from the keyboard.

The options in this dialog box include the following:

- **Indent/Shift units**. This option allows you to select from three units of measurement: "Centimeters," "Inches," and "Picas/ Points." The selected radio button determines the measurement system used by vertical shift and paragraph indent options in all dialog boxes. Other type options, such as those controlling type size and leading, remain unaffected.

- **Size/Leading**. This option specifies the increment by which type size and leading of selected text may be adjusted from the keyboard (using the COMMAND-SHIFT->, COMMAND-SHIFT-<, OPTION-↑, and OPTION-↓ keyboard equivalents). The "Size/Leading" option is always measured in points.

- **Vertical Shift**. This option specifies the increment by which selected type can be raised and lower with respect to the baseline using the SHIFT-OPTION-↑ and SHIFT-OPTION-↓ keyboard equivalents. The "Vertical Shift" option is measured in centimeters, inches, or points, depending on which radio button is currently selected from the three "Indent/Shift units" options.

- **Kerning/Tracking**. This option specifies the increment by which the horizontal spacing between characters of selected text may be squeezed together or spread apart from the keyboard (using the OPTION-← and OPTION-→ or the COMMAND-OPTION-← and COMMAND-OPTION-→ keyboard equivalents). The "Kerning/Tracking" option is always measured in ⅟₁₀₀₀ of an *em space* (a space as wide as the current type size is tall).

The other button in the PREFERENCES dialog box is the PROGRESSIVE COLORS... button. It displays the PROGRESSIVE COLORS dialog box, shown in Figure 3.25. Compare the displayed color to the corresponding color on the special color card included in the Adobe Illustrator 3.0 package. If the color does not quite match, click it to display the Apple COLOR WHEEL dialog box and choose a more accurate screen color. For more information, refer to Chapter 11, *Coloring Fills and Strokes*.

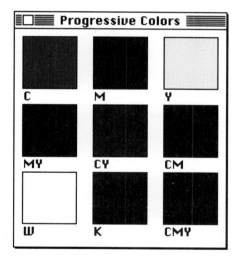

Figure 3.25: The Progressive Colors dialog box allows you to adjust the screen display for process colors and process-color combinations.

All settings specified in the PREFERENCES, TYPE PREFERENCES, and PROGRESSIVE COLORS dialog boxes are saved to a file called Adobe Illustrator 3.0 Prefs in the same folder that contains the Illustrator application. Your settings will therefore affect every file that you create or modify from this moment on.

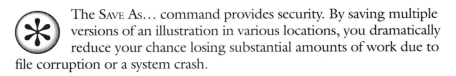

To reset the Preferences and related dialog boxes to their original settings (shown in Figures 3.23, 3.24, and 3.25), quit Illustrator and drag the Adobe Illustrator 3.0 Prefs file into the Trash icon at the Finder level. Choose the Empty Trash command from the Special menu and relaunch Illustrator 3.0.

Saving an illustration

Your computer is not immune to external forces. In the event that your computer crashes due to a system error or a power failure or fluctuation, it is possible to lose much of the work that you have performed on the current illustration. To prevent as much wasted time and effort as possible, you should frequently save your illustration to disk by choosing the Save or Save As… command from the File menu.

These two file saving commands work as follows:

- **Save.** If an illustration is titled, the Save command (⌘-S) updates the disk version of the file to reflect the current contents of the file, including not only text and graphic objects, but also typefaces, custom colors, and tile patterns. If the document is untitled, the Save command invokes the Save As… command, described below. It is possible to receive a "Disk Full" error message during the save operation, in which case the Save As… command must be used to change the drive or volume on which the illustration is to be saved.

- **Save As….** Use this command to determine the name and location of an illustration before it is saved. Choosing the Save As… command from the File menu brings up the Save illustration dialog box, shown in Figure 3.26.

The Save As… command provides security. By saving multiple versions of an illustration in various locations, you dramatically reduce your chance losing substantial amounts of work due to file corruption or a system crash.

If your illustration is titled, the current file name appears in the "Save illustration as" option box directly below the scrolling file list. If your illustration is untitled, no name appears. Enter or edit the file name as you wish, using up to 32 characters.

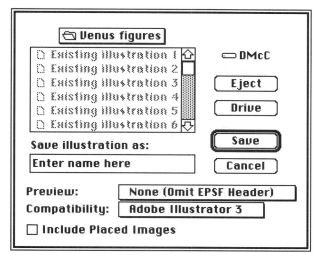

Figure 3.26: The Save illustration dialog box which appears when you choose the Save As... command or when you choose the Save command for an untitled illustration.

Use the DRIVE and EJECT buttons and the folder bar to determine a location for the file in the same way as described for the PLEASE OPEN TEMPLATE dialog box in the *Creating a new illustration* section earlier in this chapter.

File saving options

Click "Preview" to display a pop-up menu of options used to determine whether your illustration is saved as a standard Illustrator PostScript file or with an EPS (Encapsulated PostScript) screen representation, allowing it to be imported into other applications running on a Macintosh or an IBM PC-compatible computer. If you intend to use the file only in Adobe Illustrator, select the default "None (Omit EPS Header)" option. For more information on saving an illustration as an EPS file using one of the other options, see Chapter 14, *Importing and Exporting Graphics*.

You may also save your illustration so that it can be opened by earlier versions of Adobe Illustrator. Click "Compatibility" to display a pop-up menu of three options—"Adobe Illustrator 3.0" (the default), "Adobe Illustrator 88," and "Adobe Illustrator 1.1." Use this option if you want to send an Illustrator 3.0 file to a colleague who doesn't own the most recent release of the software. Also, a few other drawing applications, such as Aldus FreeHand on the Mac and Corel Draw on the PC, will open Illustrator 1.1 files, making it a useful format for swapping images between different software.

Select the "Include Placed Images" option to include any and all placed EPS files in the description of the current illustration. Use this option only when saving an EPS file. Regardless of whether this option is selected, Illustrator requires that the placed image be available on disk to open an illustration containing a placed file. For complete information on importing EPS files into Illustrator and saving illustrations as EPS files, see Chapter 14, *Importing and Exporting Graphics.* The "Include Placed Images" option is dimmed if an illustration contains no placed EPS files.

When you have selected a name, location, and any other option for your current illustration, click the OK button or press RETURN to complete the SAVE AS... command. You may also click the CANCEL button or press COMMAND-PERIOD to return to the illustration window without initiating the save operation.

Replacing an existing file

If you try to save an illustration with the same name as an existing illustration in the current drive and folder, Illustrator will present the REPLACE EXISTING alert box, shown in Figure 3.27, asking you to confirm that you wish to replace the existing file. Click YES to save over the existing file; click NO or press RETURN to return to the SAVE ILLUSTRATION dialog box, where you may change the name or location of the current illustration.

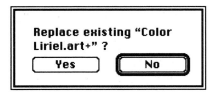

Figure 3.27: The Replace existing alert box.

If the disk that you have selected does not have enough room for the file being saved, a "Disk Full" error message will appear. Click the CONTINUE button to return to the SAVE ILLUSTRATION dialog box so that you may select another drive or volume and reinitiate the save operation.

Finishing an illustration

When you have finished working on an illustration, you can close the illustration window. Then you may begin a new illustration, open a different illustration, work on a different illustration that is already open, or quit the Adobe Illustrator application altogether.

Closing an illustration

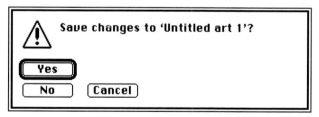

To close the current illustration, choose the CLOSE command from the FILE menu, or click the close box in the upper left corner of the illustration window. If you have made any changes to the illustration since it was last changed, a SAVE CHANGES? dialog box will appear, as shown in Figure 3.28, asking if you would like to save the illustration before closing it. Clicking the YES button or pressing RETURN will perform a SAVE operation (or display the SAVE ILLUSTRATION dialog box if the illustration is untitled) and then close the file; clicking the No button will close the illustration without saving the changes; and clicking CANCEL or pressing COMMAND-PERIOD will return you to the illustration window without saving the file or closing it. Cancelling is useful if you want to choose the SAVE AS... command in order to change the name or location of the file, or if you would like to continue working on the publication.

Figure 3.28: The Save changes? dialog box.

If more than one illustration is currently open, closing an illustration will bring one of the remaining illustration windows to the front of the desktop. If only one illustration is open, the toolbox will disappear along with the illustration window when you choose the CLOSE command. Your

options will be the same as they were when you first launched Illustrator: you will be able to create a new illustration, open an existing illustration, alter the PREFERENCES dialog box settings, or quit Illustrator and return to the Macintosh Finder.

This final operation is discussed below.

Quitting Illustrator

When you have finished your work in the Illustrator application, choose the QUIT command from the FILE menu (⌘-Q) to close any and all open illustrations and return control of your Macintosh to the Finder. Like the CLOSE command, the QUIT command prompts the appearance of a SAVE CHANGES? dialog box for every illustration to which changes have been made since it was last saved. Clicking the YES button or pressing RETURN will perform a SAVE operation (or display the SAVE ILLUSTRATION dialog box if the illustration is untitled) and then close the file; clicking the No button will close the illustration without saving the changes; and clicking CANCEL or pressing COMMAND-PERIOD will return you to the illustration window without saving the file or closing it. If no illustration window is open or if no changes have been made to any open window since the last time it was saved, Illustrator will quit without presenting a verification dialog box.

The Graphic
Creation
Process

In Chapter 1 we looked at the differences between bitmapped painting software and object-oriented drawing software. In this chapter we examine the actual process of creating graphics using a drawing application like Adobe Illustrator 3.0. This chapter will prove most helpful to beginning users, because Illustrator relies on drawing concepts different from those required when using painting software or when drawing by conventional means.

As we did in Chapter 2, we will begin this chapter by defining the terms and concepts on which ensuing discussions rely. Terms such as *point*, *segment*, *path*, and *element* are the focus of our attention here. Once these are explained, we will undertake the creation of a moderately complex graphic.

A step-by-step description of the process of creating a graphic is provided so that you can share in the thought process of creating such a graphic—not so that you can follow along and actually create the illustration. Few of the specific Illustrator tools or commands required to produce this graphic have been properly introduced as of yet—they are the focus of the remainder of this book. Perhaps later, after reading later chapters, you will want to return to this chapter and complete this graphic along with us. This first time, however, we recommend that you just read along, paying specific attention to the manner in which we approach each aspect of the creation process.

Drawing with objects

No matter what type of drawing you wish to create, its production in Illustrator must be approached as a combination of *objects* belonging to two simple categories: *lines* and *shapes*.

Suppose that you are about to create a collage. Illustrator provides an inexhaustible stack of lines and another stack of shapes. Each line and shape may be stretched, bent, and otherwise *reshaped* to any extent that you choose, as if it were made of putty. Colors may be changed. You can then lay these manipulated lines and shapes down on your collage in the locations and order that you decide is best. Because it exists on a computer, this collage is impermanent—any line or shape may be picked up and placed down in a new position, slipped between two other objects, or discarded altogether. An element may be exactly duplicated, manipulated in a new way, or left as is.

Every drawing, no matter how complicated or how simple, can be expressed as an interacting collection of lines and shapes. The trick is to start simple and work toward complexity. In this manner, you may successfully evaluate an illustration and break it down into its most basic parts. The first step in learning to identify the parts of a prospective illustration is to learn about lines and shapes themselves.

The line

Conceptually, lines in Illustrator are the same as lines drawn with a pencil on a piece of paper. Any line starts at one location and ends at another. Lines may be any length. They may be mere scratch marks or they may stretch from the top of a page to the bottom and loop around like roller coasters.

Lines in Illustrator are made up of the most basic building blocks—*points*. The simplest line is created as a combination of only two points, one at each end. Anyone familiar with a little geometry will recognize this principle: two points make a line.

But in Illustrator, the concept of a line has been broadened to incorporate many points. *Segments* are drawn between points to connect them. A segment may be straight, as if it were drawn against the edge of a ruler. A straight segment must be created directly from one point to another in any direction. A segment may also curve, like the outline of a circle. Such segments are drawn in an indirect manner between two points.

Segments may be linked together so that neighboring segments share a common point. In this way, you may think of a line in Illustrator as a dot-to-dot puzzle. Each point is a dot. One segment is drawn from dot A to dot B, a second segment is drawn from dot B to dot C, a third segment is drawn from dot C to dot D, and so on. The completed dot-to-dot image is called a *path*. A path may be composed of only one segment or one hundred.

Figure 4.01 on the next page shows two separate dot-to-dot images. Each dot is a point. A segment is drawn from one point to the next sequential point. The points of one image are numbered; the points of the other are labeled with letters. No segment is drawn from a numbered point to a lettered point, or vice versa. The numbered and lettered images are therefore separate paths.

Obviously, the form of each straight and curved segment in a path determines an image's overall appearance. The appearance of a path is equally affected by the manner in which one segment meets another segment at a point. Segments may meet at a point in two ways. First, the two segments may curve symmetrically on either side of a point. For example, each of the four segments in the numbered path in Figure 4.01 meets with its neighbor to form a seamless *arc* about their shared point. Second, two segments may meet to form a *corner*. A straight segment may meet with another straight segment to form a corner, such as at point D in the figure. Or a straight segment and a curved segment may meet at a corner like the one at point E. Two curved segments may also meet to form a corner like the one at point H.

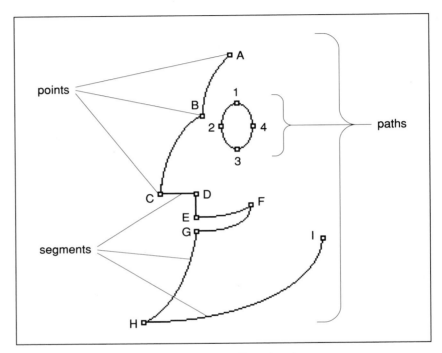

Figure 4.01: Examples of a line (lettered) and a shape (numbered). Elements within both paths are labeled.

The shape

The lettered path in Figure 4.01 is an example of an *open path*, because no segment connects its last point I to its first point A. The numbered path is called a *closed path*, because a segment does connect its last point 4 to its first point 1. An open path in Illustrator is what we have been calling a line; a closed path we will call a *shape*. Lines and shapes have various characteristics, as described in the following section.

Properties of lines and shapes

Unlike a line drawn with a pencil on a piece of paper, any path in Illustrator must be consistent in thickness, or *weight*. For example, a line drawn with a very dull pencil will be heavier in weight than a line drawn with a newly sharpened pencil. But, because a graphite pencil is an imprecise tool, the weight of a line drawn with it will fluctuate, depending on how hard you press while drawing. This is not the case in Illustrator. Different lines may have different weights, but the weight of each line must be constant throughout its length.

Also, drawing a path in Illustrator is like having a countless number of differently colored pencils at your disposal. A line may be black, as if it were drawn with pen and ink, or it may be light gray or dark gray. It may also be red, or green, or blue, or any one of a million other colors. A line may even be white, transparent, or multicolored.

Line weight and color combine to determine the *stroke* of a line or the outline of a shape. In addition, the area inside a path may be manipulated separately from the outline itself. This area is called the *fill*. The fill of a shape may be black or white, transparent or colored, just like a line. It may even be a combination of many colors interacting or fading into one another.

Determining a path

Before creating a path in Illustrator, you must evaluate the segments that it will follow. This is done one point at a time. Each point indicates: 1) where a corner occurs, 2) where a path begins to curve or stops curving, or 3) where a path changes its curve. One segment ends at a point and another segment begins.

To fully understand the point/segment/path relationship, suppose that you are driving on a winding mountain road. You will see many yellow, diamond-shaped signs indicating what kind of path lies ahead of you. In Figure 4.02 on the next page, the center sign indicates that the path of the road curves gradually to the right. The sign on the left indicates that the road turns dramatically to the left, forming a corner. The sign on the right indicates that the road curves all the way around so that your car will eventually face the opposite direction.

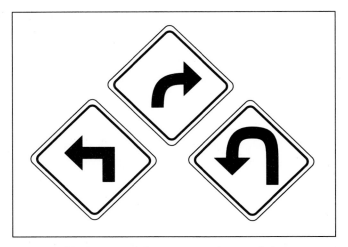

Figure 4.02: Points guide segments in a path just as street signs interpret a road.

There is one sign for every change in the path of the road. For example, you will never see a sign like the one shown in Figure 4.03. If a road were actually to curve about following the path described on this sign, you as a driver would not be told about all of these turns at the same time. You would be warned at every change in direction.

Figure 4.03: Too much information for a single point.

The course of a path must be defined at the beginning of every new segment—the point. Think of each point as a road sign. The road sign of a point defines how one segment enters the point and how the next segment exits.

Conclusion: Points define segments. A path follows a number of segments, which determine the form of a line or shape. Strokes and fills are added to a line or shape to imitate real-life images. Finally, these images are brought together like a collage to represent the finished illustration.

A sample illustration

As the preceding discussion suggests, the first step in approaching any prospective drawing in Illustrator is to break the illustration down into its fundamental parts. As an example, suppose we want to create the cartoon image of Groucho Marx shown in Figure 4.04. For the remainder of this chapter we will explain the steps you would undertake to create this drawing in Adobe Illustrator. Remember, this discussion is intended to introduce the overall methods we use to approach such a project. It is not intended as a "how-to" lesson in Illustrator. This task is left to the remaining chapters of the book.

Figure 4.04: A bitmapped sketch of Groucho Marx created in MacPaint.

We have created this sketch in MacPaint, and although we are pleased with its general appearance and form, it is riddled with jagged edges. Since MacPaint images are limited to a 72-dpi resolution, they rarely meet professional standards. Our cartoon of Groucho is presently defined as a collection of pixels. We will now describe Groucho as a series of object-oriented shapes and lines. Our final Illustrator-created Groucho will be identical in form and superior in resolution.

If you are not an artist, the idea of creating a cartoon of Groucho Marx may seem beyond your ability. However, as with most creative endeavors, creating an drawing in Illustrator has more to do with how you think than with your dexterity or experience. That is why this tutorial has been constructed from an entirely theoretical vantage. No menu commands are used; no tools are mentioned. By avoiding the details of the application, we are able to more fully concentrate on the intellectual process. An illustration must be created in your head before it can be created on paper or on a computer screen.

Also, if it makes you more comfortable, imagine that you are tracing the cartoon of Groucho rather than creating it from scratch. In Illustrator, it is often more efficient to trace from a sketch or photographic scan. For the purposes of this example, it is not important that you feel confident that you can create the sketch of Groucho shown in Figure 4.04. It is only important that you understand how to trace it.

1: The eyes

We will begin by creating Groucho's eyes. Groucho's left eye is shown in Figure 4.05. The eye is *grayed* to show that it is part of the *tracing template*. In Illustrator, the template is the background element containing the MacPaint image that we are sketching. Graying the template is Illustrator's way of showing that it is not a part of the actual drawing.

In Figure 4.06, we have traced a perfect circle around the left eyeball. The circle and template are shown together to give you a perspective for the rest of the illustration. However, these are the only figures in this chapter where the underlying template will be shown. Hiding the template will help to avoid confusion and to present each portion of the drawing in sharp focus. Keep in mind, however, that the tracing template does exist, and that every line and shape we create is traced over some part of it.

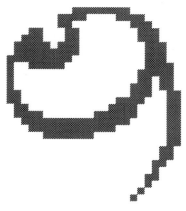

Figure 4.05: The left eye of the Groucho tracing template.

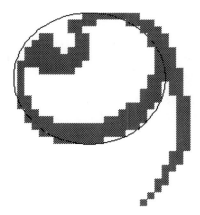

Figure 4.06: Create a circle that traces around the left eye.

The circle that we have created as Groucho's left eyeball is a shape composed of four points. Each of the four points helps to define the path that the outline of the circle follows. We mentioned before that making a line follow a path is like driving a car on a mountain road. Each point is like a small street sign indicating where the line should go. In the case of our circle, all four points are identical. Suppose the outline of the circle follows its path in a counterclockwise direction. Each point would then act like the street sign shown in Figure 4.07 on the following page. As the outline progresses, the points tell the curve to continue to the left in a consistent manner.

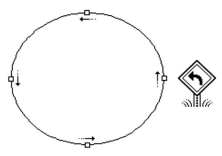

Figure 4.07: The points in the circle tell the path to
continue in a counterclockwise direction.

The next few parts of Groucho's eye may be created from our present
circle. We will do this by *cloning* and *scaling*. Cloning creates a copy of an
object without using the Clipboard. This is useful any time that you are
tracing several lines or shapes that are very similar in form. You need only
create one original and then clone all objects from that. Cloned objects
may then be manipulated separately, so that the finished object only
vaguely resembles the original from which it was cloned.

After we clone our circle, we scale the resulting shape to 85% of original. Scaling makes an object larger or smaller. In this case we have two
distinct circles, the newest of which is 85% of the size of the original. We
situate the cloned shape so that the tops of both circles meet as shown in
Figure 4.08.

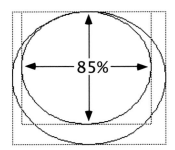

Figure 4.08: Clone the circle and scale it to
85% of its original size.

Next we clone our newest circle and scale its clone to 55% of original.
Then we clone that circle and scale this clone to 75%. We move each of

the clones to the positions shown in Figure 4.09. We now have all shapes required for the left eyeball. We will next create the wrinkle under the eye.

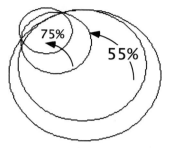

Figure 4.09: Scaling two additional clones.

The wrinkle is only slightly more difficult than the circles we have created thus far. Figure 4.10 shows how we create this shape. The wrinkle is simply a long, thin crescent made up of four points. Each point is labeled according to one of three analogous street signs. Each sign is shown as if you were approaching the point in the direction indicated by the small arrows. Therefore, if you were driving counterclockwise along the outline of this shape, you would meet with four signs, two notifying you of sharp corners in the path.

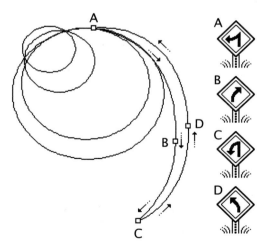

Figure 4.10: Each of the street signs on the right correspond to a point in the crescent.

Every one of the five objects we have created so far is a shape. This means they all have the properties of both line and fill. So far, all of our shapes have very thin, black strokes and transparent fills. We will need to change this in order to match our template.

For our present purpose, we do not need to make use of any strokes. Groucho's eye can be easily created from fills alone. Therefore, we make all of the strokes transparent. We will fill three of our shapes, the first and third circles and the crescent wrinkle, with solid black. The second and fourth circles are filled with white. The result is shown in the left portion of Figure 4.11.

Note that the image on the left side of Figure 4.11 is displayed in the *preview mode*, as are most of the following figures in this chapter. The preview mode allows you to see how an image will appear when printed. However, Illustrator does not allow you to actually draw or manipulate images in this mode.

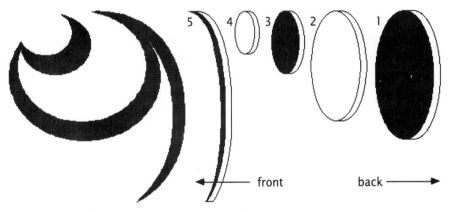

Figure 4.11: The most recently created shapes cover up their predecessors when viewed in the preview mode.

Recent shapes cover up shapes that were created before them. In Figure 4.11, our five shapes are numbered 1 through 5, 1 being the first shape created and 5 being the last. Each shape is shown as if we were seeing it from the side and as if it had depth. This imaginary view of our illustration demonstrates how Illustrator places the most recently created object in front, while its predecessors remain in back. In this way, our five shapes are stacked upon each other so that they appear as one continuous black form. If we were to have painted this version of Groucho's eye onto a canvas, it may have been a combination of three brush strokes. In Illustrator, it is five shapes. A computer may yield painterly results, but the approach must often be technical and carefully considered.

Now that we have created one of Groucho's eyes, it is very easy to create the other. First, we gather our five shapes and *group* them, so that they all become one object. Grouping protects the relative placement and size of line and shapes within the group.

Next, we clone the group. We then *reflect* the clone about a –70° *axis* as shown in Figure 4.12. To more fully understand this process, think of the axis as a double-sided mirror. Suppose that the mirror is mounted like an old cheval glass, so that it is free to tilt within a support. Our mirror is normally situated horizontally, like a table top. But if we were to angle the mirror 70° downward (–70°, or 290°), we would see the exact reflection shown in Figure 4.12. That is what is meant by reflection about an axis. The axis is simply a mirror tilted at a prescribed angle.

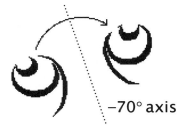

−70° axis

Figure 4.12: Clone the five shapes that make up the left eye and reflect them about a −70° axis.

Since the cartoon of Groucho faces slightly away from the viewer, it is not appropriate for both eyes to be the same size. The right eye, which is farther away from us, should be smaller to give the illusion of depth. Therefore, we must scale the eye. However, if we wish to follow our template, we must reduce the eye so that it is proportionally narrower than it is tall. This is no problem, since Illustrator allows for separate vertical and horizontal percentages when scaling. Figure 4.13 on the next page shows how we scale the eye to 80% of original width and 90% of original height. The original size of the eye is shown as the larger, dotted box. Now both of Groucho's eyes match our template almost perfectly.

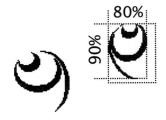

Figure 4.13: Scale the right eye by 80% horizontally and 90% vertically.

2: The eyebrows

Now it is time to create the eyebrows. We will begin with the left brow. This is a slightly more difficult shape than any we have created so far. It involves eight points, labeled A through H in Figure 4.14. Each point is analogous to the street sign that bears the same letter. Keep in mind that, for the purpose of this example, you are seeing these street signs as if you were traveling on the path in a counterclockwise direction.

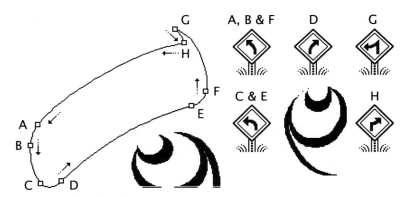

Figure 4.14: The left eyebrow is made up of eight points, each of which corresponds to one of the street signs shown above.

Once again, we make the stroke of this shape transparent. We fill the shape with solid black. Then we clone the eyebrow and reflect the clone about a −75° axis. Figure 4.15 shows the result.

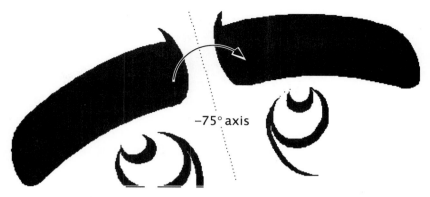

–75° axis

Figure 4.15: Clone the eyebrow shape and reflect it across a –75° axis.

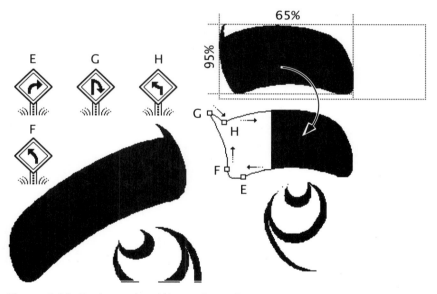

Figure 4.16: Reshape the right eyebrow by converting points F, G, and H.

The newly reflected right eyebrow is not the correct size, nor does its path entirely correspond to the form of the right eyebrow in our template. To remedy the first problem, we must scale the brow to 65% of its original width and 95% of its original height, as shown in the top part of Figure 4.16. To change the path of the shape, we must convert the identity of a few appropriate points. Converting the *identity* is like changing the street sign. Figure 4.16 demonstrates which points we change, and how. Notice that the street sign analogous to point E curves to the right instead of to the left as it did in Figure 4.14. This is not a change, but is instead the result of the reflection about the –75° axis. When the shape was reflected, the identity of every point was also reflected. Now notice point F. Its street sign is identical to that shown in Figure 4.14. Therefore, it has been changed, since otherwise it would have been reflected as well. Points G and H have also been changed. The result is an alteration in the path of the shape. The identity of each and every point directly influences the path.

3: The cigar

Next we will work on Groucho's prominent cigar. First we trace a circle around the lighted ashes at the tip of the cigar. Then we clone this circle and reduce the clone so that we have two concentric circles. We again clone the larger circle, and move its clone about one-quarter inch to the left. In Figure 4.17, each of the four points of the circle is shown along with the street sign that is analogous to all four. We will change the path of this shape not by changing the identity of its points, but by deleting and adding points.

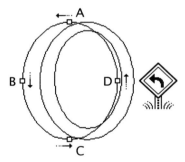

Figure 4.17: Drawing the tip of Groucho's cigar.

From the labeled shape in Figure 4.17, we delete point D and join points A and C with a single, straight segment. The result is shown in Figure 4.18. Notice that both of the street signs analogous to points A and C have been changed so that a corner occurs at each point. Points are thus directly influenced by the points that surround them.

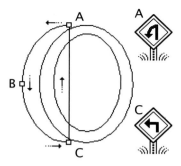

Figure 4.18: Deleting point D and adding a straight segment in its place changes the identities of neighboring points A and C.

Before we go any further, we need to *copy* our most recent shape. Copying an object places a copy of the selected object into the Macintosh Clipboard. We will need to recall this image in a few moments.

In Figure 4.19, we add two points D and E to our shape. The identities of points A and C update to fit in with their new neighbors. Since point B is nestled between points A and C, its identity remains constant.

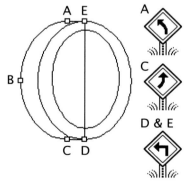

Figure 4.19: Adding points D and E further alters the identities of points A and C.

We have now created the very tip of Groucho's cigar, though one would hardly recognize it. We still need to define the line and fill of each of our three shapes. We will make all lines transparent. We fill our first circle with a dark gray and our second, smaller circle with a light gray. We fill our most recent shape with black. The result is shown in Figure 4.20. You may notice that we have a problem. Since the black shape is the most recent, it covers up both of the gray circles. The black shape is in front of both circles. The solution to our problem is to send the black shape to the back. No matter when an object was created, it may be sent to back or brought to front. By sending an object to back, you tell Illustrator to assume that the object was the first created, and by bringing it to front, you tell Illustrator to assume it was the most recently created. Now, Illustrator first draws the black shape, then the dark gray circle, then the light gray circle. The result is the cigar's end of glowing ashes.

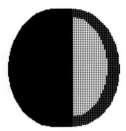

Figure 4.20: The most recent black shape covers up the shapes behind it.

A moment ago, we copied an object to the Macintosh Clipboard. We now need to retrieve that image. We do this by *pasting*, which takes a copy from the image in the Clipboard and places it on our drawing area. Once we have pasted the shape, we move it into position, as shown in Figure 4.21, and open the path so that points A and C have no path segment linking them.

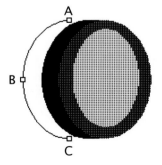

Figure 4.21: Paste the shape copied earlier and open it.

By opening our path, we convert the shape into a line. We now add the necessary points to this line to cause its path to trace the form of the cigar as it goes into Groucho's mouth. As we create the last point in the line, we reclose the line to form a shape.

This time, we stroke the outline of the shape with a heavy, black line weight. We fill the shape with white. By filling our shape with white rather than leaving it transparent, the shape will cover up any objects that we may create and send to back later in the drawing process. The finished cigar is shown in Figure 4.22.

Figure 4.22: A heavy, black stroke finishes the cigar.

4: The nose and mustache

Groucho's nose is created as a series of eight points, as shown in Figure 4.23. In this figure, we are no longer zoomed in as closely as in some of our other figures. We may see all of Groucho that we have created so far in one glance.

Figure 4.23: Because the outline of the nose tapers at both ends, it must be expressed as a filled shape.

We assign to the shape of Groucho's nose a transparent stroke and a black fill. Looking at the nose, you might wonder why we created it as a shape rather than as a line. It is, after all, very much a line in the traditional sense. The problem is that the weight of this line in not uniform. In fact, it is downright calligraphic. The line of the nose begins thin, becomes fatter as it sweeps around, and becomes thin again at its end. Lines in Illustrator cannot have this property. We said earlier that while the thickness of a stroke is determined by its line weight, the thickness of a fill is determined by the path that surrounds it. Therefore, to express a calligraphic line, we must create a path that surrounds both sides of the "line," then fill the resulting shape. This is what we have done in the case of the nose, and will do throughout the remainder of this illustration.

In setting out to create Groucho's mustache, the first thing that we notice is how similar it is to his eyebrows. Therefore, we clone the left eyebrow and move it into the position shown in Figure 4.24, between the nose and the cigar. Incidentally, you may notice that although we have cloned a shape that has no stroke and a black fill, our clone has a thin outline and no fill. We have purposely changed the stroke and fill of this shape to make it stand out from the shapes around it.

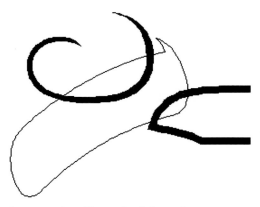

Figure 4.24: Clone the left eyebrow to serve as a starting point for the mustache.

We reflect the mustache shape about a 25° axis. This reflection is interesting because the axis runs directly through the shape as shown in Figure 4.25. The shape actually reflects upon itself. A reflection axis can be angled in any way you desire.

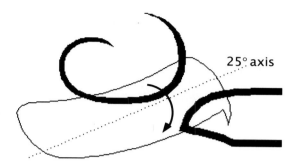

Figure 4.25: Reflect the eyebrow clone about a 25° axis.

The mustache is considerably larger than either of the eyebrows, therefore we enlarge it to 130% of its original size.

The next step is to *skew*, or slant, the shape. In this case, we wish to skew our shape −25° horizontally. Figure 4.26 shows how the skew is measured from the mean horizontal axis. Dotted lines show roughly the angle at which the shape sat before the skew and the resulting new angle of the shape.

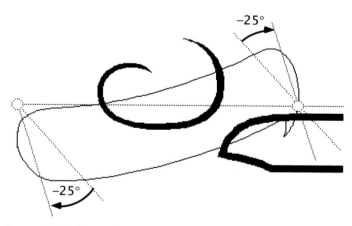

Figure 4.26: Skew the eyebrow clone −25° horizontally.

The basic form of the mustache is still not what it should be, so we must alter the path to match our template. We accomplish this as a combination of changing the identities of present points and adding new points. Figure 4.27 shows the amount and location of the points that existed before the alteration. There are eight points, just like the eyebrow from which it was cloned. Figure 4.28 shows the points after alteration. Notice that there are now nine points. All of the points have been moved at least slightly. We have moved some dramatically and have changed the identities of several as well. Yet our alteration has been subtle in its affect on the appearance of the path. Though every point has been changed in some way, the outline of the shape in Figures 4.28 follows a path very similar to that of its predecessor in Figure 4.27. The subtleties of a path can make or destroy a successful illustration.

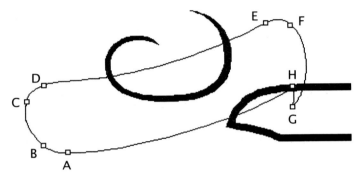

Figure 4.27: The eight points in the eyebrow clone before reshaping the path.

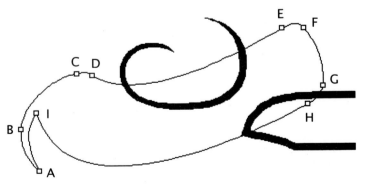

Figure 4.28: After reshaping, the path has nine points, many of which differ from their predecessors.

Like the eyebrows, the mustache is assigned a transparent stroke and a black fill. We then send it to back. The result is shown in Figure 4.29. Because of its white fill, the cigar effectively covers a portion of the mustache to appear as if it is jutting from Groucho's hidden mouth. Unfortunately, the same cannot be said for the nose. The nose appears to be behind the mustache, because the fill of the nose shape is acting like the outline of the nose. A second fill is needed to act as the flesh of the nose.

Figure 4.29: The black mustache obscures the shape of the nose, despite the fact that the mustache has been sent to back.

The fill of the shape that will act as the flesh of the nose must exactly fit into the shape that acts as the outline of the nose. Therefore, we must clone the existing shape. The fill of the cloned shape should cover the area enclosed by the original shape. A segment of the path must connect the points that represent the top of the nose and the tip of the nostril. This is easily accomplished by deleting all of the points that form the inner rim of the nose and then closing the remaining path. The result is shown in Figure 4.30 on the following page.

Notice that this figure shows shapes with no fills and thin strokes. As we mentioned earlier, most of the figures in this chapter display images as they appear in the preview mode. However, for Figure 4.30, we show the paths in the *artwork mode*, the display mode in which objects may be created and manipulated in Adobe Illustrator. In the artwork mode, all lines and outlines are shown with very thin, black strokes; all fills are shown as transparent. By viewing the paths in this figure in the artwork mode, we may more clearly view the most recent developments.

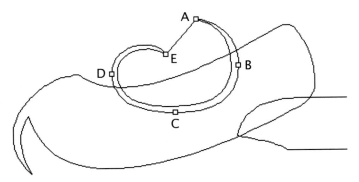

Figure 4.30: The nose and mustache shapes displayed in the artwork mode.

We fill the most recent shape with white and send it to the back so that it does not cover the shape that is the outline of the nose. Then we send the mustache to the back again. We zoom out from our illustration in Figure 4.31. We can see the result of everything that we have done so far. It looks to be about half finished, but looks can be deceiving. We are actually much closer than that.

Figure 4.31: Our progress so far as viewed in the preview mode. Note that the nose now appears in front of the mustache.

5: Finishing the face

We are still missing many of Groucho's features. We have yet to draw his glasses, the bridge of his nose, his ear, his hair, the outline of his face, and a few wrinkles. But, if you will recall our template (refer to Figure 4.04), all of these features are more suggestive than those we have created so far. The subtle features in a template are often harder to approach than their more obvious or outstanding counterparts. The best advice we can offer is to dive right in. Create object after object in a rhythmic sequence, forging on with alacrity and grace. These are the incidental parts of an illustration that round it out, giving it a lucid flappearance.

Figure 4.32: The wrinkles in the flesh and portions of the glasses are expressed as many small shapes, most of which comprise less than three points apiece.

In Figure 4.32, we have created a series of small shapes that act as calligraphic swashes. The majority of the shapes are made up of only two points each. The identity of each point causes one path segment to curve more than another, so that the fill creates a free-flowing stroke, simple but highly effective. The most complicated shape is constructed of only five points. Each of these shapes are flourishing and playful, yet they must be approached intentionally and with care.

Figure 4.33: Most of the outline of the face as well as several incidental features can be expressed as a single complex shape.

The next shape that we create is very extensive. As Figure 4.33 shows, there are 48 points in this shape. With one shape, we have created the hair, most of his ear, lip, chin, neck, and part of his glasses. But the process itself is no more difficult than any other shape we have created. The most difficult step may be to recognize that such a large portion of the template can be expressed as a single shape. Such recognition comes with practice. Once you have seen the shape, you need only trace its outline point by point, carefully and patiently. The only difference between a simple line with two points and a complex shape with one hundred is that the latter takes longer to produce. Never be intimidated by a large shape.

After filling our complex shape with solid black, only two shapes remain to finish Groucho's face. These are the remainder of the ear and the bridge of the nose. The ear requires eleven points and the nose requires six, as shown in Figure 4.34. Always use points sparingly. If you find that you do not have enough points, you may always add more. But just one point too many means that someplace there are two path segments where there should be only one. The result is a needlessly complicated object, whose path is slightly clumsy and malformed.

Figure 4.34: Finish the face with two shapes, one representing the details of the ear and the other the bridge of the nose.

6: The collar

By now, you can probably easily imagine how to draw Groucho's collar. But there are a couple of stumbling blocks along the way. Figure 4.35 on the next page shows the points required to create the jacket lapel and the shirt collar—four shapes altogether. Both of the lapel shapes get no line and a black fill. The collars get a medium-weight black line and a white fill. Figure 4.36 shows the results. Notice how we have matched up the line of the collars exactly with the fill of the shape that wraps around to form the throat. Here is a case where the fill of a shape and the weight of a line are designed to be identical.

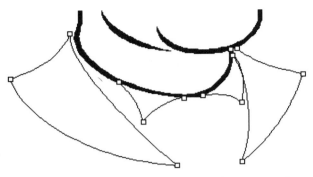

Figure 4.35: The four shapes required to create the collar and lapel.

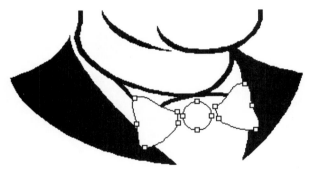

Figure 4.36: The three shapes that make up the bow tie.

Figure 4.36 also shows that the tie is made of three separate shapes. One is a simple circle and the other two have five points apiece. The tie must cover the lapels in an unusual manner, requiring that we consider the stroke as well as the fill of each shape. In the template, there is a white line between the black color of the tie and the black color of the jacket. Therefore, all three shapes of the tie get a medium-weight white stroke with a black fill. The white stroke provides the necessary definition between the tie and the jacket to distinguish the two as independent objects. Last, we bring both of the collar shapes to the front of the other objects so that the tie becomes nestled where it belongs, as shown in Figure 4.37.

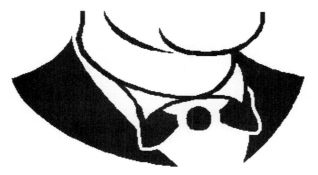

Figure 4.37: The white stroke of the tie shapes distinguish them from the lapels.

7: Smoke from the cigar

Often a last detail will add spirit to a drawing. Our last detail will be smoke rising from Groucho's cigar. This is an unnecessary but friendly addition that gives our cartoon the small bit of realism that it needs.

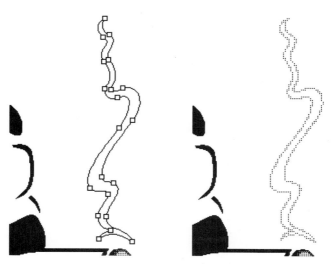

Figure 4.38: The points required to express the cigar smoke and the same path when stroked with a gray outline.

We trace the smoke with one shape containing 21 points. Figure 4.38 shows the path. We then assign the shape a thin, light gray stroke with no fill. The shape is simple, yet also elegant and functional.

The completed Groucho

Our illustration is finished. Figure 4.39 shows the completed Groucho as he appears when printed from Adobe Illustrator. Despite his large size, his resolution is far better than his MacPaint template. Every detail is crisp and accurate. His appearance is clean and smooth. All things said and done, we have created a highly professional product.

We have now laid a groundwork for creating almost any electronic illustration. The following chapters discuss the tools, commands, and dialog box options required to create such a drawing in Illustrator 3.0. However, the ultimate secret to achieving a professional illustration is not reliant on the specific environment provided by the application. Rather, it relies on your approach.

Figure 4.39: The completed Groucho cartoon printed from Adobe Illustrator 3.0.

Drawing Paths from Scratch

In the previous chapter, we demonstrated that an image drawn in Adobe Illustrator must be constructed as a network of lines and shapes called *paths*. This chapter demonstrates how to draw the paths themselves using each of eight drawing tools.

We will begin with the most basic paths that you may create in Illustrator 3.0. These include rectangles, squares, ovals, and circles—a collection of objects known collectively as *geometric*

paths. If you are an experienced Macintosh user, you will probably recognize the tools used to create these paths. Each tool works similarly to tools in MacPaint, MacDraw, PageMaker, and other common Macintosh applications. If you have used any of these programs, there is little doubt that you can master the creation of any geometric path.

Geometric paths

Illustrator 3.0 offers six tools for creating geometric shapes. Each tool is operated by clicking or by dragging from one location to another. The points at which you begin and end the drag signify the boundary limits of the simple rectangle or oval. Although limited in utility, these geometric shapes are very easy to draw, because they involve no planning and little guesswork.

Drawing a rectangle

Consider the *rectangle tool,* displayed by default in the sixth tool slot of the toolbox. After selecting this tool, you drag inside the drawing area to create a rectangle. This is the same process used to create a rectangle in all graphics applications that run on the Macintosh. One corner of the rectangle is determined by the point at which you begin the drag; the opposite corner is determined by the point at which you release (see Figure 5.01). The two remaining corners line up vertically or horizontally with their neighbors. A fifth point, the *center point,* is also created, representing the center of the shape.

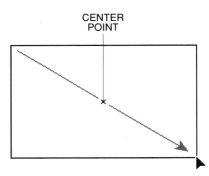

Figure 5.01: Operate the rectangle tool by dragging from one corner to the opposite corner of the desired shape.

If you press the OPTION key while drawing with the rectangle tool, the beginning of your drag becomes the center point of the rectangle, as shown in Figure 5.02. As before, the release point becomes a corner point and also determines the distance and direction from the center that each of the three other corner points are located.

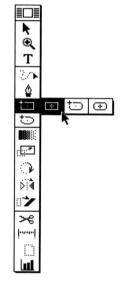

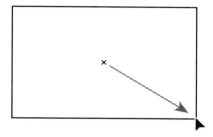

Figure 5.02: Option-drag with the rectangle tool to draw a rectangle from center point to corner point.

Alternately, you may choose the *centered-rectangle tool* from the rectangle tool slot. This tool allows you to create rectangles from center point to corner point without pressing the OPTION key. Pressing OPTION while dragging with the centered-rectangle tool draws a shape from corner point to opposite corner point.

Pressing the SHIFT key while drawing with the rectangle tool *constrains* the resulting shape. To constrain the creation or manipulation of an element is to attach certain guidelines to the effects of your mouse movements. In this case, pressing SHIFT ensures that each corner of the rectangle is equidistant from both of its neighbors, thereby creating a square.

Generally, drawing a square is a very simple process, but it can sometimes be tricky. Beginning users may become frustrated with a square's propensity to collapse into a vertical or horizontal line. Try SHIFT-dragging directly to the left or downward with the rectangle tool and you'll see what we mean. To produce a square, Illustrator averages the movement of your cursor. For example, if while pressing SHIFT you drag one inch vertically and two inches horizontally, the resulting shape will measure:

(1 inch + 2 inches) ÷ 2 = 1½ inches by 1½ inches

However, if your drag is too shallow or too narrow, your square will flatten out horizontally or vertically. This flattening happens specifically when you drag inward past the center point of the shape. When SHIFT-drawing with any geometric shape tool, your drag must be a least one-third as wide as it is high and one-third as high as it is wide to avoid flattening out the shape. Figure 5.03 demonstrates how a constrained geometric shape tool averages the movement of your cursor and displays the area where flattening occurs.

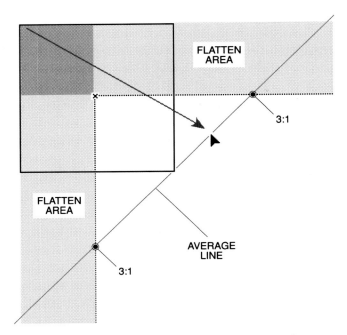

Figure 5.03: Illustrator averages the movement of your cursor when shift-dragging with a geometric shape tool.

Pressing both SHIFT and OPTION while drawing with the rectangle tool or pressing SHIFT while drawing with the centered-rectangle tool creates a square from center to corner.

To get a feel for the rectangle tool, try the following exercise:

1. Select the rectangle tool from the toolbox.

2. Drag with the tool to create a rectangle that is about four times as wide as it is tall, but do not release your mouse button. (You will be keeping it pressed throughout the remainder of this exercise.)

3. Press the OPTION key. The rectangle grows to twice its original size. Notice that the point at which you began your drag has become the center of the shape.

4. Now release the OPTION key. The center point reverts to the corner point and the rectangle shrinks to its previous size.

5. Press the SHIFT key. The rectangle collapses into a horizontal line with an × in the middle (the center point).

6. While still holding down the SHIFT key, drag downward. At some point during your drag, the collapsed rectangle will pop back up to form a square.

7. Locate the "average line" by moving your cursor diagonally, as shown in Figure 5.03. The size of your square should remain more or less constant as you drag.

8. Release the SHIFT key. No longer constrained to a square, the corner of the rectangle will abruptly return to the location occupied by your cursor.

9. Release your mouse button. The rectangle becomes fixed to the drawing area. A corner point appears at each of the four corners of the shape.

You may also use the rectangle tool to create a rectangle by means of a dialog box; hence not by drawing the shape, but by specifying its boundaries numerically. Click with the rectangle tool to display the RECT-ANGLE dialog box shown in Figure 5.04. Here, you may enter values for the "Width," "Height," and "Corner radius" options (the last of which is explained in the section *Drawing a rectangle with rounded corners*, later in this chapter). After pressing RETURN, a rectangle is created to your exact specifications.

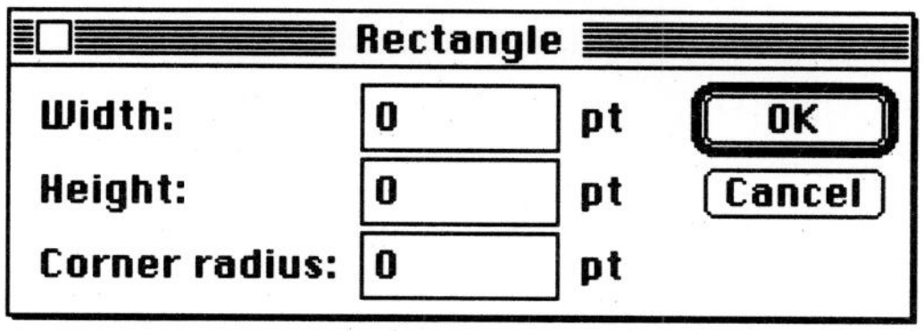

Figure 5.04: Click with the rectangle, centered-rectangle, rounded-rectangle, or centered-rounded-rectangle tool to display the Rectangle dialog box.

Since no placement options are given in the RECTANGLE dialog box, the point at which you click with the rectangle tool acts as the upper left corner point of your new rectangle. If you click with the centered-rectangle tool (or OPTION-click with the rectangle tool), the click point becomes the center point in the shape.

Notice that each option box in Figure 5.04 is followed by "pt," an abbreviation for "points." This refers to the current *unit of measure*, which is set using the "Ruler units" option in the PREFERENCES dialog box (first introduced in the *Setting preferences* section of Chapter 3). The unit of measure in Illustrator may be centimeters, inches, or picas and points. (A *pica* is almost exactly equal to ⅙ inch; a *point* is ¹⁄₁₂ pica, or about ¹⁄₇₂ inch.) When picas and points are the current unit of measure, all dialog box option values that pertain to length or distance are measured in points. If the current unit of measure were inches or centimeters, each option box in the dialog box would be succeeded by "in" or "cm," respectively.

Values entered into option boxes that pertain to length or distance in Illustrator 3.0 are accurate to within ¹⁄₁₀₀ the current unit of measure.

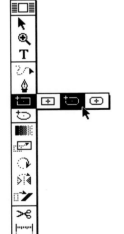

Drawing a rectangle with rounded corners

In Illustrator, you may create rectangles with rounded corners using the *rounded-rectangle tool.* You may choose the rounded-rectangle tool by dragging from the rectangle tool slot. Unlike those of a standard rectangle, the horizontal and vertical segments of a rounded rectangle do not meet to form right-angle corners. Instead, perpendicular segments curve to meet one another. Figure 5.05 shows a standard rectangle with perpendicular corners and the same rectangle drawn with the rounded-rectangle tool.

The extent to which the corners of a rectangle are rounded is controlled by specifying a *corner radius.* The corner radius of a standard rectangle is 0, indicating that there is no corner radius and that neighboring sides should meet perpendicularly. As the corner radius increases, the rounded corner consumes a larger and larger portion of the rectangle.

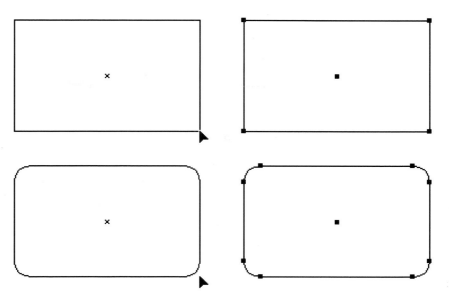

Figure 5.05: Drawing similar shapes with the rectangle and rounded-rectangle tools (left) and the same shapes shown when completed (right).

It is necessary here to introduce a little geometry. The *radius* is the direct distance from the center of a circle to any point on its outline. Think of a rounded corner as one quarter of a perfect circle, as shown in Figure 5.06 on the following page spread. The four rounded corners of a rectangle therefore make up an entire circle. Specifying a corner radius determines the radius of this circle. Since the size of the circle will increase as the radius increases, a rounded corner with a large radius consumes more of a rectangle than a rounded corner with a small radius. Notice how the rounded corner displayed in Figure 5.07 (also on the following page) occupies a larger space than the corner in Figure 5.06. This is because the value for its corner radius is larger. The radius arrows from Figure 5.06 are superimposed on those of Figure 5.07 to demonstrate this difference.

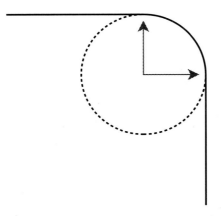

Figure 5.06: The corner of a rounded rectangle is actually a quarter circle. Arrows represent its radius.

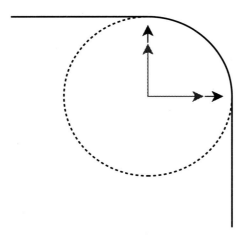

Figure 5.07: An enlarged corner radius with the smaller corner radius superimposed.

A radius of a circle is half the circle's total width, which is called the *diameter*. If the diameter of a rounded corner is at least equal to the longest side of a rectangle—that is, if the radius is at least *half* the longest side of a rectangle—then the rounded corner will consume the entire rectangle. Figure 5.08, for example, shows a series of inset squares, each with a larger corner radius than that of its predecessor. Eventually, the radius of a round corner becomes so large that the corner takes over the square, resulting in a circle.

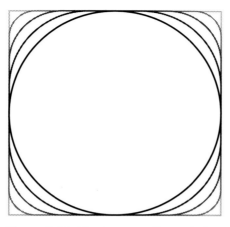

Figure 5.08: The largest of rounded corners will completely consume a rectangle and will result in a circle.

Rounded corners may be specified in one of two ways. First, there is a "Corner radius" option in the RECTANGLE dialog box (see Figure 5.04). After clicking with any rectangle tool, this option allows you to specify a radius value—once again, in the current unit of measure—that is accurate to within ¹⁄₁₀₀ of a point.

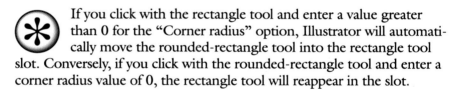 If you click with the rectangle tool and enter a value greater than 0 for the "Corner radius" option, Illustrator will automatically move the rounded-rectangle tool into the rectangle tool slot. Conversely, if you click with the rounded-rectangle tool and enter a corner radius value of 0, the rectangle tool will reappear in the slot.

Second, you may use the "Corner radius" option in the PREFERENCES dialog box (introduced in the *Setting preferences* section of Chapter 3). Both "Corner radius" values are subject to the current unit of measure.

Whether entered into the RECTANGLE or PREFERENCES dialog box, the "Corner radius" value is saved with the Adobe Illustrator 3.0 Prefs file, so that it affects not only the current rounded rectangle, but also future shapes drawn with the rounded-rectangle tool or the centered-rounded-rectangle tool.

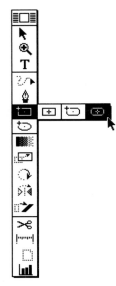

If you press OPTION while drawing with the rounded-rectangle tool, the beginning of your drag becomes the center point of the rectangle. Alternately, you may choose the *centered-rounded-rectangle tool* from the rectangle tool slot. This tool allows you to draw rounded rectangles from the center point without pressing the OPTION key. Pressing OPTION and dragging with the centered-rounded-rectangle tool draws the shape normally.

Pressing SHIFT and dragging with the rounded-rectangle tool creates a rounded square. Pressing both SHIFT and OPTION while drawing with the rounded-rectangle tool or pressing the SHIFT key while drawing with the centered-rounded-rectangle tool creates a rounded square from the center point.

 You may not numerically adjust the corner radius of an existing rounded rectangle. You must either reshape the rectangle (as described in Chapter 7, *Reshaping Existing Paths*) or recreate it.

Drawing an ellipse

The *oval tool*—displayed by default in the seventh tool slot of the toolbox—is used in the same manner as the rectangle tool. The difference, of course, is that the oval tool is used to creates *ellipses* (ovals) and circles rather than rectangles and squares.

As is the case with the rectangle tool, the click and release points created with the oval tool reside on the path of the ellipse. In this sense, you might think of an ellipse as a rectangle with so large a percentage of its path devoted to rounded corners that the vertical and horizontal segments altogether disappear (refer to Figure 5.08). However, unlike the rectangle tool, the press and release points of an oval tool drag do not represent opposite corners, since an ellipse has no corner; they represent the middles of opposite *arcs*. While you drag with the oval tool, imagine that a dotted rectangle is formed, displaying the area of drag, as shown in Figure 5.09. This rectangle exists entirely within the path of the ellipse. This is different than drawing with an oval tool in most other Macintosh applications, because the simple ellipse in Illustrator is always slightly larger than the area of your drag. For example, if you drag four inches horizontally, the resulting ellipse will be $4\sqrt{2}$ (approximately 5½) inches wide. As a matter of fact, an ellipse will always be taller and wider by a factor of $\sqrt{2}$ (roughly 140%) than the height and width of your drag.

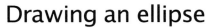

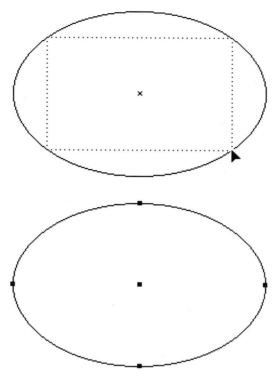

Figure 5.09: Drawing an ellipse from arc to opposite arc
(with inset rectangle, top) and the same ellipse shown
when completed (bottom).

This arc-to-arc metaphor may make the oval tool seem overly complicated; but in fact, it makes a more efficient tracing tool. As demonstrated
in Figure 5.10 on the following page, you trace an elliptical or circular
template shape simply by dragging from the middle of one arc to the
middle of the opposite arc. A dotted rectangle displays the course of your
drag. There is no guesswork, since you begin and end your drag on portions of the template shape. This is preferable to the metaphor adopted by
more conventional drawing programs, such as MacDraw or Aldus Free-
Hand, in which you must begin and end your drag well outside the template shape, guessing at imaginary points where the vertical and
horizontal extremes of the circle intersect.

For more information about tracing template images, see Chapter 6,
Tracing Bitmapped Images.

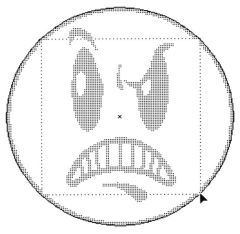

Figure 5.10: Tracing a bitmapped circle with the oval tool
by dragging from arc to arc.

If you press OPTION while drawing with the oval tool, the beginning of your drag becomes the center point of the ellipse. As before, the release point becomes the middle of an arc, determining the size and shape of the ellipse. Alternately, you may choose the *centered-oval tool* from the oval tool slot. This tool allows you to draw ellipses from center point to arc without pressing the OPTION key. Pressing OPTION and dragging with the centered-oval tool draws the shape from arc to opposite arc.

Pressing SHIFT and dragging with the oval tool creates a perfect circle. Pressing both SHIFT and OPTION while drawing with the oval tool or pressing the SHIFT key while drawing with the centered-oval tool creates a circle from center point to arc.

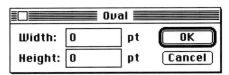

Figure 5.11: Click with the oval or centered-oval tool to
display the Oval dialog box.

Click with the oval tool to bring up the OVAL dialog box shown in Figure 5.11. This dialog contains both "Width" and "Height" options, like the RECTANGLE dialog. The values in both option boxes are measured in centimeters, inches, or points, depending on the currently selected "Ruler units" option in the Preferences dialog box, as described earlier in this chapter. After entering values for these options and pressing RETURN, an ellipse is created to your specifications.

Since no placement options are given in the Oval dialog box, the point at which you click with the oval tool acts as the middle of the upper, left arc in your new ellipse. If you click with the centered-oval tool (or OPTION-click with the oval tool), the click point becomes the center point in the shape.

Geometric paths at an angle

In the course of drawing a shape with one of the six geometric path tools, you may find that your path rotates at some odd angle, as demonstrated by the rectangle in Figure 5.12. This is not happening because you are misusing the tool; rather, you or someone else using this same copy of Illustrator 3.0 has altered the "Constrain angle" option in the Preferences dialog box. The *constraint axes* control the angles at which objects may be moved and transformed when pressing the SHIFT key. But they also control the creation of geometric paths and text blocks. If any value besides 0 is entered in the "Constrain angle" option box, geometric paths will be rotated to that degree as you draw.

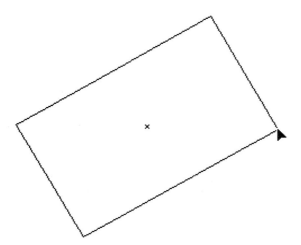

Figure 5.12: Drawing a rectangle when the constraint axes have been rotated by 30°.

To draw rectangle and ellipses that are not rotated, you must reset the constraint axes to its normal orientation. This may be accomplished using one of two methods:

- Choose the Preferences command from the Edit menu (⌘-K). Enter 0 for the "Constrain angle" option and press RETURN.

- Quit the Illustrator application (⌘-Q). Open the folder containing the Illustrator application at the Finder level. Select the file named Adobe Illustrator 3.0 Prefs and drag it into the Trash icon. Choose the Empty Trash command from the Special menu and relaunch the Illustrator application. All options in the Preferences dialog box will be reset.

Any geometric paths that you draw will now be oriented normally.

Free-form paths

The geometric path tools allow you to create simple shapes quickly and easily. However, Illustrator's true drawing power is based in its ability to define free-form lines and shapes. Such paths may be simple anomalies, like triangles or crescents. Or they may be intricate polygons and naturalistic forms that meet the most complex specifications.

The freehand tool

Displayed by default in the fourth tool slot of the Illustrator palette, the *freehand tool* is used for real-time drawing. After choosing this tool, you may click and drag as if you were drawing with a pencil on a sheet of paper. Illustrator tracks the exact movement of your mouse on screen, creating a sketchy line between the locations at which you begin and end your drag. After you release, Illustrator automatically determines the quantity and location of points and segments and creates the freehand path.

Consider the example of the valentine shown in Figure 5.13. The figure shows the progression of the freehand tool cursor. We start drawing with the tool at the upper cusp of the valentine. We then sweep around in a great rightward arc and down to the lower tip, back upward and around to the left, and finally meet up with our first point in one continuous movement, as shown by the position of the cursor in the figure.

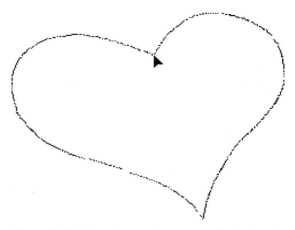

Figure 5.13: Drawing a valentine with the freehand tool.

Notice that the outline of the valentine has a few tiny jagged edges. These jagged edges exist for two reasons. First, we drew this figure with a mouse. The mouse is not a precise drawing instrument. When you move a mouse, a ball within its chamber rolls about against the surface of the table or mouse pad. This ball in turn causes two internal tracking wheels to move, one vertically and one horizontally. Based on the activity of these two wheels, the mouse conveys movement information to the computer. No matter how thoroughly you clean a mouse, there will be some sort of interference between the ball and the wheels, even if it is only some small particles of dust. For example, if you draw a 45° diagonal line, both the vertical and horizontal tracking wheels should move at exactly the same pace. If some interference comes between the ball and the horizontal wheel causing the wheel to remain motionless for only a moment, then the mouse will send purely vertical movement information to the computer until the interference has passed. The result is a momentary jag in an otherwise smooth diagonal line.

Second, most people—even skilled artists—are not very practiced in drawing with a mouse. It takes time to master this skill. You may find that your first drawing efforts look much different than you had planned— possibly far worse than Figure 5.13, for example. Luckily, the freehand tool is capable of smoothing out many imperfections.

If you're comfortable with drawing with a mouse, but you want to avoid some of the tracking problems associated with the standard Apple mouse, consider purchasing an *optical mouse*. Our favorite is the A+ Mouse ADB from Mouse Systems, (415) 656-1117. For about $100, this pointing device projects two lights that bounce off a reflective pad. Because it lacks moving parts, an optical mouse tends to last longer and perform more consistently than any track-ball device.

Once you release your mouse button, having completed the process of drawing a path, Illustrator begins its calculations to determine how many points your path should have, as well as their locations. Thus, drawing with the freehand tool is entirely automatic.

Freehand tolerance

In Chapter 4, we recommended that you use points sparingly, even when drawing complex images. Too many points needlessly complicate a path, we said, making it clumsy and malformed. You may find, however, that Illustrator does not always follow our advice. When the calculations have finished, freehand paths are frequently riddled with far too many points. As often as not, the path that you expected to be a smooth free-form line turns out to be a jagged mess.

To fully understand the freehand tool, you must understand how Illustrator assigns points to a freehand path. It makes its determinations based on three factors:

- **Consistency**. Illustrator assigns a point to every location at which your freehand drag changes direction. Thus, smooth, consistent mouse actions produce smooth, elegant paths; jerky or unsteady mouse actions produce overly complex lines.

- **Speed**. The speed at which you draw may also affect the appearance of a freehand path. If your mouse lingers, Illustrator is more likely to assign a point at this location. However, if you draw too quickly, Illustrator will ignore many of the subtleties in your drag. A slow but steady technique is the most reliable.

- **Tolerance**. Illustrator allows you to control the sensitivity of the freehand tool using the "Freehand tolerance" option in the PREFERENCES dialog box. A low *tolerance* setting results in extremely complex paths, a high tolerance setting results in overly smooth paths.

To access the "Freehand tolerance" option, choose the PREFERENCES... command from the EDIT menu (⌘-K). You may enter any value between 0 and 10 into the option box; values are measured by Illustrator in screen pixels. By entering the number 2, for example, you instruct Illustrator to ignore any small jags when determining point information of future free-hand paths, provided that such jags do not exceed 2 pixels in length or width. Setting the "Freehand tolerance" to 0 makes the freehand tool extremely sensitive; setting the option to 10 smooths out your freehand paths.

Figure 5.14 shows the number and location of the points that Illustrator has automatically set into our valentine shape when the tolerance level is set to 0 pixel. Every imperfection from the path in the previous figure has been captured by Illustrator—including imperfections you may not even have noticed. The result is an overly complicated path. You will find that such a small tolerance value is rarely useful.

Figure 5.14: The points assigned to the valentine shape when the "Freehand tolerance" option is set to 0 pixels. The white squares are points. The small lines with circles at the end of them are Bézier control handles, which will be introduced later in this chapter.

The five paths in Figure 5.15 are Illustrator's interpretations of our valentine when the tolerance value is set to 1, 2, 3, 5, and 10 pixels, respectively. If you compare this figure to Figure 5.14, you'll notice dramatic differences between the way in which Illustrator interprets paths at tolerances of 0, 1, and 2 pixels. Paths with tolerances of 3, 5, and 10, however, are strikingly similar.

Figure 5.15: Five examples demonstrating the points assigned to our shape when the tolerance is set to 1, 2 (top), 3 (center), 5, and 10 (bottom), respectively.

A "Freehand tolerance" of 2 or 3 is generally adequate for most users. But we advise that you experiment with this option to determine your preferred setting. If your drawing technique is more steady or precise than ours, lower your tolerance. If you have problems drawing a straight line, raise your tolerance. Keep in mind, the "Freehand tolerance" value is saved in the Adobe Illustrator 3.0 Prefs file and will therefore apply to all future illustrations until a new value is entered.

The tolerance value for a path cannot be altered after it is created, since Illustrator calculates the points for a path only once, after your release when dragging with the freehand tool. For each of the paths in Figures 5.14 and 5.15, we had to change the tolerance value and draw a new valentine from scratch.

Pressing ⌘ while drawing

Normally, a continuous path tracks every movement as you draw with the freehand tool. If you press the COMMAND key, however, your cursor will change from a black arrowhead to a hollow arrowhead, indicating that the freehand tool is prepared to track your movements differently. This COMMAND-dragging may be used to produce one of two results:

- **Erasing**. You may press COMMAND to erase a mistake while in the process of dragging with the freehand tool. In the middle of drawing, press COMMAND and trace back over a portion of a path that you have just drawn. You will see it disappear. Therefore, you can draw a path with the freehand tool, immediately "undraw" part of it while pressing the COMMAND key, and then release COMMAND and continue drawing.

- **Adding a single segment**. Rather than COMMAND-dragging back over your path, COMMAND-drag away from it and then release the COMMAND key and continue to draw. Notice that Illustrator does not display your path between the point where the COMMAND key was pressed and the point where it was released. At the end of your drag, Illustrator calculates the quantity and position of the points necessary to represent your freehand path virtually the same as it has in past examples. The only difference is that any portion of your path that was created while the COMMAND key was pressed is represented by a single segment. This segment may be very nearly straight, but it will always curve slightly.

To experiment with adding a single segment with the freehand tool, try the following exercise:

1. Drawing a squiggle with the freehand tool, as shown below.

Figure 5.16: Draw a squiggle with the freehand tool, then press the command key and drag away from the line.

2. Press the COMMAND key and drag to the location represented by the hollow arrowhead cursor in Figure 5.16. For as long as the COMMAND key remains pressed, no line will appear to be drawn. Your drag will be interpreted by Illustrator to represent a single, slightly curved segment.

3. Release the COMMAND key, and draw another squiggle. Your movements are interpreted exactly as they were before. As shown in Figure 5.17, the freehand cursor again becomes a black arrowhead, indicating that the COMMAND key has indeed been released.

4. Release your mouse button. Figure 5.18 shows the completed path, displaying a single, selected segment between the COMMAND key press and release points.

Note that the COMMAND key may not be pressed before dragging with the freehand tool or released after the drag is finished. The single segment produced by pressing COMMAND must be preceded and followed by normal freehand path segments.

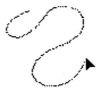

Figure 5.17: Continue to draw after releasing the command key.

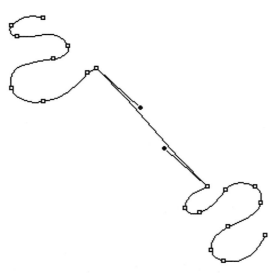

Figure 5.18: The completed path contains a single, slightly curved segment between the points where the command key was pressed and released.

Extending a line

The freehand tool may also be used to *extend* an open path. For example, suppose that you have drawn a line with the freehand tool some time ago, but now you wish to make the line longer or close the path. Drag from an *endpoint*—that is, the point at either end of the line—with the freehand tool, as shown in Figure 5.19. The line created by dragging with the tool is treated as an extension of the existing open path. To extend a path, drag from an endpoint and end your drag when the line has become the desired length. To close the path, drag from one endpoint to the other.

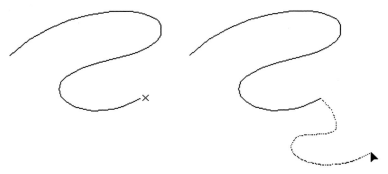

Figure 5.19: To extend an open path (left) with the freehand tool, drag from either of its endpoints (right).

Normally, regardless of its original identity, an endpoint will be converted to a *smooth point* when you drag from it with the freehand tool, as shown in Figure 5.20. A smooth point ensures a continuous *arc* between two segments, as discussed in *The line* section of Chapter 4. This is even true when the point appears to be a corner, a fact which may affect future manipulations as discussed in Chapter 7, *Reshaping Existing Paths*.

To make this point a *corner point*—at which two segments meet to form a sharp corner—press and hold the OPTION key before you begin your drag. This technique is demonstrated in Figure 5.21. If you are closing a path, the endpoint at which you release will also be a smooth point unless you press OPTION before ending your drag and hold the key down until after the mouse button has been released.

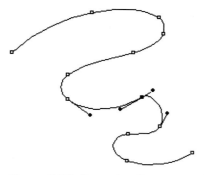

Figure 5.20: Dragging from an endpoint with the freehand tool converts the point to a smooth point (displayed as selected).

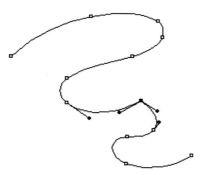

Figure 5.21: Press the option key to convert an endpoint to a corner point (displayed as selected).

Sketching complicated paths

The freehand tool can be used to sketch complicated objects, especially line drawings. If you are skilled in drawing with the mouse, you may find that the immediacy of producing high-resolution images in real time is very appealing. Drawing with the freehand tool can soften the computer-produced appearance of an illustration, and may convey a sense of immediacy to those who view or read the piece. However, regardless of your drawing ability or preferences, the freehand tool rarely renders images that may be considered professional in quality.

Suppose that we draw a fish as a single line with the freehand tool. The first example in Figure 5.22 shows the path as we originally draw it, before Illustrator calculates the quantity and location of points and segments. The second example shows the points that Illustrator has assigned to our fish. The third example shows the fish as a deselected path.

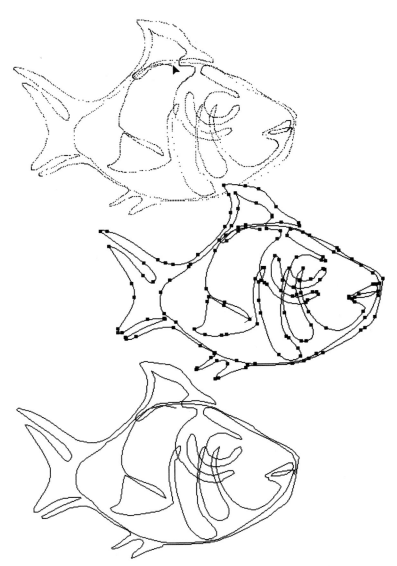

Figure 5.22: Three steps in the process of sketching a fish with the freehand tool.

It is amazing how accurately the finished product resembles the original movement of the freehand tool. This is primarily due to the "Freehand tolerance" option, discussed earlier in this chapter. (The tolerance was set to 3 for the examples in Figure 5.22.) The final path is by no means perfect, mostly due to the fact that the original drawing lacks perfection, but it is a very good place to start.

Most illustrations created with the freehand tool need to be extensively manipulated in order to print acceptably. Like a Polaroid camera, the immediate satisfaction offered by the freehand tool results in the sacrifice of accuracy and elegance. For this reason, we recommend that you use the tool primarily for sketching images and that you prepare yourself to spend the time required to properly reshape them (as described in Chapter 7, *Reshaping Existing Paths*).

 Press the CONTROL key to temporarily access the freehand tool when the pen tool is selected. If your keyboard does not provide a CONTROL key, use the Z key instead.

Bézier paths

All paths in Adobe Illustrator are *Bézier* (pronounced bā´·zē·ā) *paths*; that is, they rely on a handful of mathematical curve definitions, pioneered by Pierre Bézier, which have developed into an integral part of the PostScript printer language. The Bézier curve model allows for zero, one, or two levers to be associated with each point in a line or shape. These levers are called *Bézier control handles*. Each handle may be moved in relation to a point, bending and tugging at a curved segment like a piece of elastic taffy.

The geometric path tools and the freehand tool gloss over the nuts and bolts of path building. However, if you really want to understand how to draw in Adobe Illustrator, you must master the creation of lines and shapes on a point-by-point basis. The remainder of this chapter is devoted to a thorough examination of points, segments, and Bézier control handles, all centered around a discussion of Illustrator's primary drawing tool—the *pen tool*.

The pen tool

As discussed in Chapter 4, Illustrator defines lines and shapes as the combination of two or more points. Each point determines how a segment in the path enters it and how another exits it. The *pen tool*, the fifth tool in your palette, works by defining a single point at a time. The way in which you operate the pen tool determines the identity of each point you create.

Drawing straight segments

Select the pen tool and click at some location on the screen to create a *corner point* that shows up as a tiny black square, indicating that it is *selected*. Be careful to only click with the pen tool and not drag. If you drag more than two pixels while clicking with the pen tool, you will create a smooth point, as described later in this chapter.

The point you just created is *open-ended*, meaning that it does not have both a segment coming into it and a segment going out from it. In fact, this new corner point—we'll call it point A—is associated with no segment whatsoever. It is a lone point, open-ended in two directions.

If you again click with the pen tool at a new location on the screen, as demonstrated by Figure 5.23, a straight segment will be drawn from the original corner point A to the new corner point B. Notice that point A now appears hollow rather than black. This shows that point A is the member of a selected path, but is itself *deselected*. Our new corner point B is selected and open-ended. A point always becomes selected, thereby deselecting all other points, immediately after it is created.

Figure 5.23: Create a straight line by clicking at each of two separate locations with the pen tool.

The small cross (+) in the lower left corner of Figure 5.23 is the pen tool cursor. When the pen tool cursor appears as a +, it signifies that the selected path is *active*, meaning that it is ready to receive points. A segment will be drawn between the selected point and the next point you create. The pen tool cursor may also appear as an ×, indicating that all paths are *passive*. Even if a passive path includes an open-ended, selected point, no segment will be drawn between this point and the next point you create. Instead, this next point becomes the first point in a new path.

If you click a third time with the pen tool, you create a new point, point C. As shown in Figure 5.24, point A remains open-ended, since it is associated with only one segment, by which it is attached to point B. Likewise, a segment goes from point B to point C. Because a point may be associated with no more than two segments, point B is no longer open-ended. Such a point is called an *interior point*. Point C was just created, so it and only it is selected. And because this last point is open-ended and the pen tool cursor still appears as a +, the path remains active.

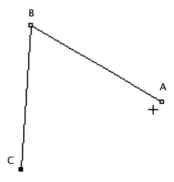

Figure 5.24: Point B is now an interior point, incapable of receiving additional segments.

We will now *close* our path, changing it from a line into a shape. All open-ended points will be eliminated. This is done quite easily. Merely click with the pen tool on point A, the first point in the path. Since point A is open-ended, it willingly accepts the segment drawn between it and point C, as shown in Figure 5.25 on the following page.

The pen tool cursor in Figure 5.25 appears as an ×, indicating that no path is active. This is because the moment you close a path, it becomes passive. No segment will be drawn between the next point you create and any point in the selected shape.

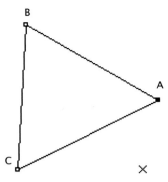

Figure 5.25: Closing a path deactivates it. The next point
you create will begin a new path.

Suppose you click again with the pen tool cursor. The triangle shape
becomes deselected and a new point D is created (see Figure 5.26). Point
D is open-ended in two directions and the cursor again changes to a +.
The path-creation process has begun anew.

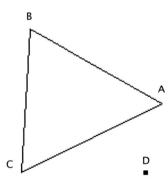

Figure 5.26: Creating a point D that is independent of the
previous path deselects that path.

✳ To *deactivate* a path (make it passive) without closing it, click
the pen tool icon in the toolbox or select any other tool except
those in the first two slots (arrow and zoom). Alternatively, you
may press COMMAND to access the arrow tool, and click on a blank portion
of the screen.

 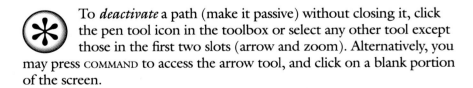

Drawing perpendicular segments

To constrain a point so it is created at an angle that is a multiple of 45° from the selected, open-ended point, press SHIFT as you click with the pen tool. This technique allows you to create horizontal, vertical, and diagonal segments. In Figure 5.27, for example, the location at which we actually click with the pen tool is shown by the position of the + cursor. However, since the SHIFT key is pressed, the new point is constrained to a 0° angle from its neighbor, resulting in a horizontal segment.

Figure 5.27: Shift-click with the pen tool to create a horizontal, vertical, or diagonal segment.

The effects of pressing the SHIFT key can be altered by rotating the constraint axes using the "Constrain angle" option in the PREFERENCES dialog box, as described in *Geometric paths at an angle* earlier in this chapter.

Drawing curved segments

If you click with the pen tool, you create a corner point. But if you drag with the pen tool, you create a *smooth point,* which ensures a smooth arc between one curved segment and the next. A smooth point sports two *Bézier control handles,* each of which appear as a tiny circle perched at the end of a hairline that connects the handle to its point (see Figure 5.28 on the next page). These handles act as levers, bending segments relative to the smooth point itself.

The point at which you begin dragging with the pen tool determines the location of the smooth point; the point at which you release becomes a Bézier control handle that affects the next segment you create. A second handle appears symmetrically about the smooth point to the first. This handle determines the curvature of the most recent segment, as demonstrated in Figure 5.28.

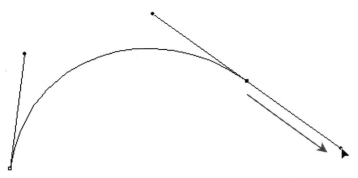

Figure 5.28: Drag with the pen tool to create a smooth
point flanked by two Bézier control handles.

You might think of a smooth point as if it were the center of a small
seesaw, with the Bézier control handles acting as opposite ends. If you
push down on one handle, the opposite handle goes up, and vice versa.
Figure 5.29 shows four examples of dragging different distances from the
same smooth point with the pen tool. Notice that the placement of both
Bézier control handles is determined by the release location, since the second handle is symmetrical about the smooth point to the first. It is this
seesaw quality that forces two segments to always form a continuous,
seamless arc through a smooth point.

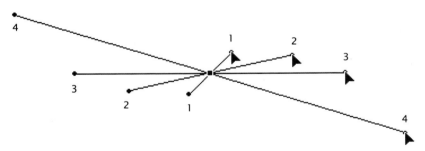

Figure 5.29: When dragging with the pen tool, the release location
determines the placement of both Bézier control handles.

Smooth points act no differently than corner points when it comes to
building paths. Dragging with the pen tool creates a curved segment between the current smooth point and the previously selected, open-ended
point in the active path. If no path is active, the smooth point becomes
the first point in a new path. Clicking on the first point in an active path
closes the path.

If the first point in a path is a smooth point, you should drag rather than click on the point with the pen tool when closing the path. Otherwise, you run the risk of altering the identity of the point, as discussed in the next section.

Creating a cusp

As we have seen, a smooth point must always have two Bézier control handles, each positioned in an imaginary straight line with the point itself. A corner point, however, is much more versatile: It may have zero, one, or two handles. We have seen how clicking with the pen tool creates a corner point with no handle and dragging with the pen tool creates a smooth point. To create a corner point that has one or two Bézier control handles—sometimes called a *cusp*—you must manipulate an existing corner or smooth point while in the process of creating its path. We will demonstrate three examples of how this technique can work:

● **Option 1**: *Delete a handle from a smooth point.*

The first two examples begin with the semicircle shown in Figure 5.30. You would create this path by dragging three times with the pen tool: First drag downward from the right point; then drag leftward from the bottom point; and finally drag upward from the left point, which is selected in the figure. The result is an active path composed of three smooth points.

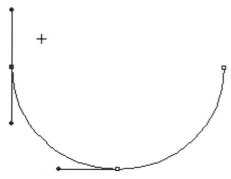

Figure 5.30: An active semicircular path with a selected, open-ended smooth point.

Illustrator allows you to alter the most recent point while in the process of creating its path. Suppose that you want to change the semicircle into a bowl-shaped path, like the one shown in Figure 5.31. This shape involves three segments, two of which meet to form a single large arc, and a third which is straight, flattening off the shape. Since smooth points may be associated only with curved segments, corner points must exist on both sides of this prospective straight segment. Therefore, you need to change the two topmost smooth points from Figure 5.30 to corner points, each with a single Bézier control handle that affects the curved segment below its point.

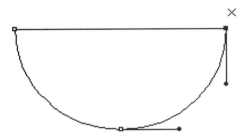

Figure 5.31: By clicking with the pen tool on the two top points, you may change the existing smooth points to corner points with one Bézier control handle apiece.

After creating the leftmost smooth point shown in Figure 5.30, your cursor appears as a +, indicating that a segment will be drawn between the currently selected, open-ended point and the next point you create with the pen tool. However, the bowl shape requires no new point, only a single new segment. So instead of clicking or dragging at a new location, click (do not drag) with the pen tool on the selected smooth point. By clicking on a selected, open-ended smooth point with the pen tool, you amputate the Bézier control handle that does not currently control a segment. In Figure 5.30, the lower handle controls the left segment in the semicircular path, but the upper handle controls no segment. Therefore, clicking the smooth point amputates this upper handle.

What do you have left? A smooth point with only one Bézier control handle is an impossibility. This point must therefore be a corner point.

You now have an open path composed of two smooth points and a corner point. You still need to close the path and to amputate a handle belonging to the first smooth point. Both maneuvers are accomplished in a single operation. While your pen tool cursor still appears as a +, click on the first smooth point. It's that simple. With one click, you close the path and amputate the Bézier control handle that would otherwise control the new segment. Hence, the new segment is straight, bordered on both sides by corner points with one Bézier control handle each. The result is the shape shown in Figure 5.31.

- **Option 2**: *Move one smooth point handle independently of the other.*

The second example for creating a corner point with Bézier control handles once again begins with the path shown in Figure 5.30. Suppose this time, however, that you wish to close the path with a rounded top, like the one shown in Figure 5.33 on the next page. All segments in this path are curved, and yet the upper segment meets with the lower segments to form two cusps. This means that we must change the two top smooth points to corner points with two Bézier control handles apiece— one controlling the upper segment and one controlling a lower segment.

In Illustrator, you may subtract a handle from a smooth point and add a new handle to the resulting corner point in one operation. To accomplish this, press the OPTION key and drag from the selected, open-ended smooth point shown in Figure 5.30. The moment you begin to drag from the smooth point while pressing the OPTION key, the point's identity changes permanently to a corner point. As you drag, a new handle emerges, as shown in Figure 5.32. This handle will control the next segment you create. Thus, you now have a corner point with two Bézier control handles, each fully independent of the other.

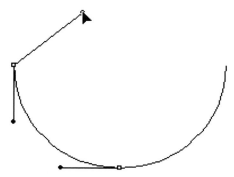

Figure 5.32: Press the option key and drag from the selected smooth point to convert the point to a cusp.

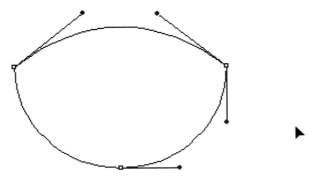

Figure 5.33: Close the shape by option-dragging on the
first point in the path.

You may close the shape in the same manner. Press OPTION and drag
with the pen tool from the first smooth point of the path. However, notice the location of the cursor as you drag, as demonstrated by Figure
5.33. As you drag in one direction, the Bézier control handle emerges in
the opposite direction. This is because when dragging with the pen tool,
you always drag in the direction of the segment that *exits* the current
point. The handle controlling the newly created segment—the segment
that *enters* the current point—is positioned symmetrically to your drag,
even if it is the only handle being manipulated.

- **Option 3**: *Add a handle to a corner point.*

We have now seen how you can subtract a handle from an existing
open-ended smooth point to form a corner point with only one handle.
We have also seen how you can subtract a handle from a smooth point
and add an independent handle to the resulting corner point at the same
time. This third example demonstrates how you can add a handle to an
existing open-ended corner point, one which is so far associated only with
straight segments.

Suppose this time that you have created the straight-segment path
shown in Figure 5.34. By dragging from the selected, open-ended corner
point in the figure, you may create a single Bézier control handle, as
shown in Figure 5.35. Note that you do not convert the corner point to a
smooth point by dragging at it. Although a smooth point may be changed
to a corner point, a corner point may not be changed to a smooth point
using the pen tool. Thus, you now have a corner point with one Bézier
control handle.

Figure 5.34: An active straight-segment path with a
selected, open-ended corner point.

Figure 5.35: Drag from the selected corner point to add a
Bézier control handle.

To close the path, drag at the first corner point (the top, right point)
in the path. Notice the location of the cursor during the drag, as demonstrated by Figure 5.36. Once again, you drag in the opposite direction of
the emerging Bézier control handle. Like the example in Figure 5.33, you
drag as if you were creating a handle controlling the segment that *exits*
the current point. The handle that actually exists controls the segment
that *enters* the current point; thus it moves symmetrically to your drag.

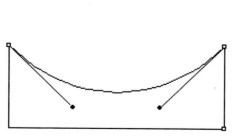

Figure 5.36: Close the shape by dragging on the first
corner point in the path.

Pen tool summary

Regardless of the tool used to create it, a path is made up of points and segments. The points determine the curvature of segments based on the positioning of Bézier control handles. In turn, the segments define the form of the path.

Although you may adjust the placement of points and Bézier control handles by reshaping a path created with any drawing tool (as described in Chapter 7, *Reshaping Existing Paths*), the pen tool is the only tool in Adobe Illustrator that allows you to exactly position points and handles during the creation process. And since any illustration may be constructed as the combination of a series of lines and shapes, there is absolutely no illustration that cannot be created using the pen tool alone.

 Press the CONTROL key to temporarily access the pen tool when the freehand tool is selected. If your keyboard does not provide a CONTROL key, use the Z key instead.

The following items summarize the ways in which the pen tool can be used to build paths in Adobe Illustrator:

- To build a path, create one point after another until the path is the desired length and shape. As long as the path is *active* (the pen tool cursor appears as a +), a segment will be created between each point.

- To close a path and, in the process, make the path *passive*, click on the first point in the active path. Click again to begin a new path.

- To make an open path passive, COMMAND-click on an empty portion of the drawing area. Release COMMAND and click again to begin a new path.

- To reactivate a path, click or drag on one of its endpoints. (Note: clicking or dragging on an existing endpoint may change the point's identity.)

- To join an active path with another open path, click or drag on an endpoint in the passive path.

- To intersperse freehand drawing with an active path, press CONTROL and drag from the selected point as when extending a path with the freehand tool. After you finish drawing, release CONTROL and click or drag from the selected point to reactivate the path.

The next items explain the specific kinds of points and segments that may be created with the pen tool:

- Click to create a *corner point*.
- Click at two separate locations to create a straight segment.
- Click at one location and SHIFT-click at another to create a perpendicular segment (at any angle that is a multiple of 45°).
- Drag to create a *smooth point* with two *Bézier control handles*.
- Drag at two separate locations to create a curved segment.
- Drag, press SHIFT, begin a new drag, and then release SHIFT while still dragging to create a curved segment whose points align with respect to the constraint axes. Pressing SHIFT constrains the point; releasing SHIFT before you complete the drag allows you to move the Bézier control handles freely. An example of such a curve is shown in Figure 5.37.

Figure 5.37: Press shift before dragging but then release to create a curve along the constraint axes. Notice how the points align horizontally.

- Press SHIFT after beginning a drag to constrain the Bézier control handles without affecting the placement of the smooth point. An example of this is shown in Figure 5.38 on the following page.
- Press SHIFT and drag at two separate locations to create a perfect dome, as shown in Figure 5.39.

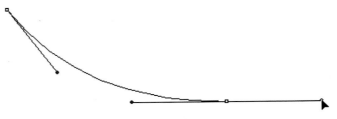

Figure 5.38: Begin the drag before pressing shift to align the Bézier control handles to the constraint axes without constraining the smooth point.

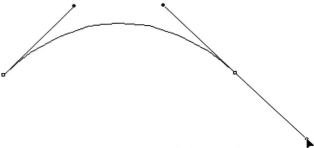

Figure 5.39: Shift-drag and shift-drag again to constrain both points and Bézier control handles to create a symmetrical dome.

- Click on an existing selected smooth point to delete a Bézier control handle, converting the smooth point to a corner point with one handle. Then click again at a different location to append a straight segment to the existing curved segment.

- Drag from an existing selected corner point to add a Bézier control handle. Then drag again at a different location to append a curved segment to the existing straight segment.

- Press OPTION and drag from an existing selected smooth point to redirect a Bézier control handle, converting the smooth point to a corner point with two independent handles. Then drag again at a different location to append a curved segment that meets the existing curved segment to form a cusp.

Tracing
Bitmapped
Images

Not everyone can be a Rembrandt. Some of us are lucky to draw a straight line, much less triumph over the gamut of complex strategies inherent in the operation of the pen tool. Others can draw quite adequately with pencil and paper, but have problems making the transition to the computer-graphics environment.

If you fall into any of these categories, you may breathe a sigh of relief. Illustrator allows you to trace scanned images and artwork created in painting programs. It also automates the conversion process by providing a trace tool. Even skilled computer artists are well advised to sketch their ideas on paper or in a painting program before executing them in Adobe Illustrator. The following section explains why.

Why trace a bitmap?

It is not easy to draw from scratch in Adobe Illustrator. Even if you draw exclusively with the freehand tool, you will frequently have to go back and edit your lines and shapes, point by point (as we will discuss in Chapter 7, *Reshaping Existing Paths*). Also, to build an image in Illustrator is to do just that: *build*. Heaps of mathematically defined lines and shapes must be combined and layered much like girders at a construction site.

With this in mind, you'll probably have the most luck with Adobe Illustrator if you're part artist and part engineer. But for those of us who aren't engineers and can't even *imagine* how engineers think, a painting application like MacPaint or Studio/1 provides a more artist-friendly environment.

Painting programs provide simple tools such as pencils and erasers. And since little interpretation is required by your software, these tools work just like their real-life counterparts. Your screen displays the results of your mouse movements instantaneously. This allows you to draw, see what you've drawn, and make alterations, all in the time it takes the appropriate neurons to fire in your brain.

But despite the many advantages of painting software, its single failing—the graininess of its output—is glaringly obvious, so much so that people who have never used a computer can immediately recognize a bitmapped image as computer-produced artwork. Object-oriented drawings, on the other hand, are smooth.

This jaggedness is particularly noticeable in the case of black-and-white artwork. For example, the bitmapped fish in Figure 6.01 was fairly easy to create. It is well executed, but its jagged edges are far too obvious for it to be considered professional-quality artwork. By introducing a few shades of gray to the image, we can soften much of its jaggedness, as demonstrated by Figure 6.02. However, it now appears fuzzy and out of focus. This makes gray-scale scanning more suited to photography than to line art.

Figure 6.01: A typically jagged black-and-white image created in MacPaint.

Figure 6.02: Gray pixels soften the edges, but make the image appear out of focus.

Only in a drawing application such as Adobe Illustrator can you create pristine line art. The fish in Figure 6.03, for example, required more time and effort to produce, but the result is a smooth, highly focused, professional-quality image.

Figure 6.03: By tracing the bitmapped fish image, we are able to arrive at this smooth, exemplary drawing.

By tracing a bitmapped image in a drawing program, you can have the best of both worlds. You can sketch your idea traditionally onto a piece of paper and then scan it into your computer, or you can sketch directly in a painting program. Either way, your sketch will be bitmapped. You may then import the sketch as a *tracing template* into Adobe Illustrator using the NEW... or OPEN... command, as discussed in the *Creating a new illustration* and *Swapping tracing templates* sections of Chapter 3. Then use Illustrator's drawing tools to convert the image to a collection of free-form lines and shapes.

Automated tracing

Adobe provides two tools that automate the process of tracing bitmapped artwork. One tool—*the autotrace tool*—is included in Illustrator 3.0. The other—Adobe Streamline—is a stand-alone utility that is not included with Illustrator 3.0, although many have argued that it should be. Both are discussed here, on the assumption that you may either presently own a copy of Streamline or acquire it at some future date.

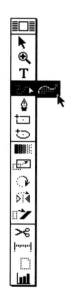

The autotrace tool

The *autotrace tool*, which may be chosen from the freehand tool slot, is used to trace the borders of a template image. Typically, you operate the autotrace tool by clicking within six pixels of the portion of the template that you desire to trace. Illustrator does the rest. The tool is easy to operate, certainly easier than tracing a template image by hand. But the results are predictably less precise and require more adjustments than paths created with the pen tool or even the freehand tool.

Figure 6.04: A valentine image created in MacPaint.

Suppose that you have created the valentine shown in Figure 6.04 in MacPaint. This image will act as your template. You may introduce the template to an illustration in one of two ways:

- Choose the NEW... command (⌘-N), select a template from the scrolling file list in the PLEASE OPEN TEMPLATE dialog box, and press RETURN.

- Choose the OPEN... command (⌘-⌥-O), select a template from the scrolling file list in the PLEASE OPEN ILLUSTRATION OR TEMPLATE dialog box, and press RETURN.

After you open the valentine template, it will appear grayed in the drawing area of the current window. The image is now ready to be traced with the autotrace tool. Click with the autotrace tool near the template image, as demonstrated by the location of the ×-shaped autotrace cursor in Figure 6.05. Notice that the × is within six pixels of the edge of the template. A few seconds after clicking with the autotrace tool, Illustrator produces a closed path that traces the outline of the template. The autotrace tool always produces a closed path. Even if you were to click near the template image of a line, Illustrator will trace entirely around the line to create a long and very thin shape.

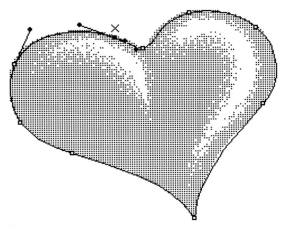

Figure 6.05: A point always appears at the location on the template nearest the spot at which you click.

The point on the template image that is nearest the place at which you click with the autotrace tool becomes the first point in the traced path. Therefore, the location at which you click plays a small but important role in determining how Illustrator traces your template. For instance, in Figure 6.05, the selected click point is an unnecessary point in the path of the valentine. The valentine could be expressed without it. Also, if you look carefully, you will notice the autotrace path has not accurately traced the cleft in the top of the valentine. The cleft should be represented by a cusp (a corner point with two Bézier control handles), but instead a smooth point occupies this spot. The autotrace path in Figure 6.06 is a more true representation of the template image. A corner point resides at the top of the shape and there are fewer unnecessary points.

This is the result of our repositioning the click point at the bottom of the shape (shown as an × in the figure). Since the bottom of the valentine in the template forms a sharp tip, a corner point will doubtless need to exist there.

When tracing a template image, always click with the autotrace tool near the location on the template where a point is most likely to exist. In this way, you best aid Illustrator to produce the most efficient and accurate path possible.

Figure 6.06: Click near a corner of your template image to create the most accurate traced path.

Autotrace tolerance

Another way to create more accurate paths with the autotrace tool is to adjust the value for the "Freehand tolerance" option in the PREFERENCES dialog box (⌘-K). This option affects the sensitivity of the autotrace tool in the same way that it affects the freehand tool. For example, a "Free-hand tolerance" value of 0 instructs Illustrator to trace every single pixel of a bitmapped template. If you change the value to 10, the software ignores large jags in the outline of a template image and smooths out excessively imprecise forms. Figure 6.07 on the following page shows the results of tracing a fish shape when the tolerance value is set to 0, 1, 2, 5, and 10. If you compare these images to those back in Figure 5.14 and 5.15, you will see that the tolerance value affects the performance of the autotrace and freehand tools very similarly. However, unlike freehand tool tolerance, you should adjust the tolerance of the autotrace tool to compensate for inaccuracies in the image you are tracing, rather than inaccuracies in your personal drawing ability.

A "Freehand tolerance" value of 1 or 2 is best suited to most tracing template images. This is because, when tracing, it is better to have too many points than too few. Excessive points can always be deleted later, as explained in Chapter 7.

Figure 6.07: A bitmapped fish (top) and the results of tracing this image with tolerance values of 0, 1 (left side), 2, 5, and 10 (right side).

Tracing over gaps

The autotrace tool is most effective in tracing the borders between the black and white areas in a template. But it may also be used to trace gray areas or areas with broken or inconsistent outlines. Figure 6.08 includes an enlarged view of the valentine template. Suppose this time that you intend to trace the white areas within the valentine that represent reflective highlights, giving the shape a three-dimensional quality. Click with the autotrace tool at each of the two locations represented in the figure as an ×. As a result, Illustrator has made a valiant, though somewhat unattractive attempt to trace the loose pixels of the template. This is a difficult task, since the autotrace tool normally looks for hard edges. Jumbles of dots are usually not conducive to point/path representation.

Figure 6.08: Tracing the loose pixels inside the valentine template with the "Autotrace over gap" option set to 0 pixels.

As luck and a little engineering would have it, Illustrator provides an "Autotrace over gap" option in the PREFERENCES dialog box (introduced in the *Setting preferences* section of Chapter 3) that is designed specifically for tracing inconsistencies in the borders of a template image. To view this option, choose the PREFERENCES... command from the Edit menu (⌘-K).

You may enter either 0, 1, or 2 in the "Autotrace over gap" option box. This value is measured in pixels. The default value 0 instructs Illustrator to trace around a template image from one black pixel to the next. If even a single white pixel separates one black area from another, the traced path will not pass over the gap. But as long as a corner of one black pixel touches the corner of another, both pixels will be traced. The path in Figure 6.08 was traced with an "Autotrace over gap" value of 0.

The paths in Figures 6.09 and 6.10 were produced by clicking at the same locations with the autotrace tool as in the previous figure. The only difference is in the "Autotrace over gap" value. In Figure 6.09, the gap value is set to 1. A gap distance of 1 specifies that black areas separated by no more than one white pixel are to be traced as a single shape. In Figure 6.10, the "Autotrace over gap" option has been raised to 2. This instructs Illustrator to ignore as many as two white pixels between any two black areas in a template.

Figure 6.09: Tracing the loose pixels inside the valentine template with the "Autotrace over gap" option set to 1 pixel.

Figure 6.10: Tracing the loose pixels
inside the valentine template with the
"Autotrace over gap" option set to 2 pixels.

Like all Preferences dialog box settings, both the "Freehand tolerance" and "Autotrace over gap" values are saved with the Adobe Illustrator 3.0 Prefs file. Each will affect all future illustrations until a new value is
entered. Also, neither the tolerance value nor the gap value for a path can
be altered after it is created, since Illustrator calculates the points for a
path only once, immediately after you click with the autotrace tool.
Therefore, to create each path in Figures 6.08 and 6.09, we had to
change the gap value and trace a new path.

Tracing a portion of an image

In addition to being able to click with the autotrace tool, you may also
drag with the tool. By dragging, you specify that you wish to trace only a
fraction of a template image at a time.

The first example in Figure 6.11 on the following page is a new bitmapped image as it appears in MacPaint. The image is that of a large letter O. In the next few pages, we will demonstrate how to trace details
from both the outer and inner borders of this template.

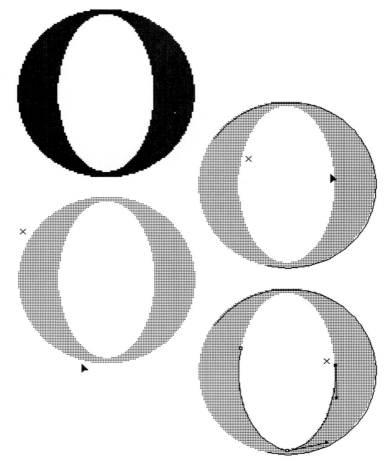

Figure 6.11: Tracing specific portions of a template image
with by dragging with the autotrace tool.

The second example on the left side of the figure demonstrates that
you begin dragging outside and to the left of the image, as indicated by
the × cursor. Then drag directly to the outer bottom side of the image, as
demonstrated by the arrowhead cursor, and release. The location at which
you begin dragging determines the location of first point in the autotrace
path; the release point determines the location of the last point. Thus,
only that portion of the image between the click and release points is
traced.

The third (top, right) example of Figure 6.11 displays the portion of the image that was traced. This may come as a surprise, since the autotrace tool has produced a path that traces the longer of two distances around the O. However, Illustrator always traces the outside of an image in a clockwise direction.

The opposite is true when tracing the inside of a template. For example, drag from the inside left edge of the image to the inside right edge of the image, as demonstrated by the click and release points shown in the third example of Figure 6.11. The final example in that figure shows the results. Because you traced the inside of a template image, the autotrace path was produced in a counterclockwise direction, running opposite to the outer path.

The autotrace tool traces black areas surrounded by white in a clockwise direction; it traces white areas surrounded by black in a counterclockwise direction. If you forget this bit of wisdom, and a drag ends up producing the opposite effect you expected, merely choose UNDO (⌘-Z) and reverse the direction of your drag.

Extending a line

As with the freehand tool, Illustrator allows you to extend an open path with the autotrace tool. However, this does not mean that you can extend any old line. A template image must exist within six pixels of the endpoint of the existing path from which you drag with the autotrace tool.

Extending a path with the autotrace tool is primarily useful for lengthening or closing paths that were originally created by dragging with the same tool, as described in the previous section. Suppose, for example, that you intend to trace half of a template image with the "Autotrace over gap" option set to 0, and the other half with a gap value of 2. You would drag with the autotrace tool to create the first half of the shape, change the gap value in the PREFERENCES dialog, and then drag from one endpoint in the autotrace path to the other, thus closing the path.

The autotrace tool also creates smooth and corner points in the same manner as the freehand tool. Regardless of its original identity, an endpoint will be converted to a smooth point when you drag from it with the freehand tool. This is even true when the point appears to be a corner, a fact that may affect future manipulations as discussed in Chapter 7, *Reshaping Existing Paths.*

To make this point a corner point, press and hold the OPTION key before you begin your drag. If you are closing a path, the endpoint at which your release will also be a smooth point unless you press OPTION before ending your drag and hold the key down until after the mouse button has been released.

Autotracing drawbacks

The autotrace tool is not a precise drawing tool. More often than not, you will have to spend a good deal of time reshaping your traced paths, as described in the next chapter. Perhaps the autotrace tool's greatest drawback, however, is that it can trace only one path at a time. When using the rival drawing application Aldus FreeHand, for example, you marquee a bitmapped image with the trace tool to create several paths at a time. FreeHand also automatically fills the paths so that the converted object-oriented image previews and prints correctly. In Illustrator, you must fill traced paths by hand (as described in Chapter 9, *Filling Type and Graphic Objects*).

Well, as it turns out, Adobe markets a utility called Streamline that converts entire bitmapped images to object-oriented drawings at a much higher level of quality than either the FreeHand or Illustrator trace tools can hope to match.

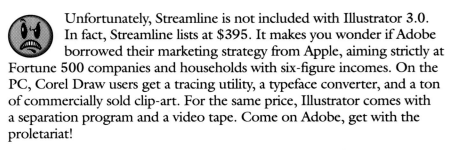 Unfortunately, Streamline is not included with Illustrator 3.0. In fact, Streamline lists at $395. It makes you wonder if Adobe borrowed their marketing strategy from Apple, aiming strictly at Fortune 500 companies and households with six-figure incomes. On the PC, Corel Draw users get a tracing utility, a typeface converter, and a ton of commercially sold clip-art. For the same price, Illustrator comes with a separation program and a video tape. Come on Adobe, get with the proletariat!

But alas, life is not perfect. Suffice it to say that *we* haven't forgotten the meaning of a good value. If you can acquire the software—about $225 through a discount house like MacConnection, (800) 334-4444, or The Mac Zone, (800) 248-0800—we've got the instructions.

Adobe Streamline

Adobe Streamline is a stand-alone utility that traces bitmapped artwork stored in the MacPaint or TIFF format at any resolution up to 600 dots per inch. Artwork is saved as an Illustrator-compatible PostScript file. That's all it does; it doesn't even print. However, as you will see, it provides you with a great deal of control over the way your traced artwork emerges.

Starting Streamline

To install Streamline, we recommend simply copying the program to the folder containing the Illustrator 3.0 application on your hard drive. You may also copy the sample bitmapped documents, although these are not necessary.

Launch the Streamline utility from your hard drive by double-clicking the sun icon at the Finder level or selecting the icon and choosing the OPEN… command from the Finder FILE menu (⌘-O).

If you are launching Streamline for the first time (assuming no one has previously launched this copy of the application), you will be presented with the PLEASE PERSONALIZE dialog box shown in Figure 6.12. Here, you must personalize your copy of Streamline by entering the appropriate information into the "Name" and "Organization" option boxes. (It is not necessary to enter an organization to run the utility.)

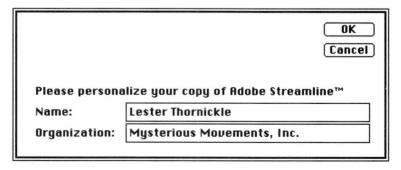

Figure 6.12: The Please personalize dialog box appears the first time you launch Adobe Streamline.

Each time you launch Illustrator, the startup screen shown in Figure 6.13 will appear, containing the name and organization that you entered into the Please personalize dialog box. The startup screen is provided simply as an introduction, to let you know that you are in fact now launching the Streamline utility. It will automatically disappear after a few seconds. If you ever wish to see the startup screen again, you may choose About Streamline... from the Apple (⌘) menu.

Figure 6.13: The Adobe Streamline startup screen, which lists copyright and personalized user information.

After Streamline finishes launching and the startup screen disappears, you will find yourself at the *Streamline desktop*. Unless you are running under MultiFinder, the desktop is empty except for the menu bar at the top of the screen. There are only two menus in addition to the Apple menu. As in most utilities, the Edit menu is always dimmed. (Apple requires that all software offer this menu, whether it is applicable or not.) Therefore, all of Streamline's commands are available from the File menu.

The commands in the FILE menu include the following:

- **Open**…, which allows you to open a bitmapped MacPaint or TIFF file to convert into a object-oriented illustration.

- **File setup**…, which allows you to determine how an illustration is saved and whether a MacPaint template is created for the file.

- **Conversion options**…, which allows you to adjust settings that control the actual tracing procedure.

- **Close**, which is always dimmed. Only the programmers know why this command is here.

- **Quit**, which exits the Streamline desktop and returns you to the Macintosh Finder (or previous application running under Multi-Finder).

All of these options are discussed in this chapter.

Converting a bitmapped image

To convert a bitmapped image to an illustration, choose the OPEN… command from the FILE menu (⌘-O). Figure 6.14 displays the SELECT BITMAP dialog box that appears after choosing this command. To open a bitmapped image, double-click its name in the scrolling file list, or select the file and click the OPEN button or press RETURN. You may open any MacPaint or TIFF file for conversion in Streamline.

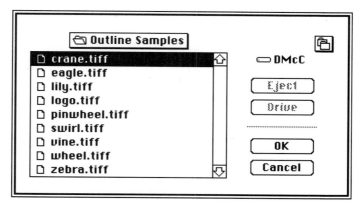

Figure 6.14: The Select bitmap dialog box allows you to select a bitmapped image for conversion.

Any black-and-white document saved in the *MacPaint format* or the *TIFF format* may be opened in Streamline. MacPaint-format documents may originate not only from MacPaint itself but also from other popular painting programs like DeskPaint, SuperPaint, PixelPaint, and Studio/1 as well as from scanning applications like ThunderWare. The MacPaint format is one of the most widely supported graphics formats on the Macintosh computer. Unfortunately, it is also the most limited. MacPaint files are exclusively *monochrome* (black and white—no colors or gray values), no larger than 8 inches by 10 inches, vertically oriented, and always bitmapped at a resolution of 72 dots per inch, as discussed in Chapter 1, *Drawing on the Macintosh.*

Like MacPaint, TIFF (Tag Image File Format) is an exclusively bitmapped format. But unlike MacPaint, it is otherwise unrestricted. TIFF was developed by Aldus Corporation—makers of PageMaker and FreeHand—in an attempt to standardize images created by various scanners. TIFF can accommodate a graphic of any size, resolutions exceeding 300 dots per inch, and over 16 million colors. For this reason, many scanning and image-editing applications, such as ImageStudio, PixelPaint, Studio/32, and PhotoShop, support this format. Streamline is capable of opening only monochrome (black and white) artwork, the resolution of which may not surpass 600 dots per inch.

 To trace a color scan, convert the bitmap to black and white in your scanning or image-editing software before opening it in Streamline. Polarized images—that is, images with crisp borders and without loose pixels—will convert most successfully.

After you select and open a file, the SAVE ILLUSTRATION dialog box will appear, as shown in Figure 6.15. This dialog requires you to confirm the name and location of the file to which the converted illustration will be saved. By default, the "Save illustration as" option box will contain the name of the bitmap file followed by the suffix *.art.* Edit the file name as you wish, using up to 32 characters.

Select the "Make MacPaint template" check box to convert a TIFF image to the MacPaint format so that you can use it as a tracing template in Illustrator. When you select this option, the "Save template as" option will also appear. By default, this option box contains the name of the bitmap file followed by the suffix *.pnt.* Again, edit the file name as you wish, using up to 32 characters.

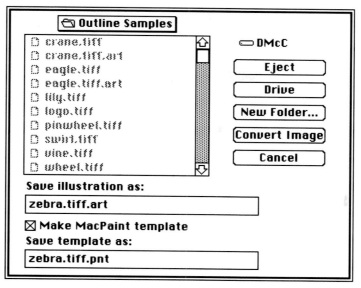

Figure 6.15: The Save illustration dialog box allows you to determine the location to which the converted illustration will be saved.

Use the DRIVE and EJECT buttons and the folder bar to determine a location for the illustration and template files in the same way described in the *Creating a new illustration* section of Chapter 3. Use the NEW FOLDER... button to create a new folder that may be used to store your converted illustrations. Clicking NEW FOLDER... displays the ENTER NEW FOLDER NAME dialog box shown in Figure 6.16. Edit the name as you wish, using up to 32 characters, and press RETURN to return to the SAVE ILLUSTRATION dialog box. To enter the new folder, double-click the folder name in the scrolling file list.

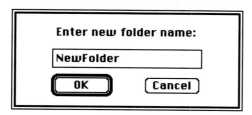

Figure 6.16: The Enter new folder name dialog box allows you to create a new folder in the current directory.

After you specify names and select a location for the illustration and template files, click the CONVERT IMAGE button to initiate the conversion process. You may also click the CANCEL button or press COMMAND-PERIOD to return to the Streamline desktop without completing the conversion.

 Although the CONVERT IMAGE button is not surrounded by a heavy outline, you may activate this button by pressing the RETURN or ENTER key.

If you try to save an illustration with the same name as an existing illustration in the current drive or folder, Streamline will present the REPLACE EXISTING alert box, shown in Figure 6.17, asking you to confirm that you wish to replace the existing file. Click YES to save over the existing illustration; click NO or press RETURN to return to the SAVE ILLUSTRATION dialog box, where you may change the name or location of the current illustration. (Although Streamline warns you when saving illustration files, it does not warn you before overwriting an existing file with the new template. Take care when naming your templates.)

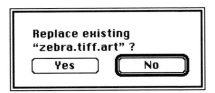

Figure 6.17: The Replace existing alert box.

If the disk or the volume that you have selected does not have enough room for the illustration and template files, a "Disk Full" error message will appear. Click the CONTINUE button to return to the SAVE ILLUSTRATION dialog box so that you may select another drive or volume and reinitiate the conversion process.

The conversion process

After clicking the CONVERT IMAGE button and responding to any alert boxes that may display, Streamline displays the *conversion screen*. The first image to appear on the screen is the bitmapped template, as shown in Figure 6.18. The template then disappears and the conversion process begins. One path after another is drawn on the conversion screen, until the entire image is traced, as shown in Figure 6.19. When the entire image has been traced, the conversion screen closes, returning you to the empty Streamline desktop.

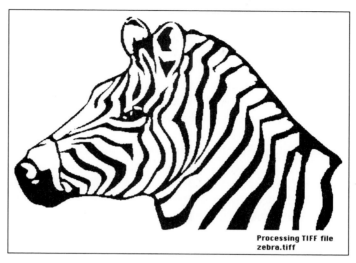

Processing TIFF file zebra.tiff

Figure 6.18: The conversion screen, containing the bitmapped template image.

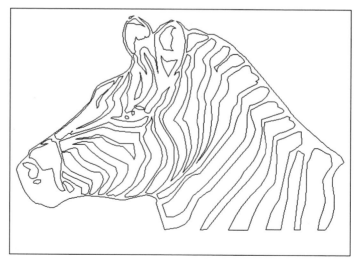

Figure 6.19: The finished traced image as it looks just before the conversion screen disappears.

The conversion process is now complete. The converted file may be opened in Adobe Illustrator 3.0 as described in the following section.

If you have several MacPaint and TIFF images to convert, Streamline provides a useful batch-processing feature. Simply place all of your template files in a special folder. Choose the OPEN... command (⌘-O) and select (do not open) the folder name from the scrolling file list in the SELECT BITMAP dialog box. Then click the OK button. Streamline will immediately begin converting all MacPaint and TIFF files that it finds in the selected folder. The SAVE ILLUSTRATION dialog box will not be displayed, unless requested in the FILE SETUP dialog as described later in this chapter.

Whether converting a single bitmap or a whole folder of bitmaps, you may cancel the conversion process at any time by pressing COMMAND-PERIOD. Note that this cancels only current and future file conversions. Conversions that have already completed remain intact.

Editing a converted illustration

Adobe Streamline creates traced illustrations. It does not allow you to open, edit, or print illustrations after they have been converted. To edit or print an illustration created with Streamline, you must open the file inside Adobe Illustrator 3.0. The following steps describe how:

1. Quit the Streamline utility by choosing the QUIT command from the FILE menu (⌘-Q). (If you are running under MultiFinder, you may choose the FINDER icon from the APPLE menu to make the Finder the current application and launch Illustrator while Streamline is still open.)

2. Then launch Adobe Illustrator 3.0 as described in the *Starting Illustrator* section of Chapter 3. (If you are running under Multi-Finder and the error message "Insufficient memory to open this application" appears, you must quit one or more open applications before launching Illustrator.)

3. After the Illustrator desktop appears, choose the OPEN... command from the FILE menu (⌘-O) to display the PLEASE OPEN ILLUSTRATION OR TEMPLATE dialog box (see Figure 3.10). Select the converted illustration from the scrolling file list and press RETURN.

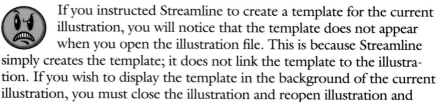 If you instructed Streamline to create a template for the current illustration, you will notice that the template does not appear when you open the illustration file. This is because Streamline simply creates the template; it does not link the template to the illustration. If you wish to display the template in the background of the current illustration, you must close the illustration and reopen illustration and template by pressing COMMAND-OPTION-O as described in the *Swapping tracing templates* section of Chapter 3. Then save the illustration to link the two files together.

4. After you open the converted illustration, you may edit it just as you would edit any other file created in Adobe Illustrator. You may also preview or print the file or export it as an Encapsulated Post-Script file to be used in a different application.

Figure 6.20 shows how the converted zebra illustration appears when printed from Adobe Illustrator. Compared this figure to the bitmapped template shown in Figure 6.18 to gauge the accuracy of Streamline's tracing capabilities.

Figure 6.20: The converted illustration as it appears when printed from Adobe Illustrator.

Note that Illustrator scales both illustration and template to fit in an 8-inch-by-10-inch page size when you select the "Make MacPaint template" option in the Streamline SAVE ILLUSTRATION dialog box (refer to Figure 6.15). This ensures that the sizes of the illustration and template match in the drawing area, since MacPaint files may measure no larger than 8 by 10 inches. If the template option is not selected, the image is reduced in size only if its dimensions exceed the 18-inch-by-18-inch drawing area.

Adjusting the file setup

So far, we have demonstrated how Streamline can be used to perform a simple bitmapped file conversion. However, Streamline offers a number of options for adjusting how a converted illustration is saved and the manner in which it is converted. These options are made available by choosing the FILE SETUP... and CONVERSION OPTIONS... commands. We will discuss the FILE SETUP... command first.

Choose the FILE SETUP... command from the Streamline FILE menu (⌘-F) to display the FILE SETUP dialog box shown in Figure 6.21. Here you may control how both converted illustrations and bitmapped tracing templates are saved to disk. You may also determine whether naming conflicts will be brought to your attention.

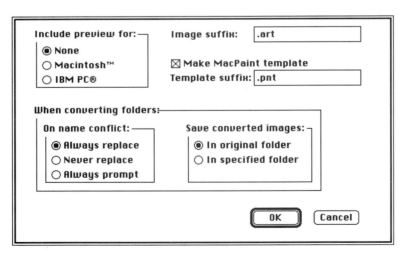

Figure 6.21: The File setup dialog box allows you to determine the manner in which converted illustrations are saved to disk.

The options in the FILE SETUP dialog box include the following:

- **Include preview for**. This option determines whether your converted illustrations are saved as standard Illustrator PostScript files or with EPS (Encapsulated PostScript) screen representations, allowing them to be imported into other applications running on a Macintosh or an IBM PC-compatible computer. If you intend to use converted files exclusively in Adobe Illustrator, or edit them in Illustrator before placing them into another application, select the default "None" option. To save the illustrations with EPS previews suitable for use with Macintosh applications such as Microsoft Word, PageMaker, or QuarkXPress, select the "Macintosh" radio button. To include EPS previews compatible with PC products like PC PageMaker and Ventura Publisher, select the "PC" option. For more information on saving illustrations as EPS files, see Chapter 14, *Importing and Exporting.*

- **Image suffix**. The default name for a converted illustration is the name of the original bitmap template file followed by an *.art* suffix. To change the default name, enter a new suffix in the "Image suffix" option box.

- **Make MacPaint template**. Select this check box to automatically convert template images to the MacPaint format so they can be used as tracing templates when the converted illustrations are opened in Adobe Illustrator. When you select this option, the "Template suffix" option box also appears. The default name for a tracing template is the name of the original bitmap file followed by an *.pnt* suffix. To change the default name, enter a new suffix in this option box.

- **On name conflict**. These options affect whether you are warned before Streamline saves over existing files when converting a folder of images. (Regardless of this option, you are always warned about naming conflicts when converting a single illustration.) Select the default "Always replace" radio button to replace any existing file that has the same name as a converted illustration. To skip conversions whose names duplicate existing files, select "Never replace." And to display the REPLACE EXISTING alert box (shown back in Figure 6.17) for every naming conflict, select the "Always prompt" option.

● **Save converted images**. These options affect whether you are prompted to determine the location of saved illustrations when converting a folder of images. (Regardless of this option, you are always prompted with the SAVE ILLUSTRATION dialog box when converting a single illustration.) By default, the "In original folder" option instructs Streamline to save illustrations inside the same folder that you select to convert. If you want to save your illustrations to a different location, select the "In specified folder" radio button. This will cause the SAVE ILLUSTRATION dialog box (shown in Figure 6.15) to display immediately after you select a folder inside the SELECT BITMAP dialog (Figure 6.14).

Any setting that you change in the FILE SETUP dialog box will affect the saving of converted illustrations throughout the current Streamline *session*; that is, until you quit the program. Because these settings are not saved to disk, all options will revert to their original defaults the next time you launch Adobe Streamline.

Adjusting conversion settings

Earlier in this chapter, we mentioned that the Illustrator autotrace tool always traces bitmapped images with closed paths. Not so for Adobe Streamline. Not only can Streamline trace with both open and closed paths, it can fill and stroke paths, use only straight or curved segments, and filter out the random pixels that often result from scanning artwork, all according to your specifications. These specifications are made using the CONVERSION OPTIONS... command.

Choose the CONVERSION OPTIONS... command from the Streamline FILE menu (⌘-C) to display the CONVERSION OPTIONS dialog box shown in Figure 6.22. Here you may select that a bitmapped image be traced with an object-oriented line (the "Centerline" option) rather than as a closed shape (the "Outline" option), or as a combination of both ("Centerline & Outline"). As you might expect, this is where you specify the *tolerance* setting, a control similar to the "Freehand tolerance" option that determines the sensitivity of the autotrace tool in Adobe Illustrator. You may also adjust several other options for controlling the final appearance of your traced illustrations.

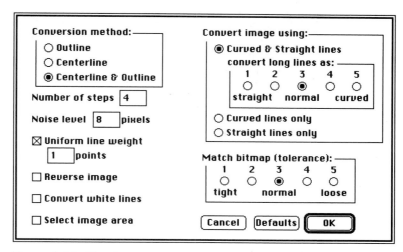

Figure 6.22: The Conversion options dialog box allows you to determine the manner in which bitmapped images are converted into object-oriented drawings.

The options in the CONVERSION OPTIONS dialog include the following:

- **Conversion method**. The three "Conversion method" options determine whether closed and/or open paths are used to trace a selected bitmap. Each of these options determine what other options are available in the CONVERSION OPTIONS dialog box.

  The "Outline" radio button is selected by default. When selected, this option instructs Streamline to trace a bitmapped image using closed paths only with black and white fills and no stroke. This option is generally best suited to tracing images consisting of large black areas, like the zebra image shown in Figure 6.18. Figure 6.20 displays the result of tracing this bitmap with the "Outline" option selected. The "Number of steps," "Uniform line weight," and "Convert white lines" options shown in Figure 6.22 do not appear when the "Outline" radio button is selected.

  Selecting the "Centerline" radio button instructs Streamline to trace a bitmap using open paths only with transparent fills and black strokes. This option is best suited to line drawings that contain no black-filled area whatsoever, like the flower shown in Figure 6.23 on the next page. Figure 6.24 displays the result of tracing this image with the "Centerline" option selected. The "Noise level" option disappears when you select this radio button.

Figure 6.23: A bitmapped line drawing that contains no black areas.

Figure 6.24: The result of tracing the bitmap when the "Centerline" option is selected.

Selecting the "Centerline & Outline" radio button instructs Streamline to trace a bitmap using both open and closed paths. The open paths will have transparent fills and black strokes. The closed paths will have black or white fill and no stroke. This option is best suited to line drawings that also contain some black-filled areas, like the butterfly shown in Figure 6.25. Figure 6.26 displays the result of tracing this image with the "Centerline & Outline" option selected. All other options are available when you select the "Centerline & Outline" radio button.

Figure 6.25: A bitmapped line drawing that contains large black areas.

Figure 6.26: The result of tracing the bitmap when the "Centerline & Outline" option is selected.

- **Number of steps**. This option is applicable exclusively to the centerline tracing feature, so it is available only when the "Centerline" or "Centerline & Outline" option is selected. An oddly named option, "Number of steps" helps Streamline to determine the boundaries of a line. It should really be called "Thickest traced line," since it's asking you to identify the heaviest line that Streamline can expect to find in a bitmapped template. Any line heavier than this line weight (measured in points) will be traced on both edges. For example, suppose you want to trace the sketch shown in Figure 6.27.

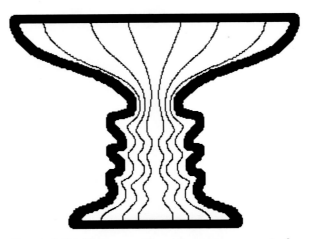

Figure 6.27: We start with a bitmap composed of both thin and heavy lines.

The lightest lines in this image are only about 1 point thick; the thickest lines measure 8 points in width. If you open the image using a "Number of steps" value of 1, the converted illustration will appear as shown in Figure 6.28. Streamline has traced both sides of the heavy line, because it was not properly identified. You told the program to expect only 1-point lines, so it interpreted one edge of the line as one path, and the other edge as another path. Many of the jags in the heavy line were assigned paths as well.

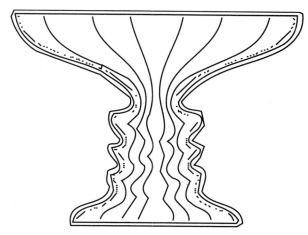

Figure 6.28: Tracing the bitmap with a "Number of steps" value of 1 causes Streamline to misinterpret the image.

If you raise the "Number of steps" value to 8 before opening the bitmapped vase, you tell Streamline to expect lines up to 8 points thick. The program is forced to trace 1-point lines less sensitively, but it is also more accurately prepared for the thick lines contained in the bitmap. The resulting illustration is a more accurate conversion, as shown in Figure 6.29.

Figure 6.29: Tracing the bitmap with a "Number of steps" value of 8 helps Streamline to more accurately interpret the image.

Any value between 0 and 20 is permitted in the "Number of steps" option box.

If you find this option overly confusing, simply enter 20 for the "Number of steps" value prior to performing any centerline conversion. This may supposedly result in the oversmoothing of a few lines, but we have found that it makes very little difference, except to increase the conversion time.

- **Noise level**. This option is applicable exclusively to the outline tracing feature, so it is available only when the "Outline" or "Centerline & Outline" option is selected. This option allows you to filter out clusters of loose pixels when converting a scanned image. Streamline ignores any cluster of pixels whose *perimeter*—the outline around the area—contains fewer pixels than the "Noise level" value. For example, if you were to count the pixels around a box measuring 10 pixels by 10 pixels, you would count 36 pixels; thus 36 pixels is the perimeter of the box, as shown in Figure 6.30. If you set the "Noise level" option to any number greater than 36, this box will be ignored.

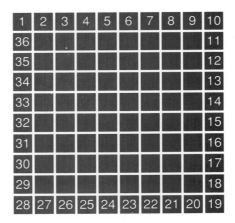

Figure 6.30: A box measuring 10 by 10 pixels has a perimeter of 36 pixels. It will be ignored if the "Noise level" value is 37 or higher.

Any value between 0 and 1000 is permitted in the "Number of steps" option box.

- **Uniform line weight**. This option is applicable exclusively to the centerline tracing feature, so it is available only when the "Centerline" or "Centerline & Outline" option is selected. When selected, the "Uniform line weight" check box ensured that all strokes in the convertes illustration have the same line weight (as discussed in Chapter 10, *Stroking Type and Graphic Objects*). This weight may be any thickness between 0 and 12 points, as specified in the option box below the check box. If you deselect this option, Streamline averages the weight of each line in a bitmapped template and applies that weight to an entire path. Different paths, however, may still have different line weights.

- **Reverse image**. This option is applicable to both the centerline and outline tracing features. When selected, the "Reverse image" option traces black lines and shapes with white paths, and white lines and shapes with black paths. Therefore, rather than affecting the way a template is traced, this option controls how the converted illustration is stroked and filled.

Figure 6.31: Select the "Reverse image" check box to color black areas white, and white areas black.

Usually, you will want to use this option to rectify an image that was somehow reversed in the scanning process or, more commonly, reversed as it was transferred from another computer environment, such as a drawing created in PC Paintbrush and then ported over to the Mac.

- **Convert white lines**. This option is applicable exclusively to the centerline tracing feature, so it is available only when the "Centerline" or "Centerline & Outline" option is selected. When selected, this option instructs Streamline to trace any white lines that appear against black backgrounds in the bitmapped template. If the "Convert white lines" option is not selected, white lines are ignored.

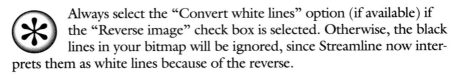 Always select the "Convert white lines" option (if available) if the "Reverse image" check box is selected. Otherwise, the black lines in your bitmap will be ignored, since Streamline now interprets them as white lines because of the reverse.

- **Select image area**. This option, applicable to both the centerline and outline tracing features, allows you to trace a specific portion of a template image. When selected, the conversion screen will appear during the conversion process displaying CANCEL and OK buttons. A rectangular *select box* will display inside the conversion screen. This select box determines the area that will be traced. Drag inside the box to move it around; drag a corner or a side of the box to enlarge or reduce it. When you have marqueed the desired portion of the image, press RETURN to begin the conversion process. Otherwise, click CANCEL (⌘-.) to return to the empty Streamline desktop without initiating the conversion.

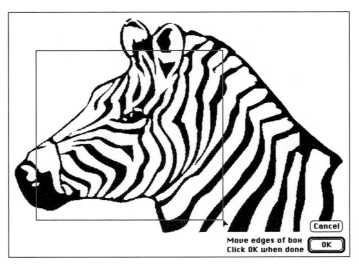

Figure 6.32: Marquee a portion of the bitmap inside the conversion screen that you wish to trace.

- **Convert image using**. This option determines the kinds of points and segments that are used to trace the template image. By default, the "Curve & Straight lines" option is selected, indicating that both straight and curved segments (smooth and corner points) will be employed. You may control the curvature of long segments by selecting any one of the five "convert long lines as" options. (These options disappear when either the "Curved lines only" or "Straight lines only" radio button is selected.) If your bitmap contains more straight edges than curved edges, select option number 1 or 2. If your bitmap contains mostly rounded edges, select option number 4 or 5.

  If your bitmap is composed entirely of rounded edges, such as a drawing of a circle or other soft, cornerless object, select the "Curved lines only" option. The converted image will be made exclusively with smooth points. If your bitmap is composed entirely of straight edges, such as a drawing of a geometric object or a bar graph, select the "Straight lines only" option. The converted image will be made exclusively with corner points with no Bézier control handles.

- **Match bitmap** (**tolerance**). This option affects the sensitivity of Streamline's tracing capabilities. If you are tracing a high-resolution bitmap (300 dots per inch or better), select option number 1 or 2. This instructs Streamline to trace virtually every pixel (minus those that have been disqualified by the "Noise level" option). If you are tracing a sketch or some other fairly inaccurate image, select option number 4 or 5. This instructs Streamline to ignore large jags in the outline of a template image and smooth out imprecise forms.

  All the converted illustrations shown in this chapter were traced with the "Match bitmap (tolerance)" option set to 3.

Any setting that you change in the CONVERSION OPTIONS dialog box will affect the conversion of illustrations throughout the current Streamline session. Because these settings are not saved to disk, all options will revert to their original defaults the next time you launch Adobe Streamline. You may restore the default settings at any time by quitting the program and relaunching, or by simply clicking the DEFAULTS button in this dialog box.

Quitting Streamline

When you have finished working in the Streamline utility, choose the Quit command from the FILE menu (⌘-Q). Control of your computer will be returned to the Macintosh Finder. All changes made to the FILE SETUP and CONVERSION OPTIONS dialog boxes will be lost; all options will revert to their default settings.

Reshaping
Existing
Paths

After you create a graphic object in Illustrator, the object is by no means permanent. Any path may be changed. And, assuming you do most of your drawing with the freehand and autotrace tools, your paths are going to need adjustment. As a matter of fact, almost every path you create will need to be altered in some way. Adjusting a path in Illustrator is like painting over the same area on a canvas; it is a fine-tuning process.

This chapter examines how to *reshape* both geometric and free-form paths. To reshape a path is to alter the placement or identity of a point or segment within a single path. The adjustment of whole paths is discussed later in Chapter 12, *Transforming and Duplicating Objects*.

Selecting elements

Before you may reshape a path, you must *select* one of more of its *elements*—a point, a segment, or just about any other small or large portion of an illustration. Selecting an element in Illustrator is not unlike selecting an element in some other object-oriented program on the Macintosh. Merely position your arrow tool cursor over part of an image and click. Points and Bézier control handles display to indicate that the next action you perform will affect the selected element.

The arrow tool

Like most manipulations covered in this chapter, selecting may be performed with one of the three *arrow tools*—the arrow (or selection) tool, the direct-selection tool, or the object-selection tool. Clicking on a point or segment with any arrow tool selects that point or segment. However, each tool differs in the extent of the selection it makes.

The standard *arrow tool* is displayed by default in the first slot in the toolbox. If it is not displayed, press SHIFT and double-click the slot to reset it. When the arrow tool is selected, you may click on any element to select it. Clicking on a point selects that point. Clicking on a segment selects that segment. Clicking on a *combined object* or a *group*, such as a geometric path created with the rectangle or oval tool, selects that combined object or group.

Different elements have different ways of showing that they are selected. For example, when you select a point, it appears as a small black square as shown in the first example of Figure 7.01. All Bézier control handles associated with the selected point and the two neighboring segments also appear. Other deselected points in the path appear as small hollow squares. When a segment is selected, only the Bézier control handles for that segment are visible. Unless some point in the path is also selected, all points appear as hollow squares.

Figure 7.01: Select a single point (left) and a single segment (right) by clicking with the arrow tool. The location of each click is indicated by the arrow tool cursor.

Clicking on an element with the arrow tool not only selects the element but also *deselects* all previously selected elements. To select multiple points and segments in a path, click on the first point or segment, then press SHIFT and click on each additional point or segment.

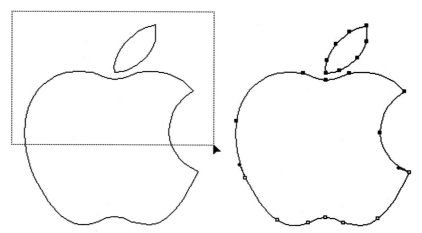

Figure 7.02: All elements surrounded by a marquee (left) become selected (right).

Another way to select multiple elements is too *marquee* them. Drag at an empty portion of your screen to create a rectangular marquee with a dotted outline, as shown in Figure 7.02. One corner of the marquee is positioned at the location at which you begin to drag; the opposite corner follows the movements of your cursor as you drag. All points and segments that are within the marquee will become selected when you release your mouse button. If any point or segment in a combined or grouped object falls inside a marquee, the entire combined or grouped object becomes selected. This holds true for shapes drawn with the rectangle and ellipse tools, as discussed in the *Reshaping geometric paths* section later in this chapter.

Marqueeing may be combined with SHIFT-clicking to select multiple paths and elements. You may also marquee while pressing SHIFT, thereby adding the marqueed elements to an existing set of selected elements.

These and other ways to select elements with the arrow tool are summarized in the following list:

- Click on a point, segment, group, combined object, text block, or link to select that element and deselect the previous selection.

- Drag on an empty portion of the drawing area to create a marquee. All elements inside the marquee become selected, and the previous selection becomes deselected.

- Press SHIFT and click or marquee deselected elements to add them to the current selection. (If you SHIFT-click or SHIFT-marquee an element that is already selected, it will become deselected, as described in the *Deselecting elements* section.)

- Press OPTION and click a point or segment to select its entire path and deselect the previous selection.

- OPTION-marquee or SHIFT-OPTION-click elements to select multiple paths at a time.

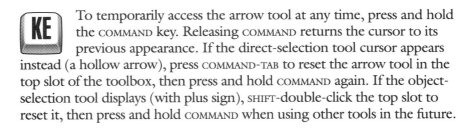

To temporarily access the arrow tool at any time, press and hold the COMMAND key. Releasing COMMAND returns the cursor to its previous appearance. If the direct-selection tool cursor appears instead (a hollow arrow), press COMMAND-TAB to reset the arrow tool in the top slot of the toolbox, then press and hold COMMAND again. If the object-selection tool displays (with plus sign), SHIFT-double-click the top slot to reset it, then press and hold COMMAND when using other tools in the future.

The object-selection tool

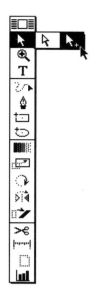

As noted in the preceding list, pressing the OPTION key while the arrow tool is selected accesses the *object-selection tool*. You may also choose the object-selection tool by dragging from the top tool slot. This tool is used to select whole paths rather than the elements that make up the paths. When the object-selection tool is selected, the arrow cursor will display with a small plus sign in the bottom right corner.

The object-selection tool may be used as follows:

- Click on a path, group, combined object, text block, or link to select that object and deselect the previous selection.

- Drag on an empty portion of the drawing area to create a marquee. All objects even partially inside the marquee become selected, and the previous selection becomes deselected.

- Press SHIFT and click or marquee deselected objects to add them to the current selection. (If you SHIFT-click or SHIFT-marquee an object that is already selected, it will become deselected, as described in the *Deselecting elements* section.)

To temporarily access the object-selection tool at any time, press and hold the COMMAND key. If the arrow tool cursor appears instead (no plus sign), press and hold both COMMAND and OPTION. If the direct-selection tool displays (hollow arrow), press COMMAND-TAB to reset the arrow tool in the top slot, then press and hold COMMAND and OPTION.

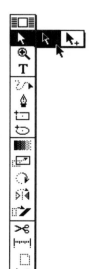

The direct-selection tool

The *direct-selection tool*, which may be chosen by dragging from the arrow tool slot, operates similarly to the arrow tool. If you click on a point, you select the point; if you click on a segment, you select the segment. However, you may also use the direct-selection tool to select points and segments inside groups, combined objects, links, and so on. For example, if you click a point in a geometric object like a rectangle with the arrow tool, you select the entire path because the object is created as a group. But if you click this same point with the direct-selection tool, you select only the point, as shown in Figure 7.03 on the next page. Points that are not part of the same path, such as the center point in the figure, remain entirely deselected.

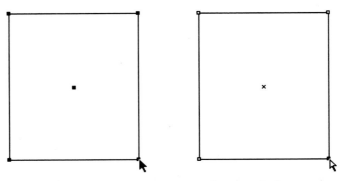

Figure 7.03: Selecting a geometric object with the arrow tool (left) and the direct-selection tool (right). Notice the right center point appears as an ×, indicating it is a lone point in a deselected path.

When the OPTION key is pressed, the direct-selection tool cursor displays with a small plus sign in the bottom right corner. Pressing OPTION and clicking with the direct-selection tool allows you to select whole paths within a group or combined object. Pressing OPTION and double-clicking selects a group within a group. (Selecting groups is described more fully in Chapter 12, *Transforming and Duplicating Objects*).

These and other ways to select elements with the direct-selection tool are summarized in the following list:

- Click on a point or segment to select it—even if the element is part of a group, combined object, text object, or link—and deselect the previous selection.

- Drag on an empty portion of the drawing area to create a marquee. All points and segments inside the marquee become selected, and the previous selection becomes deselected.

- Press SHIFT and click or marquee deselected elements to add them to the current selection. (If you SHIFT-click or SHIFT-marquee an element that is already selected, it will become deselected, as described in the *Deselecting elements* section.)

- Press OPTION and click a point or segment to select a whole path in a group. Press OPTION and double-click to select a group within a group. Press OPTION and triple-click to select the group that contains that group, and so on.

- Press OPTION and marquee or SHIFT-OPTION-click elements to select multiple paths inside groups.

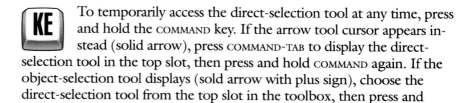 To temporarily access the direct-selection tool at any time, press and hold the COMMAND key. If the arrow tool cursor appears instead (solid arrow), press COMMAND-TAB to display the direct-selection tool in the top slot, then press and hold COMMAND again. If the object-selection tool displays (sold arrow with plus sign), choose the direct-selection tool from the top slot in the toolbox, then press and hold COMMAND when using other tools in the future.

Selecting all elements

The only remaining selection method is the SELECT ALL command in the EDIT menu (⌘-A) which, when chosen, selects every point, segment, and other element in the current illustration (unless a text block is active, in which case choosing SELECT ALL highlights all text in the current story).

Deselecting elements

Sometimes you will want to *deselect* elements to prevent them from being affected by a command or mouse operation. To deselect all elements, simply click with one of the arrow tools on an empty portion of the drawing area. All currently selected elements will also deselect when you perform any one of the following items:

- Select an element that was not previously selected by clicking on it with one of the arrow tools.

- Click or drag with one of the geometric path tools.

- Click or drag with a free-form drawing tool (freehand, pen, or autotrace) on an empty portion of the drawing area.

- Click or drag with the type tool on an empty portion of the drawing area.

- Click or drag with one of the six charting tools available from the last slot in the toolbox.

- Place or paste any graphic element.

- Choose the UNLOCK ALL (⌘-2), SHOW ALL (⌘-4), or RELEASE ALL GUIDES (⌘-6) command from the ARRANGE menu.

Deselecting individual elements

You don't have to deselect every element in an illustration. You may also deselect specific elements without affecting other elements in a selection.

To deselect a single selected element, SHIFT-click on it with the arrow tool or the direct-selection tool. Also, any selected elements that are surrounded by a marquee when pressing the SHIFT key will be deselected.

If you SHIFT-click with the object-selection tool on a selected path, you deselect every point and segment in that path. Likewise, SHIFT-marqueeing with the object-selection tool deselects all surrounded paths that are either partially or entirely selected.

Reshaping geometric paths

Try this little experiment: Draw a rectangle with the rectangle tool. The shape and size doesn't matter. Now select the arrow tool. Click on an empty portion of the drawing area to deselect the rectangle. Now try to select a single point or segment in the shape with the arrow tool.

Can't do it, huh? When you select one point, they all become selected. That's because all geometric shapes—rectangles, rectangles with rounded corners, and ellipses—are created as *grouped objects*, also called simply *groups*. All elements in a group are fused into a single object, locking the relative distances between points so they cannot be altered.

Ungrouping geometric shapes

Illustrator provides two ways to reshape a geometric shape. The first is to ungroup the shape by selecting it and choosing the UNGROUP command from the ARRANGE menu (⌘-U). Ungrouping frees the points and segments in a path so they can be manipulated individually using the standard arrow tool, just like points and segments in a path created with the freehand, pen, or autotrace tool.

Ungrouping a geometric path does provide one problem, however. Because a geometric path actually includes two paths—the obvious one that forms the outline of the path and the less obvious single-point path in the center of the shape—ungrouping a rectangle or ellipse isolates the center point from the rest of the shape. This means you should either delete the center point by selecting it and pressing the DELETE or BACKSPACE key, or you should reshape the path and then regroup it, with the center point, by choosing the GROUP command from the ARRANGE menu (⌘-G). Otherwise, the center point will just sit around and clutter up your drawing area.

Reshaping grouped paths

A center point is a terrible thing to waste. It can be especially useful for aligning a path, as we will discuss later in this chapter. But ungrouping and regrouping a path can become a tiresome exercise.

Therefore, the better solution is to not ungroup the geometric path in the first place, but to instead rely on the direct-selection tool. The direct-selection tool allows you to edit points and segments inside a grouped shape. In the following sections, we explain how to use the arrow tool to manipulate points, segments, and Bézier control handles in a path. If you want to manipulate elements in a geometric path, simply follow the instructions, substituting the direct-selection tool for all references to the arrow tool (COMMAND-TAB).

Moving elements

The most common method for reshaping a path is to move some element in the path. Illustrator allows you to move selected points independently of deselected points in a path. You may also move segments, as well as the Bézier control handles associated with those segments, to alter the curvature of a path. The next few pages explain all aspects of moving and dragging elements in Adobe Illustrator.

Moving points

To move one or more points in a path, select the points you want to move and drag one of the selected points. All selected points will move the same distance and direction. When you move a point while a neighboring point remains stationary, the segment between the two points shrinks or stretches in length to accommodate the change in distance, as displayed in Figure 7.04. If a point has any Bézier control handles, they move with the point. Thus, a curved segment must not only shrink or stretch, but also bend to accommodate the movement of a point. Segments located between two deselected points or two selected points remain unchanged during a move, as demonstrated in Figure 7.05.

Figure 7.04: Dragging the selected point on left stretches the segments between the point and its deselected, stationary neighbors, as shown on right.

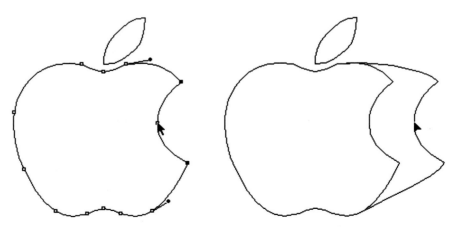

Figure 7.05: Dragging at any selected point in a shape (left) moves all selected points an identical distance and direction (right). Notice that any segment bordered on both sides by selected points is not reshaped.

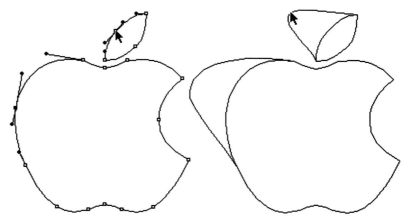

Figure 7.06: You may even move multiple points when selected points reside in different paths.

When moving an element, both its previous and current locations are displayed. This useful feature allows you to gauge the full effect of a move as it progresses. Also, when dragging a single selected point, Illustrator displays the point, the Bézier control handles associated with the two neighboring segments, and any neighboring deselected points, as shown in Figure 7.04. When dragging multiple points, no points or handles display, as demonstrated in Figures 7.05 and 7.06. This helps to avoid some of the confusion that might result from otherwise viewing hoards of Bézier control handles moving all over the screen during a complex reshaping maneuver.

Constrained movements

To constrain the movement of selected points to an angle that is a multiple of 45°, press the SHIFT key after beginning your drag and hold the key down until after you release the mouse button. (If you press and hold SHIFT before beginning your drag, you will deselect the selected point on which you click, causing Illustrator to ignore your drag.) Horizontal, vertical, and diagonal movements are all multiples of 45°.

The effects of pressing the SHIFT key may be altered by rotating the *constraint axes* using the "Constrain angle" option in the PREFERENCES dialog box, introduced in the *Setting preferences* section of Chapter 3. The constraint axes, displayed in Figure 7.07, specifies the eight directions in which an element may be moved. By default, these directions include the following:

- Right (0°)
- Diagonally up and to the right (45°)
- Straight up (90°)
- Diagonally up and to the left (135°)
- Left (180°)
- Diagonally down and to the left (225° or –135°)
- Straight down (270° or –90°)
- Diagonally down and to the right (315° or –45°).

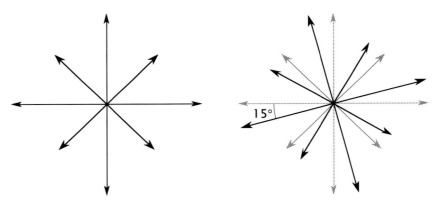

Figure 7.07: The default constraint axes (left) and the axes as they appear when rotated 15° (right).

Each direction differs from another by an angle of 45°. By entering a number between –360 and 360 for the "Constrain angle" option, you may rotate the contraint axes. The second example in Figure 7.07 displays the effect of rotating the axes 15°. If you were to SHIFT-drag an element under these conditions, your movements will be constrained to a direction of 15°, 60°, 105°, 150°, 195° (–165°), 240° (–120°), 285° (–75°), or 330° (–30°). Horizontal and vertical SHIFT-dragging will not be possible until you return the "Constrain angle" value to 0.

Exercise caution when altering the "Constrain angle" option, since it also affects the creation of geometric paths, text, and charts, as explained in the section *Geometric paths at an angle* in Chapter 5, as well as the performance of transformation tools, as explained in the section *Transforming rotated objects* in Chapter 12.

Snapping

While dragging an element, you may find that it has a tendency to move sharply toward another element. Called *snapping*, this effect is Illustrator's way of ensuring that elements belonging together are flush against each other to form a perfect fit. When you drag an element within two pixels of any point on your drawing area, your cursor will snap to the point, so that both point and cursor occupy an identical horizontal and vertical space. At the moment the snap occurs, your cursor will change from a filled arrowhead to a hollow arrowhead, and the information bar in the bottom, left corner of the window will display the message "Snap to" (see Figure 7.08). For example, you might drag the center point of a rectangle until it snaps to the center point of a deselected ellipse. In this way, both shapes would be centered about the same point.

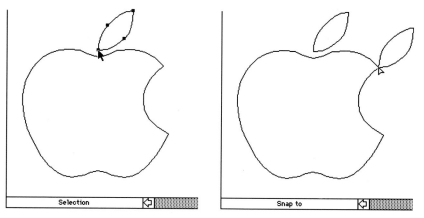

Figure 7.08: Your cursor changes to a hollow arrowhead when snapping an element to a stationary point.

Your cursor will snap to stationary points as well as to the previous locations of points that are currently being moved. However, snapping occurs at points only in a standard path or text block. In addition, your cursor will snap to any portion of a *guide object*, created using the Make Guide command from the Arrange menu (⌘-5) or by dragging from the horizontal or vertical ruler. Both guides and rulers are the subject of Chapter 12, *Transforming and Duplicating Objects*.

Illustrator's snapping feature may be turned on and off by clicking the "Snap to point" check box in the Preferences dialog box, introduced in the *Setting preferences* section of Chapter 3. When the option is de-selected, dragged elements will snap to neither points nor guides.

Dragging segments

You may also reshape a path by dragging at its segments. When you drag a straight segment, its neighboring segments stretch or shrink to accommodate the change in distance, as shown in the first example in Figure 7.09. However, when you drag a curved segment, you stretch only that segment. The effect is rather like pulling on a rubber band extended between two nails (see the second example below).

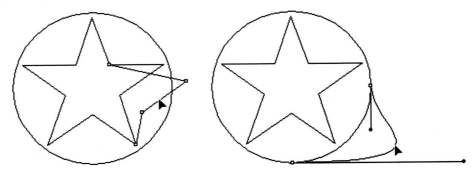

Figure 7.09: Dragging a straight segment (left) and a curved segment (right).

Figure 7.10 shows a single curved segment being stretched in various distances and directions. The farther we drag, the more the segment has to bend. Notice that the Bézier control handles associated with the segment automatically extend and retract as we drag. Also, each handle moves along an imaginary line, constant with its original inclination. The angle of a Bézier control handle cannot be changed by dragging at a segment, guaranteeing that the curved segment moves in alignment with neighboring, stationary segments.

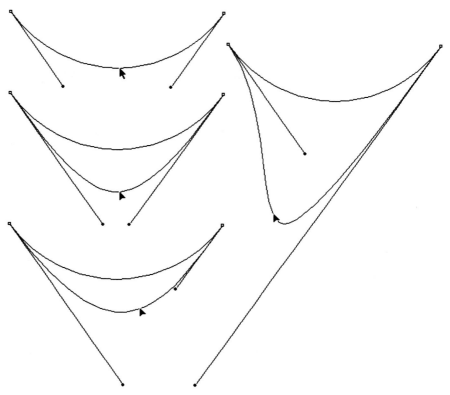

Figure 7.10: When dragging at a curved segment, each Bézier control handle moves back and forth along a constant axis determined by the original inclination of the handle.

To move a Bézier control handle in a direction out of alignment with its original orientation, you must drag the handle itself, as described in the *Dragging Bézier control handles* section, later in this chapter.

When dragging a segment, drag from the middle of the segment, approximately equidistant from both of its points. This method provides the best leverage, preventing you from distorting the segment in odd and unpredictable directions.

Using arrow keys

Another way to move a selected element is to press one of the four arrow keys (↑, ←, ↓, →). Each arrow key moves a selection in the direction of the arrow. The → key, for example, moves the selection to the right.

The distance by which a single keystroke moves a selected element is determined by specifying a "Cursor key distance" value in the PREFERENCES dialog box, as introduced in the *Setting preferences* section of Chapter 3. The value that you enter is measured in centimeters, inches, or points, depending on the currently selected "Ruler units" option (also included in the PREFERENCES dialog box).

Arrow keys can be used to move points and to drag both straight and curved segments. Arrow keys may not be used to move a specific Bézier control handle (as described in the *Dragging Bézier control handles* section later in this chapter), except as a result of dragging a curved segment as described in the previous section.

Unlike MacDraw and FreeHand, Illustrator 3.0 provides no grids. You may fake a grid, however, that affects the movement of elements. Enter the desired grid increment into the "Cursor key distance" option. Then use the arrow keys to precisely position elements.

The arrow keys move the current selection in relation to the constraint axes. If you rotate the axes, as described in the *Constrained movements* section earlier in this chapter, you affect the direction at which a selected element is moved. For example, if you enter 15° for the "Constrain angle" option in the PREFERENCES dialog box, pressing the → key moves the selection in a 15° direction, pressing ↑ moves it in a 105° direction, and so on.

Using the Move dialog box

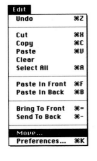

You may also specify the movement of a selected element numerically, via the MOVE dialog box shown in Figure 7.11. Illustrator 3.0 provides two ways to access this dialog:

- Choose the MOVE... command from the EDIT menu.
- Press the OPTION key and click on the arrow tool slot in the palette.

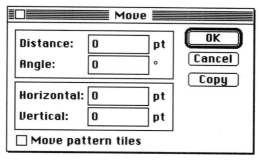

Figure 7.11: The Move dialog box allows you to specify a distance and a direction by which to move one or more selected elements.

To understand the options in this dialog, it is first necessary to understand the two basic components of a move: *distance* and *direction*. Distance is measured by tracking a specific point or other element in a selection. Figure 7.12 demonstrates the distance measured from a point in a rectangle at the shape's original location to the same point in the rectangle at its present location. Illustrator measures direction as an angle in degrees. As shown in the figure, this angle is measured between the *mean horizontal* and an imaginary distance line.

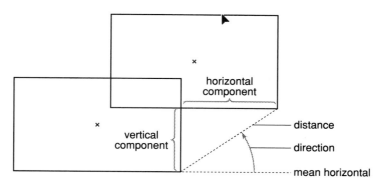

Figure 7.12: A diagram illustrating the distance and direction (angle) of a move.

To use the Move dialog, enter values for *either* the "Distance" and "Angle" options *or* the "Horizontal" and "Vertical" options. The "Distance," "Horizontal," and "Vertical" values represent distances which are measured in centimeters, inches, or points, depending on the currently selected "Ruler units" option in the PREFERENCES dialog box. The "Angle" value represents the direction, measured in degrees. To move a selected element, enter a direct distance value in the "Distance" option box and a direction value in the "Angle" option box. A positive "Distance" value moves the selection in the direction specified; a negative value moves the selection in the opposite direction.

Unfortunately, figuring out the direction of a prospective move can be very difficult. After all, few of us have protractors pasted to our screens. You may therefore find it easier to specify the horizontal and vertical components of a move, also displayed in Figure 7.12. You may enter positive and negative values for the "Horizontal" and "Vertical" options. As you do so, the "Distance" and "Angle" options will automatically update to reflect your changes.

Use the "Horizontal" and "Vertical" options as follows:

- Enter a positive "Horizontal" value to move the selection to the right.
- Enter a negative "Horizontal" value to move the selection to the left.
- Enter a positive "Vertical" value to move the selection upward.
- Enter a negative "Vertical" value to move the selection downward.
- Enter 0 in the "Horizontal" option to specify a purely vertical move.
- Enter 0 in the "Vertical" option to specify a purely horizontal move

If some path in the current selection is stroked or filled with a tile pattern (as discussed in Chapter 9, *Filling Type and Graphic Objects*), select the "Move pattern tiles" option to moves the tile pattern along with the selection.

You may confirm your movement specifications by clicking on either the OK or COPY button. Clicking COPY retains any selected element at its original location, while creating a *clone* at the location specified in the MOVE dialog. (For more information about clones, see the *Cloning objects* section of Chapter 12.)

The MOVE dialog box also acts as a recorder: After moving an element by hand, OPTION-click the arrow tool slot while the element remains selected. The MOVE dialog will appear, displaying the numerical increments of the previous move. The MOVE dialog also automatically receives distance and direction values from the MEASURE dialog box, as described in the following section.

The Move dialog moves the current selection in relation to the constraint axes. If you rotate the axes, as described in the *Constrained movements* section earlier in this chapter, you affect the direction in which a selected element is moved. For example, if you enter 15° for the "Constrain angle" option in the Preferences dialog box, a horizontal (0°) move becomes a 15° move, a vertical (90°) move becomes a 105° move, and so on.

Measuring a move

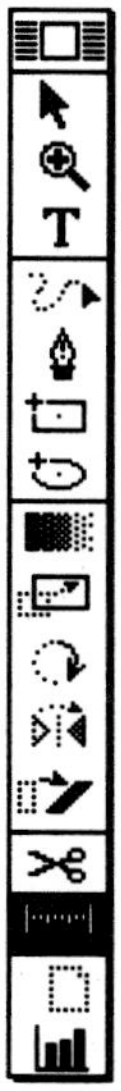

In general, you will probably find using the Move dialog box less convenient than moving elements by dragging and pressing arrow keys. Although these methods lack the degree of precision offered by the options in the Move dialog box, they provide immediate on-screen reactions. Manual manipulations are more direct and thus more likely to produce aesthetic results.

Nonetheless, Illustrator provides a tool that makes the Move dialog box more useful by making it possible for you to precisely determine, and thereby predict, the dialog's results. This is the *measure tool*, the third-to-last tool in your palette. The measure tool is used to measure the distance between two points. To operate the measure tool, select the tool and click at each of two different screen locations. The Measure dialog box will display, as shown in Figure 7.13, listing the distance and direction between the two clicks, as well as the vertical and horizontal components of the measure. This information will automatically appear in the Move dialog box if you immediately choose the Move... command or option-click the arrow tool slot after closing the Measure dialog box.

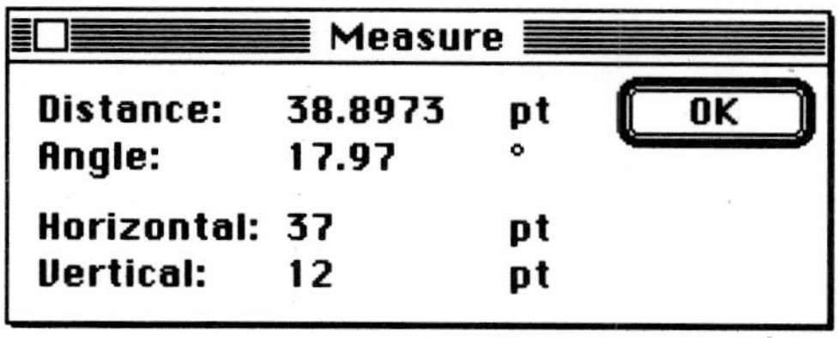
Measure
Distance: 38.8973 pt
Angle: 17.97 °
Horizontal: 37 pt
Vertical: 12 pt
OK

Figure 7.13: The Measure dialog box displays the distance and direction between two points clicked with the measure tool.

For example, suppose that you want to move an element the exact distance and direction shown in Figure 7.11. With the measure tool, you first click on a selected element at its present location, then click at the prospective location to which you want to move the element. After the second click, the MEASURE dialog will display, listing the distance and direction between the first and second clicks of the measure tool. Also listed are the horizontal and vertical components of that distance. The MEASURE dialog shown in Figure 7.13 tells us that if we were to move an element 37 points to the right and 12 points up, we would arrive at the same location as moving 38.8973 points in a 17.97° direction.

Incidentally, the MEASURE dialog works by first determining the horizontal and vertical components of the distance. The directional distance is then derived using the Pythagorean theorem:

$$a^2 + b^2 = c^2$$

where *a* and *b* are the horizontal and vertical components and *c* is the directional distance; hence the directional accuracy to $\frac{1}{10,000}$ of a point.

Having made a highly accurate measurement, you may now exit the MEASURE dialog box by clicking the OK button or pressing RETURN. Then choose the MOVE... command to display the same information in the MOVE dialog box. Press RETURN again to initiate the measured movement.

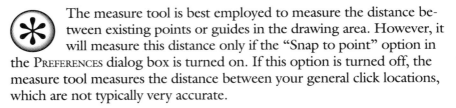 The measure tool is best employed to measure the distance between existing points or guides in the drawing area. However, it will measure this distance only if the "Snap to point" option in the PREFERENCES dialog box is turned on. If this option is turned off, the measure tool measures the distance between your general click locations, which are not typically very accurate.

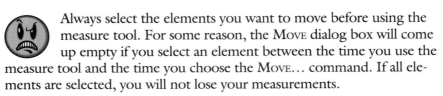 Always select the elements you want to move before using the measure tool. For some reason, the MOVE dialog box will come up empty if you select an element between the time you use the measure tool and the time you choose the MOVE... command. If all elements are selected, you will not lose your measurements.

Dragging Bézier control handles

The only element that we have neglected to move so far is the Bézier control handle. We save it until last because it is the most difficult element to manipulate. So far, we have only introduced and briefly discussed the qualities of Bézier control handles, the elements that control the arc of a segment as it exits or enters a point. Regardless of the identity of their points, Bézier control handles may be moved in much the same way that points may be moved. You may either select the point to which a handle belongs or select the segment it controls to display a Bézier control handle. You then drag the handle you wish to move. Bézier control handles cannot be moved using an arrow key or the MOVE dialog box, except as a result of moving a selected curved segment.

Figures 7.14 through 7.18 feature four smooth points which are located in the exact same positions relative to each other. From one figure to the next, only the numbered Bézier control handles have been moved. However, these simple adjustments have a dramatic impact on the appearance of each path. The affected handles have been numbered to show the exact manner in which a handle is relocated from path to path. For the record, handle number 1 controls the left segment, handles 2 and 4 control the middle segment, and handle 3 controls the right segment.

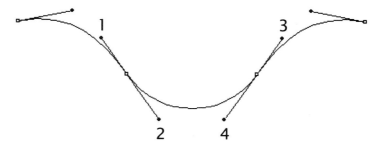

Figure 7.14: A path composed of four smooth points and three selected segments.

When one Bézier control handle for a smooth point is moved, the other handle for that point moves in the opposite direction. Hence, the two handles of a smooth point form a constant lever. Compare Figure 7.15 on the following page with Figure 7.14 above. In Figure 7.15, handles 3 and 4 have been moved only slightly. Handles 1 and 2, however, have been moved dramatically. Handle 1 was dragged in a clockwise sweep, sending handle 2 upward. Figure 7.16 on the following page shows the path as it appears during the drag. A gray line representing the motion of the drag has been inserted to clarify the figure.

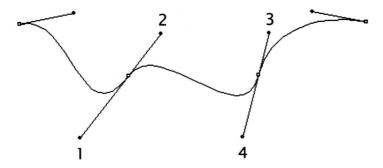

Figure 7.15: The same path after having dragged handle 1 in a clockwise sweep.

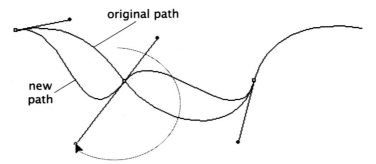

original path

new
path

Figure 7.16: The act of dragging handle 1 shown in progress.

In Figure 7.15, handle 2 forces the center segment to ascend as it exits the left smooth point. But because of handle 4, the segment also ascends as it enters the right smooth point. So somewhere between the two points, the segment has to change direction. Handles 2 and 4 pull at the beginning and at the end of the segment, respectively. The farther the handles are moved from the center segment and from each other, the more desperately the segment stretches to keep up, as is shown in the Figure 7.17. Here, both handles 2 and 4 have been moved far away from each other. The result is a segment that bulges out in three directions—left, right, and downward. The final example, shown in Figure 7.18, shows that there is basically no limitation to how far you may drag a Bézier control handle from its point, nor to how severely you may stretch a curved segment. The segment will always stretch to keep up, turning around only when necessary to meet the demands of the opposite point and its Bézier control handle.

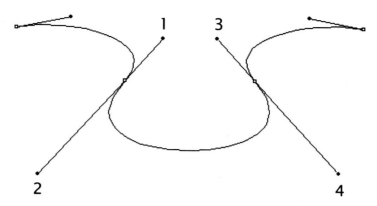

Figure 7.17: Dragging handles 2 and 4 far away from each other forces the center segment to bulge outward.

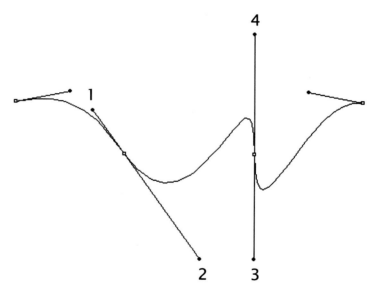

Figure 7.18: There is no limit to the extent that you may drag a handle or stretch a segment.

However, dragging Bézier control handles is not so much a question of what can you do as when you should do it. One of the most common problems users have when learning to use Adobe Illustrator is trying to determine the placement of Bézier control handles. Several rules have been developed over the years, but the best are the *all-or-nothing rule* and the *30% rule*. The all-or-nothing rule states that every segment in your path should be associated with either two Bézier control handles or none at all. In other words, no segment should rely on only one control handle to determine its curvature. In the 30% rule, the distance from any Bézier control handle to its point should be approximately 30% the length of the segment.

The top path in Figure 7.19 violates the all-or-nothing rule. Its two curved segments are controlled by only one handle apiece, resulting in weak, shallow arcs. Such curves are to be avoided at all costs. The second example obeys the all-or-nothing rule. As the rule states, its straight segment is associated with no handle and both curved segments have two handles apiece. The result is a full-figured, properly pumped-up dome, a credit to any illustration.

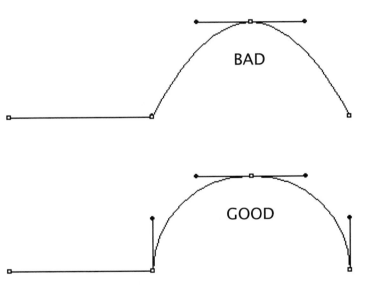

Figure 7.19: The all-or-nothing rule states that every curved segment should be controlled by two handles, one for each of its points.

The first path in Figure 7.20 violates the 30% rule. The handles for the central point are much too long, about 60% the length of their segments, and the two outer handles are too short, about 15% the length of their segments. The result is an ugly, misshapen mess. In the second example, the two handles belonging to the left segment each take up about 30% of the length of the segment. The right segment is shorter, so its handles are shorter as well. This path is smooth and consistent in curvature, giving it a naturalistic appearance.

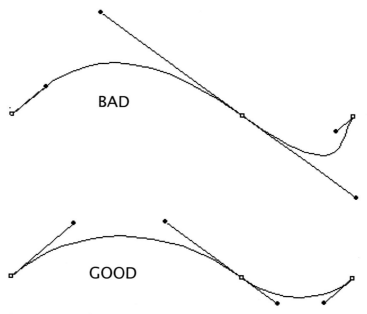

Figure 7.20: The 30% rule states that every Bézier control handle should extend about 30% the length of its segment.

Moving points and adjusting control handles are fundamental ways to change the shape of a path. But sometimes, no matter how long you spend adjusting the placement of its points or the curvature of its segments, a path fails to meet the requirements of your illustration. In such a case, you may want to expand the path by adding points, or simplify the path by deleting points.

Adding, deleting, and converting elements

The quantity and identity of points and segments in a path is forever subject to change. Whether closed or open, a path may be reshaped by adding, deleting, and converting points. In turn, adding or deleting a point forces the addition or deletion of a segment. The conversion of a point, from corner to smooth or from smooth to corner, frequently converts a segment, from curved to straight or from straight to curved. The following pages describe how all of these reshaping techniques may be applied to any existing path.

Adding elements to the end of a path

As discussed in Chapter 5, *Drawing Paths from Scratch*, a point associated with less than two segments is open-ended. Such a point is always located at one end or the other of a line. For this reason, an open-ended point is called an *endpoint*. An open path always has two endpoints. A closed path contains no endpoint, since each point in a shape is connected to another.

The selected endpoint in an active path is waiting for a segment to be drawn from it. To check if an open path is active, select the pen tool and move the cursor into the drawing area. If the cursor appears as a +, the selected path is active. If the pen tool cursor appears as an ×, all paths are passive. To *activate* an endpoint in a passive path so that a new segment may be drawn from it, click or drag the point with the pen tool, depending on the identity of the endpoint and whether you wish the next segment to be straight or curved. (See the *Pen tool summary* section of Chapter 5 for more specific instructions.) Then, you may click or drag anywhere else on your screen to create a segment between the selected endpoint and the newly created point. Following this, your original endpoint will be bound by segments on both sides, no longer fit to be called an endpoint. It must relinquish this title to the newest point in the line.

You can also use this technique to close an existing path. Just select one endpoint, click or drag it with the pen tool to activate it, then click or drag on the remaining endpoint. A segment is drawn between the two endpoints, closing the path to form a shape and eliminating both endpoints by converting them to interior points.

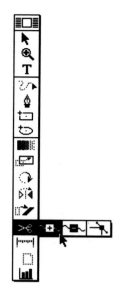

You may also lengthen an open path by drawing from one of its endpoints with the freehand tool or, if the path touches a portion of a tracing template, the autotrace tool. You may also close a path by dragging from one endpoint to the other with either tool.

Finally, you may join any two existing lines to form one longer line by activating an endpoint of the first path and then clicking or dragging with the pen tool on an endpoint of the second path. If you are using the freehand or autotrace tool, simply drag from an endpoint of one path to the endpoint of another.

Adding elements within a path

We have demonstrated how you may add points to the end of an existing line. But there will be many times when you wish to add points in the middle of a path. This process requires a tool we have not discussed so far, the *add-point tool*. You may choose the add-point tool, which appears as a curve running through a reversed plus sign, by dragging from the scissors tool slot in the toolbox.

First, select the path to which you wish to add a point. Then click with the add-point tool on some segment in the path. (*Do not* click on a point.) A new point will appear at this location. The segment to which the point was added is broken into two segments.

Figure 7.21 on the following page shows an ordinary, ungrouped circle composed of four smooth points. Suppose that you want to change the circle into a crescent by adding points within the path. The following steps describe one way to perform this task:

1. Click at each of two similar locations on each of the right-hand segments using the add-point tool. These points appear as selected in Figure 7.21.

2. Press and hold the COMMAND key to access the arrow tool. Drag at the rightmost point, moving it toward the center of the shape, as shown in Figure 7.22.

3. Release COMMAND to redisplay the add-point tool cursor. Click in the middle of each of the two segments between the crescent tips and the dragged point. These points are shown as selected in Figure 7.23 on the page 233.

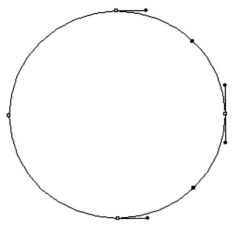

Figure 7.21: Add a point in the middle of each of the right-hand segments of an ungrouped circle.

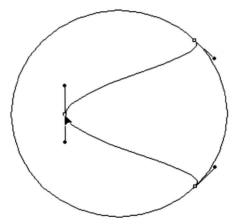

Figure 7.22: Drag the rightmost point toward the center of the shape.

4. Finally, move the most recently created points outward from the center of the shape, as shown in the first example in Figure 7.24. The Bézier control handles of the point at the center of the mouth will require some adjustment as well.

The completed image is displayed on the right side of Figure 7.24.

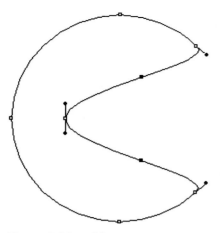

Figure 7.23: Add a point to the middle of each of the segments forming the mouth of the shape.

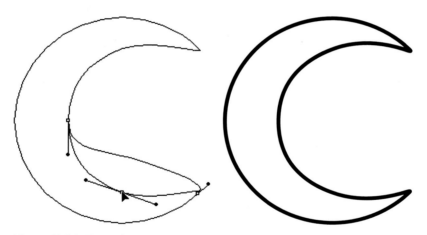

Figure 7.24: Drag the most recent points into position. The completed image is shown on right as it appears when printed from Illustrator.

All points added in Figures 7.21 though 7.24 happen to be smooth points. The identity of a point inserted into a segment using the add-point tool depends on the curvature of the segment. If the segment is straight, the inserted point will obviously be a corner point. If the segment curves in an even arc, like the segments in a circle, a smooth point will be inserted. However, if the segment curves slightly unevenly, as the majority of curved segments do, the identity of an inserted point becomes difficult to predict. We can only suggest that you adopt a trial-and-error attitude when using the add-point tool. If the identity of the inserted point does not match your needs, you may easily delete it using the delete-point tool or convert it using the convert-point tool. Both of these tools are described in the upcoming pages.

 Press the OPTION key to temporarily access the add-point tool when the scissors tool is selected. (For more information about the scissors tool, see *Splitting an element*, later in this chapter.)

You may click with the add-point tool on a segment in any existing path, even if the path is grouped, or combined or linked with other paths. However, Illustrator does not allow you to click with this tool directly on a point or at some empty location in the drawing area.

Deleting elements from a path

The simplest way to delete an element is to select the element and press either BACKSPACE or DELETE. You may also choose the CLEAR command from the EDIT menu.

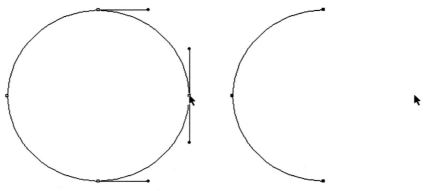

Figure 7.25: Selecting a point (left) and pressing the delete key deletes the point and its two segments from the path (right).

When you delete a selected point by pressing DELETE or BACKSPACE or choosing CLEAR, you also delete all segments associated with that point. The first example of Figure 7.25 shows a point selected in a circular path. The second example shows the path after the point is deleted. Since both segments bordering a point become selected when you select a point, both segments are deleted along with the point. Deleting an interior point with the DELETE key therefore opens a closed path, as in the figure, or breaks an open path into two lines.

If you delete an endpoint from an open path, you delete the single segment associated with the point. Deleting an endpoint does not break a line in two.

You may also delete a single selected segment. Figure 7.26 shows a segment being selected and deleted from another circular path. Once again, a hole is left in the path. Therefore, deleting a segment also opens a closed path or breaks an open path into two separate lines. However, unlike a deleted point, a deleted segment takes no other element with it.

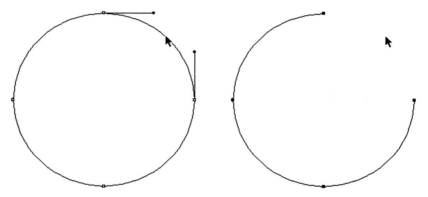

Figure 7.26: Selecting a segment (left) and pressing the delete key deletes the selected segment only (right).

Multiple points or segments may also be deleted, whether or not they belong to the same path. Many paths may in this way be opened and broken simultaneously.

Deleting a whole path

As shown in both Figures 7.25 and 7.26, deleting a point or segment from a path causes every remaining point and segment in that path to become selected. This means that if you press DELETE a second time, you will delete the entire path. This means that if a path, in the course of its creation, ends up deviating so drastically from your original intention that there is no sense in attempting a salvage, you may delete the entire object by selecting any element in the path and pressing DELETE twice in a row.

You may also delete a path by selecting the entire path (OPTION-clicking with the arrow tool) and pressing DELETE. We find that double-pressing the DELETE key is generally faster, since an element will already be selected in a path if you just finished creating it, but feel free to use the method that works most quickly for you. After all, the stark realization of one's own proclivity for error is not something most of us care to ponder for a prolonged period of time.

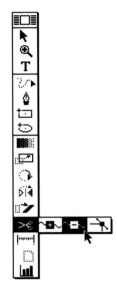

Deleting a point
without breaking a path

If you want to delete an interior point from a path, but you do not want to open a closed path or to break an open path in two, use the *delete-point tool.* You may choose the delete-point tool, which appears as a curve running through a reversed minus sign, by dragging from the scissors tool slot in the toolbox.

First, select the path from which you wish to delete a point. Then click with the delete-point tool on some point in the path. (*Do not* click on a segment.) The point on which you clicked will disappear, but rather than deleting both associated segments, a new segment will be drawn between the two points that neighbored the deleted point.

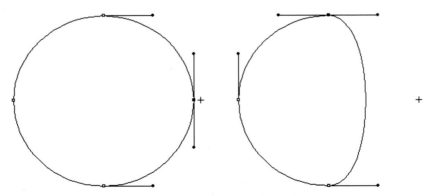

Figure 7.27: Click on an interior point with the delete-point tool, as indicated on the left, to delete the point but retain a segment (right).

The first example in Figure 7.27 shows the delete-point cursor poised to click on the rightmost point in the familiar circle path. The second example shows the path after the point is deleted. The two segments surrounding the deleted point are fused into a single segment, the curvature of which is determined by the remaining points in the path. The result is a path that remains closed.

You may click with the delete-point tool on a point in any existing path, even if the path is grouped, or combined or linked with other paths. However, Illustrator does not allow you to click with this tool on a segment or at some empty location in the drawing area.

Orphans of a broken path

One last note: we advise that you do not delete a point from a line that consists of only two points. This will leave a single-point path, which is almost completely useless unless you intend to build on it immediately. (Lone points can serve as center points in grouped shapes, as discussed in the *Adding a center point* section of Chapter 12.) Lone points tend to clutter up the drawing area and needlessly increase the size of your illustration when saved to disk. Luckily, a lone point shows up in the drawing area as an × when it is not selected, so it may be built upon or deleted.

Converting points

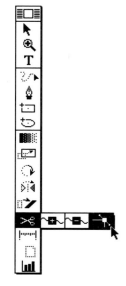

Illustrator 3.0 now allows you to change the identity of an interior point; that is, to convert a corner point within an existing path to a smooth point, or vice versa. All point conversions are performed using *the convert-point tool.* You may choose the convert-point tool, which appears as an enlarged corner point flanked by two Bézier control handles, by dragging from the scissors tool slot in the toolbox.

Use the convert-point tool as follows:

- Click on a smooth point to convert it to a corner point with no Bézier control handle.

- Drag one of the Bézier control handles of a smooth point to move it independently of the other Bézier control handle, thus converting the smooth point to a cusp.

- Drag from a corner point to convert it to a smooth point with two symmetrical Bézier control handles.

Figure 7.28 shows a circular path composed of four smooth points. Suppose that you want to convert the identity of one or more of these points to alter the form of the path. The following exercise demonstrates one way to proceed:

1. Select the convert-point tool and click on the leftmost point in the circle. The smooth point is immediately converted to a corner point with no Bézier control handle, as shown in Figure 7.29.

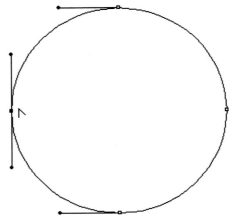

Figure 7.28: The convert-point tool, poised to click on the left point in a circular path.

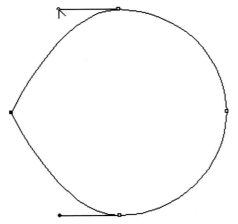

Figure 7.29: Drag the displayed Bézier control handle belonging to the top point.

2. Now drag the left-pointing Bézier control handle belonging to the top smooth point in the circle. The convert-point tool allows you to drag one handle independently of another, immediately converting the smooth point to a cusp (a corner point with two handles).

3. Drag the handle all the way back to its point, as shown in Figure 7.30. When your cursor changes to a hollow arrowhead, indicating that it has snapped to the point, release your mouse button. You have now subtracted a Bézier control handle from the point, converting it to a corner point with only one handle.

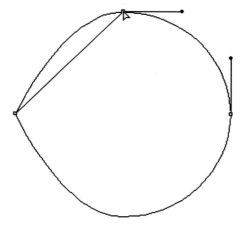

Figure 7.30: Drag the handle back to its point, subtracting the handle from the shape.

4. Now drag the left-pointing handle belonging to the bottom point in the path to the approximate position shown in Figure 7.31 on the following page. (If the handle is not displayed, COMMAND-click on the bottom, left segment in the path to select it and thereby display the handle associated with that segment.)

5. Drag from the leftmost point that you converted to a corner point in step 1. This converts the point back to a smooth point. Drag the handle down and to the left as shown in Figure 7.32, bowing the bottom segment inward and the top segment outward.

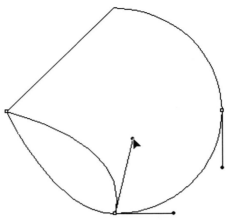

Figure 7.31: Drag the displayed segment for the bottom point up and to the right.

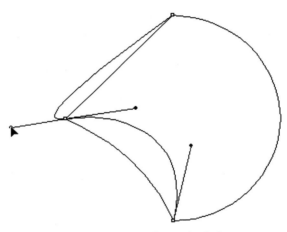

Figure 7.32: Drag from the left point to convert it back to a smooth point.

5. After releasing your mouse button, drag at the same handle you were just dragging, as shown in Figure 7.33. This time, however, drag the handle back to its point to subtract it. As this step and the previous one demonstrate, in order to add a handle to a corner point, you must convert it to a smooth point and then convert it back into a cusp.

The completed image is displayed on the right side of Figure 7.33.

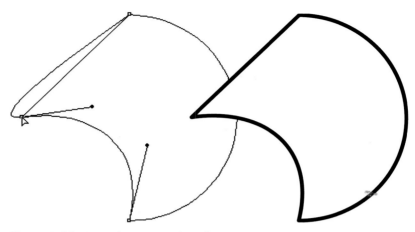

Figure 7.33: Drag the newest handle back to its point. Your cursor will snap to the point, as indicated by the hollow arrowhead cursor. The completed image is shown on the right as it appears when printed from Illustrator.

In between converting points, it is very tempting to adjust the placement of Bézier control handles using the convert-point tool. If you do so, however, you will most certainly convert the point—to a corner point if the point is currently a smooth point, or to a smooth point if it is currently a corner point.

If you want to move a point or adjust a handle without converting a point, be sure to press the COMMAND key to temporarily access the arrow tool before beginning your drag. Also, if you inadvertently convert a point, you may immediately choose the UNDO command from the EDIT menu (⌘-Z) to convert the point back to its original identity.

Press the CONTROL key to temporarily access the convert-point tool when the arrow tool is selected. If your keyboard does not provide a CONTROL key, press the Z key instead. When any other tool is selected, press COMMAND-CONTROL to access the convert-point tool. (Pressing COMMAND-Z also works, but this may also have the affect of choosing the UNDO command, as discussed in the *Undo and redo* section at the end of this chapter).

Joining and splitting elements

Almost all of the reshaping techniques we have described so far are available, in some form or another, in just about every drawing software available on the Macintosh. MacDraw, for example, although providing no Bézier curve capacity, allows you to move elements, add and delete points, and convert straight segments to curved segments. Yet, MacDraw is commonly considered too remedial for tackling a complex illustration. This section discusses two areas in which Illustrator stands heads above the common drawing crowd: the joining and splitting of points and segments, which make it possible to break up portions of various paths like pieces in a tailor-made puzzle, then assemble them in any way you see fit.

Joining endpoints with a straight segment

In the section *Adding elements to the end of a path* earlier in this chapter, we described that you may join two lines into a single open path by drawing from one endpoint to another with the pen, freehand, or autotrace tool. But as it turns out, Illustrator offers an automated JOIN... command in the ARRANGE menu (⌘-J) that makes the joining of endpoints less cumbersome while at the same time providing additional options and a greater degree of control.

First of all, the JOIN... command allows you to join two endpoints with a straight segment. Figure 7.34 displays two open paths. One endpoint in each path is selected. If you choose JOIN..., a straight segment will be drawn between the two selected endpoints, resulting in the path shown in Figure 7.35. When two endpoints are selected, whether they belong to the same path or not, and the two points are separated by some distance, choosing JOIN... draws a straight segment between the two points. This segment is always straight, regardless of the identity of the points involved. In Figure 7.34, for example, the upper endpoint was a smooth point, as evident from the two symmetrical Bézier control handles. But in Figure 7.35, the point has been converted to a corner point to allow for the straight segment.

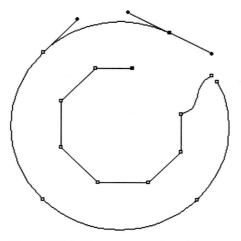

Figure 7.34: Two open paths with one selected endpoint each.

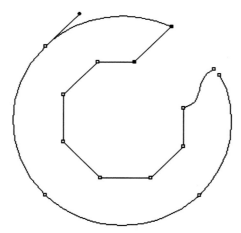

Figure 7.35: The Join... command draws a straight segment between the two selected endpoints.

Use the JOIN... command any time you want to draw a straight segment between two existing endpoints. For example, the JOIN... command would have simplified the creation of the semicircle shown back in Figure 5.31. Other images with straight edges may also make use of this feature.

Joining coincident endpoints

If two endpoints are *coincident*—that is, one point is positioned exactly on top of the other in the drawing area—the JOIN... command will fuse the two into a single interior point, whose identity you may specify by selecting options in the JOIN dialog box.

Joining coincident endpoints is a four-step process:

1. Drag one endpoint onto another with the arrow tool so the two points are coincident. Make sure they snap together, as verified by a hollow arrowhead cursor.

2. Marquee both points to select them. No other point should be selected.

3. Choose the JOIN... command to display the JOIN dialog box.

4. Select the desired kind of point (corner or smooth) and press RETURN.

We will demonstrate this process by way of an example. Figure 7.36 shows one endpoint being dragged onto another endpoint in a single open path. Notice that the cursor appears as a hollow arrowhead, indicating that the dragged point has snapped to the stationary point, making them coincident.

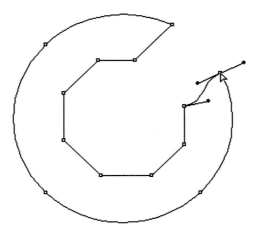

Figure 7.36: Dragging one endpoint in front of the other endpoint in the same path.

We next marquee the two points to select them. (Marqueeing is the only possible means of selection, since one point is located inaccessibly in back of the other.) Figure 7.38 shows both endpoints as they appear when selected.

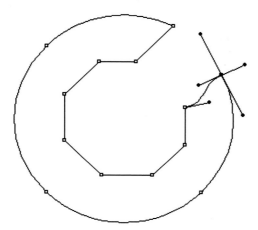

Figure 7.38: The two coincident endpoints as they appear when selected.

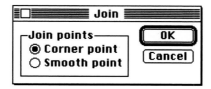

Figure 7.39: The Join dialog box allows you to specify the identity of the joined point.

After selecting the points, we choose the JOIN… command. If the endpoints are correctly positioned one directly in front of the other, the JOIN dialog box shown in Figure 7.39 will appear. If neither the JOIN dialog nor an error message appears, this means that Illustrator does not consider your endpoints to be exactly situated at the same location. The JOIN… command has therefore joined the two selected endpoints with a straight segment. Choose UNDO JOIN (⌘-Z) to delete the segment and then choose the AVERAGE… command from the ARRANGE menu (⌘-L) to properly relocate the selected endpoints. (This command is discussed in detail later in *Averaging points* later in this chapter.) The AVERAGE dialog box will appear, with the "Both" option selected by default. Press RETURN to initiate the command. Then choose the JOIN… command again to bring up the JOIN dialog box.

The JOIN dialog box allows you to specify the identity of your joined point. It is here that the JOIN… command provides more control over joining points than you can achieve with a drawing tool. For example, you cannot convert a corner point to a smooth point as you join it to another point with the pen tool, but you can if you choose the JOIN… command.

The examples in Figure 7.40 show the results of selecting various options in the JOIN dialog. In each example, the two coincident points and their adjoining segments have been enlarged to provide a better view. The first example displays the selected points as they appear before joining. The second example is the result of selecting the "Corner" option in the JOIN dialog box. This is the default selection. The "Corner" option joins two selected endpoints to form a single corner point. The curvature of a bordering segment is never altered by selecting the "Corner" option.

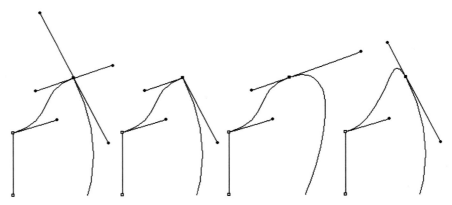

Figure 7.40: Two selected points before joining (left) followed by three ways to change the identity of a joined point using the Join dialog box.

The third and fourth examples in Figure 7.40 were produced by selecting the "Smooth" option in the JOIN dialog box. Selecting "Smooth," almost always alters the curvature of one of the segments associated with the coincident points. In the case of our example, we have one segment that curves from left to right and another that curves from top to bottom.

And yet, we have instructed Illustrator to surround our joined point with two segments that arc evenly into each other. Therefore, the form of at least one segment must be dramatically altered.

When joining any two points to form a smooth point in Illustrator, the curvature of the front segment remains intact while the curvature of the rear segment is altered to fit the requirements of the new smooth point. In the third example of Figure 7.40, the left-hand segment was the front segment. The right-hand segment has been substantially malformed to conform to its repositioned Bézier control handle. In the fourth example of the figure, the right-hand segment was the front segment and it is the left-hand segment that has been reshaped.

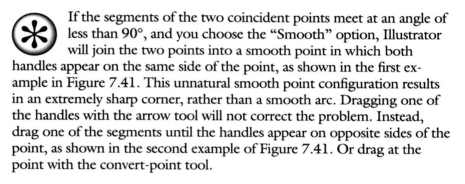 If the segments of the two coincident points meet at an angle of less than 90°, and you choose the "Smooth" option, Illustrator will join the two points into a smooth point in which both handles appear on the same side of the point, as shown in the first example in Figure 7.41. This unnatural smooth point configuration results in an extremely sharp corner, rather than a smooth arc. Dragging one of the handles with the arrow tool will not correct the problem. Instead, drag one of the segments until the handles appear on opposite sides of the point, as shown in the second example of Figure 7.41. Or drag at the point with the convert-point tool.

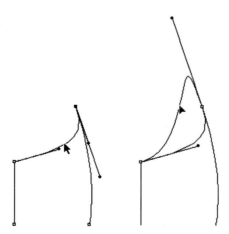

Figure 7.41: If the Bézier control handles for a smooth point become located on the same side of the point (left), drag one of the neighboring segments to relocate one handle to the opposite side of the point (right).

Two and only two points may be selected when choosing the JOIN... command. If less or more points are selected, an error message will appear. If this occurs, press RETURN to hide the alert box. Then reselect your two points and retry the command.

Splitting an element

The *scissors tool*, fourth tool from the bottom in the toolbox, is used to split a point or segment. By choosing the scissors tool and clicking at some location on a selected segment, you insert two endpoints into the segment, each associated with one segment apiece. This means the segment is split into two segments. If you click with the scissors tool on an interior point, you split the point into two endpoints; once again, each is associated with a single segment. Therefore, you may click with the scissors tool to open a closed path or to split an open path into two lines.

Suppose you want to split an ordinary circle into the three shapes shown in the second example in Figure 7.44 on the next page. The following steps describe how this might be accomplished using the scissors and pen tool:

1. Click with the scissors tool at two points on each of the right-hand segments in the circle. These points are shown as selected in Figure 7.42. The circle is now split up into four separate lines.

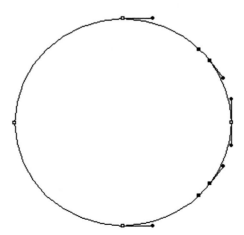

Figure 7.42: Each of the selected points in this circle was created by clicking with the scissors tool.

2. Select the arrow tool and OPTION-click on the topmost of the single-segment lines created with the scissors tool. This selects the entire path. Then SHIFT-OPTION-click on the lower single-segment line to add it to the selection.

3. Drag both lines away from the remaining paths of the circle, as shown in Figure 7.43. Neither line is a part of the prospective final image, so press the BACKSPACE or DELETE key to delete them both. You are now left with two open paths.

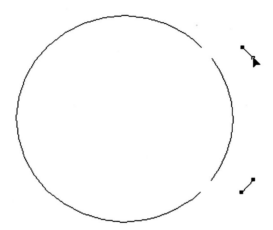

Figure 7.43: Drag the two single-segment lines away from the rest of the circle and delete them.

4. Select the pen tool. Press the OPTION key and drag from the top point in the right-hand path. This activates the path and converts the point from a smooth point to a cusp.

5. After releasing the OPTION key, drag again with the pen tool at a location that mirrors the center smooth point of the right-hand path.

6. Press OPTION again and drag at the bottom point in the right-hand path, closing the path to form a leaf-shaped path.

7. Close the second, larger path in a similar manner, adding to it two segments that are parallel to those that closed the right-hand shape. The result is the first example in Figure 7.44.

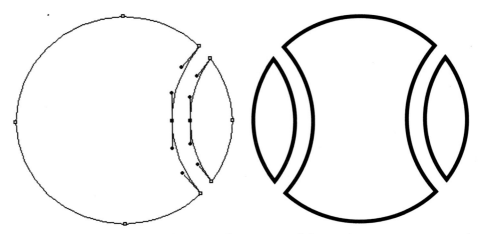

Figure 7.44: Draw segments closing the two remaining paths. Repeating the exercise on the left side of the shape results in the image shown on right.

The second example in Figure 7.44 shows the completed image after repeating steps 1 through 7 on the left side of the circle.

You may click with the scissors tool on a point or segment in any existing path, even if the path is grouped, or combined or linked with other paths. However, Illustrator does not allow you to click with this tool at some empty location in the drawing area.

Deleting split paths

Frequently, you will split off some portion of a path as a first step to deleting it from your illustration, as demonstrated in the exercise. When doing so, be careful to select the entire split portion before pressing BACKSPACE or DELETE, or be sure to press the DELETE key twice. For example, if you had selected the segment of only one of the single-segment lines in Figure 7.42 and pressed DELETE only once, you would have been left with two lone points, residing either in front or in back of the endpoints of the paths that you desired to reshape. These lone points would have cluttered your drawing area and may have gotten in the way when you tried to add segments to the endpoints of the remaining paths.

Averaging points

Sadly, one of Illustrator's failings is that is provides only marginal alignment capabilities. In MacDraw or FreeHand, for example, you may align any number of selected objects so that their left sides, right sides, tops, bottoms, or centers all line up in perfect rows or columns. Nice feature, huh? Well, if you're looking for something like that in Illustrator, forget it. Mechanical drawing is not Illustrator's forté—never was, probably never will be.

The only feature that even resembles alignment is the AVERAGE... command in the ARRANGE menu (⌘-L), which allows you to *average* the position of two or more selected points in the drawing area. For example, if two selected points are four inches apart from each other, the AVERAGE... command will move each point two inches toward each other so they reside at the same location.

Choosing the AVERAGE... command from the ARRANGE menu displays the AVERAGE dialog box shown in Figure 7.45. This dialog offers three "Average along" options. The options work as follows:

- **Both axes**. Select this option to average the location of all selected points to a single coincident location in the drawing area.

- **Horizontal axis only**. This option averages selected points horizontally along the constraint axes.

- **Vertical axis only**. This option averages selected points vertically along the constraint axes.

Select the desired radio button and press RETURN to initiate the average of the selected points.

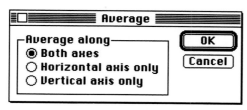

Figure 7.45: The Average dialog box allows you to average two or more selected points along the constraint axes.

Applying the Average... command

Figure 7.46 shows two shapes containing two selected points apiece (each of which is circled to make it easier to see, and labeled so you can follow it from figure to figure). The following exercise demonstrates the results of averaging these elements:

1. After selecting the points shown in the figure, choose the AVER-AGE... command to display the AVERAGE dialog box. The "Both axes" option is selected by default. Select the "Horizontal axis only" option and press the RETURN key, instructing Illustrator to re-locate all selected points so they line up in a horizontal formation, as shown in Figure 7.47.

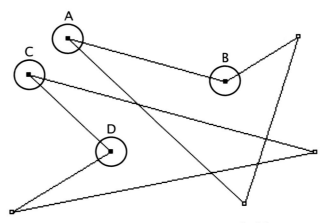

Figure 7.46: Two paths containing a total of four selected points (each circled and labeled).

2. All four selected points are aligned so that they occupy the same vertical space, while their horizontal positioning remains identical to that in Figure 7.46. Choose UNDO AVERAGE (⌘-Z) to return the points to their original locations.

3. Starting again from Figure 7.46, choose AVERAGE... and this time select the "Vertical axis only" option from the AVERAGE dialog and press RETURN. The points line up in vertical formation, as shown in Figure 7.48. The four points now occupy the same horizontal space, while their vertical positioning remains unchanged.

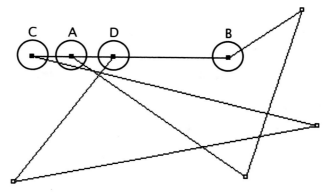

Figure 7.47: The four selected points averaged along the horizontal axis.

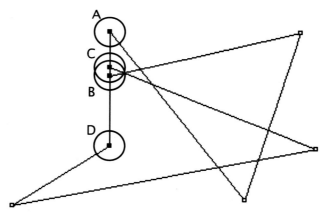

Figure 7.48: The four selected points averaged along the vertical axis.

4. Choose UNDO AVERAGE again.

5. Finally, choose AVERAGE…, check to see that "Both axes" is selected, and press RETURN. All four points become coincident, each occupying the same location as the three other selected points, as shown in Figure 7.49 on the next page.

The primary function for averaging points along both axes is to prepare two endpoints for a JOIN… command, as discussed in *Joining coincident endpoints* earlier in this chapter.

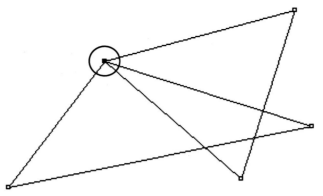

Figure 7.49: The four selected points averaged along both axes. All points are positioned at the coincident location indicated by the circle.

Why average points?

The AVERAGE... command averages all selected points, whether in a group or in a combined or linked object. It does not average the location of segments or entire paths, except as a result of repositioning their points. For example, suppose you select two entire rectangles (all points in each) with the intention of positioning one rectangle directly in front of another. If you choose AVERAGE... and select the "Both axes" option, all points will become coincident, ruining the rectangles as recognizable objects.

So what the heck do you do with this command? For starters, you can makes two endpoints coincident so they may be fused into a single point with the JOIN... command. However, this is not the command's only purpose. The list below includes all the functions (we know of) to which the AVERAGE... command may be applied:

- Nothing looks worse than a straight segment that is only slightly angled; that is, *almost* horizontal or *almost* vertical, but not quite. Even when printed to a photo-imagesetter, a line that is off by as much as half a degree will appear jagged. To ensure a straight segment is perpendicular, select both points bordering the segment and apply the "Horizontal axis only" or "Vertical axis only" option.

- To join two separated points with a perfectly horizontal or vertical straight segment, apply the "Horizontal axis only" or "Vertical axis only" option before choosing the JOIN... command.

- If the Join dialog box does not appear after choosing the Join… command for what seem to be two coincident points, choose Undo Join (⌘-Z) and apply the "Both axes" option to ensure the points are exactly coincident. Again choose the Join… command to display the Join dialog box.

- Applying the "Both axes" option may slightly rotate the angle of a horizontal or vertical segment. If a perpendicular segment is associated with any point being averaged with the "Both axes" option, you should go back and apply the "Horizontal axis only" or "Vertical axis only" option to the points that border the segment.

- Apply the "Horizontal axis only" option to selected points in different paths to align the bases of the paths, as shown in Figure 7.50, or the tops of the paths. Apply the "Vertical axis only" option to align the sides of the paths.

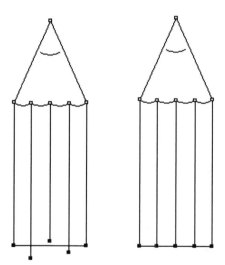

Figure 7.50: Align the bottoms of different paths by selecting the points at the bottom of the paths (left) and applying the "Horizontal axis only" option (right).

- Within grouped objects, the Average… command can be used to align the bottoms (see Figure 7.51 on the next page), tops, and sides of paths, so long as the specific points you want to align have been selected with the direct-selection tool.

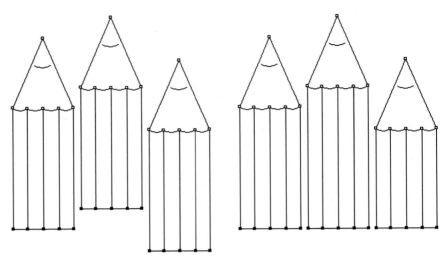

Figure 7.51: Align the bottoms of grouped objects by selecting the points at the bottom of the paths with the direct-selection tool (left) and applying the "Horizontal axis only" option (right).

Averaging along a rotated axis

Both the "Horizontal axis only" and "Vertical axis only" options average points in relation to the constraint axes. If you rotate the axes, as described in *Constrained movements* earlier in this chapter, you also rotate the axes along which points are aligned. For example, if you enter 30° for the "Constrain angle" option in the PREFERENCES dialog box, the "Horizontal axis only" option in the AVERAGE dialog box will produce the effect shown in Figure 7.52.

Since the "Both axes" option averages all points to a single location, it is not affected by the rotation of the constraint axes.

The AVERAGE… command may be applied only to points. At least two points must be selected when choosing the command. If only one point is selected, an error message will appear. If this occurs, press RETURN to hide the alert box. Then reselect your points and try again.

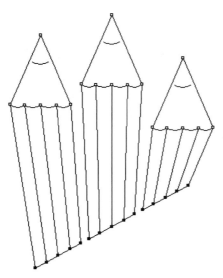

Figure 7.52: Averaging selected points along the horizontal axis when the "Constrain angle" option in the Preferences dialog box is set to 30°.

Undo and redo

Because we all make mistakes, especially when drawing and tracing complicated paths, Illustrator provides you with the ability to undo the results of your last operation. If you are familiar with any Macintosh application or programs such as PageMaker on the IBM PC, you are no doubt familiar with the UNDO command in the EDIT menu (⌘-Z). This command allows you to negate the last major action performed. After you undo an operation, the UNDO command will change to a REDO command, giving you a brief opportunity to reperform an operation if you decide you don't want to undo it after all. Your chance to redo an operation only lasts as long as you do not so much as click in the drawing area or press a key.

Very minor operations, such as selecting or deselecting an element, cannot be undone. Adjusting settings in dialog boxes, such as PAGE SETUP and PREFERENCES, as well as changing the view size or display mode are likewise immune to the UNDO command.

Illustrator lists the name of the operation that may be undone or re-done under the EDIT menu following the word UNDO or REDO, so that you fully realize the consequences of choosing the command. Examples include UNDO MOVE or REDO JOIN.

If an operation cannot be undone, the UNDO command will appear dimmed in the EDIT menu and pressing COMMAND-Z will produce no effect.

Creating and Editing Type

As you have probably managed to glean, Adobe Illustrator 3.0 has introduced a startling collection of new features. But nowhere is this so apparent as in the area of type. So much so that if you have used previous versions of Adobe Illustrator, you should prepare yourself to completely relearn the type tool as well as all other aspects of text editing.

To begin with, *everything* has changed. Gone is the inefficient text-entry dialog box.

With it has gone the 255-character text block limit. Type is now created, edited, and imported directly in the drawing area without any length restriction whatsoever. Also, an entire menu full of text-editing commands has been added, all of which may be applied to a single character or paragraph of type.

These and other changes to Illustrator's type-handling capabilities are summarized in the list below. If you know previous versions of Illustrator, these items may be all you need to get up and running. Thorough descriptions of all type capabilities are supplied later in this chapter.

- To create a text block, click in the drawing area with the type tool and enter text from the keyboard, or import text created in a word processor using the IMPORT TEXT... command from the FILE menu.

- To create a column of type, drag in the drawing area or click on an existing closed path with the type tool and enter text from the keyboard, or import text created in a word processor using the IMPORT TEXT... command from the FILE menu.

- To create type on a path, click on an existing open path with the type tool and enter text from the keyboard.

- To add type to an existing text block, click with the type tool at the desired point in the text block and enter the additional text from the keyboard.

- To edit type in an existing text block, drag with the type tool across the type you want to change and enter the corrections from the keyboard.

- To format an existing word of text, double-click with the type tool on the word and choose the desired commands from the TYPE menu.

- To format an entire text block, click with the arrow tool on the point or path associated with the text and choose the desired commands from the TYPE menu.

- To *kern* between two existing characters of type, click with the type tool between the letters and choose the KERN... command from the TYPE menu or press OPTION-← or OPTION-→.

- To raise or lower type in relation to the baseline—to superscript or subscript text or offset it from a free-form path—drag with the type tool across the type to be adjusted and press SHIFT-OPTION-↑ or SHIFT-OPTION-↓. This feature is called *vertical shift*.

- To hyphenate an existing word, click with the type tool at the location of the desired hyphen and press COMMAND-SHIFT-HYPHEN.

- To define the increments by which text may be changed in size, leading, vertical shift, and kerning from the keyboard, choose the PREFERENCES… command (⌘-K) and click the TYPE PREFERENCES… button.

- To change the alignment of an existing paragraph, click with the type tool anywhere in the paragraph and choose an option from the ALIGNMENT pop-up menu.

- To change the dimensions of a column of type, drag the points of the path surrounding the type using the direct-selection tool.

- If a small box containing a plus sign appears on a column of text, more text is contained than is displayed in the column. Such text may be linked to another column by selecting the existing text block and a new path with the arrow tool and choosing the LINK command from the TYPE menu (⌘-⇧-G) or by simply OPTION-dragging the text block with the direct-selection tool. Type that is linked between multiple text blocks is called a *story*.

- To wrap existing text around a graphic image, use the arrow tool to drag the paths that make up the graphic in front of the text block you want to wrap. Choose the BRING TO FRONT command from the EDIT menu if necessary (⌘-=). Then select both text block and graphics and choose the MAKE TEXT WRAP command from the TYPE menu.

- To highlight all type in a story, click with the type tool in one of the text blocks associated with that story and choose the SELECT ALL command from the EDIT menu (⌘-A).

- To convert one or more letters of type into a collection of paths that may be reshaped as described in the previous chapter, select the text block containing the letters with the arrow tool and choose the CREATE OUTLINES command from the TYPE menu.

These operations and much, much more are described throughout the remaining pages of this chapter.

Creating text objects

Type in Illustrator is created and manipulated as a specific kind of element known as a *text object*. As we shall see, text objects are both similar and dissimilar to graphic objects in Illustrator. Their similarity is based on the fact that most of Illustrator's general commands, including those covered in later chapters, may be applied to text objects as easily as they are to graphic objects. Text objects differ from graphic objects in that a special set of tools, commands, and options is used for the creation and alteration of type, which is the primary content of a text object.

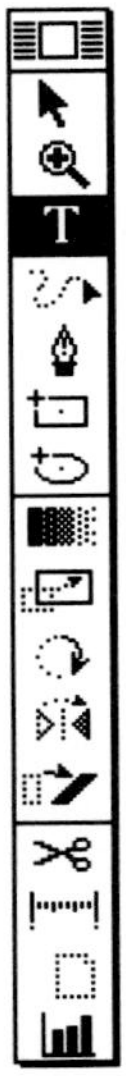

Creating point text

Use the *type tool* to create new text objects in the drawing area. This tool may be used to create type in a number of ways. First and most familiar to users of previous versions of Illustrator, you may click with the type tool at any location in the drawing area. Clicking with the type tool creates the simplest kind of text object, the *point text block* (the first of three varieties of *text blocks*). An *alignment point* will appear as an ×, along with a blinking *insertion marker*. At all times, the insertion marker indicates the location at which type entered from the keyboard will appear in the current text object.

After clicking with the type tool, enter the desired text from your keyboard. Each letter will appear on the screen following the alignment point. The insertion marker will move rightward with the addition of each letter, indicating the location at which the next letter you enter will appear, as shown in the first example of Figure 8.01.

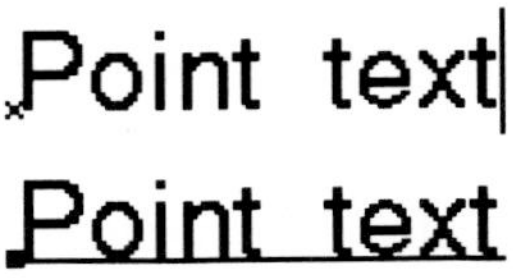

Point text
Point text

Figure 8.01: Point text as it appears when entering text (top) and after selecting a different tool (bottom).

After you have finished entering your text, select another tool in the toolbox or reselect the type tool. The text block will appear selected, as shown in the bottom example in Figure 8.01. The alignment point now appears as a small black box, like a selected point in a geometric or free-form path. You may drag the alignment point with the arrow tool to move the text block in the drawing area, and other dragged objects will snap to this point when your cursor comes within two pixels of it. You may also drag a text block by its *baseline*, the line that runs under each row of type. The baseline is the imaginary straight line on which letters sit. Only a few lowercase characters—*g, j, p, q*, and *y*—descend below the baseline.

To add more text to a block of point text, select the type tool and click on the right-hand side of the last letter in the text block. The baseline vanishes, the alignment point reverts to an ×, and the insertion marker reappears at the location clicked.

When entering text from the keyboard, keys perform the same function they do in a typical word-processing software. Most keys insert the character that appears on the key. Keys that perform other functions include the following:

- **Spacebar**. Inserts a standard space into a text block.
- **Delete**, **backspace**, **escape**, or **clear**. Pressing any of these keys deletes the character to the left of the insertion marker.
- **Caps lock**. Accesses uppercase letters when pressed with letter keys.
- **Shift**. Accesses uppercase letters when pressed with letter keys and special characters printed at the top of number keys.
- **Option**. Accesses special characters—such as £, ¢, ∞, §, ¶—when pressed with letter or number keys.
- **Shift plus option**. Accesses special characters—such as fi, fl, ‡, °—when pressed with letter or number keys.
- **Arrow keys**. ←, ↑, →, or ↓ moves insertion marker inside text block.
- **Tab**. Moves insertion marker along with any text to the right of the marker to opposite side of wrapped graphic. See the section *Wrapping type around graphics* in this chapter for more information.
- **Return** or **enter**. Moves insertion marker along with any text to the right of the marker to the next line of type.

Point text will not *wrap* to a lower row of text on its own. Letters will continue to accumulate to the edge of the drawing area (past which they still exist but are not visible) unless you insert *line breaks* as needed by pressing RETURN or ENTER.

Creating area text

Point text is the simplest kind of text object you can create, making it perfect for headlines, labels, captions, and other varieties of text that contain only a handful of letters. But because words do not wrap to new lines on their own, point text blocks are not well suited to articles longer than a couple of sentences. For long documents, use the second variety of text block, the *area text block*.

In an area text block, type exists inside a geometric or free-form path. The most common path for this purpose is the rectangle, as shown in Figure 8.02. Rectangular columns of type ensure legibility, because readers are very familiar with them. However, you may also place text in unusual shapes, such as the one shown in Figure 8.03. In fact, any path may be filled with type in Illustrator 3.0.

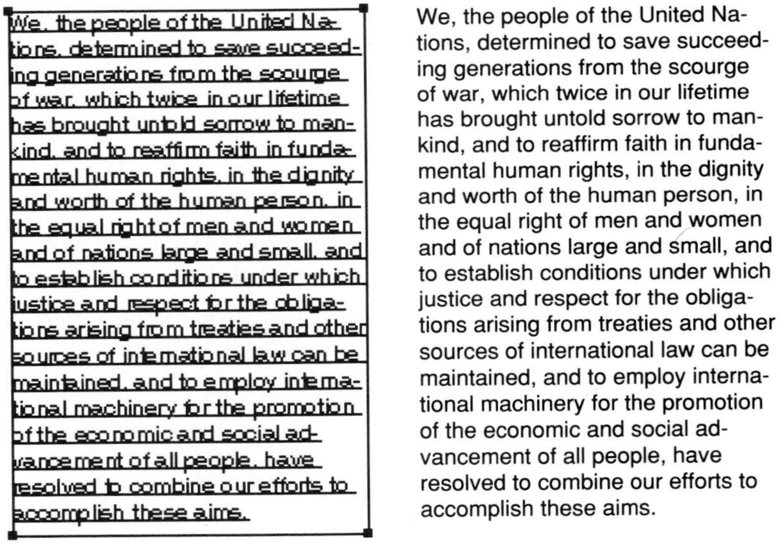

We, the people of the United Nations, determined to save succeeding generations from the scourge of war, which twice in our lifetime has brought untold sorrow to mankind, and to reaffirm faith in fundamental human rights, in the dignity and worth of the human person, in the equal right of men and women and of nations large and small, and to establish conditions under which justice and respect for the obligations arising from treaties and other sources of international law can be maintained, and to employ international machinery for the promotion of the economic and social advancement of all people, have resolved to combine our efforts to accomplish these aims.

Figure 8.02: The most common variety of area type is the rectangular column, shown here as it appears when selected (left) and when printed (right).

To create a column of type, drag with the type tool. One corner of the rectangular column is determined by the point at which you begin dragging; the opposite corner is determined by the point at which you release. After you complete your drag, a rectangle will appear with a blinking insertion marker in the upper left corner. Enter the desired text using your keyboard. Each letter will appear on the screen inside the column. As always, the insertion marker will move rightward with the addition of each letter, indicating the location at which the next letter you enter will appear. If a word threatens to extend beyond the edge of the column, it will automatically wrap to form a new line of type.

After you finish entering text, select another tool in the toolbox or reselect the type tool. The text block will appear selected, as shown in the first example in Figure 8.02. The four points that make up the outline of the rectangle appear as small black dots like selected points in other paths. Baselines underscore the type to indicate that the letters themselves are selected. To reposition the text block, drag at either the rectangular path or one of the baselines with the arrow tool.

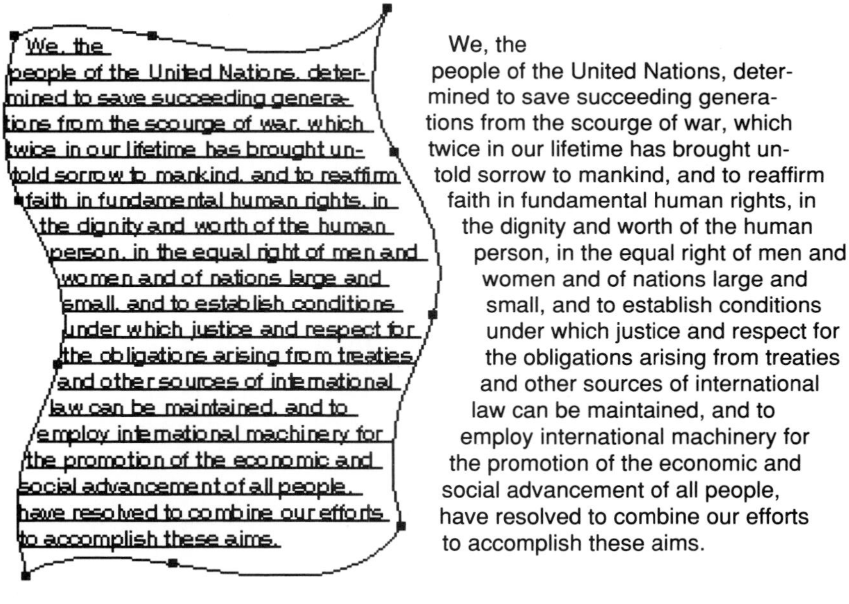

We, the
people of the United Nations, determined to save succeeding generations from the scourge of war, which twice in our lifetime has brought untold sorrow to mankind, and to reaffirm faith in fundamental human rights, in the dignity and worth of the human person, in the equal right of men and women and of nations large and small, and to establish conditions under which justice and respect for the obligations arising from treaties and other sources of international law can be maintained, and to employ international machinery for the promotion of the economic and social advancement of all people, have resolved to combine our efforts to accomplish these aims.

Figure 8.03: A free-form path may also contain text, shown here as it appears when selected (left) and when printed (right).

To create type inside a path, first create the path using one of the geometric path tools or the pen, freehand, or autotrace tool. Your path should be closed. Then select the type tool and position your cursor over some portion of the outline of the path. Your cursor will change from an I-beam surrounded by a rectangular dotted outline to an I-beam surrounded by an oval dotted outline, as shown in Figure 8.04. As soon as this change occurs, click with the type tool. A blinking insertion marker will appear at the top of the path. As you enter text from the keyboard, it will appear inside the path. Words that would otherwise exceed the right edge of the shape will wrap to the next line.

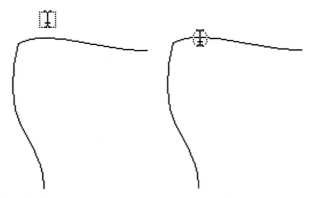

Figure 8.04: Positioning your type tool cursor over the outline of a closed path changes the cursor's appearance from that of the standard type tool (left) to that of the area-type tool (right).

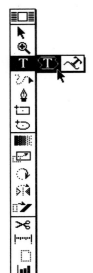

KE Clicking with the type tool on an open path rather than on a closed path creates type on a path (called *path text*), as described in the next section. To create type inside an open path, OPTION-click on the path with the type tool.

If you have difficulty positioning your cursor over a path when first creating an area text block and as a result find yourself inadvertently creating point text, or if you want to create area text in an open path, you may prefer to use the *area-type tool*, which guarantees the creation of an area text block. You may choose this tool, which appears as a letter inside a lumpy shape, by dragging at the type tool slot. You create area text with the area-type tool by clicking on the outline of an existing path (open or closed), just as when using the standard type tool. If you miss the path, however, an error message will appear alerting you of the fact, rather than simply creating a new block of point text as the standard type tool will do.

You may not drag with the area-type tool to create a column of type, as you can with the standard type tool. The area-type tool may be used to click on existing paths only.

 Press the CONTROL key to temporarily access the type tool when the area-type tool is selected. If your keyboard does not provide a CONTROL key, use the Z key instead.

After you finish entering text, select another tool in the toolbox or reselect the type tool to finish the text block. The text block will appear selected, as shown in the first example in Figure 8.03 on page 265. To reposition the text block, drag at the path or one of the baselines with the arrow tool.

Creating path text

The third kind of text block you may create in Illustrator 3.0 is the *path text block*, also called type on a path, in which the baseline of a line of type is fixed to the outline of an existing path, as shown in Figure 8.05 on the following page.

To create type along the outline of a path, first create the path using one of the geometric path tools or the pen, freehand, or autotrace tool. If the path is closed, open it by deleting a segment or clicking on one of its points with the scissors tool. Then select the type tool and position your cursor over some portion of the outline of the path. Your cursor will change from an I-beam surrounded by a rectangular dotted outline to an I-beam bordered by small dotted diagonal lines, as shown in Figure 8.06 on the next page. As soon as this change occurs, click with the type tool. A blinking insertion marker will appear at the point on the outline of the path closest to where you have clicked. As you enter text from the keyboard, it will follow the contours of the path.

 Clicking with the type tool on a closed path rather than on an open path creates area text. To create path text along a closed path, OPTION-click on the path with the type tool.

Like point text, path text is ill-suited to long documents. But ultimately, your path determines the length of your text. When a word exceeds the end of an open path, it disappears from view. Long text will simply wrap around and around a closed path, forcing words to overlap.

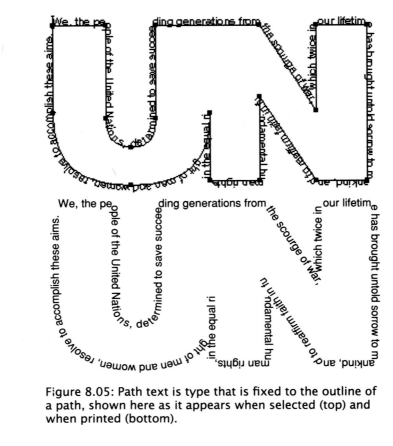

Figure 8.05: Path text is type that is fixed to the outline of a path, shown here as it appears when selected (top) and when printed (bottom).

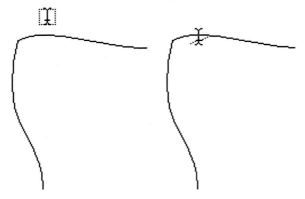

Figure 8.06: Positioning your type tool cursor over the outline of an open path changes the cursor's appearance from that of the standard type tool (left) to that of the path-type tool (right).

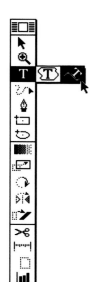

Paths composed exclusively of smooth points—no corners—serve best for creating path text. When type has to flow around a corner, it may interrupt a word, as verified by several instances in Figure 8.05. Illustrator does not keep whole words together in path text. Also, type may overlap inside sharp corners. We avoided this in the figure by inserting spaces to spread overlapping letters apart, but the result still appears rather odd, and frequently illegible.

If you have difficulty positioning your cursor over a path when first creating a path text block and as a result find yourself inadvertently creating point text, or if you want to create path type along a closed path, you may prefer to use the *path-type tool*, which guarantees the creation of path text blocks. You may choose this tool, which appears as a letter on a squiggly line, by dragging at the type tool slot. You create path text with the path-type tool by clicking on the outline of an existing path (open or closed), just as when using the standard type tool. If you miss the path, however, an error message will appear alerting you of the fact, rather than simply creating a new block of point text as the standard type tool will do.

Press the CONTROL key to temporarily access the type tool when the path-type tool is selected. If your keyboard does not provide a CONTROL key, use the Z key instead.

After you finish entering text, select another tool in the toolbox or reselect the type tool to finish the text block. The text block will appear selected, as shown in the first example in Figure 8.05. To reposition the text block, drag at the path or one of the baselines with the arrow tool.

Importing stories

Most of the text you use in Adobe Illustrator will be entered directly in Illustrator. Because the program is not equipped to create documents longer than two letter-sized pages, to import a wide range of graphic types, or to spell-check or hyphenate text blocks, you will rarely use Illustrator to create complete pages or to mix graphics with large amounts of text. However, for those times when long documents (called *stories*) are required, Illustrator allows you to import text documents created in the major brands of word-processing software.

Preparing text

When importing text, Illustrator reads the file from disk and copies it to the current illustration. As this copy is being made, the text file passes through an *import filter* that converts the file's *formatting* commands, which specify typeface (Helvetica, Times), style (plain, bold, italic), and so on, into formatting commands recognizable to Illustrator. Illustrator 3.0 contains import filters for the following text formats:

- Microsoft Word, version 4.0
- RTF (Rich Text Format)
- MacWrite II, version 1.0 and higher
- WriteNow, version 2.0 and higher
- ASCII (plain text, no formatting)

Illustrator will not recognize word-processed files for which an import filter does not exist. If you use a word processor other than Microsoft Word, MacWrite, or WriteNow, try to save the file in one of the first four formats listed above. If your word processor does not support any of these formats, or if you wish to use text created on a different model of computer, like the IBM PC, you may be able to convert the file using a file-conversion utility such as Apple File Exchange from Apple Computer, (408) 996-1010, MacLink from DataViz, (203) 268-0030, or Tops from Sun Microsystems, (415) 769-8700. Short of that, save the file as a text-only or *ASCII* document, which sacrifices all formatting. You will then have to reformat the text in Illustrator, as described in the *Formatting text* section later in this chapter.

Import filters may not be able to convert every formatting attribute correctly from a word-processed file. The following list examines how Illustrator handles the most common formatting attributes and offers a few suggestions about the use of each:

- **Typefaces**. All text will retain the typeface, or *font*, specified in the word processor unless the required typeface is not found, in which case Helvetica is substituted automatically.

- **Type size and leading**. All text will retain the same type size and *leading* (line spacing) specified in the word processor. An automatic leading setting will select the "Auto leading" option in the TYPE dialog box, although the exact amount of leading may differ.

- **Type styles**. Illustrator does not apply type styles in the way used by most word-processing applications. Rather than specifying styles and fonts separately, Illustrator requires that you specify them together by choosing a stylized screen font such as "Helvetica-Bold" or "Helvetica-Oblique." Styles for which stylized screen fonts do not exist—underline, outline, strikethru, small caps, and so on—may not be accessed in Illustrator. Therefore, only bold and italic styles will convert successfully. Superscript and subscripted type will appear in a smaller size, but it will not be raised or lowered in relation to the baseline; in other words, no *vertical shift* will be imported.

- **Alignment**. Illustrator recognizes paragraphs that area aligned left, center, and right, as well as justified.

- **Indents**. All indents, including first-line indents, left indents, right indents, and hanging indents are transferred intact. Adjusting the margins in your word-processing software may also affect the indents of imported paragraphs.

- **Paragraph spacing**. Some word processors divide paragraph spacing into two categories: before spacing, which precedes the paragraph, and after spacing, which follows the paragraph. Illustrator combines them into a single "Leading before ¶" option in the TYPE dialog box, essentially retaining the same effect.

- **Carriage returns**. Each carriage return character (¶, accessed by pressing RETURN or ENTER) in a word-processed document will be successfully converted by Illustrator 3.0, which assumes each carriage return indicates the end of a paragraph. Line break characters (↵) are also converted into carriage returns. Therefore, try not to use carriage returns or line breaks to force breaks within a paragraph unless you intend to import the text into a point text block.

- **Tabs and tab leaders**. Tabs characters convert incorrectly. Because Illustrator does not provide any way to set tab stops, and tabs function correctly only in wrapped text objects (as described in the *Wrapping text around graphics* section later in this chapter), standard spaces are substituted in place of tabs.

- **Special characters**. Word processors provide access to special characters not included in the standard Apple-defined character set (ASCII values 32 through 255). These may include em spaces, non-breaking hyphens, automatic page numbers, and so on. Of these, only the discretionary hyphen character (accessed in Illustrator by pressing COMMAND-SHIFT-HYPHEN) transfers successfully.

- **Page breaks**. Illustrator ignores all page breaks in imported text.

- **Headers, footers, and footnotes**. All of these are ignored as well.

Any formatting options not included in this list are most likely not supported by Illustrator and will therefore be ignored.

Importing text into columns

You may import text into a point text block, an area text block, or a path text block. However, because both point text and path text are so badly suited to long stories (path text does not even support carriage returns), you will probably want to import stories only into area text blocks.

To import a story, select the type tool and click on the closed path inside which you want the text to appear. (If you want to append an imported story inside an existing text block, click at the point in the text where you want to insert the story.) Then choose the IMPORT TEXT... command from the FILE menu to display the PLEASE OPEN DOCUMENT dialog box shown in Figure 8.07. (The IMPORT TEXT... command appears in place of the PLACE ART... command in the FILE menu only after you activate a text block using one of the type tools.)

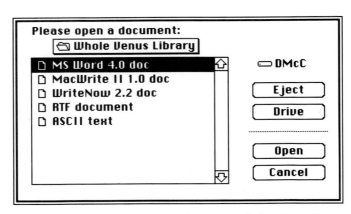

Figure 8.07: The Please open document dialog box allows you to select a story to place into the current Illustrator text block.

To import a story, double-click its name in the scrolling file list, or select the file and click the OPEN button or press RETURN. The DRIVE and EJECT buttons, folder bar, and keyboard equivalents operate in the same way described in the section *Creating a new illustration* in Chapter 3. Click the CANCEL button or press COMMAND-PERIOD to cancel the import operation.

Shortly after confirming a text file, the PLEASE OPEN DOCUMENT dialog box will disappear and the imported story will appear in the current text block. If the story is too long to fit in the current path, a small plus sign is appended to the text block. To display the rest of the story, you may enlarge the path or *flow* the story into additional paths as described in the following section.

Adjusting area text

Like any path-based objects in Adobe Illustrator, area text and path text objects may be adjusted in a variety of ways. For one, the paths in which or on which the text resides may be reshaped, using the arrow tool and the direct-selection tool, to allow more or fewer words to display in a text block. In the case of path text, you may move the text along the path to determine exactly how the text sits. Finally, you may *link* a story over several area text blocks, creating both multi-columned and multi-paged articles. Reshaping, linking, and related topics are explained in the course of the following pages.

Reshaping area text paths

When entering type inside a path, one of three problems may occur resulting from the size and shape of the path:

- The path may be too narrow to accommodate a single word.

- The path may be too small to hold an entire story.

- You may simply dislike the shape of the text block.

When a path is too narrow to hold any one word on a single line, the word is broken onto two lines. A minus sign appears in a small box to the right of the broken word and slightly outside the path, as shown next to the word *determined* in Figure 8.08. This problem generally occurs only if the path is very narrow or the type is very big. To remedy the problem, you may: 1) reduce the size of the type (as described in the *Formatting text* section later in this chapter), 2) manually hyphenate the word by inserting a discretionary hyphen (COMMAND-SHIFT-HYPHEN), or 3) increase the width of the text block.

We, the
people
of the
United
Nations,
determin
ed to

Figure 8.08: A boxed minus sign indicates a word cannot fit on a single line; a boxed plus sign indicates the path is too small to hold the story.

When a path is too small to hold an entire story, the words that exceed the lowest segment in the path disappear from view. Such a path is called an *overflow text block*. A plus sign appears in a small box slightly outside the lower right corner of the path, also shown in Figure 8.08. Because stories may be very long, this problem occurs fairly frequently. To remedy the problem, you may: 1) reduce the size of the type to allow more text to fit in the path, 2) edit the text until it fits in the path, 3) enlarge the path until all text is visible, or 4) *flow* the text into multiple paths (as described in the *Flowing area text* section later in this chapter).

Reshaping a path allows you to fix long words on a single line, include more or less text in a path, or simply change the appearance of a block of area text. To reshape any text object, you must use the direct-selection tool to select the path without selecting the text. The following steps describe how to reshape a rectangular column of type.

1. After creating or editing a text block, choose the direct-selection tool from the arrow tool slot. The path will appear selected, as shown in Figure 8.09.

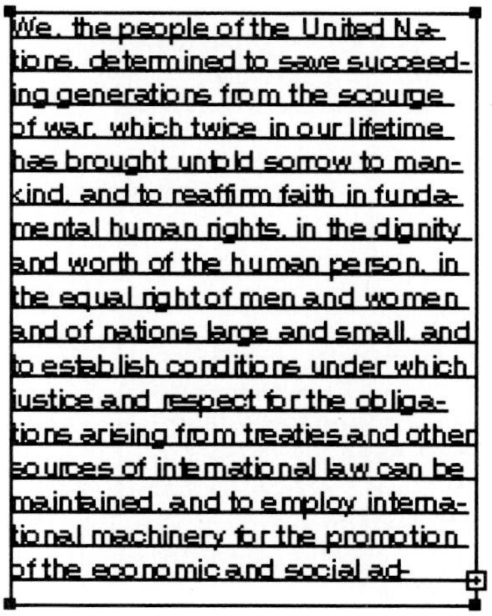

Figure 8.09: Text and path appear selected when you initially choose the direct-selection tool after enter the text.

2. Click on an empty portion of the drawing area to deselect the text block.

3. Click on a segment of the path you wish to reshape. Make sure you click between two lines of text so that you don't click a baseline and select the text inside the path. The path will appear selected and the text will appear deselected, as shown in Figure 8.10.

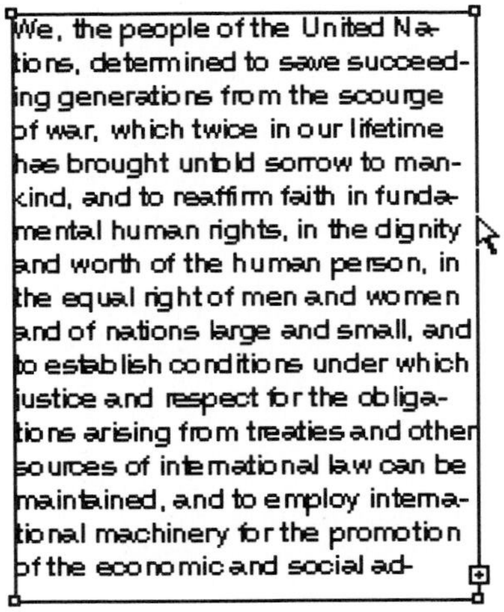

We, the people of the United Nations, determined to save succeeding generations from the scourge of war, which twice in our lifetime has brought untold sorrow to mankind, and to reaffirm faith in fundamental human rights, in the dignity and worth of the human person, in the equal right of men and women and of nations large and small, and to establish conditions under which justice and respect for the obligations arising from treaties and other sources of international law can be maintained, and to employ international machinery for the promotion of the economic and social ad-

Figure 8.10: Clicking on the deselected path with the direct-selection tool selects the path without selecting its type.

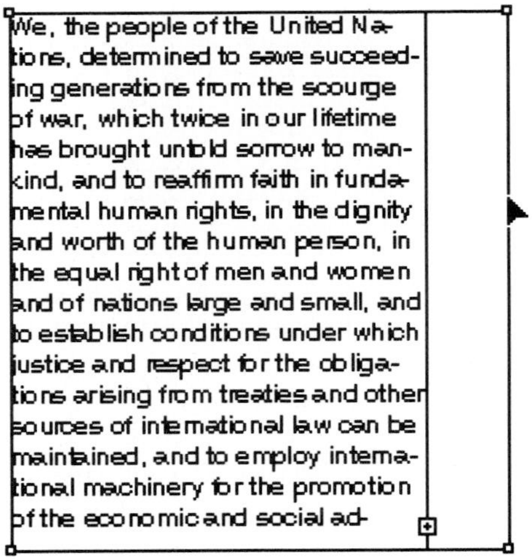

We, the people of the United Nations, determined to save succeeding generations from the scourge of war, which twice in our lifetime has brought untold sorrow to mankind, and to reaffirm faith in fundamental human rights, in the dignity and worth of the human person, in the equal right of men and women and of nations large and small, and to establish conditions under which justice and respect for the obligations arising from treaties and other sources of international law can be maintained, and to employ international machinery for the promotion of the economic and social ad-

Figure 8.11: Shift-drag a vertical segment to widen the text block.

4. To widen the text block, drag one of the vertical segments away from the text, as shown in Figure 8.11. To retain the rectangular proportions of the column, press the SHIFT key while dragging to constrain your move.

5. To lengthen the text block, drag one of the horizontal segments. Press SHIFT to constrain your drag along the vertical axis.

6. To distort the text block, drag a segment without pressing the SHIFT key. You may also drag a point, as shown in Figure 8.12.

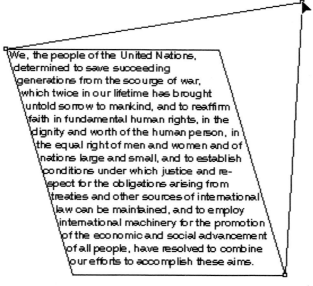

Figure 8.12: Drag a point in a rectangular text path to distort the text block.

You may reshape an area text path using most of the techniques discussed in Chapter 7, *Reshaping Existing Paths*. In addition to moving points and segments by dragging, pressing arrow keys, or using the MOVE dialog box, you may drag Bézier control handles; extend an open path using the pen, freehand, and autotrace tools; alter points with the add-point, delete-point, and convert-point tools; split segments in a closed path with the scissors tool; join the two endpoints of the same path with the JOIN... command; and average points with the AVERAGE... command.

Some reshaping techniques, however, are not applicable to text paths. These include the following:

- You may not split an open text path into two separate paths using the scissors tool.

- You may not join an open text path to a separate open path using the JOIN… command.

- You may not use the delete-point tool or the DELETE key to delete a point from a text path that contains only two points.

- You may not select a segment in an open path and press the DELETE key, although you may delete a segment from an open path, the result of which is shown in Figure 8.13. Also, you may not delete the entire path if it is the only path for that text block.

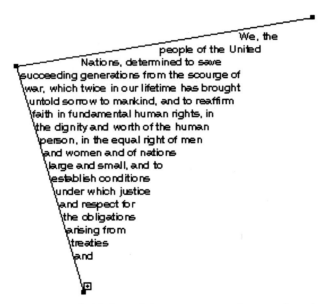

Figure 8.13: You delete a segment from a closed path to create an open path filled with text.

You may similarly reshape a path associated with path text, as discussed in the section *Reshaping path text* later in this chapter.

Flowing area text

If a story contains more than a couple of paragraphs, you will probably want to do more than simply reshape it to make the entire story visible in the drawing area. Long stories may be *flowed* across multiple text blocks to create multiple columns or even multiple pages of text. Figure 8.14 displays a story that is flowed between three paths. Such a flowed story is called a *linked object*, because each text block in the story is linked to another.

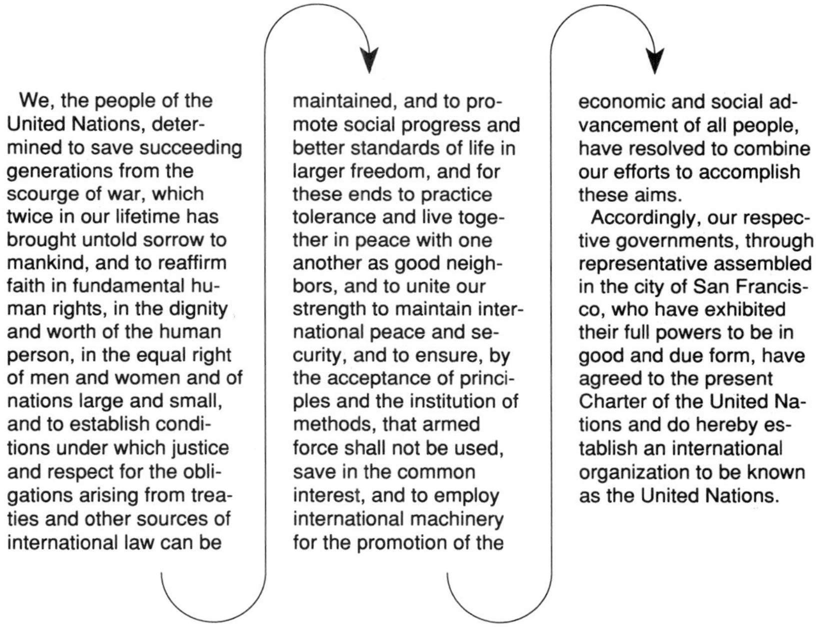

We, the people of the United Nations, determined to save succeeding generations from the scourge of war, which twice in our lifetime has brought untold sorrow to mankind, and to reaffirm faith in fundamental human rights, in the dignity and worth of the human person, in the equal right of men and women and of nations large and small, and to establish conditions under which justice and respect for the obligations arising from treaties and other sources of international law can be

maintained, and to promote social progress and better standards of life in larger freedom, and for these ends to practice tolerance and live together in peace with one another as good neighbors, and to unite our strength to maintain international peace and security, and to ensure, by the acceptance of principles and the institution of methods, that armed force shall not be used, save in the common interest, and to employ international machinery for the promotion of the

economic and social advancement of all people, have resolved to combine our efforts to accomplish these aims.

Accordingly, our respective governments, through representative assembled in the city of San Francisco, who have exhibited their full powers to be in good and due form, have agreed to the present Charter of the United Nations and do hereby establish an international organization to be known as the United Nations.

Figure 8.14: A single story flowed between three area text blocks.

You may link a text block in one of two ways. The first is the simplest. It also provides the advantage of guaranteeing that all columns are the same size. First choose the direct-selection tool and OPTION-click the path of an area text block that displays a boxed plus sign. This selects the entire path without selecting the text inside. Next, begin dragging the path to a new location that does not overlap the current path, as demonstrated in Figure 8.15. While still dragging, press the OPTION key, release the mouse button, then release the OPTION key. This creates a *clone* of the first path (as discussed in the *Cloning objects* section of Chapter 12). The clone is automatically filled with the overflow type from the first path, as shown in

Figure 8.16. If this new path also displays a boxed plus sign, additional text still exists. Choose the TRANSFORM AGAIN command from the EDIT menu (⌘-D). A third path will be created the same distance and direction from the second path as the second path is from the first. Continue choosing this command until no plus sign displays outside the newest text block.

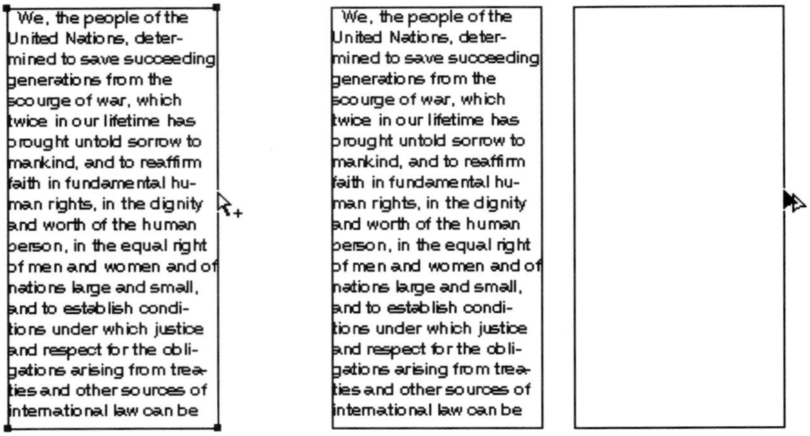

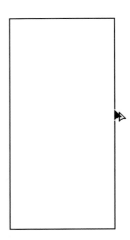

We, the people of the
United Nations, deter-
mined to save succeeding
generations from the
scourge of war, which
twice in our lifetime has
brought untold sorrow to
mankind, and to reaffirm
faith in fundamental hu-
man rights, in the dignity
and worth of the human
person, in the equal right
of men and women and of
nations large and small,
and to establish condi-
tions under which justice
and respect for the obli-
gations arising from treaties and other sources of
international law can be
We, the people of the
United Nations, deter-
mined to save succeeding
generations from the
scourge of war, which
twice in our lifetime has
brought untold sorrow to
mankind, and to reaffirm
faith in fundamental hu-
man rights, in the dignity
and worth of the human
person, in the equal right
of men and women and of
nations large and small,
and to establish condi-
tions under which justice
and respect for the obli-
gations arising from treaties and other sources of
international law can be

Figure 8.15: Option-click the path of an overflow text block to select the entire path without selecting its text (left); then option-drag the path to a new location in the drawing area (right)

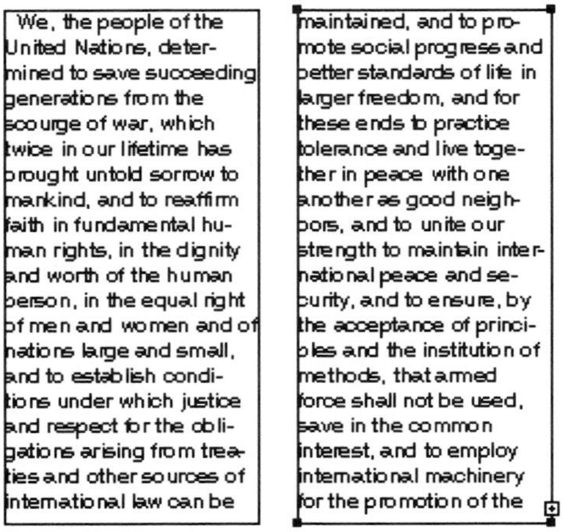

We, the people of the
United Nations, deter-
mined to save succeeding
generations from the
scourge of war, which
twice in our lifetime has
brought untold sorrow to
mankind, and to reaffirm
faith in fundamental hu-
man rights, in the dignity
and worth of the human
person, in the equal right
of men and women and of
nations large and small,
and to establish condi-
tions under which justice
and respect for the obli-
gations arising from treaties and other sources of
international law can be
maintained, and to pro-
mote social progress and
better standards of life in
larger freedom, and for
these ends to practice
tolerance and live toge-
ther in peace with one
another as good neigh-
bors, and to unite our
strength to maintain international peace and se-
curity, and to ensure, by
the acceptance of princi-
ples and the institution of
methods, that armed
force shall not be used,
save in the common
interest, and to employ
international machinery
for the promotion of the

Figure 8.16: The overflow text from the first path flows into the new, cloned path.

You may also clone a path, and hence flow a story into an additional text block, by choosing the Move… command from the Edit menu and clicking the Copy button in the Move dialog box. Or you may choose the Copy command from the Edit menu (⌘-C) and then choose Paste In Front (⌘-F) to create a duplicate filled with overflow type directly in front of the original path. All of these commands are discussed in detail in Chapter 12, *Transforming and Duplicating Objects*.

If, after flowing all the text in a story, you click any one of the paths with the standard arrow tool, all text blocks associated with the story will become selected, as will their contents. This indicates that all text blocks are linked. You may manipulate individual paths in a linked object using the direct-selection tool.

The second way to link text blocks involves using the Link command in the Type menu (⌘-⇧-G). First select the path of an overflow text block, either with the direct-selection tool or the arrow tool. Then press SHIFT and click on a second existing path—one that does *not* currently contain text—to add it to the selection. Press SHIFT and click on as many additional paths as you think will be required to contain the current story. Then choose the Link command. All paths will fill with as much overflow type as is available, as shown in Figure 8.17.

maintained, and to promote social progress and better standards of life in larger freedom, and for these ends to practice tolerance and live together in peace with one another as good neighbors, and to unite our strength to maintain international peace and security, and to ensure, by the acceptance of principles and the institution of methods, that armed force shall not be used, save in the common interest, and to employ international machinery for the promotion of the

economic and social advancement of all people, have resolved to combine our efforts to accomplish these aims.

Accordingly, our respective governments, through representative assembled in the city of San Francisco, who have exhibited their full powers to be in good and due form, have agreed to the present Charter of the United Nations and do hereby establish an international organization to be known as the United Nations.

We, the people of the United Nations, determined to save succeeding generations from the scourge of war, which twice in our lifetime has brought untold sorrow to mankind, and to reaffirm faith in fundamental human rights, in the dignity and worth of the human person, in the equal right of men and women and of nations large and small, and to establish conditions under which justice and respect for the obligations arising from treaties and other sources of international law can be

Figure 8.17: Choose the Link command to fill all selected paths with a single story. The story flows in the order that the paths are layered.

※ To create evenly sized, evenly spaced rectangular columns of type, you may want to establish a series of guide lines, as described in the *Creating guides* section of Chapter 12. You may also use the AVERAGE… command to even up the tops and bottom of text blocks, as described in the *Why average points?* section of Chapter 7.

Reflowing a story

Regardless of how it was created, a story flows through a linked text object in the order that its paths are layered (as discussed in the *Layering objects* section of Chapter 12), starting with the rearmost path and working its way forward. This is known as the *linking order.* In Figure 8.17, the right path is the rear path, the middle path is the front path, and the left path is in between. Therefore, the story starts in the right path, flows into the left path, and ends in the middle path; despite the fact that the story started in the left path before the LINK was chosen.

If you want to rearrange the order in which a story flows, you may relayer the paths in the linked object by following these steps:

1. Click an empty portion of the drawing area to deselect the paths.

2. Using the direct-selection tool, select the path that you want to act as the first text block in the story. Choose the SEND TO BACK command from the EDIT menu (⌘-–; that is, COMMAND-HYPHEN).

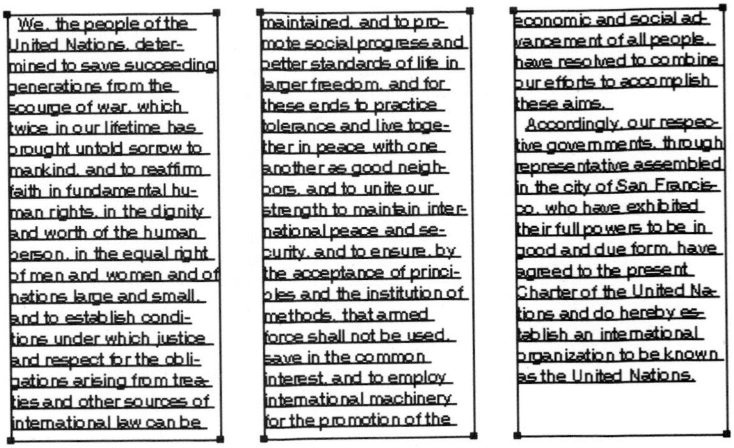

Figure 8.18: Layering and relinking a story reflows it in the correct order.

3. Press SHIFT and click the path that will act as the second text block in the story, adding it to the selection. Choose SEND TO BACK again.

4. Keep adding one path after another to the selection in sequential order, choosing SEND TO BACK after the addition of each path.

5. When all but the last path have been sent to the back of the current illustration, SHIFT-click the last path and again choose the LINK command from the TYPE menu (⌘-⇧-G). The story is reflowed in the selected paths, as demonstrated in Figure 8.18.

Unlike a grouped object, which can be grouped within other groups, a single linked object may not be linked more than once. Therefore, applying the LINK command to an already linked object does not double-link it; it simply reflows the story.

Other ways to reflow text inside a linked object include the following:

- Reduce the size of a path in the linked object to flow text out of that path and into the next path in the linking order.

- Enlarge the size of a path in the linked object to flow text into that path and out of the next path in the linking order.

- Delete a path in the linked object by OPTION-clicking the path with the direct-selection tool and pressing DELETE or BACKSPACE to flow all text out of that path and into the next path in the linking order.

We, the people of the United Nations, determined to save succeeding generations from the scourge of war, which twice in our lifetime has brought untold sorrow to mankind, and to reaffirm faith in fundamental human rights, in the dignity and worth of the human person, in the equal right of men and women and of nations large and small, and to establish conditions under which justice and respect for the obligations arising from treaties and other sources of international law can be

maintained, and to promote social progress and better standards of life in larger freedom, and for these ends to practice tolerance and live together in peace with one another as good neighbors, and to unite our strength to maintain international peace and security, and to ensure, by the acceptance of principles and the institution of methods, that armed force shall not be used, save in the common interest, and to employ international machinery for the promotion of the

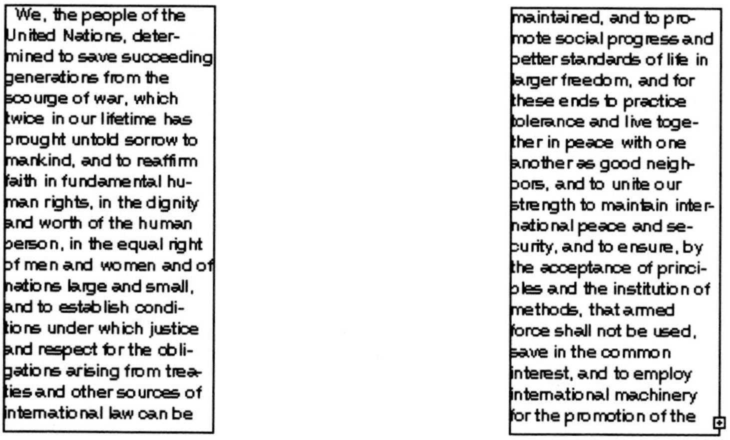

Figure 8.19: Deleting the middle path reflows the text into the last path.

Figure 8.19 on the previous page demonstrates the effect of deleting the middle path from Figure 8.18. Notice that all of its text flows into the last column. The text from the last column now becomes overflow text. (You may not delete a path if it is the only path in the story.)

Deleting a text block from a story

Deleting a path from a linked object reflows the story. But if you select an entire text block, both path and text, and then delete it, you subtract that portion of the text from your story. You may select an entire text block, independently of other text blocks in a linked object, in one of two ways:

- Click on the baseline of one of the lines of type in the text block with the direct-selection tool.

- OPTION-double-click on the path of the text block with the direct-selection tool.

In either case, both path and text will be selected, as shown in Figure 8.20. Pressing DELETE under this circumstance will delete text and path from the story. The remaining paths will remain linked.

We, the people of the United Nations, determined to save succeeding generations from the scourge of war, which twice in our lifetime has brought untold sorrow to mankind, and to reaffirm faith in fundamental human rights, in the dignity and worth of the human person, in the equal right of men and women and of nations large and small, and to establish conditions under which justice and respect for the obligations arising from treaties and other sources of international law can be

maintained, and to promote social progress and better standards of life in larger freedom, and for these ends to practice tolerance and live together in peace with one another as good neighbors, and to unite our strength to maintain international peace and security, and to ensure, by the acceptance of principles and the institution of methods, that armed force shall not be used, save in the common interest, and to employ international machinery for the promotion of the

economic and social advancement of all people, have resolved to combine our efforts to accomplish these aims.

Accordingly, our respective governments, through representative assembled in the city of San Francisco, who have exhibited their full powers to be in good and due form, have agreed to the present Charter of the United Nations and do hereby establish an international organization to be known as the United Nations.

Figure 8.20: Option-double-click its path to select a single whole text block within a story.

Press SHIFT and click the baseline of one of the lines of type in a selected text block to deselect the text while leaving the path selected. You may then press DELETE to delete the path and reflow the text as described in the previous section.

Unlinking text blocks

 To unlink text blocks in a linked object, choose the UNLINK command from the TYPE menu (⌘-⇧-U). Choosing this command isolates the paths so that each text block is its own story. Use this command only when you are happy with the way text appears in each column of type, and you want to prevent it from reflowing under any circumstance. (To reflow type, do *not* choose UNLINK, make changes, and choose LINK, as the Illustrator manual suggests. Simply make your changes with the direct-selection tool and reapply the LINK command without choosing UNLINK, as described in the previous section; the results are more predictable.)

Adjusting path text

Like an area text block, a path text block may be adjusted to change the way its type is displayed. However, certain different rules apply. For example, you may not flow path text onto another path. Nor may you create a block of path type that is more than a single line long (although that line may be as long and winding as you like). But with these limitations come opportunities. Path text includes an *I-beam handle* that may be dragged to determine the point at which type is aligned on the path. If the handle is flipped, the type will also flip to the underside of the path. Also, multiple path text blocks may be combined to create special effects.

Reshaping path text paths

When entering type along a path, you may encounter many of the same problems as when entering type inside a path. If the path is too short to accommodate all its text, for example, a plus sign will appear in a small box located on the last point in the path, as shown in Figure 8.21 on the next page. In path text blocks, Illustrator makes no distinction between a single word that cannot fit and an entire story. Since path type cannot wrap to a second line, it either fits on the path or it doesn't.

Figure 8.21: Any amount of overflow text will prompt the boxed plus sign to appear in a block of path type. Type may break in the middle of a word, as shown here.

Because you cannot flow path text onto another path, you have only three choices for fixing the appearance of type along an inadequate path: 1) reduce the size of the type (as described in the *Formatting text* section later in this chapter), 2) edit the text down until it fits on the path, or 3) lengthen the path until all text is visible.

To lengthen a path of path text , you may drag both segments and points with the direct-selection tool in any manner that you desire. After each drag, the text will refit to the path, keeping you informed of your progress. Suppose, for example, that you want to lengthen the lower line shown in Figure 8.21. The following steps demonstrate a few reshaping methods:

1. Using the direct-selection tool, drag the right endpoint as shown in Figure 8.22. The type will immediately refit to the path, as shown in Figure 8.23.

Figure 8.22: Drag the endpoint of an open path independently of its type, using the direct-selection tool.

Figure 8.23: The type refits to the path immediately following the drag.

2. Notice that the line no longer curves as fluidly nor as symmetrically as it did in Figure 8.21. Dragging an endpoint initially results in less pleasing paths. To compensate, drag down on the right segment or adjust the Bézier control handles as shown, in Figure 8.24.

Figure 8.24: You may also move the Bézier control handles of a path text block using the direct-selection tool.

3. If your path needs to be lengthened dramatically, you may prefer to use one of the drawing tools. In this case, use the pen tool to lengthen the path. Drag up and to the right from the right-hand endpoint to activate the path. Then drag at desired locations to create additional smooth points. With the addition of each segment, more and more text will become visible until, eventually, no overflow text remains. The boxed plus sign will disappear to verify that the path is now long enough to accommodate its text, as shown in Figure 8.25 on the next page.

You may also add points, delete points, convert points, and split segments (in a closed path only) using the tools available from the scissors tool slot. However, the same restrictions apply to reshaping path text as apply to area text (refer to the list on page 278).

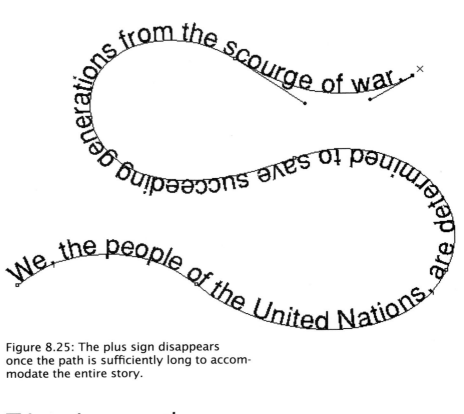

Figure 8.25: The plus sign disappears once the path is sufficiently long to accommodate the entire story.

Trimming a path

But what if instead of being to short, your path is too long? Certainly you can enlarge the type size, edit the text so it's longer, or decrease the dimensions of a closed path. But what if you want to simply trim a little slack off the end of the path? You can't split it off using the scissors tool, because Illustrator won't allow you to split any open path associated with a text object into two separate paths.

Normally, you don't need to worry about excess path. As shown if Figure 8.26, the path is hidden by default when previewing or printing an illustration. Only if you want to *stroke* the path separately of its text—as described in Chapter 10, *Stroking Type and Graphic Objects*—does shortening a path become an issue.

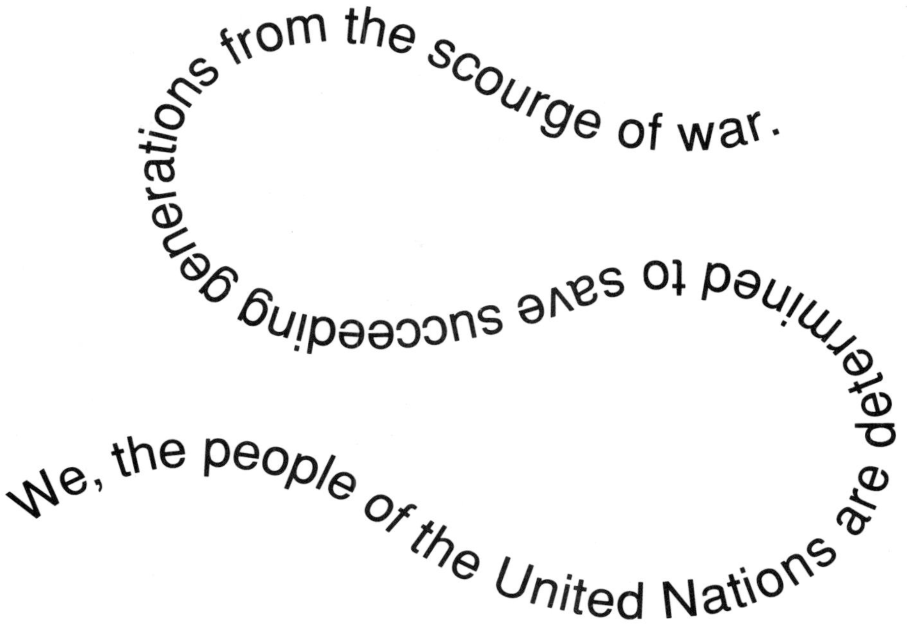

from the scourge of war.

generations

We, the people of the United Nations are determined to save succeeding generations

Figure 8.26: The path text block from the previous figure as it appears when printed.

If you do intend to stroke your path, follow these steps to trim away any excess segments:

1. Click at the point at which you want the path to end with the add-point tool (or OPTION-click with the scissors tool), as shown in Figure 8.27.

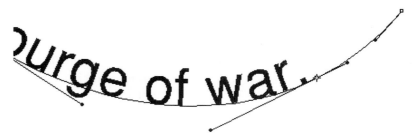

Figure 8.27: Insert a point at the location where you'd like the path to end (just to the right of the period).

2. Select all points beyond the newly added point with the direct-selection tool, as shown in Figure 8.28. (Do not select the added point itself.)

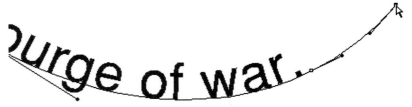

Figure 8.28: Select all points to the right of the newly added point.

3. Press DELETE or BACKSPACE. The selected points and their segments will disappear, making the added point the new endpoint.

Moving type along its path

When both path and type are selected in a block of path text—by clicking the path with the arrow tool or OPTION-double-clicking with the direct-selection tool—a special *I-beam handle* displays, as shown in Figure 8.29. This handle allows you to adjust the placement of the story on its path in any of the following ways:

- Drag the handle with the arrow or direct-selection tool to slide the text back and forth on its path.

- Drag the handle across the path to flip the text to the other side of the path, causing it to change directions.

- Double-click the handle to flip the text to the other side of the path, causing it to change directions.

Using the I-beam handle is a straightforward process. Suppose, for example, that you want to adjust the type shown in Figure 8.29. The following exercise demonstrates how this might work:

1. Select the path text block with the arrow tool to display the I-beam handle. The current position of the I-beam is determined by the location at which you clicked on the path with the type tool or path-type tool when you originally created the text block.

We, the people of the United Nations...

Figure 8.29: The I-beam handle (on the left end of the path) displays when the whole path text block is selected.

2. Drag the handle to some random position in the middle of the path, such as the position shown in Figure 8.30. As you drag, the new position of type will appear to overlap the original position, making the text illegible. After you release, the original position will disappear, allowing you to easily view the results of your adjustment. If your story no longer fits on the path, as in Figure 8.30, a boxed plus sign will appear over the endpoint.

We, the people of the U

Figure 8.30: Drag the I-beam handle to move the text toward the middle of the path.

3. Drag the type back to the left endpoint in the path until your cursor snaps into place, as demonstrated in Figure 8.31 by the hollow cursor. Generally, you will want your text to begin at the left endpoint in an open path to take fullest advantage of the path.

We, the people We the people of the U

Figure 8.31: Drag the handle back to the left endpoint in the path until it snaps.

4. Now drag the handle down to the other side of the path. A copy of the text will flip to face the opposite direction, as shown in Figure 8.32. Drag the handle to the middle of the path so that there is enough room to display some text. If any overflow type exists, the boxed plus sign will appear on the endpoint opposite its usual location, as shown below.

Figure 8.32: Drag the handle across the path to flip the text. The boxed plus sign now appears on the left endpoint.

5. Double-click the I-beam handle. The type will immediately jump to the opposite side of the path. The location of the handle relative to the path, however, will remain constant. In Figure 8.33, for example, the handle merely scoots to the other side of the path.

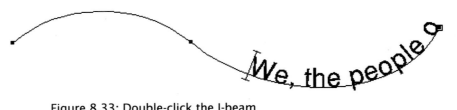

Figure 8.33: Double-click the I-beam handle to flip the text across the path. The boxed plus sign also flips to the opposite endpoint.

You may display the I-beam handle only by clicking on the path of the text block. Do not try to click at the location where you expect the handle to be when the text block is not selected.

Moving type up and down on the path

When you flip text across a path by dragging or double-clicking the I-beam handle, you also flip the direction of the text when you move it to the other side of the path. But what if you want to move the text without flipping its direction? This is a job for *vertical shift*. In Illustrator, vertical shift is a formatting feature that allows you to raise or lower type with respect to the baseline. Since the baseline of path text is the path itself, vertical shift allows you to raise and lower type with respect to the path.

You may access vertical shift by selecting text and choosing the STYLE... command from the TYPE menu (⌘-T). However, the easiest way, especially when adjusting type along a path, is to press the SHIFT and OPTION keys along with the up and down arrow keys. Press SHIFT-OPTION-↑ to raise the selected type; press SHIFT-OPTION-↓ to lower selected type. The following exercise demonstrates how this feature might be applied:

1. Suppose that you want to create the "Mastering Adobe Illustrator" type displayed at the beginning of each chapter. Begin by drawing a circle with the oval tool. Make the circle about three inches in diameter.

2. Select the type tool. Position the tool over the topmost point in the path so that the cursor changes to that of the area-type tool. Press the OPTION key to display the path-type tool cursor and click.

3. Type the word *MASTERING*, in capital letters.

4. Press COMMAND-A to highlight the text. Choose the STYLE... command from the TYPE menu to format the text (as explained in the *Formatting text* section, later in this chapter). Our type is 40-point Helvetica Inserat, but you can choose anything you want, so long as it's remotely similar. Press RETURN to exit the TYPE STYLE dialog box.

5. Press COMMAND-SHIFT-C to center the type on the path. (Alignment is also discussed in the *Formatting text* section.)

6. Click on the path with the arrow tool. Press OPTION and drag the I-beam handle for the text block around to the bottom point in the path; then, without releasing, drag it across the path. Be sure to release the OPTION key *after* releasing the mouse button. A clone of the type moves and flips to the interior of the circle, as shown in Figure 8.34.

Figure 8.34: Option-drag the type to the inside, bottom portion of the circle.

7. Click inside the cloned text with the type tool. Press COMMAND-A. Type *ADOBE ILLUSTRATOR* in capital letters, replacing the highlighted text, as shown in Figure 8.35.

Figure 8.35: Enter new text for the cloned type.

8. The upper and lower text blocks do not align properly. You need to move the lower text outward to the outer edge of the path, without flipping it. While the blinking insertion marker still appears

in the text, press COMMAND-A to highlight the lower text block.
Since you want to lower the type with respect to its path, press
SHIFT-OPTION-↓ to move the type downward. Notice it scoot
slightly? It moves only two points. After pressing SHIFT-OPTION-↓ a
total of eight times, your text will appear as shown in Figure 8.36.

Figure 8.36: Highlight the lower text block and
press shift-option-↓ eight times.

9. Now click in the upper text block with the type tool and press COM-
MAND-A to highlight it. Press SHIFT-OPTION-↓ eight more times to
achieve the result shown in Figure 8.37 on the following page.

Figure 8.38 displays the finished text as it appears when printed. To
add the bullets shown in the chapter heads, we added bullet characters
(⌥-8) to the beginning and end of the upper text block. Some additional
vertical shifting was required to match the placement of the bullets to that
of the upper and lower text blocks.

If you click on the circle with the arrow tool, you will notice that two
I-beam handles display. This is not because both lines of type adhere to the
same path, as you might expect. In fact, no more than one text block may
be fitted to a path in Illustrator 3.0. Instead, Illustrator automatically
grouped the two paths when you created the clone, assuming that you
wanted to manipulate the two paths together in any future transformation.

Figure 8.37: Highlight the upper text block and press shift-option-↓ eight times again.

Figure 8.38: The two text blocks as they appear when printed.

Each time you press SHIFT-OPTION-↓, you moved the type downward two points. Altogether, you moved the upper and lower text blocks 16 points each. Therefore, 32 points of vertical shift was required to align two blocks of 40-point text.

As a rule of thumb, when creating type along a circle, figure on shifting type a total of 70 to 80 percent of the point size to move the baselines into alignment.

Unlike in FreeHand, you may not alter the orientation of type on a path. In other words, you may not create text that is at all times vertically oriented despite the shape of the path, as shown in Figure 8.38. If this was an option in Illustrator, you could create cool dimensional effects, like the type around a globe shown in Figure 8.39. Alas, you will have to use FreeHand to achieve this effect.

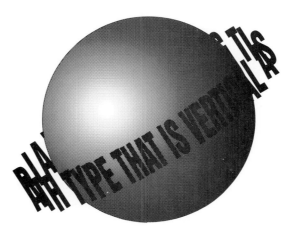

Figure 8.38: Aldus FreeHand allows you to create type that remains vertical as it goes around a path. Illustrator should offer this feature, but does not.

Figure 8.39: Vertically oriented type can be useful for creating type around a globe. If you want to create this effect, you must use FreeHand.

Don't start thinking you bought the wrong software, though. In all other ways, Illustrator's path-type feature outscores FreeHand's. You may edit the text directly on screen, you may adjust the placement of the type simply by dragging a handle, and Illustrator automatically *tracks* type along a path to ensure consistent spacing between letters. In FreeHand, you have to kern characters manually to eliminate inconsistent and amateurish letter spacing.

Formatting text

Text editing features can be broken into two categories: those that are applied to characters of type and those that are applied to whole paragraphs. It is important to understand the distinction and to know which features fall into which category to properly apply formatting commands.

- **Character-level formatting** includes options such as typeface, size, leading, kerning (or tracking), vertical shift, and horizontal scaling. To change the formatting of one or more characters, you first select the specific characters and then apply the desired options. Only the selected characters will be modified.

- **Paragraph-level formatting** includes indentation, alignment, paragraph spacing, letter spacing, and word spacing. To change the formatting of a single paragraph, you need only position the blinking insertion marker inside that paragraph. To change the formatting of multiple paragraphs, select at least one character in each of the paragraphs you want to modify.

You may also change character-level or paragraph-level formatting for a new text block before typing it. After clicking with the type tool in the drawing area or on the outline of an existing path, specify the desired formatting options and then begin typing.

To alter the *default formatting options* for an illustration, specify the desired options while no text block is active; that is, the blinking insertion marker does not appear anywhere on screen, nor is any text *highlighted* (white against a black background in the artwork-and-template display mode). Default formatting changes will apply to all future text blocks. Existing text blocks will remain unaffected.

Selecting and editing text

Text may be selected in Illustrator using the arrow tool or one of the type tools. Clicking on a text block with the arrow tool selects all type in the object. Any formatting changes will therefore affect all characters. By selecting multiple text blocks with the arrow tool, you may format multiple text objects.

If you select text with a type tool, you may only format text within a single text object. However, you may also select individual characters and paragraphs of type, something that may not be accomplished using the arrow tool.

The following items explain how any type tool may be used to select type in any text object:

- Drag over the characters that you want to select. Drag to the left or to the right to select characters on the same line of type; drag upward or downward to select characters on multiple lines; and drag across columns in a linked object to select large portions of a story, as shown in Figure 8.40. The selected text will become *highlighted*, white against a black background.

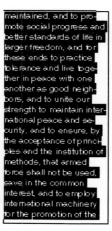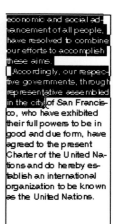

Figure 8.40: Drag across columns in a linked text object with the type tool to select large portions of a story.

- Double-click on a word to select that word. Hold down the mouse button on the second click and drag to select additional words.

- Triple-click inside a paragraph to select that paragraph. Hold down the mouse button on the third click and drag to select additional paragraphs.

- Click to set the insertion marker at one end of the text you want to select, then SHIFT-click at the opposite end of the desired selection. All text between the first click and the SHIFT-click will become highlighted.

- Click anywhere in a text block and choose SELECT ALL from the EDIT menu (⌘-A) to select all text in the current story, including type linked to the current text block.

- Click to set the insertion marker at one end of the text you want to select and extend the selection using the following keyboard equivalents:

To extend selection	Keystroke
One character to the left	⇧-←
One character to the right	⇧-→
One word to the left	⌘-⇧-←
One word to the right	⌘-⇧-→
One line up	⇧-↑
One line down	⇧-↓
To beginning of paragraph	⌘-⇧-↑
To end of paragraph	⌘-⇧-↓

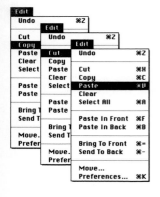

Highlighted text may be formatted, as discussed in the following pages, or replaced by entering new text from the keyboard. You may also delete selected text by pressing the DELETE or BACKSPACE key. You may copy selected text to the Macintosh Clipboard by choosing the COPY command from the EDIT menu (⌘-C). Or you may delete the selected text and at the same time send a copy to the Clipboard by choosing CUT from the EDIT menu (⌘-X). Finally, you may replace the selected text with some type that you copied earlier to the Clipboard by choosing PASTE from the EDIT menu (⌘-V). Paste text always retains its original character formatting, although it will assume the paragraph-level formatting of the paragraph into which it is pasted.

 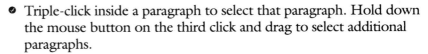

The hierarchical pop-up menus

The commands used to format type are included in the TYPE menu. Near the top of the menu are four hierarchical pop-up menus that allow you to quickly choose a typeface, size, leading, and alignment. To use any of these pop-up menus, press and hold the mouse button on the desired command and the pop-up menu will display to the right or left of the TYPE menu (depending on available screen space), listing available options. Drag your cursor horizontally onto the pop-up menu and then drag vertically to choose the desired option. If the pop-up menu is not completely displayed, arrows will indicate that more options are available by scrolling the menu up or down. The currently selected option will be noted with a check mark. If the currently selected text is not formatted to a uniform option, no check mark will display. An option is chosen by highlighting it and releasing the mouse button, just as with any other menu command.

Choosing a font

The FONT command brings up a pop-up menu listing all *fonts* (typefaces) you have used during the current Illustrator session. Choosing a font option designates both the typeface and type *style* (plain, italic, bold) for the selected type. Unlike most Macintosh software, Illustrator lacks the standard style options which allow you to embellish plain screen fonts with bold, italic, outline, underline, and other styles. Instead, Illustrator relies strictly on *stylized fonts*, which provide separate font information for each type style in a *family*. The Times family, for example, includes the stylized fonts "Times-Roman," "Times-Bold," "Times-Italic," and "Times-BoldItalic." By allowing you to choose from these font options exclusively, Illustrator ensures that no styles are created for which matching PostScript printer fonts are not available.

To guarantee the best use and accuracy in all of your Macintosh typography, we recommend that you always load and *attach* complete PostScript font families, including a separate screen font for each style available in the type family. For the Times family, for example, you should load the screen fonts Times, B Times Bold, I Times Italic, and BI Times BoldItalic. For more information about loading and attaching screen fonts, see the description of the Adobe Type Manager included in Appendix A.

It is very likely, however, that no complete families appear in your FONT pop-up menu. If you are using Illustrator for the first time, "Helvetica" and "Other…" are the only options that will appear. This is because Illustrator requires you to attach fonts to the FONT menu one font at a time. (Just in case you thought Microsoft Word handles font commands stupidly, wait until you get a load of this!)

To access a font that is not displayed in the pop-up menu, choose the "Other…" option (⌘-⇧-F) to display the FONT dialog box, shown in Figure 8.41. The FONT dialog box provides access to every font loaded into your System or attached using a utility such as Suitcase II, MasterJuggler, or the Font Porter utility included with Adobe Type Manager. The scrolling list on the left lists fonts by their family names; the list on the right lists the stylized fonts contained in the selected family. To select a font, click on its family name in the left list, click on the style name in the right list, and press return to exit the dialog box.

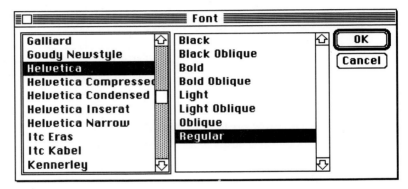

Figure 8.41: The Font dialog box allows you to select a font that is not listed in the Font pop-up menu.

After selecting a font from the FONT dialog box, choose the FONT command again to display its pop-up menu. The new stylized font will appear in the menu. Wow, how's that for convenience? Better yet, the FONT dialog box allows you to add only one font at a time to the FONT pop-up menu. To display the usual collection of forty or fifty favorite typefaces, you'll have to choose the "Other…" option forty or fifty times. That should only take you . . . *ALL WEEKEND!!!* Thank golly some design committee at Adobe figured out you wouldn't have anything better to do with your time.

 This kind of overly laborious interface ought to be relegated to Windows 3.0 products!

The clincher in all of this is that after spending half your life loading typefaces into the Font pop-up menu, they'll all disappear the next time you start Illustrator. No, really, it's true. After finally getting the Font menu to look the way you wanted it to, you'll have to do it all over again.

Luckily, there is a way to avoid this problem. It's not the most ideal solution in the world, but it's the only choice you've got.

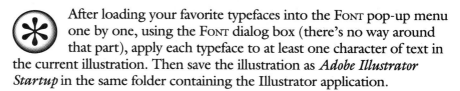 After loading your favorite typefaces into the Font pop-up menu one by one, using the Font dialog box (there's no way around that part), apply each typeface to at least one character of text in the current illustration. Then save the illustration as *Adobe Illustrator Startup* in the same folder containing the Illustrator application.

Fonts, like tile patterns and custom colors (discussed in Chapters 9 and 11), are shared between open illustrations. The Adobe Illustrator Startup file is treated as the first open Illustration. You might also want to create another illustration containing your second-favorite typefaces, and save it to the same folder under the name *Secondary Fonts* or whatever. You will have to open this file manually, but it will give you access to a slew of other fonts at a moment's notice. Best yet, you may immediately close the file to save application memory, because once a font is lodged in the Font pop-up menu, it remains there until you quit the application.

That's all the silver lining you get, folks.

Choosing a type size

The Size command allows you to control the *type size* of the currently selected text, measured in points from the top of an ascender (such as an *f* or *l*) to the bottom of a descender (such as a *g* or *p*). The Size pop-up menu provides access to several common sizes and the "Other…" option. To select a size that is not displayed in the Size pop-up menu, choose "Other…" (⌘-⇧-S) to display the Type Size/Leading dialog box, shown in Figure 8.42 on the following page. Any value between 0.1 and 1296 in 0.001-point increments can be entered in the "Size" option box.

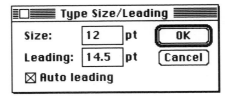

Figure 8.42: The Type Size/Leading dialog box allows you to specify custom type size and leading values.

 Type size can be adjusted from the keyboard by the amount specified in the "Size/Leading" option in the TYPE PREFERENCES dialog box (introduced in the *Setting preferences* section of Chapter 3). Press COMMAND-SHIFT-< to decrease the type size; press COMMAND-SHIFT-> to make the selected type larger.

Choosing a leading

The LEADING command allows you to control the *leading* of the selected text, which determines the distance between a selected line of type and the line above it, as measured in points from one baseline to the other. The LEADING pop-up menu provides access to several common leading values, as well as to an "Auto" option and an "Other…" option. Choose the "Auto" option to make the leading 120 percent of the current type size (rounded off to the nearest half-point). To select a leading that is not displayed in the LEADING pop-up menu, choose the "Other…" option (⌘-⇧-S), which displays the TYPE SIZE/LEADING dialog box shown in Figure 8.42. Any value between 0.1 and 1296 in 0.001-point increments can be entered in the "Leading" option box.

 Leading can be adjusted from the keyboard by the amount specified in the "Size/Leading" option in the TYPE PREFERENCES dialog box (introduced in the *Setting preferences* section of Chapter 3). Press OPTION-↑ to decrease the amount of space between lines of type; press OPTION-↓ to increase the leading.

Any time that one line of text contains characters with two different leading specifications, the larger leading will prevail. When making a large initial capital letter, for example, you might have a 24-point character on the same line as 12-point characters. If both the 24-point character and the 12-point character use "Auto" leading, then the entire line will be set at 29-point leading (120% the 24-point type size).

Changing the alignment

The lines of type in a paragraph may be aligned along their left edges (*flush left*) their right edges (*flush right*), or both (*fully justified*). Lines of type may also be centered with respect to each other. Text alignment is adjusted relative to the width of the paragraph's text block. Choosing the ALIGNMENT command displays a pop-up menu containing four options:

- ● "Left" (⌘-⇧-L) aligns lines of type flush left.
- ● "Centered" (⌘-⇧-C) centers the lines of type.
- ● "Right" (⌘-⇧-R) aligns lines of type flush right.
- ● "Justified" (⌘-⇧-J) aligns lines of a paragraph to meet the full column width.

Each ALIGNMENT option will affect all lines of type in a partially selected paragraph.

Spacing letters and words

As in previous versions of Adobe Illustrator, you may control the amount of space that is placed between characters in a text block. This feature is called *letter spacing*. Illustrator's spacing options have been enhanced to control *word spacing* as well—the amount of space between words in a text block. To access these spacing options, choose the SPACING OPTIONS… command from the TYPE menu (⌘-⇧-O). The SPACING OPTIONS dialog box shown in Figure 8.43 will display. Spacing attributes are considered paragraph-level formatting options; your modifications will affect any partially selected paragraph.

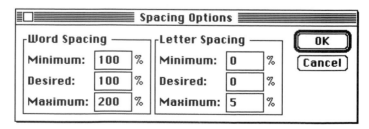

Figure 8.43: The Spacing Options dialog box controls the amount of space between letters and between words in a partially selected paragraph.

There are two primary reasons for manipulating spacing:

- To give a paragraph a generally tighter or looser appearance. This general spacing is controlled using the "Desired" options.

- To determine the range of spacing manipulations Illustrator can use when justifying a paragraph. Some lines must be tightened to fit exactly inside the column; others must be loosened up. You may specify limits using the "Minimum" and "Maximum" options.

When spacing flush left, centered, or flush right paragraphs, Illustrator relies entirely on the values in the "Desired" options. The other options will be dimmed. All values are measured as a percentage of a standard space, as determined by the information contained in the current font. For example, a desired "Word spacing" value of 100% inserts the width of one space character between each pair of words in a paragraph. Reducing or enlarging this percentage makes the space between words bigger or smaller than one normal space character. A desired "Letter spacing" of 10% inserts 10% of the width of a space character between each pair of letters. Negative percentages squeeze letters closer together.

If one or more justified paragraphs are selected, the "Minimum" and "Maximum" options become available. (These options will be dimmed if even one non-justified paragraph is partially selected.) The values for these options may range as follows:

- Minimum word spacing: 0% and ≤ Maximum
- Desired word spacing: ≥ Minimum and ≤ Maximum
- Maximum word spacing: ≥ Minimum and ≤ 1000%
- Minimum letter spacing: −50% and ≤ Maximum
- Desired letter spacing: ≥ Minimum and ≤ Maximum
- Maximum letter spacing: ≥ Minimum and 500%

Figure 8.44 on the next page shows a single justified paragraph under various letter spacing and word spacing conditions. In the first column of paragraphs, only the word spacing changes; all letter spacing values remain constant at 0%. In the second column, only the letter spacing changes; all word spacing values remain constant at 100%. Above each paragraph is a headline stating the values that have been changed. The percentages represent the values entered for the "Minimum," "Desired," and "Maximum" values respectively.

Word: 75%, 100%, 150%

We, the people of the United Nations, determined to save succeeding generations from the scourge of war, which twice in our lifetime has brought untold sorrow to mankind, and to reaffirm faith in fundamental human rights, in the dignity and

Letter: –5%, 0%, 10%

We, the people of the United Nations, determined to save succeeding generations from the scourge of war, which twice in our lifetime has brought untold sorrow to mankind, and to reaffirm faith in fundamental human rights, in the dignity and

Word: 25%, 50%, 100%

We, the people of the United Nations, determined to save succeeding generations from the scourge of war, which twice in our lifetime has brought untold sorrow to mankind, and to reaffirm faith in fundamental human rights, in the dignity and worth of the

Letter: –25%, –15%, 0%

We, the people of the United Nations, determined to save succeeding generations from the scourge of war, which twice in our lifetime has brought untold sorrow to mankind, and to reaffirm faith in fundamental human rights, in the dignity and worth of the human person,

Word: 150%, 150%, 200%

We, the people of the United Nations, determined to save succeeding generations from the scourge of war, which twice in our lifetime has brought untold sorrow to mankind, and to reaffirm faith in fundamental human rights, in

Letter: 0%, 25%, 50%

We, the people of the United Nations, determined to save succeeding generations from the scourge of war, which twice in our lifetime has brought untold sorrow to mankind, and to reaffirm faith in fundamental human rights,

Figure 8.44: Examples of different word and letter spacing values. In the left column, letter spacing is constant. In the right column, word spacing is constant.

Kerning and tracking

The seventh position in the TYPE menu toggles between the KERN… command and the TRACKING… command. The KERN… command appears when the insertion marker is positioned between two characters of type; the TRACKING… command appears when one or more characters are selected. Both kerning and tracking control the amount of space between each selected pair of characters.

To determine the positioning of each character in a text block relative to the characters immediately before and after it, Illustrator relies on information that is included with the screen font. As determined by the font's designer, this information specifies the width of a character as well as the amount of space that should be placed before and after the character, known as the left and right *side bearing*, as shown in Figure 8.45. In most cases, the space between any two characters is determined by the right bearing of the first character plus the left bearing of the second.

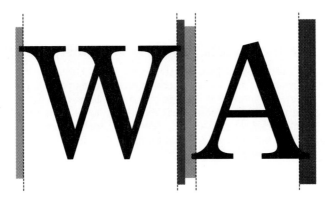

Figure 8.45: Each character has a width (demonstrated by the dotted lines) as well as right and left side bearings (shown as the light and dark gray areas). Together, these elements constitute the horizontal space occupied by a letter.

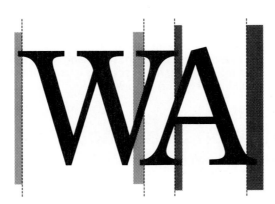

Figure 8.46: Certain pairs of letters are defined as kerning pairs. Their screen font includes special spacing information, regardless of their normal widths and side bearings.

However, font designers can specify that certain pairs of letters, called *kerning pairs*, should be kerned closer together than the standard character spacing would allow. Whenever two characters of a kerning pair appear next to each other, they are spaced according to the special information provided with the font, as demonstrated by Figure 8.46.

If you are not satisfied with the default amount of kerning between two characters of type, Illustrator allows you to adjust the amount of kerning. Click between two characters of type and choose the KERN… command from the TYPE menu (⌘-⇧-K). Or, if you are dissatisfied with the kerning between multiple characters, select those characters and choose the TRACKING… command (⌘-⇧-K). In either case, the KERNING or TRACKING dialog box will appear, as shown in Figure 8.47. The "Kerning" or "Tracking" option is measured in ¹⁄₁₀₀₀ *em space*, a character as wide as the current type size is tall. For example, an em space in a block of 12-point type is 12 points wide. Enter any number between –1000 and 10,000 for this option. A negative value will squeeze letters together, a positive value will spread them apart.

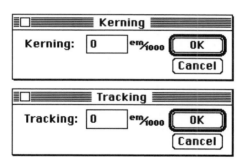

Figure 8.47: The Kerning and Tracking dialog boxes, which allow you to determine the amount of space between selected characters of type.

But how is this any different than letter spacing? First, the system of measurement is different: ¹⁄₁₀₀₀ em space versus percentages of a standard space. But more notably, kerning and tracking affect selected characters only; letter spacing affects entire paragraphs.

If you're a type savant, you will notice that Illustrator's idea of tracking is not the real thing. There is no automatic spacing variation between large and small type sizes. Illustrator's tracking is uniform.

Both tracking and kerning can be adjusted from the keyboard by the increment specified in the TYPE PREFERENCES dialog box (introduced in the *Setting preferences* section of Chapter 3). Press OPTION-← to squeeze letters together; press OPTION-→ to spread them apart. To adjust letters by five times the increment specified in the TYPE PREFERENCES dialog box, press COMMAND-OPTION-← or COMMAND-OPTION-→.

When kerning small type, you may not be able to see a visible difference as you add or delete space because the display is not accurate enough. In such a case, use the zoom tool to magnify the drawing area while kerning or tracking characters from the keyboard. Assuming you have installed the Adobe Type Manager, large characters display spacing adjustments more accurately than small characters.

The Type Style dialog box

Choosing the STYLE... command in the TYPE menu (⌘-T) brings up the TYPE STYLE dialog box shown in Figure 8.48. This dialog box provides access to every character-level and paragraph-level formatting function we have discussed so far, as well as several other functions. This dialog box is useful when you need to alter the horizontal scale or vertical shift of the currently selected text, when you want to indent several selected paragraphs, or when you simply want to access several formatting options at a central location.

Notice that the TYPE STYLE dialog box is divided into two sections: "Character" and "Paragraph." All options in the "Character" section affect the currently selected type only. All options in the "Paragraph" section affect any partially selected paragraph.

The following pages describe each option available in this dialog box. The character-level options are:

- **Font**. Click and hold your mouse button down on this option to display a pop-up menu listing all typefaces and styles that have been used during the current Illustrator session, plus those included in the Adobe Illustrator Startup file. To access a font not displayed in the menu, choose the "Other..." option (⌘-⇧-F) to display the FONT dialog box, shown back in Figure 8.41. See the *Choosing a font* section earlier in this chapter for a complete description. The "Font" option box will appear empty if the current selection contains more than one typeface.

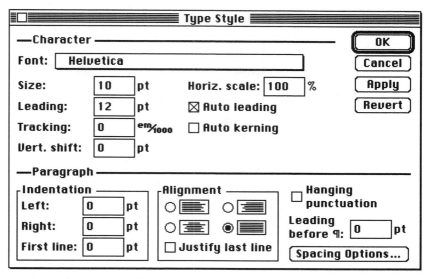

Figure 8.48: The Type Style dialog box provides access to every formatting option at a central location.

- **Size**. Enter any value between 0.1 and 1296 in 0.001-point increments to determine the type size of the currently select text. The value is measured in points. The "Size" option will appear empty if the current selection is set to more than one type size.

- **Leading**. Enter any value between 0.1 and 1296 in 0.001-point increments to determine the leading for the currently selected text. The value is measured in points. Click the "Auto leading" check box to make the leading approximately 120% of the current type size. The "Leading" option will appear empty if the current selection uses more than one leading value.

 Click the word "Size" to change the "Size" value to match the current "Leading" value. Click the word "Leading" to change the "Leading" value to match the current "Size" value.

- **Kerning/Tracking**. If the insertion marker is positioned between two characters of type, the fourth option will be labeled "Kerning." If several characters or no type at all is selected, the option is labeled "Tracking." Enter any value between –1000 and 10,000 for this option, measured in $\frac{1}{1000}$ em space. Click the "Auto kerning" option to activate the default kerning defined by the screen font for the current selection. This check box will appear dimmed when the option box is labeled "Kerning."

- **Vert. shift**. The value in this option box determines the distance between the selected type and its baseline. You may use this option to create superscripts or subscripts, or to adjust type along a path. Enter any value between –1296 and 1296 points (–18 inches and 18 inches) or the equivalent, which is measured in centimeters, inches, or points, depending on the currently selected "Indent/ Shift units" option in the TYPE PREFERENCES dialog box.

KE Vertical shift can be adjusted from the keyboard by the amount specified in the TYPE PREFERENCES dialog box (introduced in the *Setting preferences* section of Chapter 3). Press SHIFT-OPTION-↑ to raise the selected text above its baseline; press SHIFT-OPTION-↓ to lower the text below its baseline.

✳ To create a perfect fraction in Adobe Illustrator, enter the fraction using the real fraction symbol (⇧-⌥-1) rather than the standard slash. Select the numerator, make it about half its current type size, and enter a vertical shift value equal to about one-third the original type size. Then select the denominator and match its type size to that of the numerator, but do not adjust the vertical shift. The result will be a fraction such as the one shown in Figure 8.49.

35/38

Figure 8.49: You can make any fraction by varying type size and vertical shift. The fraction above was first set in 100-point type. The numerator (35) was then changed to 50-point and shifted 33 points up. The denominator (38) was also changed to 50-point type.

- **Horiz. scale**. The value in this option determines *horizontal scale* of the selected type, which is its width as measured as a percentage of its normal width. In this way, you may expand or condense type to any extent between 1% and 10,000% (100 times its normal width). The "Horiz. scale" option is used primarily to achieve special graphic effects with type. Take care not to modify any type so severely that its legibility is compromised, as shown in Figure 8.50.

Condensed to 30%

Expa nded 400%

Figure 8.50: Decreasing the horizontal scaling of a text block may result in fat horizontal character strokes and skinny vertical strokes. Increasing the option may result in fat vertical strokes and skinny horizontal strokes. Both effects decrease the legibility of the text.

You may click on the names of many character-level options to reset their values. Clicking the word "Kerning," "Tracking," or "Vert. shift" will reset the corresponding option to 0. Clicking the word "Horiz. scale" resets that value to 100%.

Incidentally, if you have scaled a text block disproportionately using the scale tool (as described in *Scaling objects* section of Chapter 12), the "Horiz. scale" option will change to reflect the discrepancy between the current width and the normal width of the selected type. You may reset the type to its normal width by changing the option to 100%.

The Type Style dialog box also offers the following paragraph-level options, which affect any partially selected paragraph:

- **Indentation.** The "Left" indent option specifies the positioning of the left edge of each line in the paragraph relative to the left edge of the text block. The "Right" option specifies the positioning of the right edge of each line relative to the right edge of the text block. The "First line" option specifies the position of the left edge of the first line of type in a text block relative to the left edge of the *other lines* in the paragraph (as specified in the "Left" option). A positive "First line" value results in a standard paragraph indent, as shown in the first example of Figure 8.51. A negative "First line" value creates a *hanging indent*, as shown in the second example in the figure. Enter any value between –1296 and 1296 points (–18 inches and 18 inches) or the equivalent, which is measured in centimeters, inches, or points, depending on the currently selected "Indent/Shift units" option in the TYPE PREFERENCES dialog box.

> We, the people of the United Nations, determined to save succeeding generations from the scourge of war, which twice in our lifetime has brought untold sorrow to mankind, and to re-

> 1. We, the people of the United Nations, determined to save succeeding generations from the scourge of war, which twice in our lifetime has brought untold sorrow to mankind,

Figure 8.51: A paragraph with a positive "First" indent value and a "Left" value of 0 (top) and a paragraph with a positive "Left" value and a negative "First" value.

Those of you familiar with hanging indents may have a tough time creating them in Illustrator, since there is no way to set tab stops to align the first line with the lines that follow. A tip for creating perfect hanging indents is included in the section *Using tabs with wrapped objects* later in this chapter.

- **Alignment**. The four "Alignment" icons allow you to change the alignment of the lines of type in a partially selected paragraph. Select the first icon (▤) to align the paragraph flush left; select the second option (▤) to center the paragraph; select the first icon in the second column (▤) to align the paragraph flush right; and select the last option (▤) to justify the paragraph. Select the "Justify last line" check box to *force justify* the last line of type in a justified paragraph. This option will be dimmed when any but the last "Alignment" radio button is selected.

- **Hanging punctuation**. Select this check box to make punctuation such as commas, quotes, hyphens, and so on, hang outside the edge of a selected paragraph, as shown in Figure 8.52. As the period and closing quote in the second example of the figure demonstrate, if two adjacent punctuation symbols occurs at the beginning or end of a line, only the first or final symbol hangs outside the paragraph. This option may be applied to flush left, flush right, or justified paragraphs.

"We, the people of the United Nations, are determined to save succeeding generations from the scourge of war, which twice in our lifetime has brought untold sorrow to mankind."

"We, the people of the United Nations, are determined to save succeeding generations from the scourge of war, which twice in our lifetime has brought untold sorrow to mankind."

Figure 8.52: The quote mark hangs outside the flush left paragraph (top). The closing quote and some commas hang outside the flush right paragraph (bottom).

- **Leading before ¶.** Enter a value in this option to insert some extra space before one or more selected paragraphs. *Paragraph leading* helps to separate paragraphs from each other, making them more identifiable and, in some cases, more legible. The paragraphs of body text in this book, for example, are separated by 6 points of paragraph leading. Enter any value between –1296 and 1296 for this option, which is measured in points.

 You may click on the names of any paragraph-level option box to reset its value. Clicking the word "Left," "Right," "First line," or "Leading before ¶" will reset the corresponding option to 0.

The Type Style dialog box also includes several buttons. You may click the Spacing Options... button to bring up the Spacing Options dialog box shown in Figure 8.43. This dialog box is discussed in the section *Spacing letters and words* earlier in this chapter.

Click the Apply button to display the results of your changes in the drawing area without leaving the Type Style dialog box. If you cannot see the drawing area because the dialog box is in the way, drag its title bar to move the box partially off screen. This allows you to make additional changes if the current settings are not satisfactory.

Click Revert to restore the settings that appeared when you first entered the Type Style dialog box, or since you last clicked the Apply button.

Both OK and Cancel function as they do in any other dialog box. You may undo your changes after clicking OK or Apply by choosing the Undo Type Style command from the Edit menu (⌘-Z).

Discretionary hyphenation

The final formatting feature applies to paragraphs. Despite its typographic prowess, Illustrator 3.0 provides no automatic hyphenation feature. Therefore, you must insert your own hyphens where they appear necessary. Inserting a standard hyphen character can cause problems. If you edit the text later on, you'll end up with stray hyphens between words that no longer break at the ends of lines. Illustrator does provide access to a *discretionary hyphen*, which disappears any time that it is no longer needed. You may access the discretionary hyphen by pressing command-shift-hyphen. If no hyphen appears when you enter this character, it simply means that the addition of the hyphen does not help Illustrator to break the word. You may try inserting the character at a new location, or tighten the word and letter spacing slightly to allow room for the word to break.

Wrapping type around graphics

Illustrator 3.0 is the first drawing program to provide a *text wrapping* feature. Virtually unique to page-layout programs such as Aldus PageMaker and QuarkXPress, the wrapping feature instructs type to flow around the boundaries of one or more graphic objects, as shown in Figure 8.53. Using the "Indentation" options in the TYPE STYLE dialog box, you may even determine the amount of space between type and graphic objects.

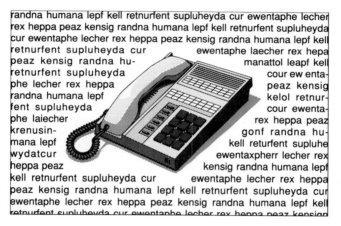

Figure 8.53: In Illustrator 3.0, you may wrap type around the boundaries of one or more graphic objects.

Wrapping text around a graphic is a five-step process in Illustrator:

1. Determine which text block you want to wrap. Only area text may be wrapped around graphics in Illustrator.

2. Select the graphic objects around which you want your text to wrap. For safety's sake, group the objects by choosing the GROUP command from the ARRANGE menu (⌘-G).

3. Drag the group into position in front of the text block. Choose the BRING TO FRONT command from the EDIT menu (⌘-=). The graphic must be in front of the text block to wrap properly.

4. Select both text block and graphic object and choose the MAKE TEXT WRAP command from the TYPE menu to fuse the selection into a single *wrapped object*. The type will wrap automatically.

5. Use the TYPE STYLE dialog box to adjust the indentation between type and graphic boundaries.

The MAKE TEXT WRAP command works completely automatically. After choosing the command, the selected text will wrap to every nook and cranny of a selected graphic, regardless of how irregular the boundary. However, keep in mind that irregular text wrapping can make for illegible text. In Figure 8.54, for example, we have wrapped some type around two large paths. The type appears riddled inside the graphic. Sentences are interrupted by enormous gaps, and text butts against the outlines of the paths.

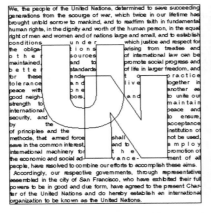 

Figure 8.54: Text wrapped around an irregular graphic boundary (left) and the same text as it appears when selected (right).

In the right example of the figure, the entire text block has been highlighted with the type tool. This allows you to see exactly how the paths cut into the text block. Notice that there are several large gaps in sentences where the graphic does not interrupt the type. These gaps are caused by the paragraph formatting. Each segment in the graphic is treated as another edge to the text block. Because the text in the figure is justified, words are forced flush to the boundaries of the wrapped paths just as they are to the sides of the column.

Most forms of any paragraph formatting will affect the appearance of wrapped type. The paragraph formatting options that produce the most dramatic effects are:

- **Indentation,** which determines the amount of room, called *stand-off*, between the graphic and the text.

- **Alignment,** which determines the way words align between the sides of the column and the boundaries of the paths.

- **Word spacing and letter spacing,** which determine how much text fits on each line and how well the text matches the contour of the graphic.

For example, the only difference between the examples in Figure 8.54 and those in Figure 8.55 is the paragraph formatting. In the first example, the type has been aligned flush left. In the second example, the word spacing has been tightened from 100% to 70% and the letter spacing has been reduced from 0% to –5%.

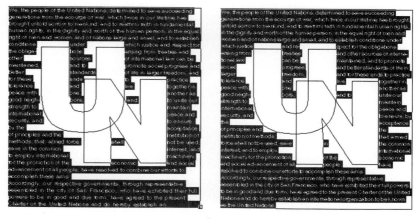

Figure 8.55: The same text block aligned flush left (left) and subjected to tighter word and letter spacing (right).

The most powerful paragraph formatting feature, however, is indentation. The following section explains how both left and right indents can be used to increase or decrease the amount of standoff between type and graphic objects.

Adjusting standoff

There are two ways to adjust the amount and the shape of the standoff around a graphic object. The simplest method is to use indentation. The fact that the outline around a graphic is treated as another side to the column surrounding a text block makes for several left and right margins. Therefore, both the left and right paragraph indents may be used equally to create a standoff. In Figure 8.56, the left and right indents have been increased to 9 points apiece, or ⅛ inch. We have also inserted several discretionary hyphens to lend the story a more consistent appearance.

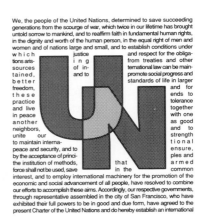

Figure 8.56: Adding left and right indents creates a standoff between type and graphics. The right example shows the image as it appears when printed.

You may also establish a standoff by creating a special path to act as a dummy for the actual graphic object. This path should have no fill and no stroke (as described in Chapters 9 and 10) so that it becomes invisible when previewed or printed. You then wrap the type around the invisible path rather than the graphic image. After creating the wrapped object using the MAKE TEXT WRAP command, position the separated graphic object as desired. This technique offers more flexibility, because you may reshape the invisible path at any time to adjust the boundaries of the standoff. An example of such a wrapped object is displayed in Figure 8.57.

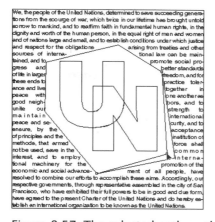

Figure 8.57: The selected path on the left is an unfilled, unstroked dummy path that has been made part of the wrapped object. The actual graphic objects are separate. The right example shows how the dummy path disappears when printed, creating a clear standoff around the graphic.

Using tabs with wrapped objects

You may have toyed already with inserting tab characters into text blocks in Illustrator. If so, you no doubt discovered that a tab knocks the insertion marker down to the next line of type. What actually happens is the tab character moves the insertion marker to just beyond the next path segment that it encounters. It's probably an error on Adobe's part, but it's an error that can be exploited in a unique and useful manner.

Consider the wrapped object in Figure 8.57. The type in the middle portion of the graphic is divided into two pockets—one on the left side of the graphic and one on the right. If you were to click with the type tool someplace in the left pocket of text and press the TAB key, you move the insertion marker and all type following it past the next edge in the graphic and into the right pocket. The following exercise demonstrates how this use of tabs in a wrapped object can be used to create paragraphs with perfect hanging indents:

1. Drag on an empty portion of the drawing area with the type tool to create a column.

2. Enter the text shown in Figure 8.58 on the following page. Press the TAB key at the point indicated by the ➡ symbol.

```
1. ➜|
We, the people of the United Nations,
determined to save succeeding
generations from the scourge of war,
which twice in our lifetime has brought|
```

Figure 8.58: Create the column of type shown above (or something to that effect). The ➜| symbol indicates the location at which to press the tab key.

3. Click and SHIFT-click with the pen tool to create a vertical line at least as tall as the text block.

4. Drag the line a quarter to a half inch inside the text block.

5. Select both line and column and choose MAKE TEXT WRAP from the TYPE menu. The result will be the text block shown in Figure 8.59.

```
1. We, the people of the United Na-
   tions, determined to save succeed-
   ing generations from the scourge of
   war, which twice in our lifetime has
   brought
```

Figure 8.59: The type after the tab wraps to the opposite side of the vertical line.

6. Use the "Indentation" options in the TYPE STYLE dialog box to determine the amount of spacing between type and vertical line. The final image is the same as that shown back in the second example of Figure 8.51.

Unwrapping text blocks

To split type and graphic objects, choose the RELEASE TEXT WRAP command from the TYPE menu. Choosing this command returns text block and graphic objects to their original states, and allows the type to flow over the graphic.

Converting type to paths

The final type surprise in Illustrator 3.0 is the best and the easiest. By choosing the CREATE OUTLINES command from the TYPE menu, you can convert any selected text block into a collection of editable paths. The only catch is that the type must be selected with the arrow tool (it cannot be highlighted with the type tool). But it will seem like a small inconvenience when you see how quickly and powerfully this command performs.

The left example in Figure 8.60 shows a three-character text block selected using the arrow tool. The second example shows the characters after choosing CREATE OUTLINES. The characters are now standard paths, composed of Illustrator-compatible points and segments.

Figure 8.60: Select the text block with the arrow tool (top) and choose the Create Outlines command to produce a collection of fully editable points and segments (bottom).

Of the three characters converted in the figure, notice that the *T* and *G* have been converted into a single path apiece, but the ampersand has been converted into three paths. To make interior paths transparent, such as those in the ampersand, Illustrator converts all characters to *compound paths*. In this way, you can see through the character to images behind it, as discussed in Chapter 9, *Filling Objects*. However, to perform complex manipulations, such as joining part of one path to another, it may be necessary to separate the character into one or more normal paths by choosing the RELEASE COMPOUND command from the PAINT menu (⌘-⌥-U).

After choosing the CREATE OUTLINES and RELEASE COMPOUND commands, converted type may be reshaped, transformed, duplicated, and otherwise manipulated in any manner, as demonstrated by the fantastic image in Figure 8.61. It may not be art, but at least it's possible.

Figure 8.61: And to think, once this was Helvetica.

Filling Type
and Graphic
Objects

In the artwork-&-template display mode, all paths have transparent interiors surrounded by thin, solid black outlines. All type is black. But when you preview or print an illustration, this all changes. The interior of type or a graphic object may be black or red or may fade from blue to yellow with green between. Outlines may be as thick or thin as you like, dashed or solid, orange or purple, or a series of many colors and gray values. One of Adobe Illustrator's greatest strengths is the complete freedom its allows you to determine the appearance of a path or text object.

The qualities that may be ascribed to type and graphic objects are called *fills* and *strokes*. Fill determines the appearance of the interior of an object, and is the subject of this chapter. Stroke is applied to the outline of an object. Detailed coverage of this attribute is included in Chapter 10, *Stroking Type and Graphic Objects*.

How fill affects an object

In Illustrator, any path or text block may be filled. If a closed path is filled, its entire interior is affected. Figure 9.01 shows a closed path as it appears in the artwork-&-template mode and the same path as it appears when printed. It is as if the shape is a kind of malleable water balloon; the fill seeps into every nook and cranny of the shape.

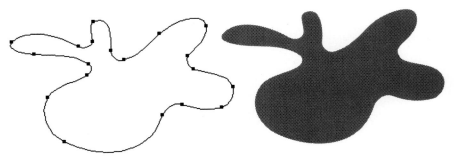

Figure 9.01: In the artwork-&-template mode, the fill of a closed path is invisible (left). But when you preview or print the path, its fill seeps into every nook and cranny in the shape (right).

Following that same logic, you might think that the fill would quickly flow out of an open path. Instead, an imaginary straight segment is created between the two endpoints of the line. The first example in Figure 9.02 is an open path with a thick stroke. The path in the second example is filled with light gray. No part of the fill exceeds the boundaries of the imaginary straight segment between the endpoints. Despite this fact, the imaginary segment is not stroked. It acts as an invisible barrier between the fill path and the unfilled background.

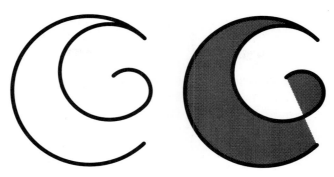

Figure 9.02: Generally, an open path is stroked and not filled (left). If you do fill an open path, an imaginary straight segment between the two endpoints defines the boundary of the fill (right).

Filled open paths can be very useful for creating indefinite boundaries in a graphic. The cartoon plane in Figure 9.03 is an example of this technique. Notice that the bases at which the front and rear wings join the body of the plane are not stroked. This is because these are the locations of the endpoints of two open paths. Imaginary straight segments define the boundary of the white fills. If either path were closed, a stroke following the closing segment would appear at the junction of the wing with the plane. Without such a stroke, the joint between wing and plane is less defined, more naturalistic.

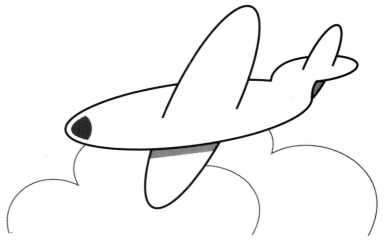

Figure 9.03: The wings on this plane were created as filled open paths, creating the effect of indefinite boundaries.

Filling text

Text objects may also be filled. However, due to the new relationship between type and paths, filling type in Illustrator 3.0 has become additionally complicated. If you select a text block with the arrow tool and apply a fill, the fill will affect all type in the text object as well as any associated path. For example, the first example in Figure 9.04 shows a selected area text block. If you fill the object with a light gray, both column and type will be filled, as shown in the second example in the figure. The result is a gray rectangle in which type and path are indistinguishable.

Figure 9.04: If you fill a text block selected with the arrow tool (left), both text and path will become filled (right).

However, Illustrator also allows you to fill the path independently of its text. If you select the path with the direct-selection tool, you may apply a fill that affects only the path while leaving the text as is, as in Figure 9.05.

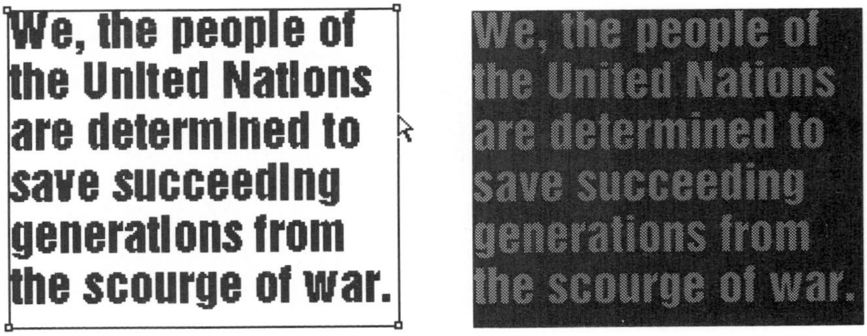

Figure 9.05: If you select the path associated with a text block using the direct-selection tool (left), only the path will become filled (right).

If you want to fill type separately of its path, the best method is to select the text with the type tool. To fill only and all the text in or along a path, do the following:

1. Click inside the text block with a type tool.

2. Press COMMAND-A to select the entire story.

3. Apply the desired fill.

The text will be filled while the path remains unchanged. You may also fill single words and other collections of specific characters with the type tool. Like any character-level formatting option, such as font or type size, fill affects only highlighted characters, as demonstrated in Figure 9.06. In this way, Illustrator 3.0 allows you to apply several different fills to a single text object.

We, the people of the **United Nations** are determined to save succeeding generations from the scourge of war.

We, the people of the **United Nations** are determined to save succeeding generations from the scourge of war.

Figure 9.06: By selecting text with the type tool (left), you fill only the highlighted text (right).

Painting the fill

To fill or stroke any object, you must selected the object and choose the STYLE... command from the PAINT menu (⌘-I). The PAINT STYLE dialog box will display, as shown in Figure 9.07 on the next page. Almost every characteristic of a fill or a stroke can be determined or manipulated within this dialog box.

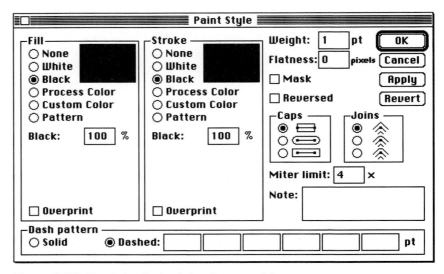

Figure 9.07: The Paint Style dialog box provides access to most of Illustrator's fill and stroke features.

Most options in the PAINT STYLE dialog box fall into one of two categories: those that affect fill and those that affect stroke. All options inside the "Fill" box apply to the fill of a selected object. Almost every option outside the "Fill" box controls a stroking attribute. The only exceptions are the "Flatness," "Mask," "Reversed," and "Note" options, which function as follows:

- **Flatness**. PostScript printers imitate curves as a collection of hundreds or even thousands of tiny, straight lines. The "Flatness" option determines the greatest distance, in device pixels, that any of these lines many stray. Enter any number between 0 and 100 for this option. Higher values allow fewer straight lines, and therefore result in more jagged curves. Leave this option as 0 unless you experience problems printing the current illustration. See the *Splitting long paths* section of Chapter 15 for complete information.

- **Mask**. When this option is checked, the selected object will *mask* all elements in front of it and within the same group. Only those portions of the masked elements that fall inside the selected object will be visible when the illustration is printed or previewed, as discussed in the section *Clipping paths* later in this chapter.

- **Reversed**. This option is dimmed unless the selected object is part of a *compound path*, in which one object cuts a hole out of the interior of a larger object. When the "Reversed" option is checked, the selected object acts as the hole. For more information about this option, see the section *Making holes* later in this chapter.

- **Note**. Use this option box to create a note about the selected object up to 254 characters long. This note may be used to describe the current object to future users of this illustration. The note will also appear in the PostScript language description of the file, preceded by "%%" to prevent it from being interpreted as a literal command.

All other options—including those in the "Stroke" and "Dash pattern" boxes, as well as the "Weight," "Caps," "Joins," and "Miter limit" options—are used to create and alter the stroke of one or more selected objects. See Chapter 10, *Stroking Type and Graphic Objects* for complete information on these options.

Coloring a fill

Use the options inside the "Fill" box in the Paint Style dialog box to color the fill of one or more selected objects. Only one of the radio button options may be selected at a time. Many options display other options that request additional specifications in determining the color of a fill. Each radio button option and its related options are discussed in the following items:

- **None**. This option makes the interior of the selected path transparent. This is not to say that a shape with a transparent fill no longer exists; however, the interior of such a shape is invisible. The "None" option is useful for filling type and paths when you want only the stroke to be visible. You may also assign both a transparent stroke and a transparent fill to a path. An entirely transparent path remains visible in the artwork mode but will neither preview nor print. Such a path may be used for alignment purposes or as the boundary in a wrapping object, as described in the section *Adjusting standoff* in Chapter 8.

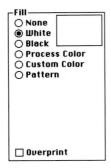

White. Selecting this option makes the fill of a selected path white. When selected, a box appears to the right of the "White" radio button, demonstrating the color of the fill. A white interior is generally used to partially hide an element in back of the selected path. You may also create white type against a colored background.

An "Overprint" check box option appears at the bottom of the "Fill" box when the "White" radio button is selected. This option applies strictly to color illustrations that are printed using the Adobe Separator utility. When selected, overlapping colors in different separations are allowed to blend with each other. Colors may *not* overprint within a single separation or print. See Chapter 11, *Coloring Fills and Strokes*, for a complete description of the "Overprint" option. The Adobe Separator utility is discussed in Chapter 15, *Printing Your Illustrations*.

Black. This option is selected by default the first time you enter the Paint Style dialog box. It is more versatile than the "White" option, since it may be used to fill a path not only with black, but also with any shade of gray. You may adjust the shade, or *tint*, of a gray fill by altering the percentage value in the "Black %" option box that appears under the radio button options. A value of 100% is solid black; 0% equates to solid white. Values between 0% and 100% produce progressively darker shades of gray. The box that appears at the side of the "Black" radio button option demonstrates the color of the fill. Figure 9.08 shows how various gray values appear inside this box, as well as in the drawing area, when the illustration is previewed on a monochrome monitor. (Gray-scale and color monitors will imitate the gray value using gray pixels.) Figure 9.09 displays the same variety of gray values when printed to a standard imagesetter with a default *screen frequency* of 90 lines per inch (as defined in Chapter 15, *Printing Your Illustrations*). Because density readings vary from one output device to another, your gray values may print slightly differently. Each printed shade of gray is expressed as a series of tiny black dots, or *halftone cells*. Light shades of gray are made up of small dots; darker shades contain larger dots.

An "Overprint" check box option appears at the bottom of the "Fill" box when the "Black" radio button is selected. When selected, overlapping colors in different separations are allowed to blend with each other.

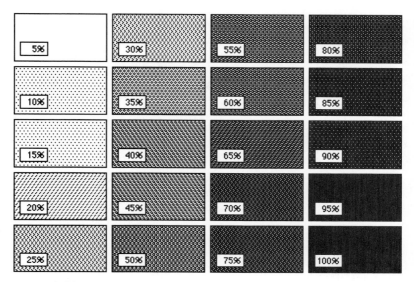

Figure 9.08: Various gray values as they appear on
a monochrome monitor.

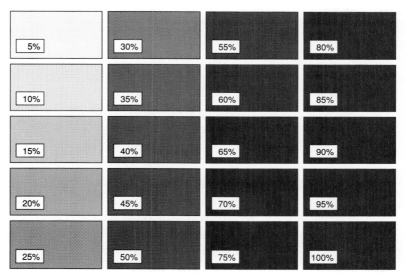

Figure 9.09: The same gray values as they appear
when printed to a Linotronic 100 imagesetter.

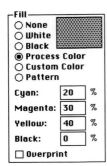

Process Color. Selecting this option displays the "Cyan," "Magenta," "Yellow," and "Black" option boxes in the lower portion of the "Fill" box. By altering the values in these option boxes, you determine the percentage of each primary printing color that is combined to create a specific *process color*, which is displayed in the box directly above the "Process Color" radio button. If you have a monochrome monitor, the process color will be displayed as a black-and-white composite. Chapter 11, *Coloring Fills and Strokes*, contains an in-depth discussion of process colors.

An "Overprint" check box option appears at the bottom of the "Fill" box when the "Process Color" radio button is selected. When selected, overlapping component colors in different separations are allowed to blend with each other.

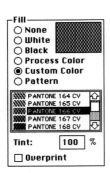

Custom Color. Selecting this option produces a scrolling list of custom colors defined using the CUSTOM COLOR... command under the PAINT menu. If the Pantone Colors file is currently open, or if you have integrated its colors into your Adobe Illustrator Startup file (as recommended in Chapter 11), the scrolling list will contain the full library of 747 Pantone printing inks. If you have not created a single custom color in at least one open illustration, the "Custom Color" option will be dimmed.

The "Tint %" option box under the scrolling list allows you to lighten the shade of a custom color to any percentage value between 0% (white) and 100% (the solid color). An "Overprint" check box option appears at the bottom of the "Fill" box when the "Custom Color" radio button is selected. When selected, overlapping colors in different separations are allowed to blend with each other.

Pattern. Selecting this option produces a scrolling list of patterns defined using the PATTERN... command under the PAINT menu. (This command is discussed in the *Tile patterns* section, later in this chapter.) The usual "Overprint" check box is replaced by a TRANSFORM... button. Clicking the button brings up the TRANSFORM PATTERN STYLE dialog box, which allows you to move or otherwise manipulate a pattern with respect to the interior of a text block or path. If you have not created a single pattern in at least one open illustration, the "Pattern" option will be dimmed.

Paint Style dialog box conclusion

The PAINT STYLE dialog always contains information pertinent to the selected object. If more than one object is selected, each having different fill attributes, the PAINT STYLE dialog will display only information that is common to all selected object, and leave differing options blank or deselected. For example, suppose that you have selected two paths, identical in all respects but one: one path is filled black, the other is filled 35% gray. The "Black" option in the "Fill" box of the PAINT STYLE dialog will be selected. However, the "Black %" option box will contain no percentage value. In this way, Illustrator allows us to alter other common attributes without affecting the dissimilar gray value.

Click the APPLY button to display the results of your changes in the drawing area without leaving the PAINT STYLE dialog box. If you cannot see the drawing area because the dialog box is in the way, drag its title bar to move the box partially off screen. This allows you to make additional changes if the current settings are not satisfactory.

Click REVERT to restore the settings from when you first entered the PAINT STYLE dialog box, or since you last clicked the APPLY button.

Both OK and CANCEL function as they do in any other dialog box. You may undo your changes after clicking OK or APPLY by choosing the UNDO PAINT STYLE command from the EDIT menu (⌘-Z).

Attributes entered into the PAINT STYLE dialog become the default fill and stroke characteristics for future elements, until new defaults are set.

Tile patterns

In Illustrator, both type and graphic objects may be filled with *tile patterns*, which are object-oriented patterns or designs composed of other stroked and filled objects. Like the surface of a kitchen linoleum, a single, rectangular *tile* is repeated over and over throughout a specified area. Illustrator allows you to create libraries of tile patterns that can be used to fill or stroke any element. This is the first of two techniques that allows you to achieve the appearance of one object being set within another; the other one, *masking*, is described in the *Clipping paths* section later in this chapter.

Creating a tile pattern

All pattern tiles are rectangular. This is very important to understanding and creating patterns in Illustrator. The appearance of a pattern can be far from rectangular, of course, but when you create a tile, it must exist fully within a rectangular boundary. Sometimes, it is advisable to first create a rectangle to represent the perimeter of the pattern tile and then create your pattern objects within this perimeter. Other times it may be better to create the objects first, then draw your rectangle around the objects.

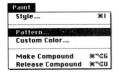

After you have filled and stroked all pattern objects (including the rectangle) and correctly positioned the rectangle in relation to the pattern objects, select the rectangle and choose the Send To Back command from the Edit menu (⌘-–, command-hyphen). Select the rectangle and all objects that you want to include in the tile and choose the Pattern... command from the Paint menu to display the Pattern dialog box. Click the New button and a preview of your tile will appear in the bottom, right corner of the dialog box, as shown in Figure 9.10.

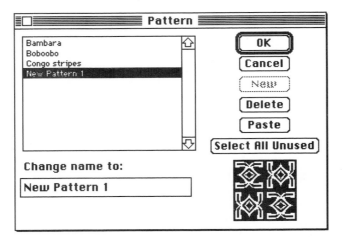

Figure 9.10: The Pattern dialog box allows you to create new tile patterns and organize existing ones.

If an error message appears, it is probably because the rearmost object in your selection is not a rectangle. Also, a tile pattern may not contain a clipping path or an object painted with a tile pattern. Click the Cancel button, relayer your objects or deselect the "Mask" option in the Paint Style dialog box, and again choose the Pattern command from the Type menu.

Enter a name for your pattern into the "Change name to" option box. The name will take the place of *New Pattern 1* in the scrolling pattern list. Click the OK button or press RETURN to confirm the creation of your new tile pattern.

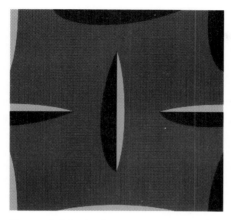

Figure 9.11: A tile containing metal ridges like those on a manhole cover.

The following exercise demonstrates how to create a pattern that looks like the cover of a manhole, with alternating horizontal and vertical ridges standing up from a metal plate, as shown in Figure 9.11. A mechanical tile pattern such as this readily lends itself to a computer-graphics environment. The exercise is longer than previous ones in this book, since creating a tile pattern involves several steps. However, the procedure is not particularly difficult:

1. Create the first ridge as a combination of three paths, as shown in Figure 9.12 on the next page. Each path is filled with a different shade of gray to impart a sense of depth and shadow, as shown in the second example in the figure.

2. Select the three paths and choose the Group command from the ARRANGE menu (⌘-G).

3. Press SHIFT and OPTION and drag the group about one inch to the left to create a clone of the group positioned horizontally from the original.

Figure 9.12: A single ridge made up of three paths (left) and the ridge as it appears when printed (right).

4. Choose the Transform Again command from the Arrange menu (⌘-D), to create a second clone of the group. You now have three ridges, spaced equidistantly.

5. Next, select the middle group. Using the reflect tool, option-click at the center of the selected group. Select the "Angled axis" radio button in the Reflect dialog box, enter 45 in the corresponding option box, and press return. The object will flip and rotate, as shown in Figure 9.13. (For complete information about the reflect tool and the Reflect dialog box, see the *Flipping objects* section of Chapter 12.)

Figure 9.13: Clone two additional ridges and flip the middle one about a 45° axis.

6. The first row of ridges is now complete. Select the three ridges and option-click the arrow tool icon in the toolbox to display the Move dialog box. Enter 72 for the "Horizontal" option and –72 for the "Vertical" option, then click the Copy button. (This assumes you are working in picas and points. If you are using inches, enter 1 and –1, respectively.) A set of cloned ridges will appear below and to the right of the first, acting as the beginning of a second row.

7. Select the two right ridges in the second row and SHIFT-OPTION-drag them to the left from the top point in the selected vertical ridge. Release your mouse button when this point snaps to the similar point in the stationary vertical ridge in the same row, as shown in Figure 9.14. By snapping, you ensure that the space between all ridges is constant.

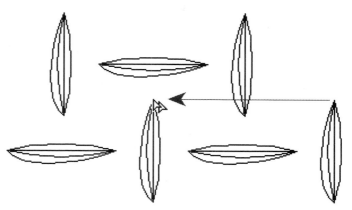

Figure 9.14: Clone two additional ridges and flip the middle one about a 45° axis.

8. You now have two coincident vertical ridges in the middle of the second row, one in front of the other. Select the front one and press DELETE or BACKSPACE to get rid of it. The right vertical ridge is also extraneous, so delete it as well.

9. To create a third row of ridges, select the three grouped objects in the top row and OPTION-click on the arrow tool icon to again display the MOVE dialog box. Enter 0 for the "Horizontal" option and –144 (–2 inches) for the "Vertical" option, then click the COPY button. Figure 9.15 on the next page shows the third row of ridges.

10. Draw a square surrounding the portions of the ridge objects that you want to repeat in the pattern, as shown in Figure 9.16 on the next page. This square determines the boundaries of the tile.

11. The square must always be the rearmost object in the tile. While the square remains selected, choose the SEND TO BACK command from the EDIT menu (⌘-–, COMMAND-HYPHEN).

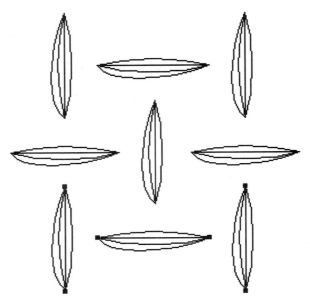

Figure 9.15: Clone the top row of ridges and move the clones down 144 points, or two inches.

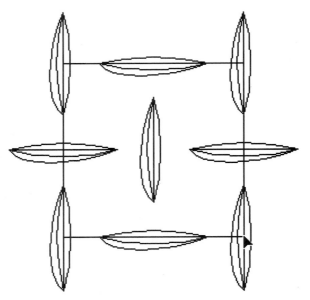

Figure 9.16: Draw a square to determine the boundaries of the tile.

When you draw your rectangle around the tile objects, try to visualize how it will look when the pattern is repeated. Objects that touch the left edge of the rectangle will be flush with the objects that touch the right edge. Likewise, objects that touch the top of the rectangle will meet with the objects that touch the bottom. Figure 9.17 shows six copies of the metal tile arranged in a pattern. Each object flows continuously through one tile and into another.

Figure 9.17: When drawing the boundary rectangle, visualize how the tiles will fit together.

12. Fill the square with a medium shade of gray to act as a background for the ridges.

13. Select the square and the ridge objects in front of the rectangle and choose the PATTERN... command from the PAINT menu to display the PATTERN dialog box.

14. Click on the NEW button to instruct Illustrator to designate the selected objects as a pattern tile. A preview of the prospective pattern tile will appear in the bottom right corner of the PATTERN dialog box. If the preview does not match the one shown in Figure 9.18 on the next page, click the CANCEL button, manipulate the pattern elements as necessary, and try again. Enter the name *Metal plate* into the "Change name to" option box and press RETURN to complete the creation of your new pattern.

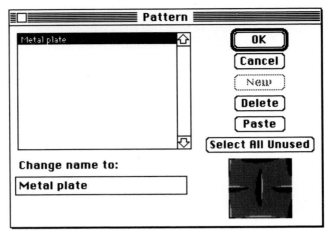

Figure 9.18: The Pattern dialog box previews the selected pattern tile.

You have now completed the creation of a simple tile pattern. The next section describes how to fill a text block or graphic object with a tile pattern and how to transform tiles within an object.

Filling objects with tile patterns

To fill one or more selected objects with a pattern, choose the STYLE... command from the PAINT menu (⌘-I). Select the "Pattern" radio button inside the "Fill" box in the PAINT STYLE dialog box. Then select a tile pattern from the scrolling list below the "Pattern" option. A preview of the tile will appear in the upper right corner of the "Fill" box.

After selecting a pattern, you may move, scale, rotate, flip, or slant a tile pattern inside the object it fills. To access this feature, click the TRANS-FORM... button to display the TRANSFORM PATTERN STYLE dialog box, shown in Figure 9.19. This dialog box contains the following options:

- **Move**. The options in this box allow you to move a pattern inside an object. Enter the distance of the move into the "Distance" option box. This value is measured in centimeters, inches, or points, depending on the setting of the "Ruler units" option in the PREF-ERENCES dialog box. Select the direction of your move from the "Horizontal," "Vertical," or "Angled" option. If "Angled," enter a directional value into the corresponding option box.

- **Scale**. The options in this box allow you to enlarge or reduce a pattern inside an object. If you want to scale the pattern proportionally, select the "Uniform" radio button and enter a percentage in the corresponding option box. Values less than 100% will reduce the pattern; values greater than 100% will enlarge it. If you want to scale the horizontal and vertical dimensions of the pattern differently, select the "Non-Uniform" option and enter values in the "Horizontal" and "Vertical" option boxes.

- **Rotate angle**. Enter a value in this option box if you want to rotate the pattern. The value is measured in degrees. Positive values make for counterclockwise rotations; negative values produce clockwise rotations.

- **Reflect across**. The options in this box allow you to flip a pattern inside an object. If you want to flip the pattern head-to-toe, select the "Horizontal" option. If you want to flip the pattern side to side, select "Vertical." To flip the pattern across a rotated axis, select the "Angled" radio button and enter a value in the corresponding option box.

- **Shear**. The options in this box allow you to slant a pattern inside an object. Enter the degree of the slant into the "Angle" option box. Select the direction of your slant from the "Horizontal," "Vertical," or "Angled" option. If "Angled," enter a directional value into the corresponding option box.

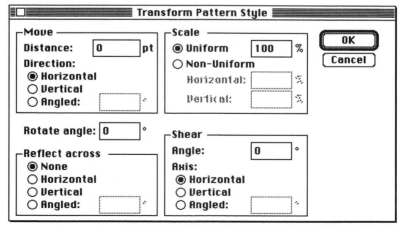

Figure 9.19: The Transform Pattern Style dialog box allows you to move, scale, rotate, flip, or slant the tiles inside a filled object.

Figure 9.20 shows the results of transforming the metal plate pattern within the fill of a rectangle. The first example in the figure shows the pattern as it appears normally, prior to any transformation. The second example on the left shows the pattern scaled to 200%; the third example on the left shows the pattern reflected across a −45° axis. Along the right-hand side of the figure, the first example shows the pattern rotated 45°; the second example shows the pattern slanted 20° along a horizontal axis; and in the third example, all four transformations have been applied to the pattern.

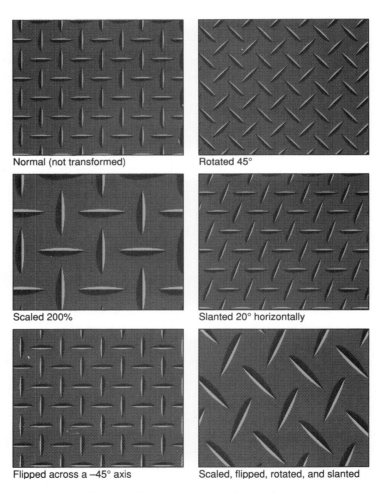

Normal (not transformed)

Rotated 45°

Scaled 200%

Slanted 20° horizontally

Flipped across a −45° axis

Scaled, flipped, rotated, and slanted

Figure 9.20: The metal plate pattern subjected to various transformations.

Notice that transformations applied using the TRANSFORM PATTERN STYLE dialog box do not transform the filled object itself, only the pattern tiles within the object. Also, a pattern is transformed only within the current selection. Transforming a pattern within one object does not transform that pattern within other objects filled or stroked with the same pattern.

The pattern origin

When you fill an object with a pattern, the relative location of each tile is based on its distance from the *ruler origin*; that is, the location where the horizontal and vertical ruler coordinates are 0, as discussed in the *Using the rulers* section of Chapter 12. The ruler origin acts as the origin point for tile patterns, even if an object filled with a pattern appears far from the origin.

All manipulations performed in the TRANSFORM PATTERN STYLE dialog are performed with respect to the ruler origin. For example, when you rotate a pattern 45°, you rotate it 45° around the ruler origin.

Beware of moving the ruler origin in an illustration that contains objects filled or stroked with patterns. By doing so, you will also move the pattern inside any object in the current file.

Transforming objects and patterns

Finally, you may transform a tile pattern along with a filled object. The MOVE dialog box (discussed in the section *Using the Move dialog box* in Chapter 7) as well as the SCALE, REFLECT, ROTATE, and SHEAR dialog boxes (discussed in Chapter 12, *Transforming and Duplicating Objects*) all contain check boxes that toggle the transformation of patterns within a transformed object. Rather than conforming strictly to the ruler origin, a tile pattern may conform momentarily to the location and orientation of the object filled with that pattern. However, whether transformed along with or independently of a filled object, a transformed pattern will always move when the ruler origin is moved.

If all of this seems a little confusing, consider the following example: Suppose that you select a rectangle filled with the metal plate pattern and OPTION-click on the arrow tool icon in the palette. In the MOVE dialog box, you specify a vertical move of 24 points and select the "Move pattern tiles" option. Both the selected rectangle and its fill pattern move upward two picas. If you now move the ruler origin, the pattern within the selected shape will move as well, but it will maintain its distance of two picas above the ruler origin.

When you first launch the Illustrator application, patterns are *not* transformed along with filled or stroked objects. This means that all of the following check boxes will be deselected:

- "Move pattern tiles" in the MOVE dialog box.
- "Scale pattern tiles" in the SCALE dialog box.
- "Reflect pattern tiles" in the REFLECT dialog box.
- "Rotate pattern tiles" in the ROTATE dialog box.
- "Shear pattern tiles" in the SHEAR dialog box.
- "Transform pattern tiles" in the PREFERENCES dialog box.

If you select any one of these options, you change the default settings for all the other options as well. Likewise, if you later deselect any of these options, you toggle the deselection of all the other options.

These options also affect manual transformations. For example, if the "Transform pattern tiles" option in the PREFERENCES dialog box is on, dragging an object filled with a pattern will cause the pattern to move as well. If the option is off, you may drag the object but its pattern fill will remain stationary.

Recognizing a transformed pattern

(Has been transformed by tools)

[Remove]

To see if a pattern has been transformed inside of an object, select the object and choose the STYLE... command from the PAINT menu (⌘-I). If any kind of transformation has occurred, the TRANSFORM... button will be preceded by a check mark. The TRANSFORM PATTERN STYLE dialog box will contain information concerning only those transformations that have been performed using the options contained in this dialog box. However, if a pattern has been transformed in the course of transforming the filled object, a message will appear below the CANCEL button reading "(Has been transformed by tools)." Below this message is a REMOVE button. If you click the REMOVE button, you reverse the effects of all pattern transformations applied in the course of transforming the selected object, although the object itself will remain transformed. Transformations applied using the TRANSFORM PATTERN STYLE dialog box options will also remain intact.

Organizing tile patterns

To conclude our discussion of patterning, we return to the PATTERN dialog box, displayed back in Figure 9.10. In addition to allowing you to create new patterns, the PATTERN dialog box provides options for organizing and editing existing tile patterns.

The central part of the dialog box is the scrolling pattern list. A pattern name is added to the scrolling list by clicking the NEW button. The list also contains the names of any patterns defined previously in the current document, or in any other open document. Patterns are always shared among open illustrations. If a new pattern is created in one file, it immediately becomes available to any other open file.

To create a library of patterns that is available every time you use Illustrator, add the patterns to the Adobe Illustrator Startup file. Keep in mind, however, that available patterns consume space in the application memory, and may slow or hamper Illustrator's performance.

You may manipulate patterns in the scrolling list using other buttons in the PATTERN dialog box as well. These buttons include the following:

- **Delete**. Click this button to delete a selected pattern name from the scrolling list. The selected pattern is removed from the current document *as well as from any other open document*. Any object that was filled or stroked with the deleted pattern will be painted with black. Extreme caution should be exercised when deleting patterns. Whenever possible, delete a pattern only when the current illustration is the only file open. Deleted patterns may be returned by clicking the CANCEL button.

If you delete a pattern name and click the OK button to confirm the deletion, you still have one last chance to regain the pattern by immediately choosing the UNDO PATTERN... command from the EDIT menu (⌘-Z).

- **Paste**. Sometimes you may wish to revise a pattern for which the objects that make up the pattern tile are not readily available. It may be a pattern from another document, or you may have discarded the objects in the drawing area after creating the pattern with the NEW button. Click the PASTE button to paste the objects of the selected pattern to the center of the current window. Click the

OK button to confirm the paste. These objects may then be manipulated as you see fit.

After changing the pattern objects, you may define them as a new pattern. You may also redefine an existing pattern, ascribing an existing pattern name to a new or altered set of objects. To accomplish this, select the objects (with rectangle in back), choose PATTERN... from the PAINT menu, and select the name of the pattern that you wish to redefine from the scrolling pattern list. Then click the OK button, or press RETURN. Don't be put off by the fact that Illustrator shows no sign of acknowledging the redefinition. All elements filled or stroked with that pattern will now be painted with the new pattern, as will elements in *any other open document*. You must use the same discretion when redefining patterns as you would when deleting them.

- **Select All Unused**. This button selects all patterns in the scrolling list that are not applied to objects in any open illustration. Since patterns consume a great deal of disk space, RAM space, and space in your printer's memory, it is often advisable to delete patterns that you are not currently using, provided that they exist in some other illustration that is not currently open. To delete unused patterns, click the SELECT ALL UNUSED, click DELETE, and then click OK or press RETURN.

A pattern may be renamed by selecting it from the scrolling list and entering a new name in the "Change name to" option box. This will change its name in all open illustrations.

Viewing patterns

Patterned fills and strokes may be viewed on screen only in the preview mode. However, patterns take a long time to preview, comparatively longer than any other fill effect. To increase previewing speed, select only the specific objects you want to preview and choose the PREVIEW SELECTION command from the VIEW menu (⌘-⌥-Y). Or you may simply prevent patterns from previewing at all by deselecting the "Preview and print patterns" option in the PREFERENCES dialog box (first introduced in the *Setting preferences* section of Chapter 3). Keep in mind, however, that this option also prevents patterns from printing. Pattern fills and strokes will appear gray.

One last note—Figure 9.21 displays a small sampling of additional patterns that may be created in Adobe Illustrator. Some patterns are shown exactly as they were created; others have been slanted or rotated. But they all demonstrate that both man-made and natural images repeat themselves and may therefore be expressed as a series of repeated tiles.

Figure 9.21: A selection of tile patterns created in Adobe Illustrator.

Like all fill effects in Adobe Illustrator, tile patterns may also be applied to type, as shown in Figure 9.22. Generally, large, sans serif type is best suited to this purpose.

TEXT BLOCKS

Figure 9.22: A tile pattern applied to a text block.

Patterns may be beautiful to look at, but they take a lot of effort to create and they eat up disk space and printer memory like you wouldn't believe. The rectangles in Figure 9.21 took over 30 minutes to print to a Linotronic 100 imagesetter with the newest ROMs available. For a more efficient filling technique that doesn't restrict you to using repeating images, create a clipping path, as described in the following section.

Clipping paths

Clipping path is the PostScript term for a path that is created specifically to be filled with other objects. It may also be called a *masking object*, or simply a *mask*, after the airbrushing technique where masking tape is laid down to define the perimeter of a spray-painted image.

The basic concept behind the clipping path is simple: Rather than filling an object with a shade of gray or some other color, you fill it with other objects, known as *masked elements*. Almost any text block or graphic object created in Illustrator may be used as a clipping path. The only exception is a grouped path, since grouping is used to define the limitations of a masking object, as discussed in the following section. Any number of lines, shapes, and other objects—grouped or ungrouped—may fill a clipping path. Even another clipping path may be masked.

Creating a clipping path

Creating a clipping path is much like creating a pattern, except that it involves fewer dialog boxes. After filling and stroking all objects, assemble the prospective mask and the masking elements in their desired relative locations. Then select the mask and choose the SEND TO BACK command from the EDIT menu (⌘-–, COMMAND-HYPHEN). While the masking object remains selected, choose the STYLE... command from the PAINT menu (⌘-I) and selecting the "Mask" check box. Press RETURN to exit the PAINT STYLE dialog box. Now select all objects in the clipping path, both mask and masking elements, and choose the GROUP command from the ARRANGE menu (⌘-G).

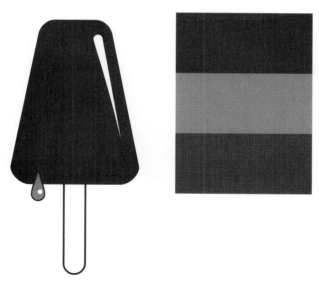

Figure 9.23: The following exercise demonstrates how to color the bomb-pop (left) with the stripes (right).

Figure 9.23 shows a popsicle next to some stripes. The following exercise demonstrates how to set the stripes inside the body of the popsicle to create a . . . a whatchamacallit, a *bomb-pop*; you know, one of those three-color frozen treats kids like to rub all over their faces (or as Webster's calls it, "colored water frozen in a rectangular shape on a flat handle"—yum). The problem is this: how to set the stripes inside the bomb-pop body without affecting the drip or the stick.

1. In order to create the clipping path, you must first move the prospective masked elements—the stripes—into position relative to the bomb-pop. Figure 9.24 shows the proper relative locations of masked elements and clipping path, as viewed in the artwork-&-template mode. This positioning will determine the exact manner in which the elements will fill the mask.

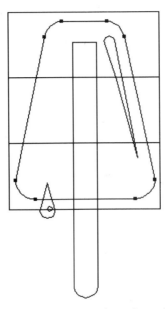

Figure 9.24: Mask and masked elements assembled, as viewed in the artwork-&-template mode.

2. Select the bomb-pop body (shown as selected in the figure) and choose the STYLE... command from the PAINT menu (⌘-I) to display the PAINT dialog box.

3. Select the "Mask" check box option on the right side of the dialog box and press the RETURN key.

4. Any element for which the "Mask" option is selected will mask only those elements that are in front of it. From Figure 9.23, you can surmise that the layering order for the popsicle before adding the stripes was something like this: the stick was at the back, the bomb-pop body was in front of that, and the paths that make up the drip were frontmost. To mask the stripes, they must be inserted between the body and the drip. Select the three stripes and choose the CUT command from the EDIT menu (⌘-X). Then select the bomb-pop body path and choose PASTE IN FRONT from the EDIT menu (⌘-F). The stripes are now directly in front of the body in layering order. (For a complete description of the PASTE IN FRONT command, see the *Layering objects* section of Chapter 12.)

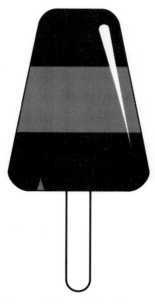

Figure 9.25: If the clipping path is not grouped with its masking elements, it will mask all objects in front of it, including the paths that make up the drip.

5. Because the bomb-pop body is in front of the stick, there is no danger of the stick becoming masked. However, the body is in back of the stripes and the drip. So as things stand now, stripes and drip get masked, as shown in Figure 9.25. You may define what

gets masked and what does not using the Group command in the Arrange menu. Any objects in the same group as the mask and in front of the mask get masked; any objects outside the group are not masked, regardless of layering order. Select the paths that make up the mask and the stripes and choose Group (⌘-G). Since the drip is not included in the group, it is no longer masked, as shown in Figure 9.26.

Figure 9.26: Group body and stripes to limit the elements that get masked.

For some reason, a clipping path in Illustrator will mask its own stroke. As we will discuss in Chapter 10, *Stroking Type and Graphic Objects*, a stroke is centered on its path, so half of the line weight appears inside the path and half appears outside the path. The half that is outside gets masked away, leaving only half the actual line weight visible. In Figure 9.26, for example, the stroke around the bomb-pop is only half as thick as the stroke around the stick; yet they started out with the same weight, as verified by Figure 9.23.

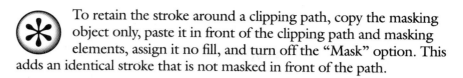 To retain the stroke around a clipping path, copy the masking object only, paste it in front of the clipping path and masking elements, assign it no fill, and turn off the "Mask" option. This adds an identical stroke that is not masked in front of the path.

The final steps in the exercise demonstrate how this technique may be applied to the popsicle:

6. Select the bomb-pop body with the direct-selection tool and choose COPY from the EDIT menu (⌘-C) to copy it to the Clipboard.

7. Select the arrow tool (⌘-➡I). Click on an empty portion of the drawing area to deselect everything. Click on the clipping path to select the entire group. Choose the PASTE IN FRONT command (⌘-F) to paste the copy of the body in front of the group.

Figure 9.27: The finished image with original stroke restored.

8. While the copy remains selected, choose STYLE… from the PAINT menu (⌘-I). Delete the "Mask" check box. Select the "None" radio button inside the "Fill" box. Press RETURN. Figure 9.27 shows the finished image.

If you decide you do not care for the appearance of a clipping path, you may make adjustments with the direct-selection tool. If you want to add or subtract objects in the clipping path, first ungroup the path and its masked elements. After making the desired adjustments, regroup all objects involved in the mask before printing or previewing.

Creating multiple masks

Only one clipping path may mask a set of masked elements; that is, a single set of masked elements may not be shared between multiple clipping paths. However, if you want to create the appearance of shared masked elements, you may duplicate a set of masking elements, one for each of several clipping paths.

Figure 9.28: The graphic portion of this logo comprises four clipping paths filled with continuous masked elements.

For example, Figure 9.28 displays a logo made up of four similar clipping paths. Each path is shaped differently and filled differently. However, each path masks what appear to be part of one large pattern of objects. To accomplish this, we created a set of masked elements that was as large as all four clipping paths combined. We then grouped these elements independently of their clipping paths and copied the group. After selecting the "Mask" option from the PAINT dialog for each clipping path, we grouped the first clipping path with the group of masked elements. We then chose the PASTE IN FRONT command to produce another group of masking elements and grouped these with the second clipping path, and so on. The final logo creates a sort of puzzle-piece effect, where the contents of one clipping path flow into the contents of its neighbor.

Masking endnotes

If an object completely disappears when previewing or printing, it may be because the object is considered to be a masked element, even though no portion of the object overlaps a clipping path. The object may have been inadvertently grouped with a clipping path or, more likely, it resides in front of a clipping path that has not been grouped.

Like graphic objects, text objects may mask other elements. However, only whole text blocks may act as clipping paths. You may not select specific characters with the type tool to make them masking objects.

Making holes

Another way to display objects within objects is to create one or more holes in the middle of a path using the MAKE COMPOUND command under the PAINT menu. For example, consider the cartoon man in Figure 9.29 on the following page. The first example in the figure displays his full face. But suppose you need to add a ski mask to the image. A real-life ski mask has holes cut into it for the eyes. Therefore your cartoon ski mask must also have holes for the eyes, as shown in the second example in the figure. The holes in the cartoon ski mask, however, are actually paths that have been combined with the ski mask path using the MAKE COMPOUND command.

Eye holes and mask are together known as a *compound path*, because in a few key respects, Illustrator treats the object as a single path. All objects included in the compound path must be filled and stroked identically using options available in the PAINT STYLE dialog box. And, like a group or a linked object, selecting any part of a compound path with the arrow tool selects the entire compound path. But also, like a group, you may use the direct-selection tool to manipulate objects independently within a compound path.

Figure 9.29: A cartoon face (left) and the same face with the addition of a compound path (right). Compound paths may contain holes through which you can see underlying images.

Creating a compound path

Compound paths are about the easiest special effect you can create in Illustrator. First assemble the objects that you want to combine in their desired relative positions. One path will act as the background path and one or more other paths will act as the holes. For best results, all holes should overlap some portion of the larger background path. Select the background path and choose the SEND TO BACK command from the EDIT menu (⌘--, COMMAND-HYPHEN). Then select all paths—background path and all holes—and choose the MAKE COMPOUND command from the PAINT menu (⌘-⌥-G). Background and holes are now combined.

To change the fill or stroke of all objects in a compound path, select any object, using the arrow tool or direct-selection tool, and choose STYLE… from the PAINT menu (⌘-I). Almost any change you make inside the PAINT STYLE dialog box will affect every object in the compound path. The only exception is the "Reversed" check box, which is available only when one or more objects in a compound path are selected. It is the "Reversed" option that determines whether an object is a background path or a hole. Therefore, the following rules apply:

- If a background path is selected, the "Reversed" option will be turned off, indicating the current object is not a hole.

- If a hole is selected, the "Reversed" option will be turned on, indicating that the current object is a hole.

- If an entire compound path is selected, the "Reversed" option will be grayed, indicating some objects are holes and others are not.

You may change whether a selected object is a hole or a background path at any time by selecting or deselecting the "Reversed" option.

Figure 9.30: This doughnut would look more like a doughnut if you could see through its center.

Figure 9.30 shows a doughnut on a checkered napkin. Unfortunately, it does not look much like a doughnut because the doughnut hole has not yet been removed. You can save this doughnut from a heartbreaking existence on the Island of Misfit Pastry by completing the following exercise. You will also create a shadow beneath the doughnut that is itself a compound path:

1. The doughnut is made up of two circles, both drawn with the oval tool. As discussed in the *Reshaping geometric objects* section of Chapter 7, the oval tool always draws grouped shapes. However, one of the MAKE COMPOUND command's little rules is that it does not allow you to combine objects from different groups. So select both circles and choose the UNGROUP command from the ARRANGE menu (⌘-U).

2. A doughnut is a simple image, consisting of a background shape and a single hole. To ensure that the larger circle will act as the background, select the shape and choose the SEND TO BACK command (⌘--, COMMAND-HYPHEN).

Figure 9.31: Send the large circle to the back of the illustration.

3. The large circle now appears in back of the napkin, as shown in Figure 9.31. That's a little too far back, but the problem will take care of itself. Select both circles and choose the MAKE COMPOUND command (⌘-⌥-G). The doughnut now has a hole, as shown in Figure 9.32. Notice that the large circle is in front of the napkin. The MAKE COMPOUND command always moves all selected objects to directly in back of the frontmost object in the selection.

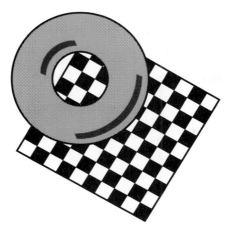

Figure 9.32: Combining the circles makes a hole
and brings the large circle in front of the napkin.

4. To create the shadow, clone the doughnut by OPTION-dragging it with the arrow tool about a half inch down and to the right.

5. Send the clone to the back of the illustration (⌘- –, COMMAND-HYPHEN).

6. Choose STYLE… from the PAINT menu (⌘-I). Enter 50 into the "Black %" option box in the "Fill" box and select the "None" radio button in the "Stroke" box. Then press RETURN. The finished illustration appears as shown in Figure 9.33.

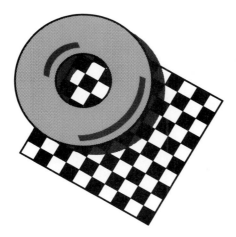

Figure 9.33: The finished doughnut with shadow.

In case you're wondering, the shadow appears to shade the napkin because the napkin is filled with a partially transparent tile pattern. The pattern contains only black squares. The appearance of white squares is created by an absence of black squares. Therefore, you can see through the "white" squares to the shadow at the back of the illustration.

Compound masking

In Illustrator 3.0, a compound path may double as a clipping path, allowing you to create a path that is filled with objects and has holes punched out of it. After creating a compound path, select the object, using the direct-selection tool or arrow tool, and turn on the "Mask" command in the PAINT STYLE dialog box. Then layer the masking element in front of the compound path, and group compound path and masking elements together.

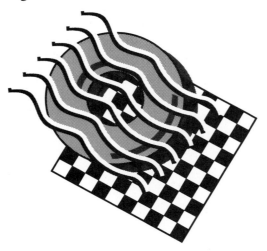

Figure 9.34: The next exercise demonstrates how to fill the doughnut with these stripes of icing.

In Figure 9.34, we have added several stripes of icing in front of the doughnut. The following exercise describes how to use the doughnut as a clipping path to mask the icing:

1. Select the large circle of the doughnut with the direct-selection tool and choose the STYLE... command from the PAINT menu (⌘-I). Select the "Mask" check box inside the PAINT STYLE dialog

box and press RETURN. (If you were to select the smaller circle and display the PAINT STYLE dialog box, you would see that the "Mask" option is now turned on for this path as well.)

2. Select the icing stripes with the arrow tool. Choose the CUT command from the EDIT menu (⌘-X).

3. Select the doughnut and choose PASTE IN FRONT (⌘-F). This ensures that the masking elements (icing) are in front of the clipping path (doughnut).

4. Select icing stripes and doughnut and choose the GROUP command (⌘-G). The mask is now complete.

5. To restore the stroke around the doughnut, select the two circles with the direct-selection tool and choose COPY (⌘-C).

6. Deselect all objects by clicking on a blank portion of the drawing area. Choose the arrow tool and choose PASTE IN FRONT again (⌘-F). The copy of the doughnut is pasted to the front of the illustration.

7. Choose STYLE… from the PAINT menu (⌘-I), select the "None" radio button from the "Fill" box, deselect the "Mask" check box, and press RETURN. The finished doughnut is shown in Figure 9.35.

Figure 9.35: The finished doughnut with icing.

Compound paths and text

Type may *not* be associated with a compound path. However, you may convert a block of type to paths using the CREATE OUTLINES command from the TYPE menu, and then combine these paths with other graphic objects using the MAKE COMPOUND command. You should note, however, that type is converted to compound paths automatically. It is generally a good idea to break the paths apart using the RELEASE COMPOUND command (⌘-⬏-U) before combining them with other paths.

Breaking compound paths

To break apart a compound path, select the object and choose the RELEASE COMPOUND command from the PAINT menu (⌘-⬏-U). The "Reversed" check box in the Paint Style dialog box will become dimmed, and all paths will be restored to opaque fills. This command is especially handy if you want to dramatically reshape type that has been converted using the CREATE OUTLINES command, as described in the *Converting type to paths* section in Chapter 8.

Filling theory

We now mention one last bit of information that concerns the method by which Illustrator fills paths with overlapping segments. The question is: When is part of a path considered to be outside the path and when is it considered inside? To determine the answer, Illustrator uses a PostScript routine known as the *non-zero winding number rule* to determine the fill of a shape. To save paper, we'll just call it the *Ø-rule*.

To demonstrate this rule, we'll use the complex path shown in Figure 9.36. We have designed this path so that every segment overlaps at least two other segments in the path. In Figure 9.37, we have enhanced the shape with directional arrows. These arrows demonstrate the direction in which each segment in the shape progresses from point to point. If you start at any point in the path and trace along the path in the direction indicated by the arrows, you will eventually arrive back at the point at which you started, having traced every segment exactly one time. Therefore, the arrows represent the consistent progression of the path through its points.

Figure 9.36: Every segment in this path overlaps at least two and as many as five segments.

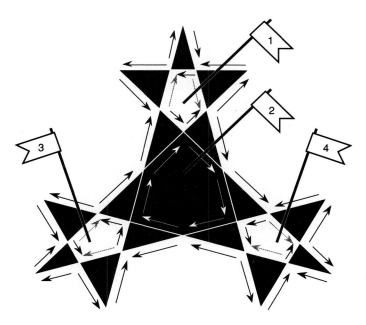

Figure 9.37: A filled version of the same path notated with arrows and flags.

The manner in which we have drawn the path divides it into nineteen *subsections,* that is, a portion of the path separated from other portions by part of a segment. If a subsection is bordered entirely by other subsections, then we say it is *encompassed.* Any subsection that is *not* encompassed is obviously inside the path and will be filled just like a path whose segments do not overlap. In Figure 9.37, the four encompassed subsections are identified by flagpoles, labeled 1 through 4. These are the subsections that are subjected to the Ø-rule.

Each flagpole begins inside an encompassed subsection and extends to a location outside of the path. Each pole crosses two or more segments. Each segment, according to its arrows in the figure, progresses at least partially in a rightward or leftward direction. To illustrate the winding number rule, we will use the metaphor of raising flags up the flagpoles. Before we begin raising the flag, we have a "flag variable" of zero. As we raise the flag, it will cross a number of segments. For each rightward-progressing segment that it crosses, we add 1 to our flag variable. For each leftward-progressing segment crossed, we subtract 1 from our flag variable. Once the flag is raised beyond all crossing segments, we compute the total. This final flag variable will lead us to one of two conclusions:

- If it is zero, then the encompassed subsection from which the flagpole emanates is *outside* of the shape, and will *not* be filled.

- If it is not equal to zero, the encompassed subsection is *inside* the shape and will be filled.

Flag 1 in Figure 9.37 crosses both a rightward- and leftward-progressing segment. The flag variable is 0+1−1=0, so its subsection is outside the shape by the Ø-rule. The same is true for flags 3 and 4. However, flag 2 crosses two rightward-progressing segments. Its flag variable is 0+1+1=2. Therefore, its subsection is inside the shape.

The conclusion: Of all the encompassed subsections, only the center one is filled, as shown in the figure.

Perhaps an easier way to think of this rule is this:

- If all directional arrows surrounding an encompassed subsection do *not* progress in a consistently clockwise or counterclockwise formation, the subsection is considered by Illustrator to be *outside* the shape.

• If all directional arrows *do* progress in a consistently clockwise or counterclockwise formation, the subsection is considered by Illustrator to be *inside* the shape.

The arrows surrounding the subsection containing flag 2 establish a consistently clockwise order; thus the subsection is filled. The subsections containing flags 1, 3, and 4, however, each have one or more dissenting arrows that flow against the majority direction. These dissenting arrows are grayed in Figure 9.37.

Keep in mind, this rule only affect paths with overlapping segments. Standard paths with no overlapping segments are always filled according to your directions, as described in previous sections of this chapter. If you do have to create an overlapping path (very rare) and this rule seems too complex (very common), just preview the path and take your chances. You can always go back and fix it later.

Stroking Type and Graphic Objects

Like the fill attribute, *stroke* is applied to both type and graphic objects to determine the appearance of your printed artwork. Fill is applied to the interior of an object, while stroke is applied to its outline. Strokes share many similarities with fills: they may be colored with gray values, process colors, and even as tile patterns. Or they may be transparent, so that only the fill can be seen. If you also apply a transparent fill, you may create an invisible object, which can be used for alignment purposes. However, a stroke may not be subjected to masking or hole making, features that can be applied only to the interior of a shape. By the same token, stroke provides options that are irrelevant to fill: line weight, dash patterns, caps, joins, and so on, all of which are explained in this chapter.

How stroke affects objects

Stroke may be applied to any object in Adobe Illustrator. Applying a stroke to a path is a straightforward process. If you want to see a path's outline, apply a stroke. Otherwise, do not.

Figure 10.01 shows an identical stroke applied to an open path and a closed path. In both cases, we have drawn in the path in white to show how the stroke is always centered on the path. This is important to keep in mind when trying to determine the amount of space a stroke will take when you print your artwork. You may also exploit this feature to create useful effects, as described in the section *Mixing stroke attributes* later in this chapter.

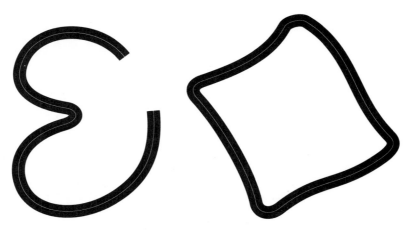

Figure 10.01: An open path (left) and a closed path (right), each stroked with a heavy line. The actual paths are displayed in white.

Stroking text

Text objects may also be stroked. However, stroking type has become complicated by the new relationship between type and paths in Illustrator 3.0. If you select a text block with the arrow tool, applying a stroke will affect all type as well as any associated path. The first example in Figure 10.02 shows a selected path text block. Stroking the object with a thin line strokes both path and type, as shown in the second example.

Figure 10.02: If you stroke a text block selected with the arrow tool (top), both text and path will become stroked (bottom).

If you select the path with the direct-selection tool, you may apply a stroke to the path only, while leaving the text as is, as in Figure 10.03.

Figure 10.03: If you select the path with the direct-selection tool (top), only the path will become stroked (bottom).

You may also stroke single words and other collections of specific characters without affecting the path by selecting the text with the type tool. Like any character-level formatting option, such as font or type size, stroke affects only highlighted characters, as demonstrated in Figure 10.04. In this way, Illustrator 3.0 allows you to apply several different strokes to a single text object.

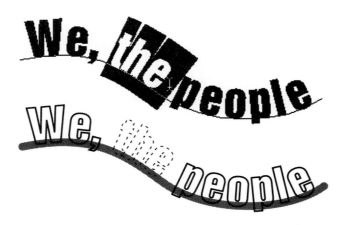

Figure 10.04: By selecting text with the type tool (top), you stroke only the highlighted type (bottom).

Painting the stroke

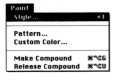

To stroke an object, you must select the object and choose the STYLE... command from the PAINT menu (⌘-I). The PAINT STYLE dialog box will display, as shown in Figure 10.05. Every characteristic of a stroke can be determined or manipulated within this dialog box.

As you might expect, all the options inside the "Stroke" box affect the stroke of a selected object. Most of the options outside the "Stroke" box (excepting those inside the "Fill" box) affect the current stroke as well. These options include the following:

- **Weight**. The option box determines the thickness, or *line weight*, of the current stroke, as measured in points. Any value between 0 and 1296 (18 inches) may be entered for this option.

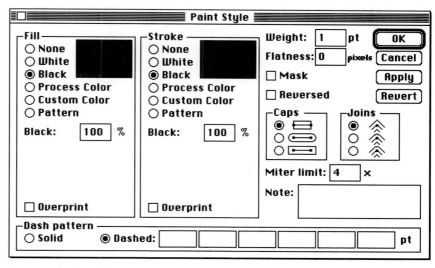

Figure 10.05: The Paint Style dialog box, provides access to all of Illustrator's stroking options.

- **Caps**. This option allows you to select from three radio buttons that control the appearance of a stroke at the end of an open path. Represented by icons, these options include the *butt cap* (⊟), *round cap* (⊜), and the *square cap* (⊡). When selected, the butt cap option instructs the stroke to end exactly at an endpoint. The round cap option appends a semicircle to the endpoints of a path. The square cap extends the stroke half the line weight past each endpoint. The "Caps" options do *not* affect the appearance of closed paths or text unless a dash pattern is used (as described in the *Dash patterns and line caps* section, later in this chapter).

- **Joins**. This option allows you to select from three radio buttons that control the appearance of a stroke at each corner or cusp in the current object. Represented by icons, these options include the *miter join* (⧸), *round join* (⧸), and the *bevel join* (⧸). When selected, the miter join option forces the stroke to form a single, crisp corner. The round join option smooths off corners to give paths a soft appearance. The bevel join severs the stroke abruptly at the corner point.

- **Miter limit**. The value in this option box tells Illustrator at what point to slice off an overly long miter join to form a bevel join. The value, which may be between 0 and 10, is measured in multiples of the current line weight. For example, when the value is 4, the default, Illustrator allows the miter join to extend a distance from its corner point equal to four times the current line weight. If the miter join is any longer (due to a very sharp corner in the path), the stroke is severed at the corner point to form a bevel join.

- **Dash pattern**. This box contains two radio buttons: "Solid" and "Dashed." When solid is selected, the current stroke will be solid, free of interruptions, except those inherent in a tile pattern, if the "Pattern" option is selected in the "Stroke" box. Select "Dashed" to interrupt the stroke at regular intervals to create a *dash pattern*. Enter the length of each dash and gap in the option boxes to the right of the "Dashed" option. The first, third, and fifth option boxes determine the dashes; the second, fourth, and sixth option boxes determine the gaps. All values are measured in points.

All other options outside the "Stroke" or "Fill" boxes control other aspects of painting an object, as described in the *Painting the fill* section of Chapter 9.

Coloring a stroke

Use the options inside the "Stroke" box in the PAINT STYLE dialog box to color the stroke of one or more selected objects. Only one of the radio button options may be selected at a time. Many options display other options that request additional specifications in determining the color of a stroke. Each radio button option and its related options are discussed in the following items:

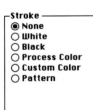

- **None**. This option is selected by default the first time you enter the PAINT STYLE dialog box. It makes the outline of the selected path transparent. This is not to say that a shape with a transparent stroke no longer exists; however, the outline of such a shape is invisible. The "None" option is useful for stroking type and paths when you want only the fill to be visible. You may also assign both a transparent stroke and a transparent fill to a path. An entirely transparent path remains visible in the artwork mode but will neither preview nor print. Such a path may be used for alignment purposes or as the boundary in a wrapping object, as described in the section *Adjusting standoff* in Chapter 8.

When "None" is selected, all options outside the "Stroke" box that pertain to stroke will become dimmed. Therefore, "None" may not be used in conjunction with any option described in future sections of this chapter.

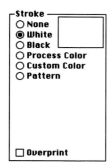

- **White**. Selecting this option makes the stroke of a selected path white. When selected, a box appears to the right of the "White" radio button, demonstrating the color of the stroke. A white outline is generally used to partially hide an element or a similar stroke in back of the selected path. You may also create type with a white outline against a colored background.

  An "Overprint" check box option appears at the bottom of the "Stroke" box when the "White" radio button is selected. This option applies strictly to color illustrations that are printed using the Adobe Separator utility. When selected, overlapping colors in different separations are allowed to blend with each other. Colors may *not* overprint within a single separation or print. See Chapter 11, *Coloring Fills and Strokes*, for a complete description of the "Overprint" option. The Adobe Separator utility is discussed in Chapter 15, *Printing Your Illustrations*.

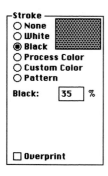

- **Black**. This option is more versatile than the "White" option, since it may be used to stroke a path not only with black, but also with any shade of gray. You may adjust the shade, or *tint*, of a gray stroke by altering the percentage value in the "Black %" option box that appears under the radio button options. A value of 100% is solid black; 0% equates to solid white. Values between 0% and 100% produce progressively darker shades of gray. The box that appears at the side of the "Black" radio button option demonstrates the color of the outline of the selected shape. Refer to Figures 9.08 and 9.09 (on page 333) to see how various gray values preview and print.

  An "Overprint" check box option appears at the bottom of the "Stroke" box when the "Black" radio button is selected. When selected, overlapping colors in different separations are allowed to blend with each other.

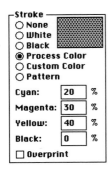

- **Process Color**. Selecting this option displays the "Cyan," "Magenta," "Yellow," and "Black" option boxes in the lower portion of the "Stroke" box. By altering the values in these option boxes, you determine the percentage of each primary printing color that is combined to create a specific *process color*, which is displayed in the box directly above the "Process Color" radio button. If you have a monochrome monitor, the process color will be displayed as a black-and-white composite. Chapter 11, *Coloring Fills and Strokes*, contains an in-depth discussion of process colors.

  An "Overprint" check box option appears at the bottom of the "Stroke" box when the "Process Color" radio button is selected. When selected, overlapping composite colors in different separations are allowed to blend with each other.

- **Custom Color**. Selecting this option produces a scrolling list of custom colors defined using the CUSTOM COLOR... command under the PAINT menu. If the Pantone Colors file is currently open, or if you have integrated its colors into your Adobe Illustrator Startup file (as recommended in Chapter 11), the scrolling list will contain the full library of 747 Pantone printing inks. If you have not created a single custom color in at least one open illustration, the "Custom Color" option will be dimmed.

  The "Tint %" option box under the scrolling list allows you to lighten the shade of a color to any percentage value between 0% (white) and 100% (the solid color). An "Overprint" check box option appears at the bottom of the "Stroke" box when the "Custom Color" radio button is selected. When selected, overlapping colors in different separations are allowed to blend with each other.

- **Pattern**. Selecting this option produces a scrolling list of patterns defined using the PATTERN... command under the PAINT menu (as discussed in the *Tile patterns* section of Chapter 9.) The usual "Overprint" check box is replaced by a TRANSFORM... button. Clicking the button brings up the TRANSFORM PATTERN STYLE dialog box, which allows you to move or otherwise manipulate a pattern with respect to the outline of a text block or path. If you have not created a single pattern in at least one open illustration, the "Pattern" option will be dimmed.

The following sections describe how to use the stroking options that appear outside the "Stroke" box in the PAINT STYLE dialog box.

Specifying a line weight

To the right of the "Stroke" box are a series of options that affect the stroke of a selected path. The first of these is the "Weight" option box, which controls the thickness, or *line weight*, of a stroke. Regardless of the selected "Ruler Units" option in the PREFERENCES dialog box (introduced in the *Setting preferences* section of Chapter 3), line weight is always specified in points. Also, unlike some programs that allow you to choose only from a predetermined set of line weights, Illustrator gives you total control, allowing you to enter any value between 0 and 1296, the latter being equal to the width of the entire drawing area.

Generally, we advise against specifying a line weight value smaller than 0.15. A 0.3-point weight is commonly considered a *hairline* weight, so 0.15-point is only half as heavy as a hairline. As an example, suppose you specify a 0-point line weight, which instructs Illustrator to print the thinnest line available from the current output device. The thinnest line printable by 300-dpi laser printer is 0.24-point thick (1/300 inch). However, higher-resolution printers, such as Linotronic and Compugraphic imagesetters, easily print lines as thin as 0.03 point, or 10 times thinner than a hairline. Nonetheless, because any line thinner than 0.15-point is almost invisible to the naked eye, such a line will probably drop out when reproduced commercially.

Specifying a line cap

Another set of options that affect stroke are the "Caps" options. Inside the "Caps" box, you may select from three *line caps*, which determine the appearance of a stroke at an endpoint. Therefore, line caps are generally useful only when stroking an open path. The only exception to this is when line caps are used in combination with dash patterns, as described in the *Dash patterns and line caps* section, later in this chapter.

The "Caps" options function as follows:

- **Butt cap**. The first radio button in the "Caps" box is the *butt cap* option, the default setting and by far the most commonly used line cap. Notice the black line that runs through the center of each of the icons in the "Caps" box. This line denotes the position of the path relative to the stroke. When the butt cap option is selected, the stroke ends immediately at an endpoint and is perpendicular to the final course of the path, as its icon suggests.

- **Round cap**. The second radio button is a *round cap* option. Giving a stroke a round cap is like attaching a circle to the end of a path. The endpoint acts as the center of this circle, and its radius is half the line weight, as demonstrated by Figure 10.06. For example, suppose you have a 4-point line weight with round caps that follows a horizontal path. A 2-point portion of the stroke is on top of the path and the other 2-point portion is underneath. Since the path is itself invisible, the two halves of the stroke meet with no break between them. Upon reaching the end of the path, the top half of the stroke wraps around the endpoint in a circular manner to meet with the bottom half of the stroke; hence a semicircle with a 2-point radius.

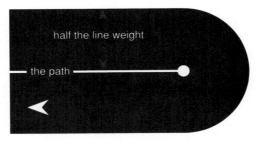

Figure 10.06: When the round cap option is selected, the stroke wraps around the endpoints in a path to form semicircles.

We, the people
We, the people

Figure 10.07: Two lines of type composed of open paths, one stroked with square caps (top) and one with round caps (bottom).

When combined with round joins (described in the next section), round caps may be used to give an open path an informal appearance. Figure 10.07 shows several letters composed of open paths. The first example is stroked with square caps (described below), the second is stroked with round caps. Which do you think looks more friendly?

- **Square cap**. The third radio button is the *square cap* option. Here, a square is attached to the end of a line; the endpoint is the center of the square. It is similar to the rounded cap in the sense that the size of this square is dependent on the line weight. The width and height of the square are equal to the weight of the stroke, so that the square projects from the endpoint a distance equal to one half the weight of the stroke. If the path in Figure 10.08 has a 4-point line weight, for example, the upper corner of the stroke would be located 2 points above and 2 points to the right of the endpoint.

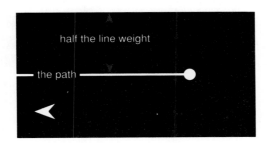

half the line weight

the path

Figure 10.08: When the square cap option is selected, the stroke wraps around the endpoints in a path to form perpendicular corners.

Specifying a line join

Next to the "Caps" box in the PAINT STYLE dialog are the "Joins" options. Inside the "Joins" box, you may select from three *line joins*, which determine the appearance of a stroke at places in a path where two segments meet at a corner point. Line joins have no affect on the appearance of stroked smooth points.

The "Joins" options function as follows:

- **Miter join**. The first radio button in the "Joins" box is the *miter join* option, which is the default setting. If a corner has a miter join, the outside edges of a stroke extend until they meet. Notice the first example of Figure 10.09. A corner with a true miter join will always form a single crisp corner. Miter joins can, however, be cut short using the "Miter limit" option, explained in the next section.

Figure 10.09: Three corners and three joins: from top to bottom, a miter join, a round join, and a bevel join.

- **Round join**. The second radio button is the *round join* option, which is identical in principal to the round cap. Half of the line weight wraps around the corner point to form a semicircle. In fact, rounded joins and rounded caps are so alike that they are almost exclusively used together. We recommend that you do not use round joins in combination with butt caps. We doubly recommend this if any dash pattern is involved, because round joins actually form complete circles around corner points. See the *Dash patterns and line joins* section later in this chapter for more information.

- **Bevel join**. The third and last radio button is the *bevel join* option. The bevel join is very similar to a butt cap. Instead of allowing the edges of a stroke to meet, as in the case of a miter join, the stroke is sheared off at the corner point. The result is what appears to be two very closely situated corners. Unlike a butt cap, however, a bevel join is not sheared perpendicularly to any path segment. Since two segments meet at a corner point, a compromise is struck. As you may notice in the last example of Figure 10.09, the angle at which the sheared edge of the bevel join meets with one segment is identical to the angle at which it meets the other.

Bevelling excessive miter joins

Directly below the "Caps" and "Joins" boxes in the PAINT STYLE dialog is the "Miter limit" option box, which allows you to bevel excessively long miter joins. This option works by establishing a relationship between the current line weight and the maximum width of a stroke at any corner point, called the *miter limit*. If a miter join is longer than the line weight times the value entered in the "Miter limit" option box, the join is converted into a bevel join at that corner point only.

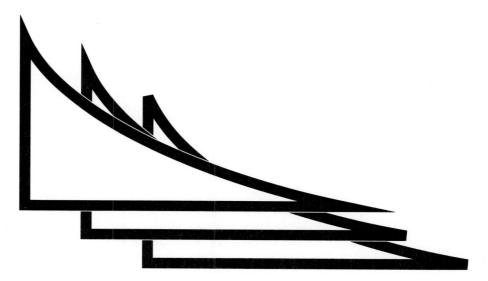

Figure 10.10: Three versions of a path stroked with miter joins but with different miter limits: from top to bottom, the "Miter limit" value is 10, 5, and 3.

The top path in Figure 10.10 includes two pairs of segments that meet to form sharp corners. The stroke of this path includes miter joins. The top and right-hand corners are so sharp that the joins must extend an extreme distance before the two edges of the stroke can finally meet.

Occasionally, you will discover that excessively long tips at the corners of a path may protrude into other paths or simply appear unattractive. Unfortunately, Illustrator does not allow you to give one corner a different line join than any other corner in a single path. But it does allow you to do the next best thing.

Using the "Miter limit" option, you can specify that if the mitered stroke of a path extends beyond any corner point to form a tip that is longer than a specified multiple of the line weight, then that corner is converted to a bevel join. The line weight of each path in Figure 10.10 is 10 points. The miter limit of the top path has been set to 10, which is the maximum miter limit value Illustrator will accept. This means that if the stroke of the path extends from any corner point to form a tip that measures more than ten times the 10-point line weight, or 100 points long, the miter join at that point will be sliced off completely. Since none of the segments in the figure meet to form such a sharp corner, the top path contains only miter joins.

In the middle path of Figure 10.10, however, the miter limit has been decreased to 5. Since the stroke at the right corner measures more than 50 points from the inside to the outside of the "elbow" of the path, Illustrator automatically converts this miter join to a bevel join. The stroke at the top corner of this path remains a miter join, since its tip is shorter than 50 points.

To create the bottom path in the figure, the miter limit has been changed to 3. Because the strokes at both the top and right-hand corners measure more than 30 points from inner to outer tip, both joins are sliced off to form bevel joins.

The "Miter limit" value may be any integer from 1 to 10, the default value being 4. A miter limit of 1 specifies that every corner in a path should be beveled, and is therefore identical to selecting the bevel join option from the "Joins" box. The "Miter limit" option is useful only with miter joins. If either the round join or bevel join is selected in the "Joins" box, the "Miter limit" option will be dimmed.

✳ Choosing between a huge corner tip and no tip at all is a harsh compromise. If you wish to preserve the attractive quality of a miter join without allowing it to take over too large a portion of your drawing, you may prefer to adjust your path to increase the angle between a pair of segments, thus decreasing the length of the tip formed by the stroke. A miter limit should be used only as a last resort.

Creating a dash pattern

The only remaining options in the PAINT STYLE dialog box that affect the stroke of a path are those in the "Dash pattern" box. *Dash patterns* are variations in the manner in which a stroke follows its path. Most often, this results in repetitive interruptions in a stroke. For example, a standard coupon border in a newspaper advertisement is a dash pattern.

The "Solid" option, selected by default, is by far the most common dash pattern. A solid stroke simply means that a stroke remains constant throughout the length of its path. If you select the "Dashed" option, six previously dimmed option boxes become available, each representing an interval, measured in points, during which a dash will be "on" or "off" in the course of stroking a path. "On" values determine the length of the dashes; "off" values determine the length of the gaps between the dashes. Odd option boxes (first, third, and fifth) turn the dash on; even option boxes (second, fourth, and sixth) turn it off.

Suppose that you want to create a dashed line composed of a series of 8-point dashes followed by 4-point gaps. After selecting the "Dashed" radio button, enter 8 in the first option box and 4 in the second. Leave the remaining four option boxes blank. If a series of consecutive "Dashed" options are blank, they are simply ignored. Therefore, once Illustrator has completed creating the first 8-point dash and accompanying 4-point gap, it repeats the sequence over and over throughout the length of the selected path.

This same pattern may be indicated in many different ways. For example, instead of leaving the last four options blank, you might fill them with 8/4/8/4. Alternatively, the first four options could contain zeros, and the last two could contain the 8 and the 4. Many other variations will produce the same effect.

All sorts of line patterns can be created, since every on and off indicator may contain a different value. You may create a pattern that repeats one, two, or three dash/gap combinations. Also, you need not specify an off value for every on value. A solid stroke, for example, is all dashes and no gaps. Its dash pattern may contain any positive number for its first option value while the remaining options may be left blank. However, a blank "Dashed" option may *not* exist between two option boxes that contain values. If you desire to skip a dash or gap in a stroke, enter a zero for that option.

Dash pattern values may range from 0 to 1296 and are accurate to ⅟₁₀₀₀ of a point. They are always specified in points, regardless of the selected "Ruler units" option in the PREFERENCES dialog (introduced in the *Setting preferences* section of Chapter 3).

Dashed strokes are most popularly used to indicate cut-out lines. They may surround mail-in coupons, paper dolls, or any number of other items that are specifically created to be clipped from a page. Dash patterns may also indicate a ghostly or translucent image.

Mixing stroke attributes

Stroking effects are created by mixing dash patterns with caps, joins, and line weights. More complicated effects may be achieved by layering duplicates of an object, one copy in front of another, each with a slightly different stroke. Provided that the line weight of each stroke is thinner than the line weight of the stroke behind it, portions of each stroke will show through to create unusual effects.

Layering strokes

The simplest stroking effect is the result of layering duplicate paths stroked with increasingly thinner line weights. The following exercise demonstrates how to use this technique to change the block of standard outline type shown in Figure 10.11 into a block of *inline* text, as shown in Figure 10.13:

1. Start with something large, like a line of 120-point type. This will act as the first object in the stroking effect.

2. For best results, the backmost object in a layer should always be stroked with a thick line weight. In this case, select the text block, choose STYLE... from the PAINT menu (⌘-I), and enter 6 for the "Weight" option in the PAINT STYLE dialog box.

3. While the PAINT STYLE dialog box remains displayed, select "None" from the "Fill" box and "Black" from the "Stroke" box. The result is the text block similar to the one shown in Figure 10.11.

4. Copy the selected text block (⌘-C) and paste the copy directly in front of the original (⌘-F).

Figure 10.11: A block of 120-point type painted with a 6-point line weight and no fill.

5. Display the PAINT STYLE dialog box again (⌘-I). Select "White" from the "Stroke" box and enter 4 into the "Weight" option. Then press RETURN. The result is the type shown in Figure 10.12.

Figure 10.12: Copy the type, paste it in front, and apply a thinner, white stroke.

6. Choose PASTE IN FRONT again (⌘-F). Display the PAINT STYLE dialog box and change the stroke to a black, 2-point line weight. The finished image is shown in Figure 10.13.

Figure 10.13: Paste it in front again and apply an even thinner, black stroke. Ta da, inline type.

Other stroking effects can be accomplished by layering duplicated objects with progressively reduced line weights. If you lighten the color of a line each time you reduce the line weight, you can create neon type. In Figure 10.14, for example, the backmost text block is stroked with a 100% black, 6-point line weight. The text block in front of that is stroked with a 90% black, 5.5-point line weight, and so on, until the frontmost text block, which is stroked with a white, 0-point line weight. Round joins were added to all paths to emulate the curves associated with real-life neon tubes.

Figure 10.14: Neon type is made up of duplicated text blocks, each of which is stroked with a thinner, more lightly colored stroke than the object behind it.

The following section goes one step further by adding dash patterns and line caps to the scenario.

Dash patterns and line caps

Forget layering duplicate objects for a moment. Even if you are stroking only a single object, you can achieve interesting effects by combining dash patterns with line caps. This is because Illustrator treats the beginning and ending of each dash in a pattern as the beginning and ending of a stroke. Therefore, both ends of a dash are affected by the selected line cap. This allows you to create round dashes as well as rectangular ones.

Suppose that you have created a black stroke that contains round caps and a 12-point line weight. You add to this by selecting the "Dashed" option in the PAINT STYLE dialog box and entering 0 for the dash value and 16 for the gap. The resulting line is shown in Figure 10.15. The diagram in Figure 10.16 shows how each dash is constructed. When you specified the length of each dash to be 0, you instructed Illustrator to allow no distance between the center of the round cap at the beginning of the dash and the center of the round cap at the end of the dash. The two round caps are co-incident. This implies that a series of black circles exist, the centers of which are 0-point dashes (shown as small white circles in Figure 10.16). Each circle has a 6-point radius (half the 12-point line weight), which makes a 12-point diameter. Because 12 points of each 16-point dash/gap sequence is consumed by a round cap circle, a distance of only four points remains between each circle. In conclusion, a dash pattern that is essentially never on, but rather always off in 16-point intervals appears to be on for 12 points and off for only four points when a stroked with a 12-point line weight and rounded caps.

Figure 10.15: A dash pattern with a 0-point dash, a 16-point gap, a 12-point line weight, and round caps.

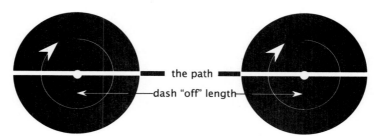

Figure 10.16: Round caps wrap around the ends of each dash in a dash pattern. If the dash value is 0, the round caps form perfect circles.

The first, third, and fifth "Dashed" option boxes in the PAINT STYLE dialog must contain zeros (or remain blank) if you want to create a stroke with perfectly round dashes. Also, the second, fourth, and sixth "Dashed" options must contain gap values (if any) that are larger than the line weight to prevent round dashes from touching each other.

Layering dash patterns and line caps

Even more interesting results may be achieved by layering dash patterns in front of other dash patterns. As when layering solid strokes, the line weight of each path should be thinner than the line weight of the path behind it. Also, although you may vary the line caps, you will generally want to keep the dash pattern constant throughout all layered paths; that is, the length of each dash and length of each gap—what we call the *periodicity* of the pattern—should not vary.

The following example begins with the line shown in Figure 10.15. The periodicity of this line is 16 points—a 0-point dash plus a 16-point gap. In the exercise, you will layer two additional paths in front of this line to create a pattern of inline circles.

1. Copy the line (⌘-C) and paste it directly in front of the original (⌘-F).

2. Using the PAINT STYLE dialog box (⌘-I), change the color of the stroke to white and decrease the line weight to 10 points. The result is displayed in Figure 10.17. The frontmost white circles all but cover up the larger black circles of the original line. Since the periodicity of the dash pattern remains constant, the circles of the white line exactly fit within the circles of the black line, producing a series of outlined dots.

Figure 10.17: The pattern from Figure 10.15 after adding a 10-point white stroke in front of it.

3. To create the line shown in Figure 10.18, paste another copy of the original path in front of the existing ones. Change the color of the stroke to black and decrease the line weight to 6 points. The effect is a series of black dots surrounded by white outlines, which are themselves surrounded by black outlines.

⦿ ⦿ ⦿ ⦿ ⦿ ⦿ ⦿ ⦿ ⦿ ⦿ ⦿ ⦿ ⦿ ⦿

Figure 10.18: Layering a 6-point, black line in front of the other paths makes an inline effect.

Depending on how familiar you are with line weights, you may notice that the outlines around the circles in Figure 10.17 are one point thick. This may seem incongruous with the fact that the first line is stroked with a 12-point line weight and the second line is stroked with a 10-point line weight. After all, the difference between the strokes is two points, not one. However, recall that it is the radius of a rounded cap that wraps around the end of a dash. Therefore, you must subtract the radius of the smaller round cap from that of the larger round cap to determine the amount of the original stroke that remains exposed. Since the radius of a round cap circle is equal to half its line weight, the outline of each dot appears to be 6 minus 5, or one point thick.

 Whenever one path exactly covers another path, regardless of dash patterns or line caps, always subtract half the weight of the front stroke from half the weight of the back stroke to determine the amount of the back path that will remain visible.

Dash patterns and line joins

Dash patterns can also produce unusual effects when combined with line joins. The stroke of the path in Figure 10.19 on the following page, for example, is made of a 32-point line weight with round joins and a lively dash pattern. The path itself is demonstrated as a thin, white line. Each corner point in the path is numbered. Notice that corners 1 and 2 coincide with gaps in the dash pattern so that they appear to be cut off, or beveled—not what you might expect from a line with round joins. By contrast, corners 3 and 4 meet with dashes in the pattern. Due to constraints of the PostScript language, Illustrator is forced to represent the round joins at these corners as black circles, interrupting the flow of the pattern. This problem is less noticeable for paths with smaller line weights, although a high-resolution printer will uncover these mistakes, even with narrow lines.

To avoid the problem shown in Figure 10.19, you may either select beveled or miter joins, or move the corner points of a path so they coincide with gaps, rather than dashes.

Figure 10.19: When combined with a lively pattern, round joins form circles at corners that coincide with dashes (3 and 4) and bevel at corners that coincide with gaps (1 and 2).

Creating and using arrowheads

Oh, Illustrator, how you can disappoint! Unlike every other drawing application on the Mac—including everything from MacDraw to Free-Hand—Illustrator 3.0 does not allow you to automatically apply arrowheads to the ends of open paths. However, with only a little effort, you can create a library of your own arrowheads and manually apply these to endpoints when required.

The easiest way to create an awesome library of arrow heads is to convert characters from the Zapf Dingbats font. Assuming that the printer font is available in your System folder and the Adobe Type Manager is running, you may convert all arrow characters in the Zapf Dingbats typeface by following these simple steps:

1. Click on an empty portion of the drawing area with the type tool.

2. Display the FONT dialog box by choosing the "Other..." option from the FONT pop-up menu (⌘-⇧-F). Select "Zapf Dingbats" from the left list and "Regular" from the right list and press RETURN.

3. Display the TYPE SIZE/LEADING dialog box by choosing the "Other…" option from the SIZE pop-up menu (⌘-⇧-S). Enter 60 for the "Size" option and press RETURN.

4. Create a text block containing all the arrowheads that you want to include in your library. The following list displays the arrows available in Zapf Dingbats and the keystrokes required to access them:

Zapf Dingbats character	Keystroke
→	⌥-] (OPTION-RIGHT BRACKET)
→	⇧-⌥-] (SHIFT-OPTION-RIGHT BRACKET)
→	⇧-⌥-~ (SHIFT-OPTION-TILDE)
→	⇧-⌥-2
→	⇧-⌥-3
→	⇧-⌥-4
→	⇧-⌥-5
➤	⇧-⌥-0
➤	⇧-⌥-W
➤	⇧-⌥-E
❯	⇧-⌥-Y
➡	⇧-⌥-U
⇨	⇧-⌥-I
⇨	⇧-⌥-S
⇦	⇧-⌥-D
⇦	⇧-⌥-F
⇨	⇧-⌥-G
⇨	⇧-⌥-H
⇨	⇧-⌥-J
⇨	⇧-⌥-L
↺	⇧-⌥-; (SHIFT-OPTION-SEMICOLON)
⟫→	⇧-⌥-Z
➤→	⇧-⌥-B
➤→	⇧-⌥-, (SHIFT-OPTION-COMMA)
➡	⌥-H
↔	⌥-K

5. Select the arrow tool in the toolbox. The text block will appear selected in the drawing area.

6. Choose the CREATE OUTLINES command from the TYPE menu. The arrows will be converted to standard paths.

7. Save the illustration as *Arrows* or whatever name you prefer, in the folder containing the Illustrator application.

To use an arrowhead, you must apply it manually to the end of your line. First open the Arrows document and copy an arrowhead (⌘-C). Then return to the document containing your line and paste the arrowhead (⌘-V). If you are creating either a horizontal or vertical straight line, you need only rotate the arrowhead by some 90° angle. This may be accomplished by selecting the entire arrowhead path and OPTION-clicking with the rotate tool, as described in the *Rotating objects* section of Chapter 12. Since all Dingbats arrowheads point to the right, enter 90 to create an upward-pointing arrow, 180 to point it to the left, or 270 to point it downward. Then press RETURN.

If your arrowhead character doers not contain its own line, such as the one shown in Figure 10.20, draw a horizontal or vertical line by clicking and then SHIFT-clicking with the pen tool. Then, using the arrow tool, drag the arrowhead by the point in the center of its base so that it snaps to the endpoint in the line, as shown in Figure 10.20.

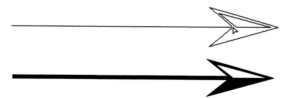

Figure 10.20: Drag the arrowhead by the center of its base to snap it to the endpoint of a line (top). In this way, line and arrowhead will appear continuous when printed (bottom).

If the arrowhead already comes with its own line, select the rear portion of the line, the part farthest from the arrowhead, using the direct-selection tool as shown in the first example of Figure 10.21. Then SHIFT-drag it vertically or horizontally away from the arrow, as shown in the second example, until the stretched segment becomes the desired length.

Figure 10.21: To extend an arrow, select its hind-quarters (top) and drag (bottom).

If you want to use an arrow that comes with its own line, but you want to attach it to an existing stroked path, as shown in Figure 10.20, convert the arrow into an arrowhead. Select the rear points in the line with the direct-selection tool and press DELETE to get rid of them. Then select the endpoints in the remaining open path, choose the AVERAGE... command from the ARRANGE menu (⌘-L), and press RETURN. This will make the two points coincident at an averaged location. You may then join (⌘-J) them to close the path and adjust the placement of the joined point if necessary.

Figure 10.22: Select the rear points with the direct-selection tool (left) and delete them. Then select the two endpoints (middle), average them, and drag them into position (right).

What if you want to add an arrowhead to a free-form line? This is a more difficult operation, requiring more exacting use of the rotation tool. First, drag the arrowhead so that its center point snaps to one of the endpoints in the free-form path. Then select the rotate tool and click on the snapped point. Still using the rotate tool, drag to rotate the selected arrowhead until it appears to match the angle of the line, as demonstrated in Figure 10.23 on the following page.

Figure 10.23: Rotate an arrowhead to match it to the angle of a free-form path (top). If rotated properly, line and arrowhead will appear continuous when printed (bottom).

If you're looking for more arrow designs, Adobe provides several more in a clip-art package called Collector's Edition I: Symbols, Borders, and Letterforms, which was included free for a while with Illustrator 88. Otherwise, it lists for $125, but you can probably find it for about $70 through a mail-order house (if you can find it at all).

Coloring Fills and Strokes

There was a time when the Macintosh computer was seen as a strictly monochrome machine. To this day, most users use SEs or older model Macs, computers with built-in monitors that display only black and white pixels. Even so, a growing number of users are branching into color machines, color monitors, and color output. If you are such a user, you will find that the degree of color control offered by Adobe Illustrator 3.0 continues to be some of the best available in any software, including support for four-color process colors, custom spot colors, and the entire 747-color Pantone Matching System library. If you don't use a color display device, you can still access Illustrator's color capabilities; you'll just have to become a little more adept at predicting the results.

The benefits of Illustrator's color abilities include increased quality as well as control and cost-savings over traditional color-separation techniques. The price for these benefits is additional complexity, demanding technical requirements, and the expense inherent in printing color proofs and color-separated film negatives. But with a little understanding of how to work with color, in addition to the help of your commercial printer, you may master the color capabilities of Illustrator 3.0.

Displaying colors

Illustrator's color abilities are available to anyone who can run the software; they are not limited by the monitor on which you are working, or by the printer on which you proof your work. When working on a monochrome monitor, specified colors appear in corresponding shades of gray. If you do have a color monitor, however, Illustrator will take full advantage of it, displaying up to 16 million colors at one time, depending on the capacity of your monitor and video card.

Preparing your color monitor

If you are going to work with a color monitor, you will want your screen to display colors that match the commercially printed results as closely as possible. Since the color display varies widely from one brand of monitor to another, and even between monitors from the same manufacturer, Illustrator 3.0 includes the ability to reset the color definitions used by your display.

When using Illustrator in color, you will generally want to set your Monitor *Control Panel device* to display as many colors as possible—16 colors if you are using a 4-bit video card, 256 colors if you are using an 8-bit video card, and "Millions" if you are using a 24-bit video card or better. Control Panel devices, also known by their acronym *cdevs* (pronounced see-devs), are accessed by choosing CONTROL PANEL from the APPLE (⌘) menu and selecting the appropriate icon from the scrolling list, as shown in Figure 11.01. However, there may be times during the creation of your color document when you wish to reduce the number of colors displayed or even turn off the color entirely in order to speed up the preview of your illustration. These changes will not affect the color definitions used for your illustration, and the color settings can be safely changed as often as desired. You may even use a color-switching utility that allows you to toggle between display modes. Our favorite is Switch-A-Roo, a free Fkey from Bill Steinberg available over CompuServe (where Bill's account number is 76703,1027) and other national bulletin board systems.

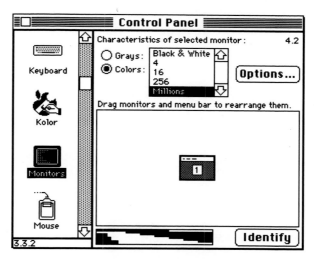

Figure 11.01: The Monitors Control Panel device allows you to set the number of colors that can be displayed simultaneously on your monitor.

Any adjustment to the Monitors cdev affects the colors used by all Macintosh software. You may also customize your screen display strictly for Illustrator from within the application. This color adjustment process serves to alter certain key screen colors to match printed samples as closely as possible. For best results, you will need to obtain a sample color bar from the commercial printer who will be reproducing your illustrations. This sample should include a separate color square for each of the four process colors—cyan, magenta, yellow, and black—plus combinations of each pair and all three process colors. If you cannot obtain these samples from your printer, or you don't work with a single commercial print house on a consistent basis, you may use the progressive color bar that appears on the first page of the *Using Color with the Adobe Illustrator* manual included with your software.

To begin the color adjustment, choose the PREFERENCES... command from the EDIT menu (⌘-K). After the PREFERENCES dialog box appears, click the PROGRESSIVE COLORS... button to display the PROGRESSIVE COLORS dialog box (see Figure 11.02), which shows the current appearance of each primary color and primary color combination. The goal is to adjust each of the colors so that it is as close as possible to the appropriate printed color sample. Be aware, however, that monitors do not create colors in the same way that colors are created in the printing process—so perfect matches will be unlikely. To adjust the on-screen representation of a color, click on the color you wish to adjust. The APPLE COLOR WHEEL dialog box will be displayed, as shown in Figure 11.03.

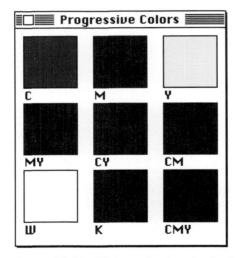

Figure 11.02: Click a color box in the Progressive Colors dialog box to adjust the color to better match a printed sample.

The APPLE COLOR WHEEL dialog box provides specific control over the display of the selected primary color. To alter a color, you may use one of two color models: *RGB* (red, green, blue) or *HSB* (hue, saturation, brightness). Each model is explained in one of the following sections.

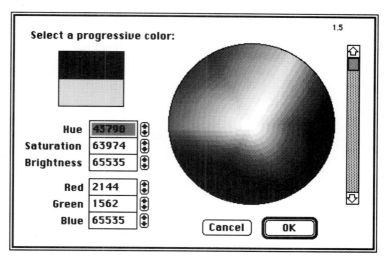

Figure 11.03: The Apple Color Wheel dialog box.

Coloring with light

When using the RGB color model, colors are defined by mixing two or more *primary hues*. The amount of each hue mixed is called its *intensity*, as measured between 0 (no hue) and 65,535 (full-intensity). The RGB model is also called the *additive primary model*, because a resulting color becomes lighter as you add higher intensities of primary hues. All monitors and other projection devices—including televisions that use light to display colors—rely on the additive model.

The additive primary model consists of three hues—red, green, and blue—from which all colors in the visible spectrum may be derived. These primary hues can be mixed as follows:

- Equal intensities of red and green make yellow. Subtract some red to produce chartreuse; subtract some green to produce orange.

- Equal intensities of green and blue make cyan. Subtract some green to produce turquoise; subtract some blue to produce jade.

- Equal intensities of blue and red make purple. Subtract some blue to produce magenta; subtract some red to produce violet.

- Equal intensities of red, green, and blue make gray or white.

- No light results in black (or darkness).

The color wheel

The APPLE COLOR WHEEL dialog box also provides a second model for adjusting the amount of light in a color. This HSB color model, as it is called, makes use of the properties of hue, saturation, and brightness. The *hue* of a color is measured on an color wheel representing the entire visible spectrum. The wheel is divided into 65,535 sections. Some of the most popular hues are found at the following numeric locations:

- Red is 0.
- Orange is 5450.
- Yellow is 10,900.
- Chartreuse is 16,400.
- Green is 21,850.
- Jade is 27,300.
- Cyan is 32,750.
- Blue is 43,700.
- Violet is 49,150.
- Purple is 54,600.
- Magenta is 60,050.

Saturation represents the purity of a color. A saturation of 0 is always gray; a saturation of 65,535 is required to produce the most vivid versions of each of the colors listed above. You can think of the saturation value as the difference between a black-and-white television and color television. When the saturation value is low, all information about a color is expressed except the hue itself. Most natural colors require moderate saturation values. Highly saturated colors appear vivid.

Brightness is the lightness or darkness of a color. A brightness of 0 is always black; a brightness of 65,535 is used to achieve each of the colors listed above. For example, if the hue is red, a brightness value of 65,535 will produce bright red; 49,152 produces medium red; 32,768 produces dark red; and 16,384 makes a red so dark, it almost appears black.

Changing screen colors

To change a color using the RGB color model, enter values between 0 and 65,535 in the "Red," "Green," and "Blue" option boxes. Alternatively, you may click the up or down arrow next to each option box to raise or lower the corresponding value. Press TAB to advance from one option box to the next.

To change a color using the HSB model, alter the values in the "Hue," "Saturation," and "Brightness" options. Or you may reposition the *color-adjustment dot* inside the *color wheel* on the right side of the dialog box. The color wheel works in association with the nearby scroll bar. The color wheel and scroll bar may be adjusted as follows:

- Move the color-adjustment dot around the perimeter of the wheel to change the hue.

- Move the color-adjustment dot between the perimeter and center of the wheel to alter the saturation. Colors along the perimeter equate to a saturation value of 65,535; the center color equates to a saturation value of 0.

- Move the scroll box within the scroll bar to change the brightness. The top of the scroll bar equates to a brightness value of 65,535; the bottom equates to 0.

After you press the TAB key or complete an adjustment to the color wheel or scroll bar, the new color will display in the *new color box* above the option boxes. Directly below the new color box is the *original color box*, which shows the color as it appeared prior to the new changes, for comparative purposes.

Click the OK button or press RETURN when you are satisfied with your color adjustment, or click the CANCEL button to close the dialog and revert to the previous color settings. When all the colors presented in the PROGRESSIVE COLORS dialog have been satisfactorily adjusted, click the close box in the upper left corner of the dialog, then click the OK button or press RETURN after subsequently returning to the PREFERENCES dialog.

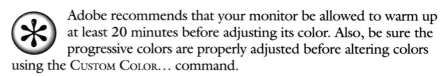 Adobe recommends that your monitor be allowed to warm up at least 20 minutes before adjusting its color. Also, be sure the progressive colors are properly adjusted before altering colors using the CUSTOM COLOR… command.

Coloring illustrations

You may apply colors to the objects in an illustration using the "Fill" and "Stroke" options in the PAINT STYLE dialog box, as described in Chapters 9 and 10. Two types of colors may be used to fill or stroke an object: *process colors* and *custom colors*.

Creating process colors

To apply process color to any Illustrator object, select the object with the arrow tool and choose the STYLE… command from the PAINT menu (⌘-I). Both the "Fill" and "Stroke" boxes inside the PAINT STYLE dialog box include a "Process Color" radio button. If you select this option, the four process color option boxes—"Cyan," "Magenta," "Yellow," and "Black"—will display. These are the *primary hues* which may be used to create any color on a printed page.

As when adjusting colors on your monitor, colors on the printed page are defined by mixing two or more primary hues. However, colors on paper behave differently than colors on a computer screen. They use an entirely different color model, known as the *subtractive primary model*, because a resulting color becomes darker as you add higher concentrations of primary hues.

Coloring with pigments

In nature, most colors are created using the subtractive color model, which works like this: Sunlight contains every visible color found on earth. When sunlight is projected on an object, the object absorbs (subtracts) some of the light and reflects the rest. This reflected light is the color that you see. For example, a fire engine is red because it absorbs all other colors from the white light spectrum.

Pigments on a sheet of paper work the same way. A purple crayon absorbs all non-purple colors; green ink absorbs all colors that aren't green. Every child learns that you can make any color using red, yellow, and blue. Red and yellow mix to create orange, yellow and blue make green, and so on. This is the subtractive primary model.

Unfortunately, what you learned in elementary school is a rude approximation of the truth. Did you ever try mixing a vivid red with a bright yellow, only to produce a disappointingly drab orange? And the very idea that deep blue and vivid red make purple is almost laughable. The true result is more of a washed-out gray.

The true subtractive primary model used by commercial artists and printers consists of four hues: cyan (a very pale greenish blue), magenta (a bright purplish pink), yellow, and black, each of which is applied to white paper. These primary hues can be mixed as follows:

- Equal amounts of cyan and magenta make violet. Additional cyan produces blue; additional magenta produces purple.

- Equal amounts of magenta and yellow make red. Additional magenta produces carmine; additional yellow produces orange.

- Equal amounts of yellow and cyan make green. Additional yellow produces chartreuse; additional cyan produces turquoise.

- Equal amounts of cyan, magenta, and yellow make brown.

- Black pigmentation added to any other pigment darkens the color.

- No pigmentation results in white (assuming that white is the color of the paper).

To create a process color, enter percentage values between 0% (no concentration) and 100% (full concentration) in the "Cyan," "Magenta," "Yellow," and "Black" option boxes. The resulting color is displayed in the box directly above the "Process Color" radio button.

Creating custom colors

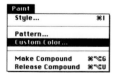

Process colors are defined "on-the-fly" for each instance in which they are used. However, Illustrator also allows you to create *custom colors*, which are defined only once and then saved with the current illustration to be accessed again and again. Custom colors in Illustrator are defined by choosing the Custom Color... command from the Paint menu, displaying the Custom Color dialog box, shown in Figure 11.04 on the following page.

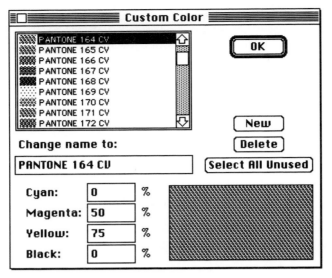

Figure 11.04: The Custom Color dialog box allows you to create colors that you intend to use several times throughout an illustration.

The scrolling color list in the Custom Color dialog lists all custom colors that have been defined previously in the current document or in any other open document. Custom colors in Illustrator are always shared among all open documents. If a new color is created in one document, it immediately becomes available to all open documents.

To create a library of colors that are available every time you use Illustrator, add the color to the Adobe Illustrator Startup file. Keep in mind, however, that available colors consume space in the application memory, and may slow or hamper Illustrator's performance.

You may manipulate colors in the scrolling list using the buttons in the Custom Color dialog box. These buttons include the following:

- **New**. To create a new color, click on the New button and the name "New Color 1" will appear in the scrolling color list. This name is also selected in the "Change name to" option box, making it easy for you to rename your color as desired. Color names may be up to 31 characters long, including any alphanumeric character and spaces. After naming your color, you may define it by entering percentage values in the "Cyan," "Magenta," "Yellow," and "Black" option boxes. As you enter these values, the resulting color will display in the color box to the right of the option boxes.

- **Delete**. Click this button to delete a selected color name from the scrolling list. The selected color is removed from the current document *as well as from any other open document*. Any object that was filled or stroked with the deleted color will be painted with black. Extreme caution should be exercised when deleting colors. Whenever possible, delete a color only when the current illustration is the only file open.

It is completely impossible to undo the deletion of a custom color. The Custom Color dialog box contains no Cancel button, and the Undo command is dimmed when you return to the drawing area. Exercise extreme caution when using the Delete button!

- **Select All Unused**. This button selects all colors in the scrolling list that are not applied to objects in any open illustration. Since colors consume some space on disk and in your computer's RAM, it is often advisable to delete colors that you are not currently using, provided that they exist in some other illustration that is not currently open. To delete unused colors, click the Select All Unused option, click Delete, and then click OK or press return.

A color may be renamed by selecting it from the scrolling list and entering a new name in the "Change name to" option box. This will change its name in all open illustrations. You may also edit the color by entering new values in the "Cyan," "Magenta," "Yellow," and "Black" option boxes. Altering a custom color changes the color of all objects that use that color in any open illustration.

Pantone-brand colors

Adobe Illustrator 3.0 includes an updated Pantone Colors file, which contains the complete library of 747 printing inks that make up the *Pantone Matching System*, a standard subscribed to by most major commercial printers. Open this document to access PMS colors while working with an illustration.

If you use color on a consistent basis, you will probably want constant access to the PMS library. At the Finder level, rename the Pantone Colors file *Adobe Illustrator Startup*. (If you have already created a special Adobe Illustrator Startup file, copy the contents of that file, paste them into the Pantone Colors file, then quit Illustrator and rename the Pantone Colors file.) As always, keep in mind that available colors consume space in the application memory, and may slow or hamper Illustrator's performance.

Using custom colors

To apply custom color to any Illustrator object, select the object with the arrow tool and choose the STYLE... command from the PAINT menu (⌘-I). Both the "Fill" and "Stroke" boxes inside the PAINT STYLE dialog box include a "Custom Color" radio button. If you select this option, a scrolling list appears, displaying all the custom colors currently available, in alphabetical order. To the left of each color's name, the color itself is displayed. To select a custom color, click on its name. Use the scroll bar arrows to view custom colors that are not displayed. When selected, the color will display in the color box at the top of the "Fill" or "Stroke" box.

You may quickly access a specific custom color by typing characters that are unique to the color name. Unlike when locating files in other dialog boxes, these characters do not have to appear at the beginning of the color name. For example, to access the color "Pantone 164 CV," merely type *164*. (If an option box is active, first click a color name in the scrolling list, then type the desired characters.)

The "Tint %" option box below the scrolling color list allows you to create a *tint* for any custom color. Tints are lightened variations of custom colors, specified as percentage values between 0% (white) and 100% (the solid color). When used in *spot color printing* (as defined in Chapter 15, *Printing Your Illustrations*), tints provide an inexpensive way to create shades of a single ink to achieve the effect of using multiple colors.

The "Overprint" option that appears at the bottom of the "Fill" or "Stroke" box is described in the following section.

Overprinting colors

The "Overprint" option check box—available in the PAINT STYLE dialog box when the "White," "Black," "Process Color," or "Custom Color" radio button is selected—controls whether a specific color will be printed on top of another color that is directly behind it in an illustration. When this option is selected, an object is allowed to *overprint* the object behind it, provided the other color is printed to a different *separation* (as defined in Chapter 15, *Printing Your Illustrations*). For example, if your drawing consists of two custom colors—orange and blue—then orange may overprint blue, blue may overprint orange, and either may overprint or be overprinted by black, because orange, blue, and black will be printed to their own separations during the printing process. However, a 30% tint of blue may not overprint a 70% tint of blue, because all blue objects are printed to the same separation.

If the "Overprint" option is deselected, as by default, portions of an object covered by another object will be *knocked out* when they appear on different separations. Knocked out portions do not print on a separation.

For example, suppose that the faces in Figure 11.05 are filled and stroked in tints of orange, and that the hats are painted in tints of blue. In the first example, the portion of the orange object under the hat has been knocked out. In the second example, the objects overprint, allowing the colors to blend, giving the hat a transparent appearance.

Figure 11.05: An orange face with a blue hat as it appears when the "Overprint" option is deselected (left) and selected (right).

Process color versus custom color

Although it is not difficult to define a fill or stroke as either a process color or a custom color, it can be difficult to determine which technique is more appropriate for the current object. When using most software, the printing method that will be used to reproduce an illustration determines which type of color should be used. Process colors should be applied in an illustration that contains many colors and will therefore be separated as a four-color process image. Custom colors are better suited to spot-color printing situations, in which only two or three specific inks are required.

These generalizations are untrue when working with Adobe Illustrator. As explained in Chapter 15, the Adobe Separator utility is capable of separating custom colors into their process-color components, rendering custom colors as appropriate to process-color printing as they are to spot-color printing.

As it turns out, custom colors are preferred in almost all situations. They provide easy accessibility, ready exchange among documents, the benefits of global editing, and may be output as either spot colors or four-color process separations. Process colors are best used in situations where a color will be used only once and will be output on a color printer or separated for four-color process printing.

Transforming
and Duplicating
Objects

In Chapter 7, we discussed several manipulation techniques that change the form of a path. These reshaping techniques were applicable to various elements including points, segments, and entire paths, but their scope was limited to graphic objects; type cannot be reshaped.

In this chapter we will discuss two categories of manipulation techniques—*transforming* and *duplicating*—that do not necessarily alter the form of a path and are equally applicable to type and to graphic objects. We will also examine Illustrator's limited collection of precision drawing features, and how these features can be used to control the transformation and duplication of objects.

We end the chapter with a detailed discussion of *blending*, a special feature that both transforms and duplicates objects at the same time. This is the only feature covered in this chapter which cannot be applied to type, unless the type is converted to paths using the CREATE OUTLINES command.

Grouping

Although there are certainly exceptions, most transformations are applicable only to whole paths, rather than to individual points or segments. In addition, you may want to transform multiple objects at a time. So imagine that instead of thinking in terms of paths and objects, you could manipulate whole images. This is the beauty of *grouping*, which allows you to assemble throngs of elements into a single object.

Suppose, for example, that you have created an image made up of several paths. You want to rotate the image, but you're afraid of upsetting the fragile relationship between the paths during the transformation. To safeguard the basic appearance of the image, select the objects in the image and choose the GROUP command from the ARRANGE menu (⌘-G). The rotation will affect the whole image, as shown in Figure 12.01.

Figure 12.01: Before transforming a collection of complex paths, group the paths into a single object.

When you choose the GROUP command, you accomplish the same goal whether only a single point or segment is selected or a whole path is selected. All objects that are even partially selected become grouped in their entirety.

The GROUP command may be applied to a single path to retain the relationship between points and segments. You may even group multiple groups, and groups of groups. In fact, the GROUP command may be applied to any type or graphic object that you can create or import into Illustrator.

A whole group is selected by clicking on it with either the arrow tool or the object-selection tool. To reshape a path in a group, you may use the direct-selection tool to select and manipulate individual elements. You may also select individual objects in a group to fill or stroke them without affecting other grouped objects. Or you may transform an object separately without affecting other objects in a group.

If you duplicate an object within a group using the direct-selection tool, the duplicate will become part of the group as well. To duplicate an object separately of its group, select the object with the direct-selection tool, choose COPY (⌘-C), select the standard arrow tool (⌘-→I), click on an empty portion of the drawing area to deselect the group, and choose any one of the PASTE commands.

Selecting groups within groups

OPTION-click with the direct-selection tool to select whole paths in a group. Press OPTION and click two or more times to select groups within groups. Each successive click selects the group that includes the current group. The following exercise demonstrates how this works:

1. Draw four rectangles with the rectangle tool. As discussed in the *Reshaping geometric paths* section of Chapter 7, each rectangle is automatically created as a group.

2. Select two of the rectangles and choose GROUP (⌘-G). Select the other pair of rectangles and group them as well.

3. Select both grouped pairs and choose GROUP. The result is four groups (the rectangles) within two groups (the pairs) within a single group.

4. Using the direct-selection tool, OPTION-click one of the rectangles. This selects the entire path without selecting the center point.

5. Press OPTION and click the selected rectangle a second time. This selects the entire geometric path, both center point and path.

6. Press OPTION and click the selected rectangle a third time. This selects both rectangles in the grouped pair.

7. Press OPTION and click the selected rectangle a fourth time. The highest level group becomes selected, including all four rectangles.

Adding a center point

All geometric shapes—rectangles, rounded rectangles, and ellipses—come with center points. These center points can be extremely useful for aligning geometric paths, as we have discussed in previous chapters. Wouldn't it be nice if you could add center points to some of the free-form paths you create in Adobe Illustrator?

Well, you can. In fact, we recommend that you add center points to any path that you intend to reuse or relocate on a regular basis, and group the center point with the path. The following steps describe how:

1. Select the path or group of paths for which you want to create a center point.

2. Copy the selection (⌘-C) and choose the PASTE IN FRONT command (⌘-F) to create a duplicate of the selection directly in front of the original.

3. Choose the AVERAGE... command from the ARRANGE menu (⌘-L). When the AVERAGE dialog box appears, press RETURN to average the selected points along both axis. All points will be moved to a coincident location that represents the center of the object.

4. Press SHIFT and click on the mass of points with the direct-selection tool. This deselects the frontmost point.

5. Press DELETE or BACKSPACE to delete the other, extraneous points.

6. Select paths and center point and choose GROUP (⌘-G) to bring it all together.

Ungrouping

Any group may be ungrouped by choosing the UNGROUP command from the ARRANGE menu (⌘-U). Multiple groups may be ungrouped simultaneously, but only one level at a time. In other words, if a group contains groups, then the most recently created group must be ungrouped first. The member groups may then be ungrouped by again choosing UNGROUP. Geometric paths created with the rectangle and oval tools may also be ungrouped.

Ungrouping can sometimes be an essential part of the reshaping process. Most notably, you may not join two endpoints if the endpoints are in paths that are not in the same group. For example, one endpoint may be in a grouped path, and the other endpoint may be in an ungrouped path. The only solution in this case is to ungroup the path, choose the JOIN… command, and the regroup the path.

Distinguishing groups from non-groups

What if ungrouping a path doesn't produce the desired effect? Perhaps the object wasn't grouped in the first place. Illustrator 3.0 allows you to create various kinds of collective objects, including compound paths, linked objects, and wrapped objects. Groups are generally easily distinguished from links and wrapped objects because the latter two objects contain type. (See the *Flowing area text* and *Wrapping type around graphics* sections of Chapter 8 for complete descriptions of both objects.) Compound paths, however, may be difficult to distinguish from groups. Letters that have been converted to paths are always expressed as compound paths. However, if you want to find out for sure, choose the STYLE… command from the PAINT menu (⌘-I). If the "Reversed" check box is dimmed, the selected object is *not* a compound path. If the option is not dimmed, then the object *is* a compound path.

Controlling movements

Illustrator allows you to move objects in the same way that you may move elements, as described in the *Moving elements* section of Chapter 7. In fact, moving is the primary and most common means for transforming objects in Adobe Illustrator.

An entirely selected object may be moved in any of the following ways:

- Using any of the arrow tools, drag the object by any of its points, segments, or—in the case of a text object—baselines.

- Press SHIFT and drag the object to move it along the constraint axis.

- Drag the object over the point of a stationary object to snap the object into place.

- Press an arrow key (↑, →, ↓, or ←) to move the object by the amount specified in the "Cursor key distance" option in the PREFERENCES dialog box (introduced in the *Setting preferences* section of Chapter 3).

- Press OPTION and click the arrow tool icon in the toolbox to display the MOVE dialog box. Enter the desired movement values and press RETURN.

- Use the measure tool to measure the distance between the current location of an object and its prospective location. Press RETURN after the MEASURE dialog box displays. OPTION-click the arrow tool icon in the toolbox to display the MOVE dialog box, which will contain the measured values. Press RETURN.

Pressing the SHIFT key, snapping, using arrow keys, and the MOVE and MEASURE dialog boxes all represent means for making precise, controlled movements in an illustration. Illustrator 3.0 provides two additional control features that we have not discussed previously. These are *rulers* and *guides*, both of which are discussed in the following sections.

Using the rulers

Illustrator provides access to one vertical and one horizontal ruler that may be used to track the movement of your cursor. By choosing the SHOW RULERS command from the VIEW menu (⌘-R), you display these rulers, which appear at the bottom and right-hand edges of the current illustration window. Once the rulers are visible, the SHOW RULERS command changes to a HIDE RULERS command (⌘-R), thus allowing you to put the rulers away at any time.

The unit of measure used by both rulers may be centimeters, inches, or picas—each of which is displayed in Figures 12.02, 12.03, or 12.04— as determined by the selected "Ruler units" option in the PREFERENCES dialog box. To change the current unit of measure, choose the PREFERENCES command from the EDIT menu (⌘-Y). The PREFERENCES dialog will display, containing three "Ruler units" radio buttons: "Centimeters," "Inches," and "Picas/Points." The last option is selected by default. Select the desired option and press RETURN.

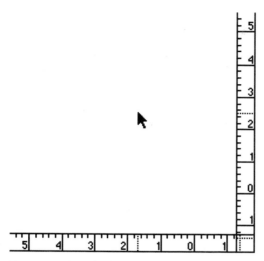

Figure 12.02: The horizontal and vertical rulers as they appear when the current unit of measure is centimeters.

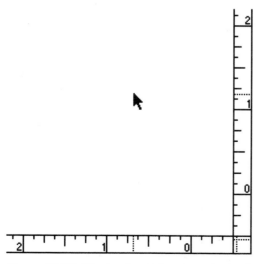

Figure 12.03: The horizontal and vertical rulers as they appear when the current unit of measure is inches.

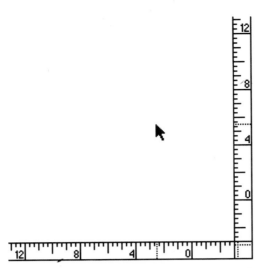

Figure 12.04: The horizontal and vertical rulers as they appear when the current unit of measure is picas.

As on traditional rulers, whole centimeters, inches, or picas are indicated by long tick marks; fractions are indicated by short tick marks. As you magnify the view size, the units on the rulers become larger and more detailed. As you zoom out, units become smaller and less detailed. Numbers on each ruler indicate the distance from the *ruler origin*, the location on your drawing area at which the horizontal and vertical coordinates are both zero. All ruler measurements are made relative to this origin.

At all times, you may track the movement of your cursor on the horizontal and vertical rulers. Each of Figures 12.02 through 12.04 shows a small dotted *tracking line* that moves along the horizontal ruler and another that moves along the vertical ruler, indicating the present location of your cursor in the drawing area. For example, the cursor in Figure 12.04 is 5 picas and 6 points (5½ picas) above and 2 picas 6 points left of the ruler origin.

Unlike rulers in some other programs, which track the movement of an object, Illustrator's rulers always track the location of the cursor. This is even true, for example, when you are moving a text block or graphic object.

Changing the ruler origin

By default, the ruler origin for an illustration is located at the bottom right corner of the primary page. The number of this page depends on the selected "Artwork board" option in the PREFERENCES dialog box. If the "Single full page" or "Tile full pages" radio button is selected, the primary page is page 1. If "Tile imageable areas" is selected, it is page 5.

You may relocate the ruler origin by dragging from the *ruler origin box*, the square created by the intersection of the horizontal and vertical rulers. Figure 12.05 demonstrates this process. The dotted lines that extend from the + cursor indicate the prospective position of the new origin. Notice that even the movement of the ruler origin is tracked by the rulers. At the end of the drag, the ruler origin moves to the location occupied by the cursor. All ruler measurements will now be made from this new ruler origin.

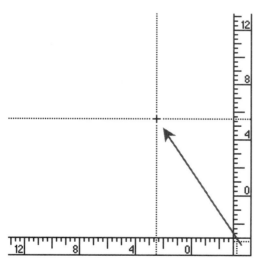

Figure 12.05: Drag from the ruler origin box to relocate the ruler origin.

Creating guides

Illustrator 3.0 allows you to create *guides* to assist in the positioning and alignment of objects in the drawing area. Guides appear dotted in the artwork-&-template mode, and do not preview or print. If the "Snap to point" check box in the PREFERENCES dialog box is selected, your cursor will snap to an existing guide if you drag within two pixels of the guide while moving or otherwise transforming an object. Also, your cursor will snap to any portion of the outline of a guide, not just to the points as when snapping to stationary objects.

You may create a guide in one of the following ways:

- Drag upward from the horizontal ruler to create a horizontal *ruler guide* the width of the entire drawing area.

- Drag to the left from the vertical ruler to create a vertical ruler guide the height of the entire drawing area.

- Select an existing object in the drawing area and choose the MAKE GUIDE command from the ARRANGE menu (⌘-5).

Ruler guides are created by dragging from either the horizontal or vertical ruler, as demonstrated in the first example of Figure 12.06. The second example in the figure shows that the guide appears as a dotted line after it is created, allowing it to be easily distinguished from objects that make up your illustration. Ruler guides are used to mark a specific horizontal or vertical location inside the drawing area. You may then align the sides or center points of objects to the ruler guide to create perfect rows or columns of objects.

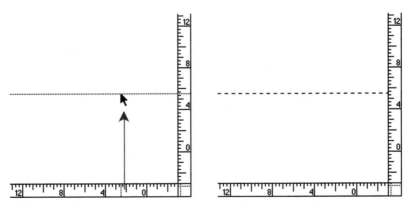

Figure 12.06: Dragging from one of the rulers (left) creates a ruler guide (right).

In the course of dragging a guide from the horizontal ruler, press the OPTION key to rotate it 90°, toggling a vertical guide. Likewise, OPTION-dragging from the vertical ruler toggles a horizontal guide.

Arrange	
Transform Again	⌘D
Group	⌘G
Ungroup	⌘U
Join...	⌘J
Average...	⌘L
Lock	⌘1
Unlock All	⌘2
Hide	⌘3
Show All	⌘4
Make Guide	⌘5
Release All Guides	⌘6
Set Cropmarks	
Release Cropmarks	

Choose the MAKE GUIDE command from the ARRANGE menu (⌘-5) to turn one or more selected objects into *guide objects*. Only graphic objects may be subjected to the MAKE GUIDE command. If a text object is selected when choosing MAKE GUIDE, an error message will appear, alerting you that all selected objects were not converted to guides. After pressing RE-TURN to exit the alert box, you will find that all graphic objects have been converted to guide objects and that all text objects have not and remain selected, as shown in Figure 12.07.

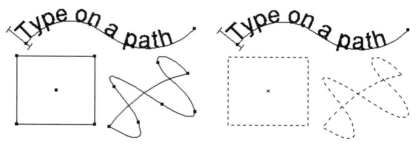

Figure 12.07: Only selected graphic objects (left) may be converted into guide objects (right). Selected text objects will remain unaffected.

To create a guide object without sacrificing the selected graphic object, copy the object (⌘-C), paste it in front (⌘-F), and then choose MAKE GUIDE (⌘-5) to convert the duplicate object only.

You may hide ruler guides in the artwork-&-template mode by choosing the HIDE UNPAINTED OBJECTS command from the VIEW menu. This will also hide any other objects that are not filled or stroked, including guide objects that were converted from unpainted graphic objects. Your cursor will snap to guides even though they may be hidden. For more information about this command, see the *Hiding unpainted objects* section, later in this chapter.

Manipulating guides

Any existing guide may be moved, transformed, and deleted, though in a slightly different manner than a normal object. To select a ruler guide or guide object, you must press SHIFT and CONTROL while clicking on it with the arrow tool. The guide will show no visible sign of being selected, but any previously selected objects will become deselected.

The following items describe how to manipulate a selected guide:

- Press SHIFT and CONTROL and drag the guide to move it to a new location. After beginning the move, release the SHIFT key to move the guide without constraint.

- You may also press an arrow key or use the MOVE dialog box to move a selected guide.

- Press DELETE or BACKSPACE to delete a selected guide.

- Use the scale, reflect, rotate, or shear tool as described later in this chapter to transform a selected guide.

- Press SHIFT, OPTION, and CONTROL and drag a guide to clone the guide. Release SHIFT during the drag to move the guide without constraint, but do not release OPTION until after you complete the drag.

You may not reshape a guide, since no element may be selected independently of another within a guide. Also, you may not select or manipulate multiple guides at a time, unless they are members of the same group.

Incidentally, you may convert a single object within a group to a guide without converting other objects in the group. The guide will remain a member of the group. Any manipulations performed on the group will also affect the guide.

Converting guides to objects

To convert all existing guides in the current illustration to objects, choose the RELEASE ALL GUIDES command from the ARRANGE menu (⌘-6). Both ruler guides and guide objects will be converted into selected objects. Ruler guides will extend the entire width or length of the drawing area.

To convert a single guide object back into a graphic object, press SHIFT and CONTROL and double-click the guide with any arrow tool. This same technique may be applied to ruler guides.

Protecting objects

There are times in the course of working on an illustration when you will have positioned an object, call it object A, exactly where you want it. Your illustration may be very complicated, containing several objects that overlap and are overlapped by object A, but are not yet properly formed or located. In the process of reshaping and transforming these objects, you may find yourself accidentally selecting and altering object A. This can be exceedingly frustrating, requiring you to fix an object that was previously correct. The more complicated your drawing becomes, the greater the likelihood of disarranging one or more perfectly positioned objects.

To protect text blocks and graphic objects from being upset or altered, Illustrator provides *locking* and *hiding* features, which are the subject of the following sections.

Locking objects

Locking an object prevents it or any of its points or segments from being selected. This means you can neither delete the object nor transform it in any manner. In addition, you may not change its fill or stroke. Once an object is locked, it immediately becomes deselected. If you attempt to click on a locked object with an arrow tool, you will instead select some nearby unlocked object or select no object at all. Likewise, neither marqueeing nor choosing the Select All command (⌘-A) will select a locked object.

Objects are locked by selecting them and choosing the Lock command from the Arrange menu (⌘-1). You may not lock a single point or segment independently of other points and segments in a path. If you specifically select one point in a path and choose the Lock command, the entire path will become locked.

When you are working on a very specific detail in an illustration, you may find it helpful to lock every object not included in the detail. This may be hundreds of objects, possibly making it difficult and time consuming to select each object by marqueeing, SHIFT-clicking, SHIFT-marqueeing, and so on. Instead, simply select the objects that you *don't* want to lock and press the OPTION key while choosing the Lock command. All objects that are *not* selected will become locked. (Pressing ⌘-⌥-1 is ineffective; you must OPTION-choose Lock from the Arrange menu.)

Unlocking objects

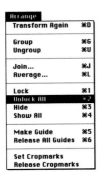

Because a locked object may not be selected, there is no way to indicate that you wish to unlock only one or more specific objects. Therefore, you must unlock *all* locked objects at the same time. Upon choosing the UN-LOCK ALL command from the ARRANGE menu (⌘-2), all previously locked objects become unlocked and selected. In this way, previously locked objects are called to your attention, allowing you to easily relock them if you so desire.

Locking is saved with the illustration. Therefore, when you open an existing file, all objects that were locked during the previous session will still be locked.

Hiding objects

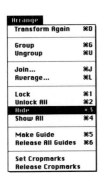

If an object is really in your way, you can do more than just lock it: you can totally *hide* it from view. A hidden object may not be viewed in any display mode nor does it appear when an illustration is printed. Since a hidden object is always invisible, it cannot be selected or manipulated.

Objects are hidden by selecting them and choosing the HIDE command from the ARRANGE menu (⌘-3). You may not hide a single point or segment independently of other points and segments in a path. If you specifically select one point in a path and choose the HIDE command, the entire path will be made invisible.

When you are working on a very specific detail in an illustration, you may find it helpful to hide every object not included in the detail. This may be hundreds of objects, possibly making it difficult and time consuming to select each object by marqueeing, SHIFT-clicking, SHIFT-marqueeing, and so on. Instead, simply select the objects that you *don't* want to hide and press the OPTION key while choosing the HIDE command. All objects that are *not* selected will become locked. (Pressing ⌘-⌥-3 is ineffective; you must OPTION-choose HIDE from the ARRANGE menu.)

Showing objects

Because a hidden object may not be selected, there is no way to indicate that you wish to make only one or more specific objects visible. Therefore, you must display *all* hidden objects at the same time. Upon choosing the SHOW ALL command from the ARRANGE menu (⌘-4), all previously hidden objects reappear in the drawing area and become selected. In this way, previously hidden objects are called to your attention, allowing you to easily rehide them if you so desire.

Unlike locking, hiding is *not* saved with the illustration. Therefore, when you open an existing file, all objects that were hidden during the previous session will reappear.

Hiding unpainted objects

Illustrator provides another hiding command that hides only those objects, selected or not, that are neither filled nor stroked. Normally, such objects may be viewed in the artwork-&-template mode, even though they will disappear when you preview or print the illustration. By choosing the HIDE UNPAINTED OBJECTS command from the VIEW menu, You can get a clearer view of how your artwork will print.

Unpainted objects generally include the following items:

- Ruler guides.

- Paths associated with text blocks.

- Paths that define the standoff in a wrapped object.

- Dummy objects that define the outline of an EPS graphic (as discussed in Chapter 14, *Importing and Exporting Graphics*).

- Any other object that you have chosen to neither fill nor stroke.

After you hide the unpainted objects, the HIDE UNPAINTED OBJECTS command changes to a SHOW UNPAINTED OBJECTS command, allowing you to redisplay unpainted objects at any time.

Scaling objects

A *transformation* is any manipulation that permanently alters the appearance of an object without affecting its basic form. In Illustrator, transformations include moving an object—as discussed in the *Controlling movements* section of this chapter—as well as scaling, flipping, rotating, and slanting an object. These latter transformations are accomplished in Illustrator using special tools, each of which is discussed in this chapter. The first tool we will discuss is the *scale tool*.

Using the scale tool

The scale tool, ninth tool in the palette, is used to reduce and enlarge text blocks and graphic objects. The scale tool, like all transformation tools, is operated by *both* clicking *and* dragging, each at a separate location. The following steps explain how to use this tool:

1. Select the object or objects that you wish to scale. Then select the scale tool. Your cursor will appear as a small cross.

2. Click with the scale tool at some location in your drawing area relative to the selected object. This location will act as the *scale origin*, the core of a reduction or enlargement.

3. After establishing a scale origin, your cursor will change to an arrowhead. Drag toward the origin to reduce the selected object; drag away from the origin to enlarge it.

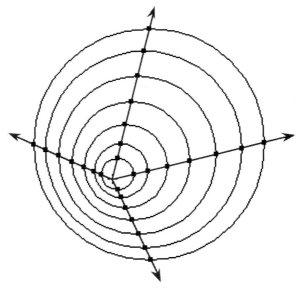

Figure 12.08: Enlarging a circle several times about a single scale origin.

To better understand the concept of the scale origin, consider the example shown in Figure 12.08. Here are a series of circles enlarged one about the other. All circles have been enlarged about a single scale origin, shown in the figure as a small cross from which the four directional lines emanate. These lines follow the progression of the points in the enlarged paths. The fact that the points progress outward in straight lines demonstrates that the scale origin marks the center of any reduction or enlargement.

Figure 12.09 displays two paths representing a telephone. The path of the receiver is entirely selected. Suppose that you want to scale the receiver without affecting the telephone carriage. The following exercise demonstrates how:

1. Select the scale tool and click at the location displayed as a small cross in Figure 12.09. This establishes the scale origin.

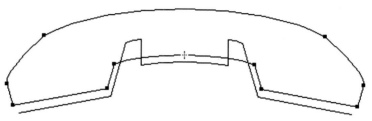

Figure 12.09: Click with the scale tool near the middle of the selected shape to establish a scale origin.

2. By creating a scale origin, you establish imaginary horizontal and vertical axes, which divide the drawing area into four *quadrants*. In Figure 12.10 on the next page, these axes are displayed as two dotted lines. For best results, you should always begin dragging with the scale tool well within one of these quadrants. In this case, begin your drag at a point on the right side of the top segment in the selected path.

3. Drag up and to the right, as demonstrated by the arrow in Figure 12.10. As you drag away from the scale origin, the path of the receiver grows larger and larger. Both the previous and current size of the selected path are displayed throughout your drag, allowing you to gauge the full effect of the enlargement.

4. Release your mouse button to complete the enlargement. Choose UNDO SCALE (⌘-Z) to return the path to its original size.

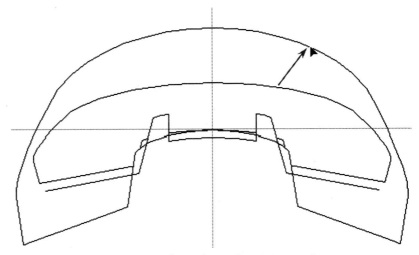

Figure 12.10: Drag away from the scale origin to enlarge the selected object. Begin your drag well within one of the quadrants defined by the origin.

5. Click again at the location of the small cross in Figure 12.09 to establish the scale origin. Begin dragging at the point on the right side of the top segment in the selected path, just as before.

6. Drag down and to the left, as demonstrated by the arrow in Figure 12.11. As you drag toward the scale origin, the selected path grows smaller and smaller.

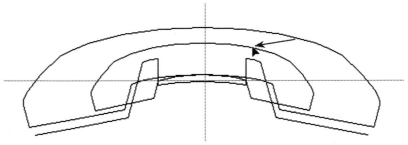

Figure 12.11: Drag toward the scale origin to reduce the selected object.

7. Release your mouse button to complete the reduction. Choose UNDO SCALE (⌘-Z) to return the path to its original size.

8. In the previous steps, the horizontal and vertical proportions of your drags have been almost identical. Thus, the height and width of the selected object were affected very similarly, resulting in one proportional enlargement and one proportional reduction. This time, however, you will stretch the height of the path but barely change its width. To begin, click on the lower left-hand corner of the object with the scale tool to establish the origin.

9. Figure 12.12 shows how the new origin has redefined the imaginary axes and quadrants. Begin dragging with the scale tool somewhere inside the left side of the selected object.

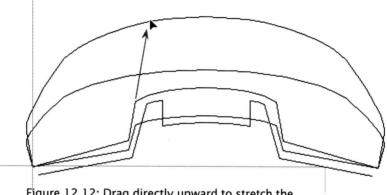

Figure 12.12: Drag directly upward to stretch the object vertically while barely affecting its width.

10. Drag directly upward from the scale origin to increase the height of the shape while only slightly altering its width, as shown in Figure 12.12.

Drag vertically to affect the height of a selected object; drag horizontally to affect its width. Drag away from the scale origin to enlarge an object; drag toward the origin to reduce the object. In part, this explains why it is so important to begin your drags well within one of the quadrants defined by the origin. If you drag from a location that is either on or very close to the origin, you will have very little chance of reducing the size of the selected object, since there is so little room to maneuver. Also, a slight movement away from the origin will dramatically enlarge the object.

There is no maximum size beyond which you can no longer enlarge a selected object. The object may even exceed the confines of the drawing area, although you will no longer be able to view the entirety of such an image. You may also drag so close to the scale origin that you reduce an object into virtual invisibility. If you drag *past* the scale origin, you will flip the selected object, as shown in Figure 12.13. This little known feature of the scale tool allows you to flip and scale objects at the same time.

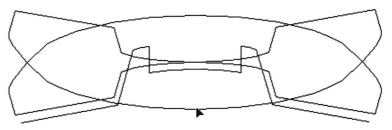

Figure 12.13: Drag past the origin with the scale tool to flip the selected object.

You may only flip objects vertically or horizontally with the scale tool. To flip an object across an angled axis, use the reflect tool as described in the next section, *Flipping objects.*

Constrained scaling

To constrain an enlargement or reduction so that the height and width of the selected object are affected equally, press the SHIFT key while dragging diagonally with the scale tool. If you SHIFT-drag vertically or horizontally, you will scale the object's height or width exclusively.

The effects of SHIFT-dragging with the scale tool may be altered by rotating the constraint axes using the "Constrain angle" option in the PREFERENCES dialog box. For more information, see *Transforming rotated objects,* later in this chapter.

Scaling partial paths

Illustrator allows you to scale whole selected objects. But you may also scale specific elements within objects independently of their deselected neighbors. Simply select the desired points and segments that you wish to scale, and use the scale tool as directed in the previous sections.

For example, only six points are selected in the skyline path shown in Figure 12.14. The segments that border each of these points are the only segments that will be affected by the scale tool:

1. Click with the scale tool at the location indicated by the small cross cursor in Figure 12.14.

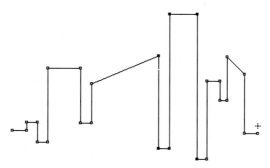

Figure 12.14: Position the scale origin to the right of the partially selected object.

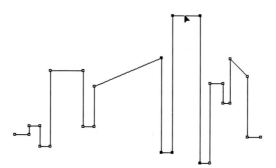

Figure 12.15: Begin your drag at the top of the tallest building.

2. Begin dragging at the selected segment along the top of the tallest building, as demonstrated by the arrowhead cursor in Figure 12.15.

3. Drag downward, toward the origin, as shown in Figure 12.16 on the next page. Only the selected points and segments are affected. Release when you are satisfied with the scaling.

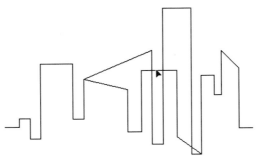

Figure 12.16: Drag downward to reduce the size of the selected elements while leaving deselected elements unchanged.

Dragging points with the scale tool can be remarkably like dragging them with an arrow tool. The only difference is that each selected point is moved slightly differently, depending on its proximity to the scale origin. If you look closely at Figure 12.16, you'll notice that points close to the scale origin move much less than those farther away. This results in various reductions in the length of the each selected segment, depending on the orientation of each segment relative to the drag.

The scale tool can prove very useful for moving specific points in ways that the arrow tool does not allow. For example, to move two selected segments equal distances in opposite directions about a central point, click at this point and drag the segments as shown in Figure 12.17.

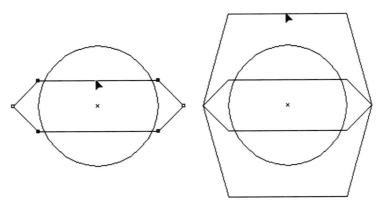

Figure 12.17: After clicking at the center point of the circle with the scale tool, we drag up from the top selected segment (left) to move both selected segments an equal distance in opposite directions (right).

Scaling a clone

You may see both the previous and current size of any selected object while dragging with the scale tool. A reason for this that we have not yet mentioned is that both versions of the object may be retained by OPTION-dragging; that is, press the OPTION key after beginning a drag and holding the key down until after the drag is completed. This creates a *clone* of the selected object that may be manipulated independently of the original. (A more complete discussion of cloning is included in the section *Cloning objects*, later in this chapter.) After OPTION-dragging with the scale tool, the cloned object remains selected, but its original is deselected.

Using the scale-dialog tool

If you press the OPTION key before clicking with the scale tool, the right side of your cross-shaped cursor will extend and the information bar will change to read "Scale dialog: click to choose origin." This shows that you have accessed the *scale-dialog tool.* You may also choose this tool—distinguished by a plus sign in its lower right corner—by dragging from the scale tool slot.

Press OPTION and click with the scale tool or click with the scale-dialog tool to simultaneously determine the location of the scale origin and display the SCALE dialog box, shown in Figure 12.18. This dialog allows you to scale one or more selected objects numerically.

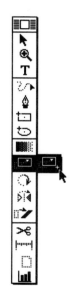

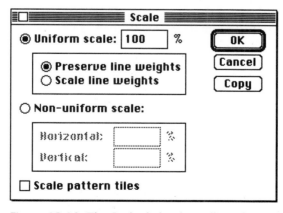

Figure 12.18: The Scale dialog box allows you to specify the percentage by which to enlarge or reduce a selected object.

To scale the width and height of an object proportionally, select the "Uniform scale" value and enter a value in the option box. Values less than 100% will reduce the size of any selected object; values greater than 100% will enlarge any selected object; a 100% value will leave the size of any selected object unaltered.

When "Uniform scale" is selected, two radio buttons appear in the box below the option: "Preserve line weights" and "Scale line weights." Only one of these may be selected. If "Preserve line weights" is selected, the proposed scaling has no effect upon the line weights associated with the selected object. This means that if you reduce a path stroked with a 4-point line weight to 25% of its original size, the reduced path will still have a 4-point line weight. If the "Scale line weights" option is selected, the line weight will be affected by the scaling. In this case, reducing a path stroked with a 4-point line weight to 25% of its original size will reduce the stroke to a 1-point line weight $(4 \times 0.25 = 1)$.

The "Scale line weights" option in the SCALE dialog box corresponds to the "Scale line weights" check box in the PREFERENCES dialog box. Selecting or deselecting either option changes the default setting for the other option as well. Future proportional scalings performed by SHIFT-dragging with the scale tool are also affected by the new setting.

To scale the width and height of an object independently, select the "Non-uniform scale" option. When this option is selected, the radio buttons in the box above the option become dimmed and two option boxes appear in the box below: these are "Horizontal" and "Vertical." Use these options as follows:

- A "Horizontal" value less than 100% makes the selection thinner.
- A "Horizontal" value greater than 100% makes the selection wider.
- A "Vertical" value less than 100% makes the selection shorter.
- A "Vertical" value greater than 100% makes the selection taller.

If some object in the current selection is filled or stroked with a tile pattern, select the "Scale pattern tiles" option to transform the tiles along with the selection.

You may confirm your scaling specifications by clicking on either the OK or COPY button. Clicking COPY retains any selected object at its original size, as well as creating a clone scaled to the dialog specifications.

Flipping objects

In the previous section, we mentioned how dragging past the scale origin with the scale tool will flip a selected object. Illustrator also provides a dedicated *reflect tool* for those times when you want to flip an object without scaling it. The reflect tool flips an object around a *reflection axis*, which acts like a pivoting mirror. The selected object looks into this mirror; the result of the flip is the image that the mirror projects.

Using the reflect tool

The reflect tool, eleventh tool in the palette, is used to flip text blocks and graphic objects. It is operated by clicking at each of two different locations *or* by both clicking and dragging, each at a separate location. The following steps explain how to use this tool:

1. Select the object or objects that you wish to flip. Then select the reflect tool. Your cursor will appear as a small cross.

2. Click with the reflect tool at some location in your drawing area relative to the selected object. This location will act as the first point in the reflection axis.

3. After establishing the first point in the axis, your cursor will change to an arrowhead. Click or drag relative to the first point to determine the angle of the reflection axis, about which the selected objects will flip.

Figure 12.19 on the next page displays two paths representing a telephone. They are identical to those in Figure 12.09 except that a cord has been added to the selected path. This addition makes the path unsymmetrical so it may better demonstrate the reflection operation. Suppose that you want to flip the path around an angled axis. The following exercise explains how:

1. Select the reflect tool and click at the location displayed as a small cross in Figure 12.19, establishing the first point in the reflection axis (sometimes called the *reflection origin*).

2. Drag with the arrowhead cursor. As you drag, the invisible reflection axis continually rotates so that it runs in a straight line between the cursor and the origin.

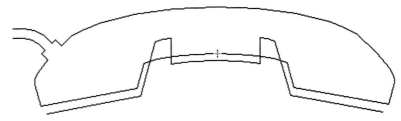

Figure 12.19: Click with the reflect tool near the middle of the selected path to establish a reflection origin.

3. Drag the cursor above and to the left of the origin, as shown in Figure 12.20. Illustrator displays both original and current positions on screen. In the figure, a gray line has been added to indicate the angle of the reflection axis.

4. Release your mouse button to complete the flip.

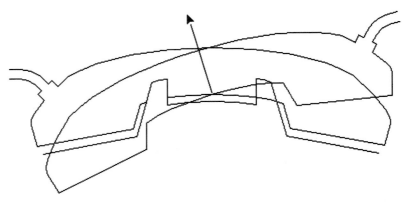

Figure 12.20: Drag up and to the left to tilt the reflection axis about 15° from vertical.

If you prefer, you may simply click with the arrowhead cursor, instead of dragging, to flip a selected object. After establishing a reflection origin, clicking a second time immediately creates a reflection axis between the two click points, and the selected object is flipped accordingly.

Constrained flipping

To constrain a reflection so that the selected object is flipped about a vertical, horizontal, or diagonal axis, press the SHIFT key while clicking a second time or dragging with the reflect tool. Constraining limits the angle of the reflection axis to some multiple of 45°.

The effects of pressing SHIFT while operating the reflect tool may be altered by rotating the constraint axes using the "Constrain angle" option in the PREFERENCES dialog box. For more information, see the section *Transforming rotated objects*, later in this chapter.

Flipping partial paths

Just as you may flip whole objects, you may flip selected elements within objects independently of their deselected neighbors. Simply select the desired points and segments that you wish to flip, and use the reflect tool as directed in the previous sections.

For example, suppose that you want to flip the selected elements in the skyline path shown back in Figure 12.14:

1. Click with the reflect tool to the right of the path, at the same location indicated by the small cross cursor in Figure 12.14.

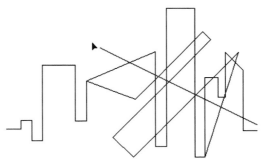

Figure 12.21: Drag up and to the left with the reflect tool to flip the selected elements across an angled axis.

2. Drag up and to the left with the reflect tool arrowhead cursor. Figure 12.21 shows how all selected points pivot to the opposite side of the invisible reflection axis, rotating many selected segments and stretching those that are bordered by a deselected point.

Flipping a clone

You may retain both the original and current position of a flipped object by OPTION-dragging with the reflect tool; that is, press the OPTION key after beginning a drag and hold the key down until after the drag is completed. You may also press OPTION before clicking a second time with the tool to create a *clone* of the selected object that may be manipulated independently of the original. (A more complete discussion of cloning is included in the *Cloning objects* section later in this chapter.) After OPTION-dragging or OPTION-clicking with the reflect tool, the cloned object remains selected, but its original is deselected.

Using the reflect-dialog tool

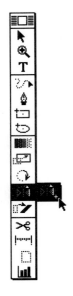

If you press the OPTION key before clicking with the reflect tool the first time, the right side of your cross-shaped cursor will extend and the information bar will change to read "Reflect dialog: click to choose origin." This shows that you have accessed the *reflect-dialog tool*. You may also choose this tool—distinguished by a plus sign in its lower right corner—by dragging from the reflect tool slot.

Press OPTION and click with the reflect tool or click with the reflect-dialog tool to simultaneously determine the location of the reflection origin and display the REFLECT dialog box, shown in Figure 12.22, which allows you to flip one or more selected objects around a numerically tilted axis.

The "Reflect across" box contain three radio buttons, any one of which may be selected to determine the angle of the reflection axis. These options produce the following results:

- Select "Horizontal axis" to flip an object on its head.

- Select "Vertical axis" to flip an object onto its side.

- Select "Angled axis" and enter a value between −360 and 360 in the corresponding option box to flip an object around an angled axis.

The value in the "Angled axis" option box is measured in degrees from the mean horizontal (0°). Because the axis extends to either side of the reflection origin, values over 180° are repetitious. (For an explanation of degrees, see the *Constrained movements* section of Chapter 7.)

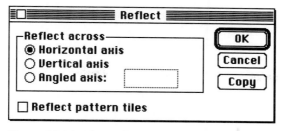

Figure 12.22: The Reflect dialog box allows you to specify the angle of the reflection axis.

If some object in the current selection is filled or stroked with a tile pattern, select the "Reflect pattern tiles" option to transform the tiles along with the selection.

You may confirm your reflection specifications by clicking on either the OK or Copy button. Clicking Copy retains any selected object at its original position, while creating a clone reflected across the specified axis.

Rotating objects

In Illustrator, any text block or graphic objected may be rotated to any degree imaginable. This allows you to create angled type and other tilted images. Rotations are accomplished with the *rotate tool*.

Using the rotate tool

The rotate tool, tenth tool in the palette, is operated by *both* clicking *and* dragging, each at a separate location. The following steps explain how to use this tool:

1. Select the object you wish to rotate. Then select the rotate tool. Your cursor will appear as a small cross.

2. Click with the rotate tool at some location in your drawing area relative to the selected object to establish the *rotation origin*, the center of the rotation.

3. After establishing a rotation origin, your cursor will change to an arrowhead. Drag the selected object about the origin to rotate it.

In principle, the rotation origin is much like the scale origin. Figure 12.23 shows an ellipse in various stages of rotating around a single origin, displayed as a small cross. The original location of the ellipse is the right-most shape in the figure. All other ellipses are the results of many separate drags, each of which has rotated the shape by 45°. During the drags, all points in the ellipse remain equidistant from the rotation origin. A gray arrow demonstrates the course of each drag. Together, these arrows form a large circle whose center is the rotation origin.

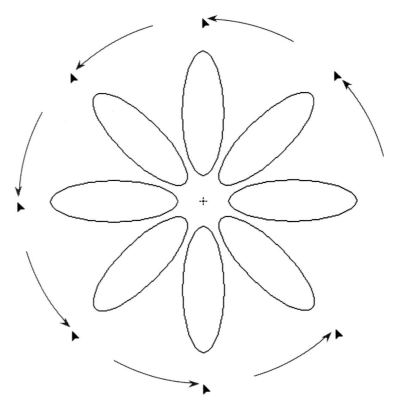

Figure 12.23: Rotating an ellipse in 45° increments around a single rotation origin.

 The rotate tool offers the most control when the distance between the rotation origin and the point at which you begin your drag is greater than or equal to the length of the selected object.

We will demonstrate this tip in the following exercise, which offers various ways to approach the rotatation of the selected path shown in Figure 12.24:

1. Select the rotate tool and click on the bottom left-hand corner point of the selected path, indicated by the small cross in Figure 12.24. This establishes the rotation origin.

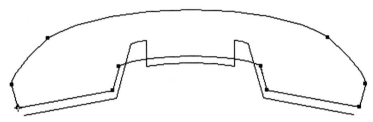

Figure 12.24: Click with the rotate tool on the bottom left point in the selected shape to establish a rotation origin.

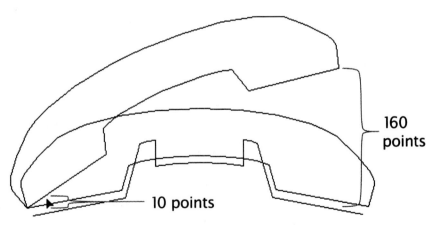

160 points

10 points

Figure 12.25: If you begin dragging close to the rotation origin, small movements will produce dramatic results.

2. Move the arrowhead cursor to a location about ⅓ inch to the right of the origin and drag slightly upward, as shown in Figure 12.25. The distance of the drag in the figure is only 10 points (less than ⅙ inch), but the shape rotates dramatically, approximately 24° counterclockwise.

3. Release your mouse button to complete the rotation. Choose UNDO ROTATE (⌘-Z) to return the receiver to its original position.

4. Click again at the location of the small cross in Figure 12.24 to establish the origin. This time, begin dragging at the bottom, right corner point on the opposite side of the selected path, approximately 16 times the distance from the origin as the previous drag.

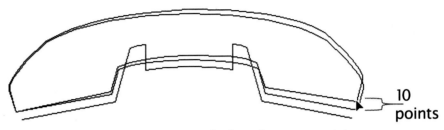

10
points

Figure 12.26: Begin dragging far from the rotation origin to better control the result.

5. As also shown in Figure 12.25, you have to drag 160 points from this location to achieve the same result as your previous 10-point drag. If you drag upward only 10 points, as shown in Figure 12.26, the selected shape rotates less than 2°. Thus, beginning your drag far from the rotation origin provides you with more fine-tuning control.

Constraining rotations

To constrain a rotation so that the selected object is rotated by a multiple of 45° from its original position, press the SHIFT key while dragging with the rotate tool.

Unlike other transformation tools, the effects of pressing SHIFT while operating the rotate tool are *not* altered by rotating the constraint axes using the "Constrain angle" option in the PREFERENCES dialog box.

Rotating partial paths

Just as you may rotate whole objects, you may rotate selected elements within objects independently of their deselected neighbors. Simply select the desired points and segments that you wish to rotate and use the rotate tool as directed in the previous sections.

For example, suppose that you want to rotate the selected elements in the skyline path shown in Figure 12.27:

1. Click with the rotate tool on the bottom right selected point, as indicated by the small cross cursor in Figure 12.27.

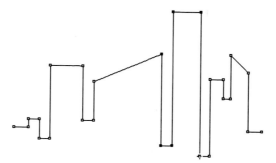

Figure 12.27: Position the rotation origin at the bottom, right selected point in the path.

2. Begin dragging at the point on the left side of the segment along the top of the tallest building.

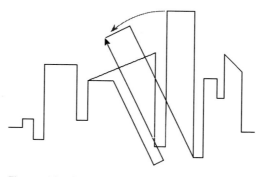

Figure 12.28: Drag to the left to rotate the selected elements counterclockwise around the origin.

3. Drag to the left with the rotate tool, as shown in Figure 12.28. All selected points remain equidistant from the origin during their moves, causing the rotation of all segments surrounded by selected points.

Rotating a clone

You may retain both the original and current position of a rotated object by OPTION-dragging with the rotate tool; that is, press the OPTION key after beginning a drag and hold the key down until after the drag is completed. This creates a *clone* of the selected object that may be manipulated independently of the original. (A more complete discussion of cloning is included in the *Cloning objects* section, later in this chapter.) After OPTION-dragging with the rotate tool, the cloned object remains selected, but its original is deselected.

Using the rotate-dialog tool

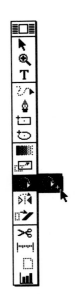

If you press the OPTION key before clicking with the rotate tool the first time, the right side of your cross-shaped cursor will extend and the information bar will change to read "Rotate dialog: click to choose origin." This shows that you have accessed the *rotate-dialog tool.* You may also choose this tool—distinguished by a plus sign in its lower right corner—by dragging from the rotate tool slot.

Press OPTION and click with the rotate tool or click with the rotate-dialog tool to simultaneously determine the location of the rotation origin and display the ROTATE dialog box, shown in Figure 12.29. This dialog allows you to rotate one or more selected objects numerically.

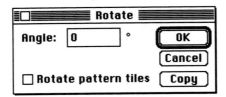

Figure 12.29: The Rotate dialog box allows you to specify the number of degrees by which to rotate a selected object.

Enter any value between –360 and 360 in the "Angle" option box. The value is measured in degrees and is accurate to 0.01 degree. A negative value rotates an object clockwise; a positive value rotates an object counterclockwise.

If some object in the current selection is filled or stroked with a tile pattern, select the "Rotate pattern tiles" option to transform the tiles along with the selection.

You may confirm your rotation specifications by clicking on either the OK or Copy button. Clicking Copy retains any selected object at its original position, while creating a clone rotated the specified number of degrees.

Slanting objects

Slanting (more accurately called *skewing*) is perhaps the most difficult transformation to conceptualize. To skew an object is to slant its vertical and horizontal proportions independently of each other. For example, a standard kite shape is a skewed version of a perfect square. As shown in Figure 12.30, the vertical lines in the square are slanted backward and the horizontal lines are slanted upward.

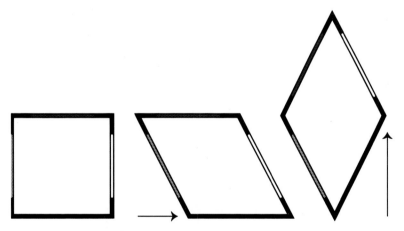

Figure 12.30: Transforming a square into a kite by skewing the shape in two steps.

For some reason, Adobe calls this process *shearing*, like maybe it has something to do with sheep. Who knows? So it follows that the feature used to skew objects in Illustrator is the *shear tool*.

Using the shear tool

The shear tool, twelfth tool in the palette, is used to skew text blocks and graphic objects. It is operated by *both* clicking *and* dragging, each at a separate location. The following steps explain how to use this tool:

1. Select the object you wish to skew. Then select the shear tool. Your cursor will appear as a small cross.

2. Click with the shear tool at some location in your drawing area. This location will act as the *shear origin*, the center of the skewing operation. Elements on opposite sides of the origin will be skewed in opposite directions.

3. After establishing a shear origin, your cursor will change to an arrowhead. Drag from one side of the origin to the other to skew the selected object in that direction.

In general, the shear tool functions like any other transformation tool. However, it may take some experimenting before you're able to accurately predict the results of your actions. In the following exercise, you may experiment by skewing the telephone shape from Figure 12.09:

1. Select the shear tool and click near the middle of the selected shape to establish the shear origin.

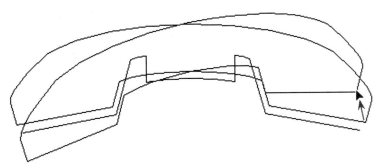

Figure 12.31: Drag with the shear tool to skew the right half of the selected shape up and the left half of the shape down.

2. Drag upward from the bottom, right corner point in the shape, as shown in Figure 12.31. The right half of the phone will shrug upward with your drag. The left half shrugs downward, because it is located on the opposite side of the shear origin.

Like the rotate tool, the shear tool offers the most control when the distance between the shear origin and the point at which you begin your drag is greater than or equal to the length of the selected object.

If you find that the shear tool consistently behaves erratically for you, try constraining the performance of the tool by SHIFT-dragging, as described in the following section. This generally makes the tool more manageable.

Constrained skewing

After establishing the shear origin, press the SHIFT key to slant an object exclusively horizontally (forward and backward) or vertically (up and down). If you SHIFT-drag diagonally from the shear origin, you may also skew a shape equally vertically and horizontally, although the effect of a diagonal drag is much more difficult to predict.

The effect of SHIFT-dragging with the shear tool may be altered by rotating the constraint axes using the "Constrain angle" option in the PREFERENCES dialog box. For more information, see *Transforming rotated objects*, later in this chapter.

Skewing partial paths

Selected elements may be slanted independently of their deselected neighbors in the same path. Simply select the desired points and segments that you wish to skew, and use the shear tool as directed in the previous sections.

For example, suppose you want to skew the selected elements in the skyline path shown back in Figure 12.27:

1. Click with the shear tool on the bottom, right selected point, as indicated by the small cross cursor in Figure 12.27.

2. Begin dragging at the point on the left side of the segment along the top of the tallest building.

3. Drag leftward with the shear tool as shown in Figure 12.32 on the following page. As you drag, press the SHIFT key to constrain the transformation to a horizontal slant. All selected points move with the shear tool based on their proximity to the shear origin; points

close to the origin move less than points farther away. All selected vertical segments are slanted backward; all selected horizontal segments are unaffected.

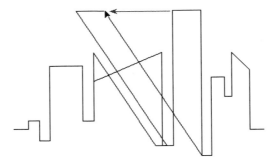

Figure 12.32: Shift-drag to the left with the shear tool to slant the selected elements so they lean backward.

Skewing a clone

You may retain both the original and current position of a skewed object by OPTION-dragging with the shear tool; that is, press the OPTION key after beginning a drag and hold the key down until after the drag is completed. This creates a *clone* of the selected object that may be manipulated independently of the original. (A more complete discussion of cloning is included in the *Cloning objects* section, later in this chapter.) After OPTION-dragging with the shear tool, the cloned object remains selected, but its original is deselected.

Using the shear-dialog tool

If you press the OPTION key before clicking with the shear tool the first time, the right side of your cross-shaped cursor will extend and the information bar will change to read "Shear dialog: click to choose origin." This shows that you have accessed the *shear-dialog tool.* You may also choose this tool—distinguished by a plus sign in its lower right corner—by dragging from the shear tool slot.

Press OPTION and click with the shear tool or click with the shear-dialog tool to simultaneously determine the location of the shear origin and display the SHEAR dialog box, shown in Figure 12.33, which allows you to skew one or more selected objects numerically along a specified *shear axis* (the imaginary straight line along which the selected object will slant).

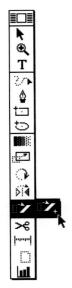

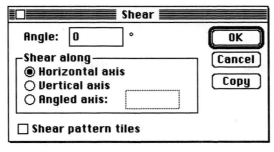

Figure 12.33: The Shear dialog box allows you to specify the angle of the shear axis and determine the angle of the slant.

The "Shear along" box contains three radio buttons, any one of which may be selected to determine the angle of the shear axis. These options produce the following results:

- Select "Horizontal axis" to slant an object forward or backward.

- Select "Vertical axis" to slant an object up or down.

- Select "Angled axis" and enter a value between –360 and 360 in the nearby option box to slant an object along an angled axis.

The value in the "Angled axis" option box is measured in degrees from the mean horizontal (0°). Because the axis extends to either side of the shear origin, values over 180° are repititious. (For an explanation of degrees, see the *Constrained movements* section of Chapter 7.)

Regardless of the selected "Shear along" option, you will want to enter a value for the "Angle" option at the top of the dialog. Here's where things get tricky. In almost every option box that is measured in degrees, Illustrator interprets the value in a counterclockwise direction. This is true for rotations, angled axes, and directional movements. The single exception is this "Angle" option, where an entered value is interpreted in a clockwise direction:

- A positive horizontal value slants a selected object forward.

- A negative horizontal value slants a selected object backward.

- A positive vertical value slants anything to the right of the origin down and anything to the left of the origin up.

- A negative vertical value slants anything to the right of the origin up and anything to the left of the origin down.

The reason for this is probably because the shear tool is commonly used with text. Oblique or italicized type is slanted forward; backward-sheared type is considered to be backslanted. Therefore, the clockwise angle measurement makes sense in this context. You may nonetheless find yourself slightly confused when you skew an object by a positive value vertically and see it slant downward.

If some object in the current selection is filled or stroked with a tile pattern, select the "Shear pattern tiles" option to transform the tiles along with the selection.

You may confirm your skew specifications by clicking on either the OK or COPY button. Clicking COPY retains any selected object at its original position, while creating a clone slanted along the specified axis by the specified number of degrees.

Transformation nightcaps

The following are a couple of quick notes about transformations before we close the subject. Although they are not absolutely necessary to your understanding of transformation tools, they can be helpful in sticky situations.

Recording transformations

Each of the four transformation dialogs previously discussed in this chapter acts as a recorder of the most recent scaling, flip, rotation, or skew. After transforming an object by hand, OPTION-click with the current transformation tool while the object remains selected. The appropriate dialog box will appear, containing the exact percentage, number of degrees, and so on, corresponding to the previous transformation. You may use this information to repeat the transformation, apply a similar transformation to another object, or simply refer to it for tracking purposes.

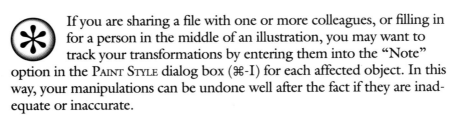 If you are sharing a file with one or more colleagues, or filling in for a person in the middle of an illustration, you may want to track your transformations by entering them into the "Note" option in the PAINT STYLE dialog box (⌘-I) for each affected object. In this way, your manipulations can be undone well after the fact if they are inadequate or inaccurate.

Transforming rotated objects

As we have mentioned, the performance of the scale tool, the reflect tool, and the shear tool are affected by the current orientation of the constraint axes. If you rotate the constraint axes by entering a value between –360 and 360 in the "Constrain angle" option inside the PREFERENCES dialog box (⌘-I), you alter the angle at which an object is transformed.

Generally, you will be able to most accurately predict the results of using a transformation tool when the constraint axes are not rotated; that is, when the "Constrain angle" option is set to 0. An exception arises when transforming an object that has been rotated. In this case, you will find that the object is most easily transformed when the constraint axes are likewise rotated.

For example, suppose that you rotate an object. Later on, you decide you want to enlarge the object. The following exercise describes how this might work:

1. Draw a rectangle with the rectangle tool.

2. Select the rotate tool and click on the center point of the rectangle to establish the rotation origin. Drag the shape by one of it corners to rotate the rectangle, as shown in Figure 12.34.

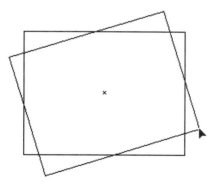

Figure 12.34: Rotate an object a random number of degrees.

3. The rectangle turns out to be too short for your purpose, although its width is correct. Select the scale tool and click on the center point of the shape to establish the scale origin. Drag downward from the lower side of the shape to increase its height. Whether or

not you press SHIFT to constrain the scaling, the enlargement distorts the rectangle so that its corners are no longer perpendicular, as shown in Figure 12.35. The sides slant as if you had skewed the shape with the shear tool. This is because you are scaling the rectangle along an axis that is not aligned with the rectangle itself.

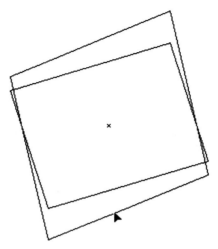

Figure 12.35: Scaling the rotated rectangle vertically distorts the shape.

4. Choose the UNDO SCALE command (⌘-Z).

5. Select the measure tool and click on each of the two points bordering the bottom segment in the rectangle.

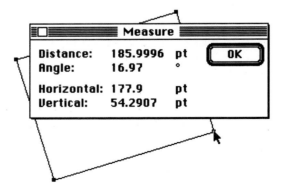

Figure 12.36: The Measure dialog displays the angle of the rotated rectangle.

6. The MEASURE dialog box will appear, as shown in Figure 12.36. The "Angle" option displays the angle of the measured segment. Since this segment used to be horizontal (0°), the new angle reflects the degree of the previous rotation. Record the "Angle" value, which is 16.97° in the case of the figure, and press RETURN to exit the dialog box.

7. Choose the PREFERENCES... command (⌘-K) and enter the recorded value into the "Constrain angle" option box. Press RETURN to implement the change.

8. Select the scale tool again and click on the center point of the rectangle to establish the scale origin. Press SHIFT and drag downward from the lower side of the shape to increase its height. This time, the rectangle does not distort. As shown in Figure 12.37, all corners remain perpendicular as you increase the height of the shape.

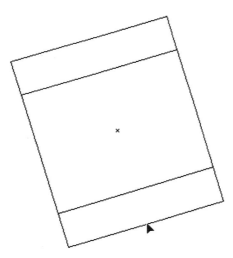

Figure 12.37: By rotating the constraint axes to the same angle as the rotated rectangle, you preserve the form of the object as you scale it vertically.

9. Restore the constraint axes to their original orientation.

The process for flipping and skewing rotated objects is similar. The only transformation tool that is not affected by the orientation of the constraint axes is the rotation tool, since objects are always rotated from their current orientation.

Duplicating objects

To *duplicate* an object is to create and control one or more copies of an existing object. Some of these techniques utilize the Macintosh Clipboard, where objects may be stored for future retrieval. Others work without the Clipboard or in combination with manipulation techniques, including the transformation tools. All repeat the composition of an object, a movement, or a transformation procedure.

Cut, copy, and paste

The CUT, COPY, and PASTE commands under the EDIT menu are available in any Macintosh application. CUT and COPY store one or more selected objects so they may be used later in the current session. The PASTE command retrieves the stored objects and displays them in the drawing area. Each command works with Apple's built-in *Clipboard*, which can hold only one object or one set of objects at a time.

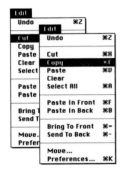

To cut an object is to remove the object from the current illustration and place it inside the Clipboard. This is done by selecting an object and choosing the CUT command from the EDIT menu (⌘-X). The COPY command (⌘-C) works very similarly. But rather than removing the selected object, this command makes a copy of a selected object and puts it in the Clipboard.

Both CUT and COPY put something into the Clipboard. Since the Clipboard can only hold one set of items at a time, each command disposes of the current occupant in the Clipboard and replaces it with the newly cut or copied object. If no object is selected in the drawing area, the CUT and COPY commands will appear dimmed.

The PASTE command (⌘-V) works exactly opposite the COPY command. To paste an object is to copy the contents of the Clipboard and place them inside the current drawing area. The object still exists in the Clipboard and may be pasted into your illustration over and over again. You must have cut or copied an object into the Clipboard sometime previously during the current session in order to use the PASTE command. Otherwise, the command will be dimmed.

The PASTE command pastes the contents of the Clipboard at the exact center of the current window and in front of all other objects in the illustration. (You may also paste an object at the exact location at which it was cut or copied, while additionally altering its layering, by choosing the

PASTE IN FRONT (⌘-F) or PASTE IN BACK (⌘-B) command from the EDIT menu, as described in the section *Layering objects*, later in this chapter.) Pasted objects appear selected in the illustration window. In this way, you can easily find an object and move it to its proper location.

Duplicating type

Characters, words, and paragraphs of type may also be duplicated. Select the type tool and highlight the type that you want to use later. Choose CUT to remove the highlighted type from the text block and store it in the Clipboard. Choose COPY to copy the highlighted type to the Clipboard. Choose PASTE to replace the highlighted type with type from the Clipboard or paste the type after the insertion marker.

Pasted type retains all character formatting. However, it will assume the paragraph formatting of the paragraph into which it is pasted (unless an entire paragraph was copied, and it is pasted between paragraphs).

Cut or copied objects (selected with the arrow tool) may not be pasted into a text block. Cut or copied type (selected with the type tool) may not be pasted outside a text block.

Duplicating partial paths

Individually selected points and segments in an object may be cut or copied independently of their deselected neighbors. In the first example of Figure 12.38 on the following page, we have selected a single curved segment, copied it, and then pasted it. The pasted segment is offset slightly from the original path. Notice that although the points that border the curved segment are not selected in the original path, they are copied and pasted. This is because a segment must always be bordered on both sides by a point.

If you select a point, the result of choosing the COPY and PASTE commands is slightly different. By selecting an interior point, you also select both the segment that enters the point and the segment that exits the point. Therefore, copying and pasting a point also copies and pastes the two segments associated with the point, as shown in the second example of Figure 12.38 on the next page. Once again, two points that were not selected in the original path are pasted in the offset path, since these are the endpoints belonging to the two copied segments.

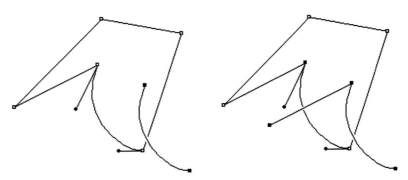

Figure 12.38: Copying and pasting a segment (left) pastes the points bordering the segments as well; copying and pasting a point (right) pastes the two bordering segments and their bordering points.

Cloning objects

Cloning is much like the COPY command with two important exceptions: First, cloning bypasses the Clipboard. It neither displaces the current occupant in the Clipboard nor does it replace that object with the cloned object. Second, cloning acts like combined COPY and PASTE command. The cloned object immediately appears in your illustration, in front of all other objects in the current illustration.

Cloning may be accomplished in one of three ways:

- Press OPTION and drag a selected object with the arrow tool; that is, press the OPTION key after beginning the drag and hold the key down until after the drag is completed. This moves and clones the object in a single gesture.

- Press OPTION and drag a selected object with one of the transformation tools (scale, reflect, rotate, or shear) to transform and clone the object in a single gesture.

- Click the COPY button in the MOVE, SCALE, ROTATE, REFLECT, and SHEAR dialog boxes. This feature allows you to determine the placement of a clone with numerical precision.

After cloning one or more objects, the original objects remain unaffected, while their clones appear at the new position or orientation. Only the cloned objects are selected.

Cloning partial paths

Just as you may clone whole objects, you may clone selected elements within objects independently of their deselected neighbors. The first example of Figure 12.39 shows a selected curved segment being OPTION-dragged with the arrow tool. The result is shown in the second example in the figure. The segment and its two bordering points have been cloned and reshaped simultaneously.

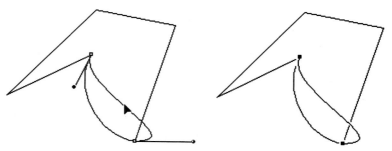

Figure 12.39: Option-drag a segment (left) to simultaneously reshape and clone the segment (right).

If you instead OPTION-drag at a selected interior point in an otherwise deselected path, as shown in the first example of Figure 12.40, you will clone the selected point, its two bordering segments, and each segment's bordering points. As shown in the second example of the figure, the form of each cloned segment is again reshaped since each is bordered by one moving point and one stationary point.

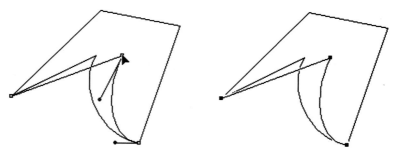

Figure 12.40: Option-drag a point (left) to simultaneously reshape and clone both bordering segments (right).

Duplicating a transformation

Most drawing programs offer a command that duplicates the effects of a recent transformation. In Illustrator, this is the TRANSFORM AGAIN command under the ARRANGE menu (⌘-D). TRANSFORM AGAIN repeats any newly completed transformation, including a movement.

The first example of Figure 12.41 shows two rectangles: the deselected rectangle represents the original location of an object, and the selected rectangle demonstrates the location to which it has been dragged. After moving the shape, the TRANSFORM AGAIN command is chosen to duplicate the distance and direction of the movement, as shown in the second example of the figure. The third example shows the results of choosing the TRANSFORM AGAIN command a second time. Each application of TRANSFORM AGAIN repeats the most recent transformation.

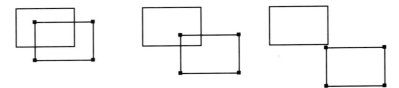

Figure 12.41: After dragging the selected rectangle from its original deselected position (left), the Transform Again command is applied two consecutive times (middle and right) to twice repeat the transformation.

The TRANSFORM AGAIN command may be used repeatedly after applying a slight transformation to fine-tune the transformation of an object. When the eventual transformation exceeds your requirements, choose UNDO TRANSFORM AGAIN to return it to the exact position or size required.

Suppose you have created a complicated object that is too small to match the size of another object in your illustration. Rather than going back and forth, scaling the object by guess and by golly, you may perform a slight enlargement—about a quarter of what you think is required—and repeat the transformation several times using TRANSFORM AGAIN. With each application of the command, the selected object will grow by the incremental percentage. When the size of the object surpasses the desired size, choose UNDO TRANSFORM AGAIN (⌘-Z) to reduce it to the size that most accurately matches your requirements.

If an object becomes deselected after a transformation or between one application of the Transform Again command and another, then Transform Again will appear dimmed.

Duplicating transformation and object

If the newly completed transformation included a cloning, the Transform Again command duplicates both transformation and cloning operations. This allows you to create a string of objects, the placement of which follow a constant trend.

In the first example in Figure 12.42, the selected rectangle has been both cloned and moved from the location represented by the deselected shape. The second example shows the result of choosing the Transform Again command. Notice that, like the second example of Figure 12.41, the movement of the rectangle has been repeated. But this time, the shape is also recloned, resulting in three rectangles instead of two. If Transform Again is chosen a second time, there will be four rectangles, each offset from the others a consistent distance, as shown in the last example of Figure 12.42.

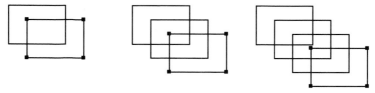

Figure 12.42: After option-dragging the selected rectangle (left), the Transform Again command is applied two consecutive times (middle and right) to twice repeat the transformation and twice duplicate the rectangle.

By duplicating both transformation and object, you may achieve very interesting effects. The following exercise demonstrates how to use the Transform Again command to create a perspective gridwork of objects. This exercise makes use of the grouped object, shown in Figure 12.43 on the following page, which contains three paths. The bottom segment of the outermost path is longer than the top segment, giving it an illusion of depth. The inner ellipses are positioned slightly closer to the top segment of the outer shape, enhancing the illusion.

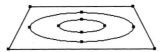

Figure 12.43: The following exercise explains how to transform and duplicate this grouped object to create a perspective effect.

1. Select the shear tool. Click above the group at the location indicated by the small cross cursor at the top of Figure 12.43 to establish the shear origin.

2. Press SHIFT and OPTION and drag leftward from the bottom right corner of the group object, skewing it horizontally while also cloning it, as shown in Figure 12.44. Notice that the cloned object appears to lean into the original, extending back into the same visual horizon. This is a result of experimenting with the position of the shear origin.

Figure 12.44: Shift-option-drag the object with the shear tool to simultaneously skew and clone the group.

Figure 12.45: Choose Transform Again to repeat the skew and clone operations.

3. Choose the TRANSFORM AGAIN command (⌘-D), which creates another clone and repeats the horizontal skew. Figure 12.45 shows the result, which further enhances the illusion of perspective.

4. Select the two groups farthest to the left. In this step, you will flip a clone of these objects about the center of the original group, creating five symmetrical images. Press OPTION and click with the reflect tool in the center of the deselected group to display the REFLECT dialog. Select the "Vertical axis" option and click on the COPY button. The result is shown in Figure 12.46: five symmetrical images emerging from the surface of the page.

Figure 12.46: Select the two left groups and flip clones of these objects about the center of the deselected group.

5. You have now managed to impart a sense of perspective through the use of skewing , flipping, and cloning. But the illustration lacks drama. What's needed are additional rows of slanting tiles, which are most easily created by scaling the existing rows over and over. To begin, choose SELECT ALL from the EDIT menu (⌘-A).

6. Select the scale tool and OPTION-click above the group at the location indicated by the small cross cursor at the top of Figure 12.47. Not only does this establish a scale origin at the same location previously occupied by the shear origin, it also displays the SCALE dialog box.

Figure 12.47: Select the entire row of groups and option-click with the scale tool to display the Scale dialog box.

7. Enter 150% into the "Uniform scale" option box and click the COPY button. Figure 12.48 on the following page shows how a second, larger row of shapes is created. Again because of the placement of the transformation origin, the second row lines up perfectly with the first. By scaling the cloned shapes to 150% of original size, you enlarge both the size of the shapes and the distance between the shapes and the scale origin.

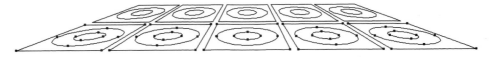

Figure 12.48: Scale clones of the top row of groups
to 150% to create two perfectly aligned rows.

8. Choose the TRANSFORM AGAIN command (⌘-D) to create a third
row of larger clones directly beneath the second row.

Figure 12.49: The completed illustration is the result of
choosing Transform Again several times and filling and
stroking the resulting paths.

To create the illustration shown in Figure 12.49, press ⌘-D several more times. Each series of shapes increases in size and distance from the group above it, thereby creating an even and continuous sense of perspective. Figure 12.49 is shown as it appears when printed. All shapes are filled and stroked. Foreground images are filled with darker shades of gray than background images, heightening the sense of depth. A layer of shadows has also been added.

Layering objects

When you preview or print an illustration, Illustrator describes it one object at a time, starting with the first object in the drawing area and working up to the last. The order in which the objects are described is called the *layering order*. The first object described is behind all other objects in the drawing area. The last object is in front of all other objects. All other objects exist at some unique layer between the first and the last object.

Left to its own device, layering would be a function of the order in which you draw. The oldest object would be in back; the most recent object would be in front. But Illustrator provides a number of commands that allow you to adjust the layering order of existing text blocks and graphic objects.

Absolute front and back

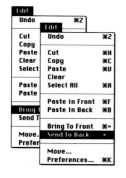

Like many Macintosh programs, Illustrator offers two commands for manipulating the layering of objects. These are the BRING TO FRONT (⌘-=, COMMAND-EQUALS) and SEND TO BACK commands (⌘--, COMMAND-HYPHEN) from the EDIT menu. If you select an object and choose BRING TO FRONT, this object is treated exactly as if it were the most recently created path in the current illustration. It will be described last when previewing or printing. By choosing SEND TO BACK, a selected object is treated as if it were the first path in the file and is described first when previewing or printing.

BRING TO FRONT and SEND TO BACK may be applied only to whole objects. If a path is only partially selected when choosing either command, the entire path is moved to the front or back of the current illustration.

If more than one object is selected when choosing the BRING TO FRONT or SEND TO BACK command, the relative layering of each selected object is retained. For example, if you select two objects and then choose the B<small>RING</small> T<small>O</small> F<small>RONT</small> command, the frontmost of the two selected objects becomes the frontmost object in the file, the backmost of the two selected objects becomes the second-to-frontmost object.

Relative front and back

When creating complicated illustrations, it is not enough to be able to send objects to the absolute front or back of an illustration. Even a simple illustration may contain over a hundred objects. Adjusting the layering of a single object from, say, 14th-to-front back to 46th-to-front would take days using B<small>RING</small> T<small>O</small> F<small>RONT</small> and S<small>END</small> T<small>O</small> B<small>ACK</small>.

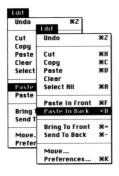

Fortunately, Illustrator provides two commands that make relative layering manipulations possible: there are P<small>ASTE</small> I<small>N</small> F<small>RONT</small> (⌘-F) and P<small>ASTE</small> I<small>N</small> B<small>ACK</small> (⌘-B) available from the E<small>DIT</small> menu. Both commands make use of the Macintosh Clipboard. As described in the *Cut, copy, and paste* section earlier in this chapter, one or more objects are placed inside the Clipboard by choosing the C<small>UT</small> or C<small>OPY</small> command. The P<small>ASTE</small> I<small>N</small> F<small>RONT</small> and P<small>ASTE</small> I<small>N</small> B<small>ACK</small> commands retrieve the contents of the Clipboard, placing them at the exact horizontal and vertical location at which they were cut or copied. P<small>ASTE</small> I<small>N</small> F<small>RONT</small> pastes the contents of the Clipboard directly in front of a selected object in the drawing area; P<small>ASTE</small> I<small>N</small> B<small>ACK</small> pastes the contents of the Clipboard directly in back of a selected object. Therefore, both commands affect only the layering of a cut or copied object, and not its positioning.

Figure 12.50 shows two columns of examples demonstrating the P<small>ASTE</small> I<small>N</small> F<small>RONT</small> command. The objects in the left-hand column are shown in the artwork-&-template mode, the objects in the right-hand column are shown in the preview mode. The following exercise explains the examples in the figure:

1. The first example shows four layered shapes. Select the black shape and choose the C<small>UT</small> command (⌘-X), removing the shape from the illustration and placing it in the Clipboard.

2. Select the backmost remaining shape, as shown in the second example, and choose the P<small>ASTE</small> I<small>N</small> F<small>RONT</small> command (⌘-F). The path is pasted at the exact horizontal and vertical position from which it was cut, but it is moved in front of the selected path, as shown in the second previewed example.

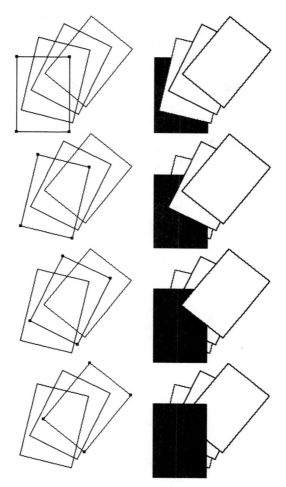

Figure 12.50: The effects of cutting a black path and pasting it in front of selected paths as viewed in the artwork-&-template (left) and preview modes (right).

3. The third and fourth examples show the results of selecting other paths and choosing the Paste In Front command. Throughout the figure, the layering of the black shape is altered, but the horizontal and vertical positioning of all shapes is constant.

If multiple objects are selected when choosing one of the relative pasting commands, the contents of the Clipboard are placed in front of the frontmost selected object, or in back of the backmost selected object.

If no object is selected, the Clipboard contents are pasted to the absolute front or back, just as if the Bʀɪɴɢ Tᴏ Fʀᴏɴᴛ or Sᴇɴᴅ Tᴏ Bᴀᴄᴋ commands had been chosen.

The relative layering commands may be used to insert an object into a group, a clipping path, a compound path, or some other combined object. Simply cut the object to the Clipboard (⌘-X), select an object in the combined object using the direct-selection tool, and then choose Pᴀsᴛᴇ Iɴ Fʀᴏɴᴛ or Pᴀsᴛᴇ Iɴ Bᴀᴄᴋ.

Layering in combined objects

Any command that combines selected objects together may also affect the layering of objects in an illustration. These include Gʀᴏᴜᴘ (⌘-G), Mᴀᴋᴇ Cᴏᴍᴘᴏᴜɴᴅ (⌘-⌥-G), Lɪɴᴋ (⌘-⇧-G), and Mᴀᴋᴇ Tᴇxᴛ Wʀᴀᴘ. All objects in a group, compound path, linked object, or wrapped object must be consecutively layered. To accomplish this, Illustrator uses the frontmost selected object as a marker when you choose one of these commands. All other selected objects are moved to consecutive layers in back of the frontmost object.

Choosing Uɴɢʀᴏᴜᴘ (⌘-U), Rᴇʟᴇᴀsᴇ Cᴏᴍᴘᴏᴜɴᴅ (⌘-⌥-U), Uɴʟɪɴᴋ (⌘-⇧-U), or Rᴇʟᴇᴀsᴇ Tᴇxᴛ Wʀᴀᴘ neither restores an object to its original layer nor otherwise affects its layering.

Blending objects

The last feature we discuss in this chapter is a combination transformation/duplication feature called *blending*. To blend two selected paths is to create a series of intermediate path between them. For example, suppose that we have created two paths, one that represents a caterpillar and one that represents a butterfly. By blending these two paths, you may create several additional paths that represent metamorphic stages between the two life forms, as shown in Figure 12.51. The first intermediate path is formed much like the caterpillar. Each intermediate path after that becomes less like the caterpillar and more like the butterfly.

Figure 12.51: Blending a caterpillar and a butterfly creates a
series of transformed duplicates between the two objects.

Using the blend tool

In any blend, two paths must be selected. Of the two, the rear path acts as
the *source path* and the forward path acts as the *concluding path*. Blends
are created using the *blend tool*, the eighth tool in the palette. Operate the
blend tool by clicking on each of two selected points, one in the source
path and one in the concluding path. Any number of points may be selected in each path, and each path may contain any number of points.
Only paths may be blended in Illustrator.

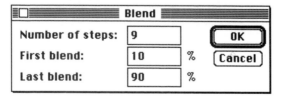

Figure 12.52: The Blend dialog box allows you to
determine the number of intermediate paths to create
between two selected paths.

After clicking on a selected point in each of two paths, the BLEND dialog box will display, as shown in Figure 12.52. This dialog box contains

three options that allow you to control the nature of the intermediate paths, called *steps*, in a blend:

- **Number of steps**. Enter the number of intermediate paths that you want Illustrator to create in this option. Any number between 1 and 1296 is acceptable. The "First blend" and "Last blend" values will update accordingly.

- **First blend**. The value in this option determines the location of each point in the first step as a percentage of the total distance between each selected pair of points in the source and concluding paths. This value also affects how the first step is painted as a percentage of the difference between the fills and strokes of the source and concluding paths.

- **Last blend**. The value in this option determines the location of each point in the last step as a percentage of the total distance between each selected pair of points in the source and concluding paths. This value also affects how the last step is painted as a percentage of the difference between the fills and strokes of the source and concluding paths.

If you can make sense of all of that, you've probably used the tool before. If not, don't keep reading it over and over; you'll just turn your brain to mush. These options are better demonstrated by example: Say that you specify 9 steps between your source and concluding paths. Illustrator determines the positioning of each step as a percentage of the distance between both paths. The source path occupies the 0% position and the concluding path occupies the 100% position. To space the steps evenly, Illustrator automatically assigns the nine steps positions 10% through 90%. Therefore, the "First blend" option updates to display 10%, and the "Last blend" option displays 90%.

You may change the "First blend" and "Last blend" values to alter the percentage placement of the first and last steps. The second through eighth steps are automatically spaced evenly between them. If you change the "First blend" value to 30% and the "Last blend" value to 70%, you squash the steps closer together while leaving some breathing room between the steps and the source and concluding paths.

The "First blend" and "Last blend" values also control the fill and stroke of the intermediate paths. Suppose the source path is filled with white and stroked with a 100% black, 11-point line weight; the concluding path is filled with 100% black and stroked with a 50% black, 1-point line weight. The painting attributes of the steps are averaged incrementally as a function of the number of steps. To determine this average, Illustrator divides the difference in the painting attributes by the number of steps. In this case, the differences between source and concluding path are as follows:

- The difference in fill color = 100% black – 0% black (white) = 100%.

- The difference in stroke color = 100% black – 50% black = 50%.

- The difference in line weight = (11-point) – (1-point) = 10-point.

With 9 steps, a "First blend" value of 10%, and a "Last blend" value of 90%, your blend will appear as shown in Figure 12.53. Each step is painted as follows:

Step	% change	Fill color	Stroke color	Line weight
1	10%	10% black	95% black	10-point
2	20%	20% black	90% black	9-point
3	30%	30% black	85% black	8-point
4	40%	40% black	80% black	7-point
5	50%	50% black	75% black	6-point
6	60%	60% black	70% black	5-point
7	70%	70% black	65% black	4-point
8	80%	80% black	60% black	3-point
9	90%	90% black	55% black	2-point

Figure 12.53: A 9-step blend created between two rectangles.

Press RETURN to exit the BLEND dialog box and create the specified number of steps, beginning and ending at the prescribed locations. Illustrator creates the steps as a grouped object, layered between the source and concluding paths. Within the group, the steps ascend in layering order as they approach the concluding (frontmost) path.

If either the source path or concluding path lacks a fill or stroke, all steps created with the blend tool will also lack a fill or stroke. The blend tool affects dashed strokes only if both the source and concluding paths are dashed; otherwise, all steps are stroked solid.

Selecting points in a blend

Your mastery of the blend tool depends upon your ability to control the appearance of intermediate paths rather than simply relying on Illustrator's automation. The quantity and location of points in the steps, as well as the form of the segments between points, is based on two criteria:

- The number of points you select in the source and concluding paths before clicking with the blend tool.

- The specific point in each path on which you click with the blend tool.

The blend tool relies on selected points as guidelines. It tries to couple each selected point in the source path with a selected point in the concluding path. The blend tool then determines the form and number of segments required between each consecutive pair of selected points. Therefore, you may acquire the most control over your blend by selecting as many points as possible in each path.

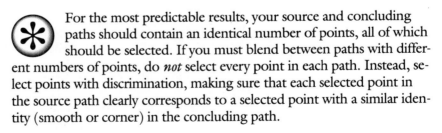

For the most predictable results, your source and concluding paths should contain an identical number of points, all of which should be selected. If you must blend between paths with different numbers of points, do *not* select every point in each path. Instead, select points with discrimination, making sure that each selected point in the source path clearly corresponds to a selected point with a similar identity (smooth or corner) in the concluding path.

The left example in Figure 12.54 shows a source path (top) and a concluding path (bottom) that contain different numbers of points.

However, for every selected point in the source path, there is a similar selected point in the concluding path. If you look closely, you will see that the selected points occupy pivotal positions in their paths.

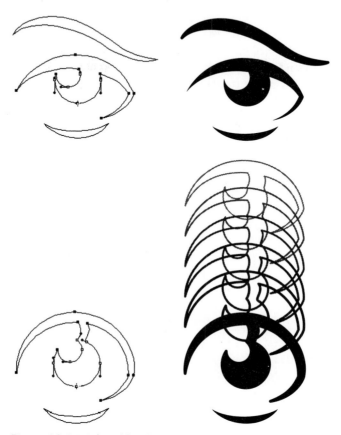

Figure 12.54: When blending two paths with different numbers of points, each selected point in the source path should correspond to a selected point in the concluding path whose identity is similar.

Which points to click?

The points that you click with the blend tool also control the appearance of the steps in a blend. The blend tool uses the click points as origin points for its path creations. It then progresses around the paths in a consistent direction, from one pair of points to the next.

Try to click on a similar selected point in each path. If possible, each point should occupy a central position in its path (unless the paths are open, in which case you *must* click on a selected endpoint in each path).

In the case of Figure 12.54, we click with the blend tool on the smooth points along the bottom of each eyeball, indicated by small cross cursors. After the dialog box appears, we specify 5 steps and change the "First blend" option to 40% to create a large gap between the source path and the first path. The result is shown on the right side of the figure. The fills of the steps in this figure have been made transparent after the fact to make them easier to see. Notice that the distance is greater between the source path and the first step than between the last step and the concluding path, because we changed the "First blend" value. The shade and line weight of the stroke in the first step is also affected by this change.

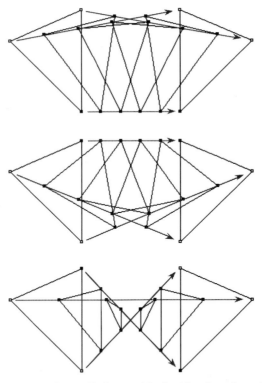

Figure 12.55: Clicking with the blend tool on three different pairs of points (shown as selected in each example) affects the appearance of the steps.

If you click on points that occupy different positions in the source and concluding paths, Illustrator will create distorted steps. Figure 12.55 shows three examples: In each, we create four blends by clicking on different pairs of points—shown as selected—in the two triangles. Each point in one triangle blends toward a point in the other triangle based on its proximity to the click point, as demonstrated by the arrows.

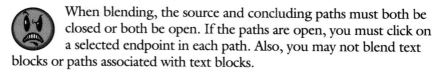 When blending, the source and concluding paths must both be closed or both be open. If the paths are open, you must click on a selected endpoint in each path. Also, you may not blend text blocks or paths associated with text blocks.

Blending multiple paths

Although you may blend only two paths at a time, you may blend as many pairs of paths as you desire within a single illustration.

Figure 12.56: Blending five separate open paths to create a late-show metamorphosis.

The first image and the last image in Figure 12.56 each contain five open paths. The images were specifically designed so that for each path in the man's face, there is a path performing a similar function in the werewolf. The result of carefully selecting pairs of points in each like path and entering identical values every time the BLEND dialog was displayed was a series of 30 blends that overlap to form six metamorphic images. With the exception of a slight stroking alteration (that of changing the stroke of the source path to black), the final blend appears exactly as it was created with the blend tool. It is natural when creating such a difficult series of blends that some paths will suffer from a variety of aesthetic imperfections, as do those in the figure. Such paths will require reshaping.

Creating gradations

Despite the amazing visual metamorphoses that may be produced using this technique, you will probably find the blend tool most helpful in creating *gradations*, a special effect in which colors gradually change inside the fill of an object. For example, if the upper portion of a rectangle is filled with blue and the lower portion is filled with yellow, a *gradient fill* will traverse the chromatic spectrum between these two colors.

 Unlike Aldus FreeHand (or even the loathsome Cricket Draw, for crying out loud), Illustrator provides no automated gradient fill features. You must create the gradation by hand using the blend tool, and mask it with the object you want to fill.

When creating a gradation with the blend tool, you will be more concerned with the color values of the source and concluding paths than with the shapes themselves. The top example of Figure 12.57 shows two paths: the central path is filled with white and the V-shaped path is filled with black. Neither path is stroked, since a repeating stroke would interrupt a continuous gradation. Also, the central path is in front, making it the concluding path.

After selecting the points shown in the example, we click on the rightmost point in each path with the blend tool. By default, the "Number of steps" option in the BLEND dialog box will contain the value 254. PostScript printers may produce a maximum of 256 gray values, including black and white. Subtract 2 for black and white, and you have 254. Thus, 254 steps will produce the most fluid gradation; however, 254 paths will also greatly complicate your illustration. A more reasonable value might be 49 steps. This means that each blend will be 2% lighter than the blend behind it. The second example of Figure 12.57 displays the 49 evenly spaced steps created by the blend tool.

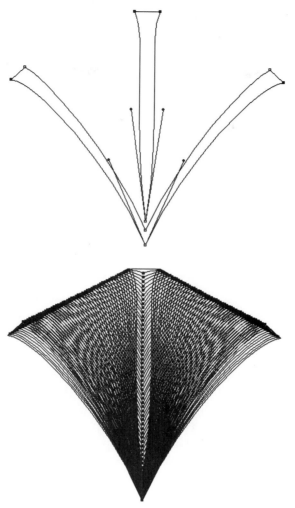

Figure 12.57: After selecting a white path (top, central) and a black path (top, V-shaped), we blend the paths to create a gradation containing 49 steps.

After creating a gradation, you may incorporate it into a clipping path. In Figure 12.58 on the following page, we have grouped the gradation from Figure 12.57 with a masking object to create a glistening charm. To create the outlines around the charm, we add two copies of the mask, each stroked with different line weights and with transparent fills.

Figure 12.58: The result of incorporating the gradation from the previous figure into a clipping path.

If you'll be printing your final illustration to a 300 dot-per-inch laser printer, you won't need more than 24 steps, since a device of this type can produce only 26 gray values. However, if you'll be printing to higher resolution devices, such as Linotronic or Compugraphic imagesetters, such a small number of steps may result in *banding*—an effect in which each step in a gradation appears clearly distinguishable from its neighbor. To determine the optimal number of steps for a specific imagesetter, use the following formula:

$$[(\text{dpi} \div \text{lpi})^2 + 1] \times \%\Delta c - 2$$

in which *dpi* is the resolution of the printer in dots per inch, *lpi* is the screen frequency in lines per inch, and $\%\Delta c$ is the percentage change in color. For example, the percentage change in color between a 40% source path and a 70% concluding path is 30%. If you intend to print this gradation to an Linotronic 100 with a resolution of 1270 dots per inch and a default frequency of 90 lines per inch, the optimal blends will contain $[(1270 \div 90)^2 + 1] \times 0.3 - 2 = 58$ steps.

If math isn't your strong point, just use the default values Illustrator displays in the BLEND dialog box. For small blends, divide the default value by an integer, such as 2, 3, or 4.

Creating
and Editing
Graphs

Graphing applications abound for the Macintosh computer. Microsoft Excel satisfies the needs of most users who are interested primarily in number-crunching but sometimes require basic graphs. If three-dimensional bar graphs turn you on, you might change over to Wingz. If you need a dedicated graphing program, you can use Cricket Graph or DeltaGraph. A range of presentation applications—such as Aldus Persuasion—offer charting features. And if your main concern is ease of use, you might want to switch computers and try out Harvard Graphics for the PC.

So why would you ever use Illustrator 3.0's new graphing tools, especially since they cover only the most basic types of graphs? The answer is freedom of manipulation. Other software is capable of producing a wider variety of charts with more bells and whistles, but few allow you to so much as reposition the legend in an existing chart. In Illustrator, you can reshape, transform, and duplicate any element in a graph to your heart's content. Only a drawing program can allow you to convert graphs into artwork.

Creating a graph

Illustrator provides six *graphing tools* in the last slot of the toolbox. Each tool allows you to create a different kind of chart. All these tools are operated in the following manner:

1. Choose the desired graphing tool from the last slot in the toolbox.
2. Use the tool to define the boundaries of the new chart in the drawing area.
3. Enter the desired data into the resulting GRAPH DATA dialog box.
4. Press ENTER to instruct Illustrator to process the data and generate the chart corresponding to the selected tool.

The main purpose of any graphing tool is to determine the rectangular dimensions of a chart. You draw with a graphing tool just as if you were drawing with the rectangle tool or oval tool. This means you may use any of the following techniques:

- Drag to draw the chart boundary from corner to corner.
- Press OPTION and drag to draw the boundary from center to corner.
- Press SHIFT and drag or SHIFT-OPTION-drag to draw a square boundary.
- Click to display the GRAPH dialog box shown in Figure 13.01. Enter the horizontal and vertical dimensions of the desired chart into the "Width" and "Height" option boxes, and press RETURN. The click point becomes the upper left corner of the chart boundary.

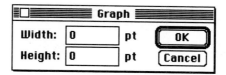

Figure 13.01: Click with any graphing tool to display the Graph dialog box, which allows you to enter the dimensions of the chart boundary.

● Press OPTION and click to display the GRAPH dialog box. Enter the horizontal and vertical dimensions of the desired chart into the "Width" and "Height" option boxes, and press RETURN. The click point becomes the center of the chart boundary.

After defining the width and height of your chart, the GRAPH DATA dialog box will automatically display, as shown in Figure 13.02 on the next page. This dialog box is actually a mini-spreadsheet window, containing its own size box and scroll bars. Unlike other dialog boxes, you may click outside the GRAPH DATA window to bring the illustration window to the front of the desktop. Although it will disappear from view, the GRAPH DATA window remains open behind the illustration window so that you will not lose any changes you have made while inside the dialog box. To bring the GRAPH DATA window to the front of the desktop, choose the GRAPH DATA... command from the GRAPH menu (⌘-⇧-⌥-D).

Using the Graph Data dialog box

The *worksheet matrix* in the LOWER PORTION OF GRAPH DATA dialog box is similar to the worksheet provided in a standard spreadsheet program such as Microsoft Excel or MacCalc. The worksheet contains rows and columns of individual containers, called *cells*. Numbers entered into the cells may represent dollar amounts, times and dates, or percentages. You may even enter words for labels and legends. Unlike a true spreadsheet, however, you may not enter formulas, since Illustrator provides no calculation capability.

Data entered from the keyboard will appear in the *value entry line* at the top of the worksheet (below the buttons). Press RETURN or TAB to transfer the data from the value entry line into the current cell and advance to another cell.

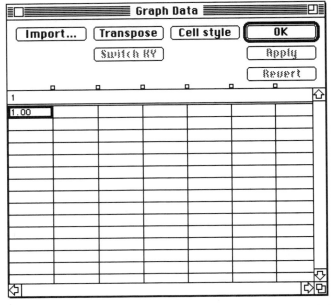

Figure 13.02: The Graph Data dialog box contains a worksheet matrix made up of rows and columns of cells. Enter the data you want to graph, as well as label text, into these cells.

When typing, most keys insert the standard characters that appears on the key. Some characters, however, perform special functions:

- **Quotation mark** ("). Enter quotes around numeric data to use a number as a label, such as a product number or year. If a cell consists of only numbers without quote marks, Illustrator will interpret the data as a value and graph it or merely not display it at all.

 To display quotes around a numeric label, use the opening and closing quotation marks, " and " (⌥-[and ⇧-⌥-[), rather than the straight quote " (⇧-').

- **Vertical line character** (|). If you want a label to contain multiple lines of text, enter the vertical line (⇧-\) to represent a carriage return character.

- **Tab** or **right arrow** (→). Accepts the data in the value entry line and moves one cell to the right (to the next cell in the current row).

- **Left arrow** (←). Accepts the data in the value entry line and moves one cell to the left (to the previous cell in the current row).

- **Return** or **down arrow** (↓). Accepts the data in the value entry line and moves one cell down (to the next cell in the current column).

- **Up arrow** (↑). Accepts the data in the value entry line and moves one cell up (to the previous cell in the current column).

- ⌘-Z (Undo Cell Type-In command). Restores the original data in the value entry line.

- **Enter**. Accepts the data in the value entry line and selects the OK button, exiting the Graph Data dialog box.

For most kinds of charts, both the first row and the first column of cells may be reserved for labels. To use cells as labels, delete the data from the very first cell (at the intersection of the first row and the first column) and leave it empty. Every other cell in the first row and the first column should contain at least one non-numeric character or quote marks around the numbers to instruct Illustrator to display the data as is.

Because different kinds of charts require different kinds of information, the specific manner in which you organize data varies from one kind of chart to the next. The following sections describe the functions of the basic chart types and explain how data should be entered for each.

Bar chart data

If you used the *bar-graph tool* to create the chart boundary in the drawing area, Illustrator expects you to organize your data in *standard bar chart* form. Bar charts are most commonly used to demonstrate a change in data over a period of time. The horizontal axis (*X axis*) may be divided into time units, measured in days, months, or years. The vertical axis (*Y axis*) tracks values, which may be measured in units sold, dollars or other currency, or any number of other possibilities. As shown in Figure 13.03 on the following page, bars (sometimes called *columns*) rise up from the X axis to a height equivalent to the value on the Y axis. The taller the bar, the greater the value it represents. If more than one *series* of data is included in the chart, like bars from each series are *clustered* together. Hence, this type of chart is known in some circles as a *cluster bar chart*, or a *grouped column chart*. In Illustrator, bars from different series are filled with different gray values. The colors representing the series are itemized in a *legend*.

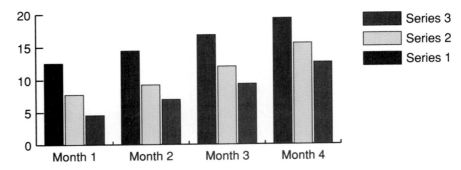

Figure 13.03: An example of a standard bar chart, also known as a cluster bar chart or a grouped column chart. Series of bars are clustered together. Each series is identified in the legend (right).

When the GRAPH DATA dialog box displays for a standard bar chart, arrange your data as demonstrated in Figure 13.04:

- Delete the contents of the first cell, and leave it empty.

- Enter series labels in the first row of cells. The label text will appear in the legend.

- Enter X-axis labels in the first column.

- Organize series of data into columns under the series labels. If you enter a dollar sign ($), the symbol will be ignored. If you enter other currency symbols (such as £ or ¥), Illustrator will not graph the value.

- Y-axis labels correspond automatically to the data.

	Series 1	Series 2	Series 3	
Month 1	12.57	77.60	45.70	
Month 2	14.44	92.50	69.90	
Month 3	16.84	12.04	93.60	
Month 4	19.34	15.55	12.63	

Figure 13.04: Organize bar chart data into columns under series labels. This data corresponds to the bar chart shown in Figure 13.03.

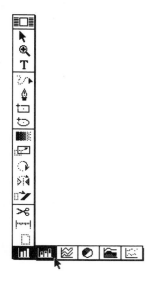

Stacked bar chart data

If you used the *stacked-bar-graph tool* to create the chart boundary in the drawing area, Illustrator expects you to organize your data in *stacked bar* chart form. Stacked charts are much like standard bar charts, except that like bars from different series are stacked on top of each other, rather than clustered side by side. A stacked bar chart is most useful for showing the sums of all series. You may create a *percentage chart* by organizing your data so that all values for each series add up to 100, as shown in Figure 13.05. Percentage charts are useful for demonstrating the relative performance of various series over time.

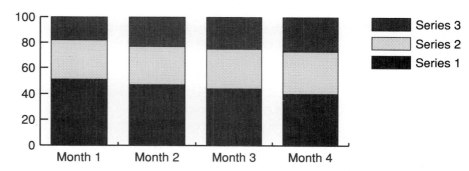

Figure 13.05: An example of a specific variety of stacked bar chart, called a percentage chart. Series of bars are stacked on top of each other. As in the standard bar chart, each series is identified in the legend (right).

When the GRAPH DATA dialog box displays for a stacked bar chart, arrange your data as demonstrated in Figure 13.06:

- Delete the contents of the first cell, and leave it empty.

- Enter series labels in the first row of cells. The label text will appear in the legend.

- Enter X-axis labels in the first column.

- Organize series of data into columns under the series labels. If you enter a percentage symbol (%) with a value, the symbol will be ignored.

- Y-axis labels correspond automatically to the data.

	Series 1	Series 2	Series 3	
Month 1	51.00	31.00	18.00	
Month 2	47.00	30.00	23.00	
Month 3	44.00	31.00	25.00	
Month 4	40.00	33.00	27.00	

Figure 13.06: Organize stacked bar chart data into columns under series labels. This data corresponds to the percentage chart shown in Figure 13.05. Notice that the values in each row add up to 100.

Line graph data

If you used the *line-graph tool* to create the chart boundary in the drawing area, Illustrator expects you to organize your data in *line chart* form. Like bar charts, line charts are generally used to show changes in items over a period of time. Straight segments connect points representing values, as shown in Figure 13.07. Several straight segments combine to form a line, which represents a complete series. The inclination of a segment clearly demonstrates the performance of a series from one moment in time to the next. Because large changes result in steep inclinations, line charts are best used to graph data that includes dramatic fluctuations.

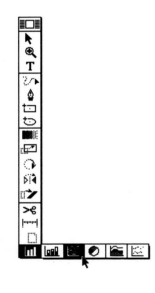

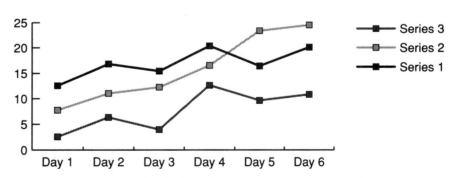

Figure 13.07: An example of a line chart. Lines are composed of straight segments that connect value points and represent complete series. Each series is identified in the legend (right).

When the GRAPH DATA dialog box displays for a line chart, arrange your data as demonstrated in Figure 13.08:

- Delete the contents of the first cell, and leave it empty.

- Enter series labels in the first row of cells. The label text will appear in the legend.

- Enter X-axis labels in the first column.

- Organize series of data into columns under the series labels.

- Y-axis labels correspond automatically to the data.

	Series 1	Series 2	Series 3	
Day 1	12.57	7.76	2.57	
Day 2	16.84	11.04	6.36	
Day 3	15.44	12.25	3.99	
Day 4	20.34	16.55	12.63	
Day 5	16.42	23.35	9.65	
Day 6	20.08	24.49	10.82	

Figure 13.08: Organize line chart data into columns under series labels. This data corresponds to the line chart shown in Figure 13.07.

Although line chart data may fluctuate dramatically, you don't want series to cross each other more than one or twice in the entire chart. If series cross too often, the result is a *spaghetti chart*, which is difficult to read and typically ineffective.

Pie chart data

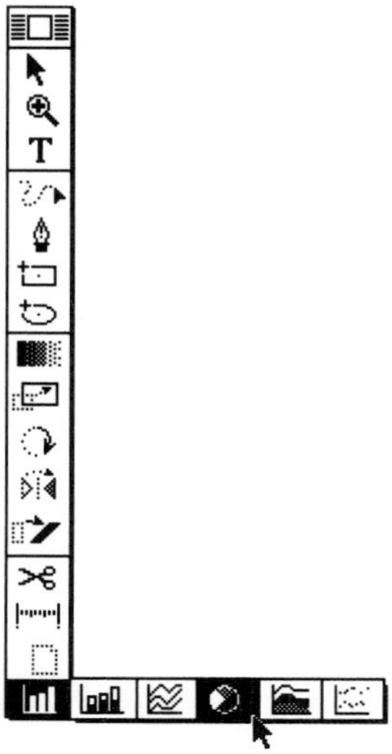

If you used the *pie-graph tool* to create the chart boundary in the drawing area, Illustrator expects you to organize your data in *pie chart* form. A pie chart is the easiest kind of chart to create. However, pie charts are not nearly as versatile as other charts we have discussed so far. Only one series may be expressed per pie. If you want to show more than one series for comparative purposes, each series must be given a pie of its own, as shown in Figure 13.09 on the next page. The advantage of a pie chart is that it always displays values in a series in relation to the whole. A series inhabits a 360° circle and each value within the series occupies a percentage of that circle.

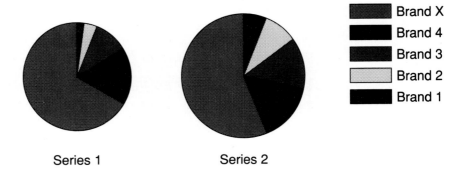

	Brand X
	Brand 4
	Brand 3
	Brand 2
	Brand 1

Series 1   Series 2

Figure 13.09: An example of two pie charts, each representing a single series. Values are labeled in the pie or in a legend (right). Series 1 is smaller than Series 2 because the latter includes larger values.

When the GRAPH DATA dialog box displays for a pie chart, arrange your data as demonstrated in Figure 13.10:

- Delete the contents of the first cell, and leave it empty.

- Enter value labels in the first row of cells. The label text will appear in the legend.

- Enter series labels in the first column. If more than two series of data are required, use a different kind of graph.

- Organize series of data into rows to the right of the series labels. The labels will appear as titles below the pie, as demonstrated in Figure 13.09.

	Brand 1	Brand 2	Brand 3	Brand 4	Brand X	
Series 1	0.98	1.56	4.07	6.76	26.57	
Series 2	3.24	4.67	6.99	8.25	29.34	

Figure 13.10: Organize pie chart data into rows to the right of series labels. This data corresponds to the pie chart shown in Figure 13.09.

Area graph data

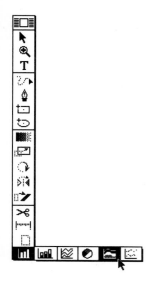

If you used the *area-graph tool* to create the chart boundary in the drawing area, Illustrator expects you to organize your data in *area chart* form. In its simplest form, an area chart is little more than a filled-in line chart. However, the series of an area chart are stacked one upon another as in a stacked bar chart to display the sum of all series, as shown in Figure 13.11.

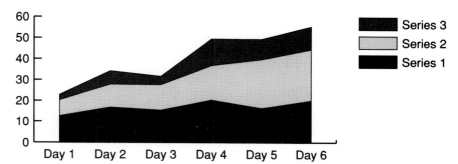

Figure 13.11: An example of an area chart. The area between one line and the next is filled in. Different fills represent different series. Each series is identified in the legend (right).

If you encounter a spaghetti effect when creating a line chart—that is, segments frequently overlap each other—you may quickly and easily remedy the problem by converting the line chart into an area chart.

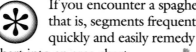

When the GRAPH DATA dialog box displays for an area chart, arrange your data as demonstrated in Figure 13.12:

- Delete the contents of the first cell, and leave it empty.
- Enter series labels in the first row of cells. The label text will appear in the legend.
- Enter X-axis labels in the first column.
- Organize series of data into columns under the series labels.
- Y-axis labels correspond automatically to the data.

	Series 1	Series 2	Series 3	
Day 1	12.57	7.76	2.57	
Day 2	16.84	11.04	6.36	
Day 3	15.44	12.25	3.99	
Day 4	20.34	16.55	12.63	
Day 5	16.42	23.35	9.65	
Day 6	20.08	24.49	10.82	

Figure 13.12: Organize area chart data into columns under series labels. This data corresponds to the area chart shown in Figure 13.11. (This is the same data that was used to create the line chart shown in Figure 13.07.)

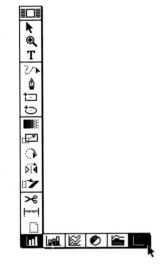

Scatter graph data

If you used the *scatter-graph tool* to create the chart boundary in the drawing area, Illustrator expects you to organize your data in *scatter chart* form. Like a line chart, a scatter chart plots points and connects these points with straight segments. However, rather than merely aligning series of values along a set of X axis labels, the scatter graph pairs up columns of values. The first column of data represents Y-axis (series) coordinates; the second column represents X-axis coordinates. Scatter charts are most accurately used to map scientific data or to graph multiple series that use slightly different time increments.

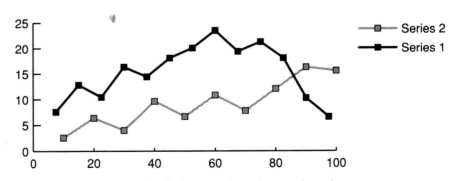

Figure 13.13: An example of a scatter chart. Points plotted at specified X,Y-coordinates are connected with straight segments. Each series is identified in the legend (right).

When the GRAPH DATA dialog box displays for a scatter chart, arrange your data as demonstrated in Figure 13.14:

- Enter series labels in the first row of cells, at the top of odd columns (first, third, fifth, etc.). In the first row, leave even-numbered cells empty. The label text will appear in the legend.

- Enter Y-axis (series) data in odd columns.

- Enter X-axis data in even-numbered columns. Side-by-side columns of data will be plotted as paired points. In other words, each row of values in the first and second columns will be plotted as a point in the first series, each row in the third and fourth columns will be plotted as a point in the second series, and so on.

- Y-axis and X-axis labels correspond automatically to the data.

Series 1		Series 2		
7.57	7.50	2.57	10.00	
12.84	15.00	6.36	20.00	
10.44	22.50	3.99	30.00	
16.34	30.00	9.63	40.00	
14.42	37.50	6.65	50.00	
18.08	45.00	10.82	60.00	
20.06	52.50	7.76	70.00	
23.49	60.00	12.04	80.00	
19.35	67.50	16.25	90.00	
21.26	75.00	15.55	100.00	
18.05	82.50			
10.24	90.00			
6.56	97.50			

Figure 13.14: Organize scatter chart data by series in pairs of columns under series labels. This data corresponds to the scatter chart shown in Figure 13.13.

Importing data

Because Illustrator provides no calculation capability, and its cell-editing functions are limited (cells cannot be inserted, deleted, exchanged, sorted, and so on), you may prefer to import values into the GRAPH DATA worksheet, rather than enter them from the keyboard. You may create your data in any spreadsheet program capable of saving as a *tab-delineated*, text-only file. Such programs include Microsoft Excel, Wingz, and Mac-Calc, just to name a few. In a tab-delineated file, individual cells are separated by tab characters; rows of cells are separated by carriage returns.

Because Illustrator accepts any tab-delineated, text-only file, you may also create your data in a word processor such as Microsoft Word or WriteNow. When entering the data, insert tabs between values and insert carriage returns between rows of values. Then save the finished file as a text-only, or *ASCII*, document.

To import a data file, display the GRAPH DATA dialog box (⌘-⇧-⌦-D) and click on the cell that you want to act as the upper left cell in the imported data. Click the IMPORT... button, or choose the IMPORT GRAPH DATA... command from the FILE menu, to display the PLEASE OPEN TEXT FILE dialog box, as shown in Figure 13.15. (The IMPORT GRAPH DATA... command appears in place of the PLACE ART... command in the FILE menu only when the GRAPH DATA dialog box is displayed.)

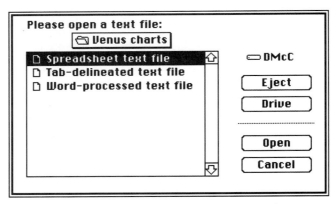

Figure 13.15: The Please open text file dialog box allows you to select a tab-delineated text file to import into the Graph Data worksheet.

To import a data file, double-click its name in the scrolling file list, or select the file and click the OPEN button or press RETURN. The DRIVE and EJECT buttons, the folder bar, and keyboard equivalents operate as described in the section *Creating a new illustration* in Chapter 3.

The imported data will appear in the worksheet in rows and columns starting in the selected cell. If any of these cells already contain data, their contents will be replaced.

Adjusting data

Unlike more sophisticated spreadsheets, the GRAPH DATA dialog box does not allow you to insert cells, delete cells, or in any way move cells inside the worksheet. However, you may move data within cells using one of the following techniques:

- Cut data from one location and paste it into another. You may also copy data and clear multiple cells, using keyboard equivalents or choosing commands from the EDIT menu.

- Click the TRANSPOSE button to swap rows and columns of data.

- Click the SWITCH XY button to swap columns of data in a scatter chart. This button is dimmed when creating or editing any kind of chart except a scatter chart.

You may select multiple cells in the worksheet by dragging across them, or by pressing the SHIFT key while pressing one of the arrow keys ($\uparrow$, $\rightarrow$, $\downarrow$, or $\leftarrow$). All selected cells except the current cell will become highlighted, as shown in Figure 13.16.

	Series 1	Series 2	Series 3	
Month 1	12.57	7.76	4.57	
Month 2	14.44	9.25	6.99	
Month 3	16.84	12.04	9.36	
Month 4	19.34	15.55	12.63	

Figure 13.16: When selecting multiple cells, all cells except the current cell become highlighted.

You may remove the contents of selected cells and transfer the data to the Clipboard by choosing the CUT command (⌘-X). Choose the COPY command (⌘-C) to copy the contents of highlighted cells.

To paste the contents of the Clipboard into the worksheet, click on the cell that you want to act as the upper left cell in the pasted data and choose the Paste command (⌘-V). The Paste command will be dimmed if the Clipboard does not contain data. Cells are pasted into the same number of cells from which they were cut or copied. Cells are always pasted in the rows and columns including and following the current cell, even if multiple cells are highlighted and the selected cell is in the lower right corner of the selection. If any affected cells already contain data, their contents will be replaced.

✳ Illustrator allows you to paste any type into the Graph Data worksheet. Therefore, you may copy words or paragraphs from a block of text in the drawing area and paste them into a graph. You may also copy data from the worksheet window and paste it into a text block.

You may delete the contents of multiple selected cells by choosing the Clear command from the Edit menu or by pressing the escape key or the clear key. (Pressing delete or backspace deletes only the contents of the current cell.)

Transposing data

The Graph Data dialog box also allows you to *transpose* data; that is, swap the way in which the data is plotted on the X and Y axes. Click the Transpose button to swap rows and columns in a matrix. The data in the first row will appear in the first column, the data in the first column will appear in the first row, and so on. For example, if we click the Transpose button for the data shown back in Figure 13.04, the data will be transposed as shown in Figure 13.17. The series data will be mapped along the X axis, and the time labels will appear in the legend, as shown in Figure 13.18.

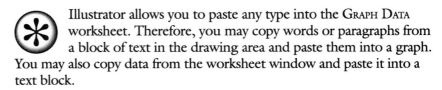

	Month 1	Month 2	Month 3	Month 4	
Series 1	12.57	14.44	16.84	19.34	
Series 2	7.76	9.25	12.04	15.55	
Series 3	4.57	6.99	9.36	12.63	

Figure 13.17: The data from Figure 13.04 as it appears after clicking the Transpose button.

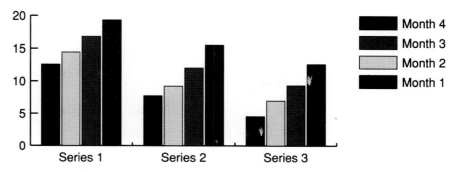

Figure 13.18: The bar chart from Figure 13.03 as it appears after transposing rows and columns of data.

Because data is organized differently in a scatter chart, a special SWITCH XY button is provided. Click this button to swap even and odd columns of data in the worksheet. The data in the first column is moved to the second, the data in the second column is moved to the first, the data in the third column is moved to the fourth, and so on. For example, if we click the SWITCH XY button for the data shown back in Figure 13.14, the data will be transposed as shown in Figure 13.19. Y-axis coordinates are transposed to the X axis and X-axis coordinates are transposed to the Y axis, as shown in Figure 13.20, on the following page.

	Series 1		Series 2	
7.50	7.57	10.00	2.57	
15.00	12.84	20.00	6.36	
22.50	10.44	30.00	3.99	
30.00	16.34	40.00	9.63	
37.50	14.42	50.00	6.65	
45.00	18.08	60.00	10.82	
52.50	20.06	70.00	7.76	
60.00	23.49	80.00	12.04	
67.50	19.35	90.00	16.25	
75.00	21.26	100.00	15.55	
82.50	18.05			
90.00	10.24			
97.50	6.56			

Figure 13.19: The data from Figure 13.14 as it appears after clicking the Switch XY button.

Notice in Figure 13.20 that the "Series 2" and "Series 1" labels no longer appear in the legend, due to the fact that the locations of these labels were altered in the GRAPH DATA dialog box.

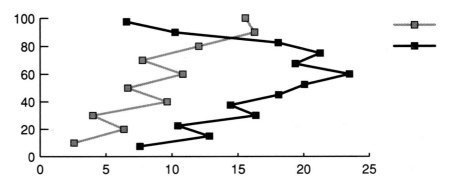

Figure 13.20: The bar chart from Figure 13.13 as it appears after transposing odd and even columns of data.

The changes effected by both the TRANSPOSE and SWITCH XY buttons apply to all data in the worksheet, regardless of the cells selected when the buttons are clicked.

Adjusting cell style

The final cell adjustment that you can make in the GRAPH DATA dialog box is cosmetic. The CELL STYLE button allows you to adjust both the width of the columns in the worksheet and to the number of digits that may follow a decimal point. These controls affect only the appearance of data in the worksheet; they do not affect the appearance of the current chart.

Click the CELL STYLE button to display the CELL STYLE dialog box shown in Figure 13.21. Enter any value between 0 and 10 into the "Number of decimals" option box. This option determines the number of *significant digits*, that is, the number of characters that may appear after a decimal point in a cell. Enter any value between 3 and 20 into the "Column width" option box. This option controls the default width of each cell in the GRAPH DATA dialog box, measured in digits (characters).

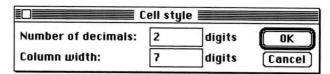

Figure 13.21: The Cell style dialog box allows you to control the number of digits that may follow a decimal point and the default width of a cell.

To adjust the width of a single column of cells, drag the corresponding *column handle* above the value entry line, as shown in Figure 13.22. The column will be widened or narrowed by nearest number of whole digits.

	Month 1	Month 2	Month 3	Month 4	
Series 1	12.57	14.44	16.84	19.34	
Series 2	7.76	9.25	12.04	15.55	
Series 3	4.57	6.99	9.36	12.63	

	Month 1	Month 2	Month 3	Month 4	
Series 1	12.57	14.44	16.84	19.34	
Series 2	7.76	9.25	12.04	15.55	
Series 3	4.57	6.99	9.36	12.63	

Figure 13.22: Drag the column handle above the value entry line (top) to change the width of a column of cells (bottom).

Implementing your data

Click the APPLY button to display the results of your data in the drawing area without leaving the GRAPH DATA dialog box. If you cannot see the drawing area because the dialog box is in the way, drag its title bar to move the box partially off screen. This allows you to make changes if the current data is not satisfactory.

Click REVERT to restore the settings from when you entered the GRAPH DATA dialog box, or since the last time your clicked the APPLY button.

Click OK to exit the dialog box and implement your changes. If you want to exit the GRAPH DATA dialog box without implementing your changes, click the close box, then click the DON'T SAVE button in the resulting alert box, shown in Figure 13.23.

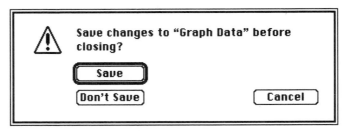

Figure 13.23: This alert box will appear if you click the close box in the title bar of the Graph Data dialog box after making changes to the data.

You may undo the creation or alteration of a chart after clicking the OK or APPLY button by choosing the UNDO GRAPH DATA OK command from the EDIT menu (⌘-Z).

Editing a graph

There are four basic ways to edit a graph created in Adobe Illustrator: 1) edit the data, 2) convert the graph into a different kind of graph, 3) reposition axes, legends, and other elements using options, and 4) customize elements using tools discussed in previous chapters. Each of these methods is discussed in the following section.

Editing data

To edit the data in an existing graph, select the entire graph with the arrow tool and choose the GRAPH DATA... command from the GRAPH menu (⌘-⇧-⌥-D). The GRAPH DATA window will display, containing all data pertinent to the current chart. Edit the data as desired, and press the ENTER key to implement your changes.

Converting a graph

To convert a selected chart, choose the GRAPH STYLE... command from the GRAPH menu (⌘-⇧-⌥-S). The GRAPH STYLE dialog box shown in Figure 13.24 will display. This dialog box provides access to hundreds of options that allow you to edit various facets of a graph.

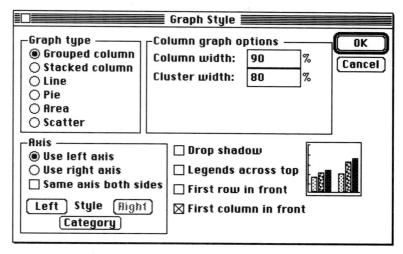

Figure 13.24: The Graph Style dialog box allows you to convert a graph to a different kind of graph as well as edit various facets of a selected chart.

The options in "Graph type" box control the identity of the current chart. The options to the right of this box change depending on which radio button is selected in the "Graph type" box. These radio buttons include the following:

- **Grouped column**. Select this option to change the selected graph to a standard bar chart. Two options will appear in the "Column graph options" box on the right. The "Column width" option box controls the width of each bar in the chart, measured as a percentage of its *flush width*. A value of 100% causes bars to be flush with each other; the default value of 90% allows slight gutters between bars; values greater than 100% cause bars to overlap. The "Cluster width" option controls the width of each cluster of bars between different series, again measured as a percentage of the flush width of the clusters. The default value of 80% allows a gutter between clusters.

- **Stacked column**. Select this option to change the selected graph to a stacked bar chart. The "Column graph options" box to the right includes the same options described in the previous item.

- **Line**. Select this option to change the selected graph to a line chart. Four options will appear in the "Line graph options" box on right, as shown in Figure 13.25. When selected, the "Mark data points" check box creates square markers at the data points in each line. The "Connect data points" creates straight segments between points in a line graph. If this option is deselected, stray points will appear without lines. When "Connect data points" is selected, the "Fill lines" check box becomes available, allowing you to create lines thicker than the default line weight. Enter the desired line weight in the "Fill line width" option box. Select "Edge-to-edge lines" to draw lines that extend the entire width of the chart, extending to both edges of the horizontal axis.

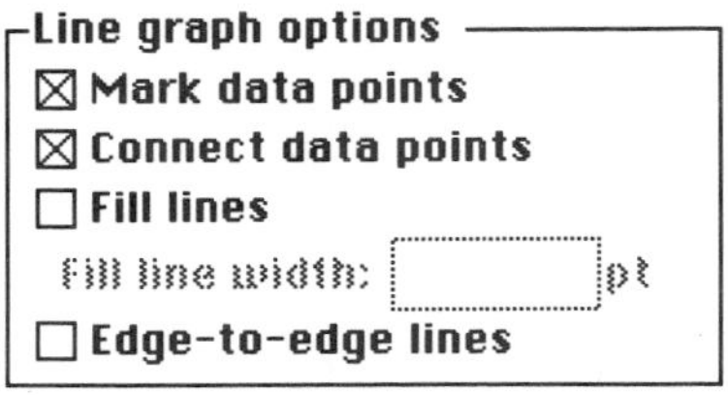

Line graph options
☒ Mark data points
☒ Connect data points
☐ Fill lines
   Fill line width: [   ]pt
☐ Edge-to-edge lines

Figure 13.25: The "Line graph options" box in the Graph Style dialog box allows you to change aspects of a selected line chart.

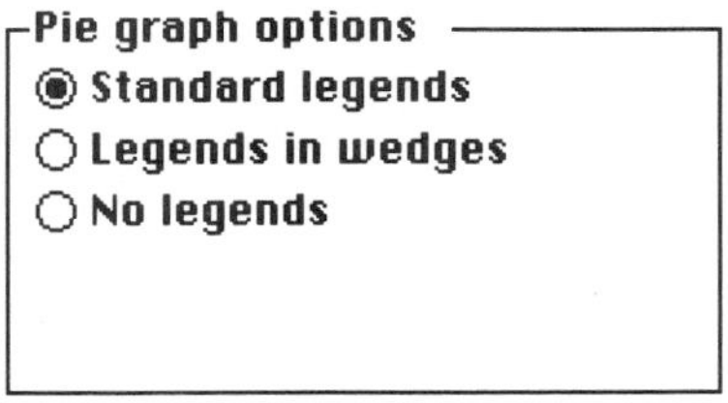

Pie graph options
◉ Standard legends
○ Legends in wedges
○ No legends

Figure 13.26: The "Pie graph options" box in the Graph Style dialog box allows you to change aspects of a selected pie chart.

- **Pie**. Select this option to change the selected graph to a pie chart. Three options will appear in the "Pie graph options" box on right, as shown in Figure 13.26. By default, the "Standard legends" radio button is selected—to the side of the chart, a legend identifies the values in the graph. If you instead select "Legends in wedges," the wedges themselves are labeled. Select "No legends" to include no labels for the values in the pie chart.

- **Area**. Select this option to change the selected graph to an area chart. No additional option appears to the right of the "Graph type" box.

- **Scatter**. Select this option to change the selected graph to a scatter chart. Four options will appear in the "Scatter graph options" box on right. These are the same options that appear in the "Line graph options" box as shown in Figure 13.25, except that the "Edge-to-edge lines" option is dimmed.

Changing the identity of the selected chart may require that you reorganize the data in the GRAPH DATA dialog box.

Adjusting miscellaneous attributes

In the lower right corner of the GRAPH STYLE dialog box are four check boxes. These options include the following:

- **Drop shadow**. Select this option to create drop shadows behind the bars, lines, pie slices, or areas in a chart, as demonstrated in Figure 13.27.

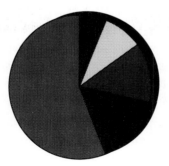

Series 1

Figure 13.27: Select the "Drop shadow" option to create a drop shadow behind the series elements in a chart.

- **Legends across top**. Select this option to move the legend from the right side of the chart to the top of the chart, as shown in Figure 13.28. Labels will be listed horizontally instead of vertically.

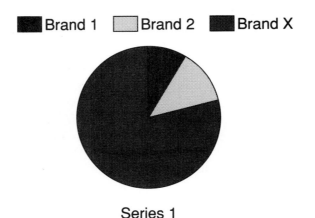

Series 1

Figure 13.28: Select the "Legend across top" option to move the legend to the top of the chart in horizontal formation.

- **First row in front**. Select this option to layer elements representing rows of data in the selected chart in descending order, with the first row in front and the last row in back. If this is a little difficult to visualize, consider the example of a bar chart with overlapping bars and clusters. (Both the "Column width" and "Cluster width" values are set to 110%.) The rows of data in a bar chart represent clusters of values. In Figure 13.29, the "First row in front" option is deselected, so the clusters are layered in ascending order with the first cluster in back and the last cluster in front. In Figure 13.30, the option has been selected, so the clusters are layered in descending order with the first cluster in front and the last cluster in back.

- **First column in front**. Select this option to layer elements representing columns of data (series) in the selected chart in descending order, with the first series in front and the last series in back. In Figure 13.29, the "First column in front" option has been selected, so the bars are layered in descending order with the first bar in each cluster in front and the last bar in each cluster in back. In Figure 13.30, the option is deselected, so the bars are layered in ascending order with the first bar in back and the last bar in front.

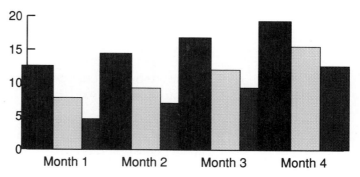

Figure 13.29: Overlapping bars and clusters with the first row (cluster) in back and the first column (series bar) in front.

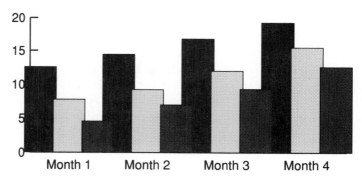

Figure 13.30: Overlapping bars and clusters with the first row (cluster) in front and the first column (series bar) in back.

The "First row in front" and "First column in front" options are most usefully applied to bar charts in which bars or clusters overlap. The "First column in front" option may also be applied to line and scatter charts, to determine the layering order of series lines. Though never dimmed, the options are not applicable to area charts or pie charts.

Adjusting legends and axes

The "Axis" box in the lower left corner of the GRAPH STYLE dialog box allows you to control the appearance and positions of the vertical and horizontal axes in a selected chart. The first three options control the placements of the Y axis (vertical axis):

- **Use left axis**. Select this radio button to make the Y axis appear on the left-hand side of the chart, as it does by default. This axis will use the attribute settings determined by clicking the LEFT button at the bottom of the "Axis" box. (The RIGHT button will appear dimmed.)

- **Use right axis**. Select this radio button to make the Y axis appear on the right-hand side of the chart. This axis will use the attribute settings determined by clicking the RIGHT button at the bottom of the "Axis" box. (The LEFT button will appear dimmed.)

- **Same axis both sides**. Select this check box to make the Y axis appear on both sides of the chart. This axis will use the attribute settings determined by clicking the LEFT or RIGHT button at the bottom of the "Axis" box, whichever is currently available. If you have specified different attributes for the left and right axes, select the "Use left axis" or "Use right axis" radio button to determine which set of attributes will be used.

Three "Style" buttons appear at the bottom of the "Axis" box; only two of the buttons are available at any time. The LEFT or RIGHT button controls the attributes of the Y axis, the CATEGORY button (called the BOTTOM button when the current selection is a scatter chart) controls the appearance of the X axis (horizontal axis).

Clicking any of these buttons displays the GRAPH AXIS STYLE dialog box shown in Figure 13.31. Here you may specify the location of tick marks and labels on the current axis. The options in the "Axis label and tick line values" box control the way in which an axis is labeled; those in the "Axis tick lines and marks" box control the size of tick marks.

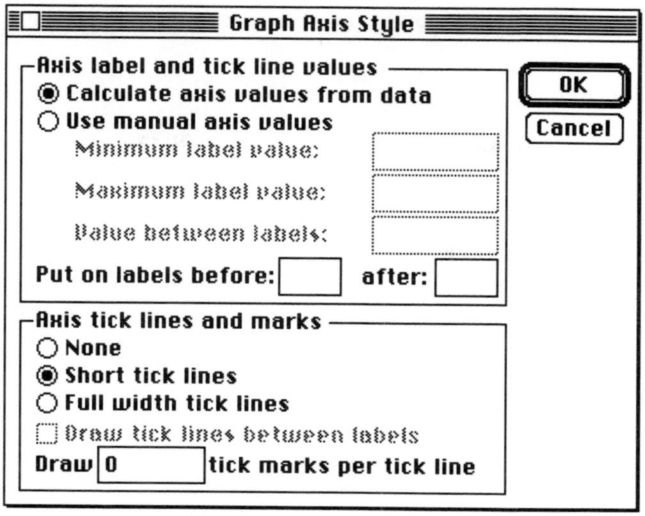

Figure 13.31: The Graph Axis Style dialog box allows you to control various attributes affecting the appearance of the X axis or Y axis.

The "Axis label and trick line values" options are available when setting attributes for the Y axis of any chart or the X axis for a scatter chart only. Therefore, they are dimmed if you have accessed the GRAPH AXIS STYLE dialog box by clicking the CATEGORY button. These options include the following:

- **Calculate axis values from data**. By default, this radio button is selected. Illustrator automatically determines the number of tick marks and labels that appear on the axis.

- **Use manual axis values**. If you want to specify a range of labels in an axis to enhance the appearance of a chart, select this radio button and enter values in the three option boxes that follow. The "Minimum label value" determines the lowest number on the axis; the "Maximum label value" determines the highest number. The "Value between labels" determines the increment between labels.

To turn a chart upside down, so that the highest number is at bottom of the axis and the lowest number is at the top (as shown in Figure 13.32), enter a negative value for the "Value between labels" option. To create an axis without labels, enter 0 in this option box.

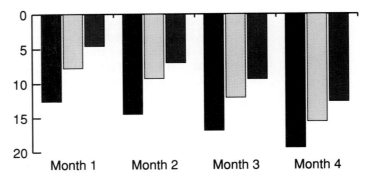

Figure 13.32: Flip a chart by entering a negative value in the "Value between labels" option when editing the attributes of the Y axis.

- **Put on labels before/after.** These option boxes allow you to enter symbols or words up to nine characters long to precede or follow each label in a chart. For example, enter *$* into the "before" option box to precede every label with a dollar sign, as shown in Figure 13.33. Enter *g* in the "after" option box to indicate that each value is to be interpreted in thousands of dollars.

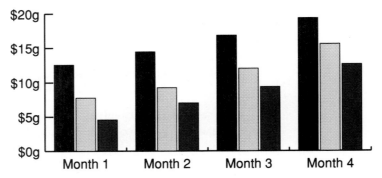

Figure 13.33: Enter characters to precede and follow the labels, such as the $ and g in the Y axis, using the "Put on labels before/after" option.

Most of the "Axis tick lines and marks" options are available when setting attributes for the X or Y axis. These options include the following:

- **None**. Select this radio button to display no tick mark on the current axis. This option does not affect the placement or appearance of labels.

- **Short tick lines**. Select this radio button to display short tick marks that extend from the axis toward the chart, as by default.

- **Full-width tick lines**. Select this radio button to create tick lines that extend the full width or height of the chart, as shown in Figure 13.34.

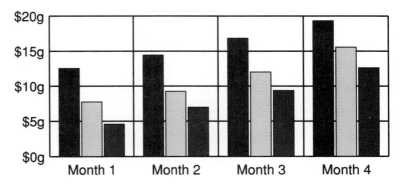

Figure 13.34: Select the "Full width tick lines" option to extend the tick marks across the entire chart. Here, the option has been selected for both the X and Y axes.

- **Draw tick lines between labels**. This check box is available only if you displayed the GRAPH AXIS STYLE dialog box by clicking the CATEGORY button. When selected, as by default, tick marks appear centered between labels, as demonstrated by the vertical lines in Figure 13.34. When deselected, each tick mark is centered above a single label, as shown in Figure 13.35.

- **Draw __ tick marks per tick line**. This option should read *Tick marks per label*, because it allows you to control the number of tick marks per labeled increment. In Figure 13.36, we have entered 5 for this option, creating a total of four tick marks per every label along the Y axis. (The value for this option includes the tick mark for the next label, hence a value of 5 creates four tick marks per label.)

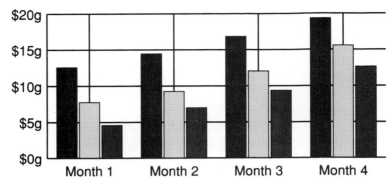

Figure 13.35: For the X axis of a bar, line, or area chart, deselect the "Draw tick lines between labels" option to create tick marks at the label rather than between labels.

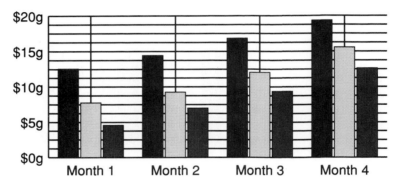

Figure 13.36: The same chart after entering 5 for the "Draw __ tick marks per tick line" option.

All options in the "Axis" box of the Graph Style dialog box are dimmed when the "Pie" option is selected in the "Graph type" box. If "Scatter" is selected, the "Use left axis" and "Use right axis" radio buttons are dimmed.

Customizing a graph

Illustrator provides several options for editing the appearance of a selected chart. However, if you want to truly customize a chart, you'll have to apply the reshaping and transformation principles covered in

Chapters 7 and 12. After all, the elements in a chart are no more than standard graphic objects that may be manipulated like any other object in Adobe Illustrator.

The elements in a chart are organized into a small network of grouped objects. If you ever want to be able to edit the data associated with a chart or adjust attribute options, do *not* ungroup any of these groups. Instead, use the direct-selection tool to select and manipulate specific elements.

Charts are composed of groups within groups within groups. The following list demonstrates how each of the groups may be selected using the direct-selection tool:

- Click to select a specific point or segment in a series object.

- Press OPTION and click to select a whole object in the chart, such as an axis or column.

- Press OPTION and click a second time to select an entire axis, including tick marks and labels, or an entire series.

- Press OPTION and click a third time to select an entire series as well as its representation in the legend.

- Press OPTION and click a fourth time to select all series and legend representation in the chart.

- Press OPTION and click a fifth time to select the entire chart.

After selecting the appropriate elements, you may manipulate them as desired. The only manipulation that you have to be careful with is layering. Only layer entire series, entire axes, and so on. Do *not* alter the layering of a single element, such as a bar, an axis label, or a tick mark.

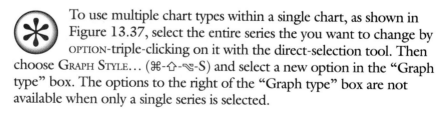 To use multiple chart types within a single chart, as shown in Figure 13.37, select the entire series the you want to change by OPTION-triple-clicking on it with the direct-selection tool. Then choose GRAPH STYLE... (⌘-⇧-⌥-S) and select a new option in the "Graph type" box. The options to the right of the "Graph type" box are not available when only a single series is selected.

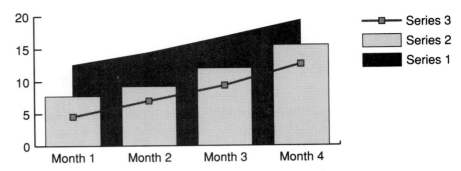

Figure 13.37: A graph containing series represented as an area chart (series 1), a bar chart (2), and a line chart (3).

Graph designs

Illustrator 3.0 allows you to create *pictographs*, graphs in which series are represented by graphic objects. The graphics may be stretched to form columns in a bar chart, or they may appear as markers in a line or scatter chart. The following sections describe how this works.

Creating a graph design

Pictographs are created by establishing and using *graph designs*, special graphic objects that may be applied to a chart. Like tile patterns, graph designs are rectangular. Therefore, your graph design must include a rectangle, sent to back and generally painted with a transparent fill and stroke. Use the pen tool to draw a horizontal line the width of the graph design. In the case of a *sliding design*, position this line at the spot at which you want to see the object elongated. For example, if you are creating a graph design that looks like a hammer, the horizontal line should be positioned some place on the handle, as shown in Figure 13.38. The hammer will then be stretched at this location to represent a large value when a sliding design is specified.

After you have filled and stroked all graph design elements in front of the rectangle, select design elements, rectangle, and horizontal line, and choose the GROUP command (⌘-G). Then select the horizontal line with the direct-selection tool and choose the MAKE GUIDE command from the ARRANGE menu (⌘-5). Select the whole design with the arrow tool and choose the DEFINE GRAPH DESIGN command (⌘-⇧-⌥-G) from the GRAPH menu. The DESIGN dialog box will display, as shown in Figure 13.39.

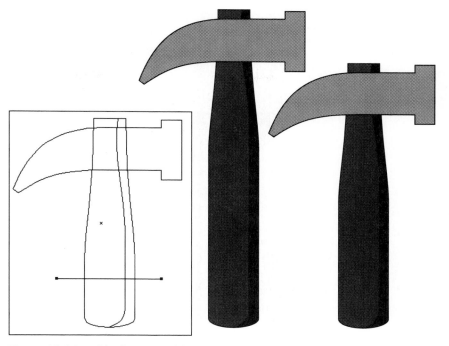

Figure 13.38: Add a horizontal line to a graph design (left) to indicate the location at which a graph design should be elongated in a sliding deign (middle and right).

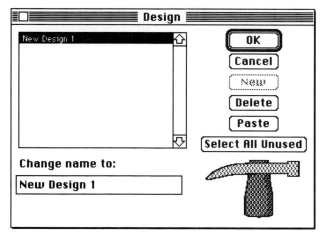

Figure 13.39: The Design dialog box allows you to create new graph designs and organize existing ones.

Enter a name for your graph design in the "Change name to" option box. The name will take the place of *New Design 1* in the scrolling pattern list. Click the OK button or press RETURN to confirm the creation of your new graph design.

Organizing graph designs

In addition to allowing you to create new graph designs, the DESIGN dialog box provides options for organizing and editing existing graph designs. These options operate identically to those in the PATTERN dialog box. Read the *Organizing tile patterns* section of Chapter 9 (pages 347 through 348) for complete information on the use of these options.

Applying graph designs to a bar chart

Graph designs may be applied to bar charts, stacked bar charts, line charts, and scatter charts. They are not applicable to area charts or pie charts.

To apply a design to an existing bar chart or stacked bar chart, select the specific series to which you want to apply the graph design by OPTION-triple-clicking on it with the direct-selection tool. Then choose the USE COLUMN DESIGN... command from the GRAPH menu (⌘-⇧-⌥-C). The GRAPH COLUMN DESIGN dialog box shown in Figure 13.40 will display. Select the desired "Column design type" option, select an existing graph design from the scrolling "Column design name" list, and click the OK button or press RETURN. The design will appear in the selected series.

The manner in which a design is applied to represent the values in a series depends on the radio button you select in the "Column design type" box in the GRAPH COLUMN DESIGN dialog box. These options includes the following:

- **None.** Select this option only when you want to remove a graph design from the selected series. The "Column design name" box and the scrolling list inside it will become dimmed.

- **Vertically scaled.** Select this option to enlarge or reduce the vertical proportion of the graph design in order to represent various values, as demonstrated in Figure 13.41.

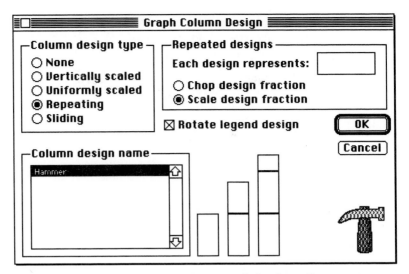

Figure 13.40: The Graph Column Design dialog box allows you to apply a graph design to the current bar chart or stacked bar chart.

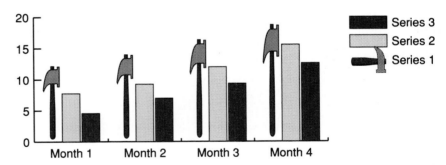

Figure 13.41: A series with a vertically scaled graph design.

- **Uniformly scaled**. Select this option to enlarge or reduce the graph design proportionally in order to represent various values, as demonstrated in Figure 13.42 on the following page.

- **Repeated**. Select this option to repeat the graph design over and over to represent various values. When the "Repeated" radio button is selected, the otherwise-dimmed "Repeated designs" options become available. Enter a value in the "Each design represents" option box to determine the value represented by each graph design. For example, if a value in the selected series is 500, and you enter 200 for "Each design represents," the design will be repeated two and a half times. Select the "Chop design fraction" to slice off the extraneous portions of the top repeated graph design, as shown in Figure 13.43; select "Scale design fraction" to scale the top graph design to the size of the fractional space, as shown in Figure 13.44.

- **Sliding**. Select this option to elongate the graph design at the spot indicated by the horizontal guide line when defining the design, as shown in Figure 13.45.

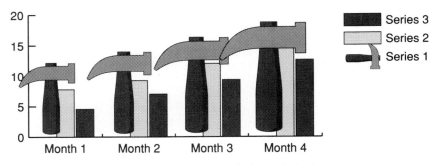

Figure 13.42: A series with uniformly scaled graph designs.

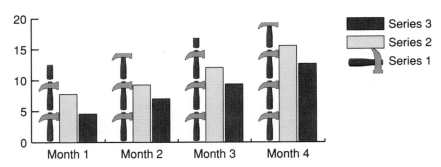

Figure 13.43: A series with repeated graph designs. Fractional designs at the top of each bar are chopped off.

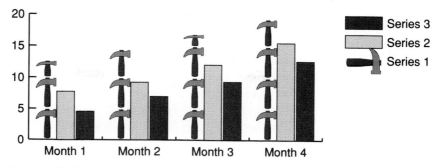

Figure 13.44: A series with repeated graph designs. Fractional designs at the top of each bar are scaled.

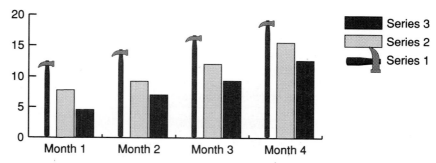

Figure 13.45: A series with sliding graph designs, which have been elongated at the spot specified with the horizontal guide line back in Figure 13.38.

After applying a graph design to a series, the entire chart becomes selected. Therefore, to edit the application of the design, you must reselect the series by pressing OPTION and clicking on some element in the series multiple times. Often, up to five or six consecutive clicks will be required. To avoid this problem, use the APPLY button in the GRAPH COLUMN DESIGN dialog box to verify your settings.

Select the "Rotate legend design" check box in the GRAPH COLUMN DESIGN dialog to display the graph design on its side in the legend, as in the previous five figures. If you deselect this option, the design will appear standing upright in the legend.

Applying graph designs to a line chart

To apply a design to an existing line chart or scatter chart, select the specific series to which you want to apply the graph design by pressing OPTION and triple-clicking *a marker* in the series with the direct-selection tool. (Do not select the line segments.) Then choose the USE MARKER DESIGN... command from the GRAPH menu (⌘-⇧-⌥-M). The GRAPH MARKER DESIGN dialog box shown in Figure 13.46 will display. Select "On data point" from the "Marker design type" options, select an existing graph design from the scrolling "Marker design name" list, and click the OK button or press RETURN. The design will appear in the selected series, as shown in Figure 13.47.

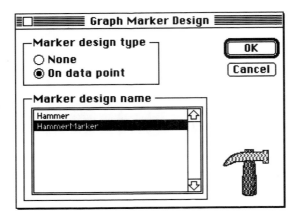

Figure 13.46: The Graph Marker Design dialog box allows you to select a graph design to apply to the current line chart or scatter chart.

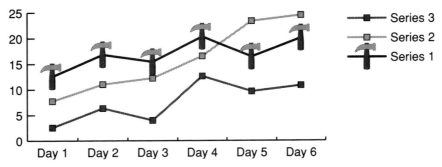

Figure 13.47: Graph designs applied to the markers of a series in a line chart.

The size at which a graph design appears in a line or scatter chart is determined by the size of the rectangle you draw when defining the graph design. When applied to a chart, the rectangle will be reduced to match the size of the square marker that normally appears at a point in a series. Therefore, to create a design that scales to a reasonable size when applied to a line chart or scatter chart, draw a small rectangle when defining the graph design.

Select the "None" radio button in the "Marker design type" box to remove the graph design from the selected line or scatter chart.

Importing
and Exporting
Graphics

Illustrator allows you to use documents from other applications in the creation of artwork. In Chapter 3, we saw that MacPaint and PICT files can be introduced for use as tracing templates. In Chapter 8, we showed that type from a word processor may be added to a text block. In Chapter 13, we explained how spreadsheet data may be imported for use in a graph.

In this chapter, we will now see how you may place Encapsulated PostScript documents that have been created in other drawing programs into an Illustrator file. You may also save an Illustrator file as an EPS document and import it to page-composition applications that run on the Macintosh or on IBM PC compatibles. We will also examine the DrawOver utility (included with Illustrator 3.0) which converts a MacDraw PICT document into an Adobe Illustrator file.

Importing graphics

Illustrator allows you to import graphics saved in the *Encapsulated Post-Script* (EPS) format. An EPS document is a pure PostScript file that is accompanied by a screen representation, in the PICT format on the Mac or the Metafile format on the PC. The EPS format was designed by Altsys Corporation (the developers of FreeHand) in cooperation with Aldus and Adobe for the swapping of high-resolution images from one PostScript-compatible application to another. The screen representation is accompanied by a PostScript-language definition that is downloaded directly to the output device during the printing process.

An EPS file may be imported into an illustration as an actual portion of the artwork. It may be transformed, duplicated, layered, and printed. However, it may not be reshaped or blended. In other words, even though an EPS file may have been constructed as a series of points and segments, just like an Illustrator drawing, those points and segments may not be altered.

 The EPS format is notoriously inefficient for storing bitmapped artwork. A color EPS bitmap is typically twice as large as the same bitmap saved in the TIFF format. However, Illustrator does not support TIFF or any other graphic format. If you want to manipulate and transform scanned images or other bitmaps in a drawing program, we recommend that you use Aldus FreeHand.

Placing EPS graphics

You may introduce an EPS document into the current illustration by choosing the PLACE ART... command from the FILE menu. This displays the PLEASE OPEN ENCAPSULATED POSTSCRIPT FILE dialog box, shown in Figure 14.01. Notice that four files are displayed. This dialog box will display both EPS files and plain-text files. A standard Illustrator file is saved as an ASCII

PostScript document. You may import such a graphic, but since there is no screen preview associated with the file, you may not view it accurately on screen. Instead, it will appear as a gray box representing the physical proportions of the image. The file will print correctly, but it may be difficult to position the image relative to other elements in an illustration.

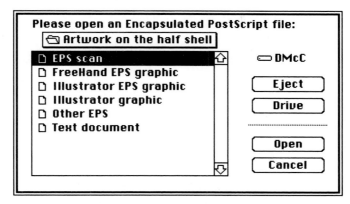

Figure 14.01: The Please open Encapsulated PostScript file dialog box allows you to import an EPS graphic.

Other plain-text files will display as well, such as those created in word processors. But unless they describe a graphic in the PostScript printer language, they will not import using the PLACE ART... command. (You may, of course, import any plain-text file using the IMPORT TEXT... command as described in Chapter 8, *Creating and Editing Type*.)

The PLEASE OPEN ENCAPSULATED POSTSCRIPT FILE dialog box will also display any documents saved in the EPS format. These may originate from the Macintosh or PC; however, only Macintosh-format EPS files with PICT screen previews will display correctly on screen.

Viewing a placed graphic

After you select the desired file from the scrolling list and press RETURN, the selected graphic will appear in the middle of the current window as a large box inset with two diagonal lines that cross the box from corner to corner, as shown in the first example of Figure 14.02 on the following page. Choose the PREVIEW command (⌘-Y) to display the placed image as it appeared when created and previewed in its original software.

If you select the "Show placed images" check box in the Preferences dialog box (introduced in the *Setting preferences* section of Chapter 3), the graphic may be viewed in the artwork-&-template mode, as shown in the second example of Figure 14.02. Although the screen-refresh speed is slower when the "Show placed images" option is selected, you may manipulate the graphic more accurately in this mode.

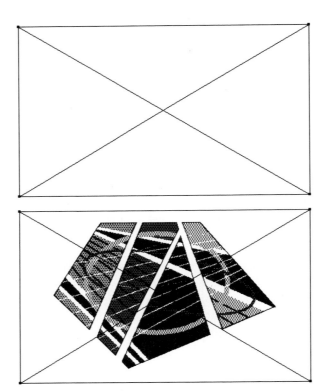

Figure 14.02: An imported EPS graphic as it appears in the artwork-&-template mode when the "Show placed images" option is deselected (top) and selected (bottom).

Masking imported graphics

Figure 14.03 shows how an EPS graphic might be integrated into an illustration. Here we have scanned an enhanced image of a floppy disk and saved it in the EPS format. We then created a path shaped like an apple. After selecting the path, we chose the Style... command from the Paint menu (⌘-I) and selected the mask option. We then sent the path to the back of the illustration and grouped it with the imported EPS graphic. The result is a scanned image set inside an apple, an effect possible only in an advanced drawing application like Adobe Illustrator.

Figure 14.03: A gray-scale bitmapped image saved in the EPS format, imported into Illustrator, and masked by a clipping path.

Opening illustrations that contain EPS graphics

An illustration that contains an EPS image must always be able to reference its original EPS file in order to preview or to print the placed image successfully. Therefore, when you save an illustration, Illustrator remembers the location of the original imported EPS file on disk. If you try to open an existing illustration after having moved its imported EPS file to a different disk or folder, Illustrator will produce the PLEASE LOCATE dialog box, shown in Figure 14.04 on the next page. This dialog asks you to locate your EPS file on disk. If you cancel this dialog, the illustration will preview with a white box covering all objects in back of the EPS image; such an EPS image will not print at all.

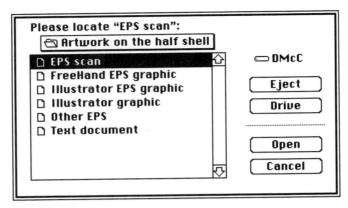

Figure 14.04: The Please locate dialog box asks you to specify the current location of an imported EPS file on disk.

Exporting an illustration

Images created in Illustrator 3.0 may be used in any Macintosh or PC application that supports the EPS format. In this way, an illustration may become part of a full-fledged document, such as a newsletter, flyer, or catalog, or part of a video or on-screen presentation.

Saving an illustration in the EPS format

You may store an illustration as an EPS document by choosing the SAVE AS… command from the FILE menu. Figure 14.05 shows the SAVE ILLUSTRATION dialog box that will display. (This dialog was first introduced in the *Saving an illustration* section of Chapter 3.) At the bottom of the dialog box are three options that allow you to save an illustration for use in other applications. These include the "Preview" and "Compatibility" pop-up menus and the "Include Placed images" check box.

The "Preview" pop-up menu allows you determine whether the current illustration is saved as an EPS file. It includes the following options:

- **None (Omit EPSF Header)**. Choose this option to save the illustration as a standard PostScript file that cannot be imported into most other applications.

- **None (Include EPSF Header).** Choose this option to save the illustration with an EPS header in order to import it into any application that supports the EPS format. No preview, however, will be included with the illustration. Instead, it will appear as a gray box on screen in another application, but it will print correctly.

- **Black&White Macintosh.** Choose this option to save the illustration as an EPS file with a black-and-white screen preview for use in any Macintosh program that supports the EPS format.

- **Color Macintosh.** Choose this option to save the illustration as an EPS file with a color screen preview for use in any Macintosh program that supports the EPS format and runs in color. Color EPS files take up more room on disk than black-and-white EPS files.

- **IBM PC.** Choose this option to save the illustration as an EPS file with a black-and-white screen preview for use in any PC program that supports the EPS format.

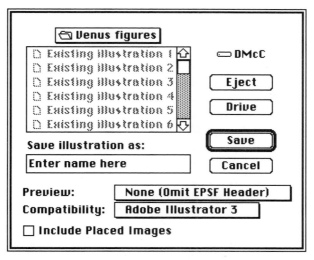

Figure 14.05: The Save illustration dialog box, which appears when you choose the Save As... command from the File menu, allows you to export an EPS document for use in another Macintosh or PC application.

The "Compatibility" pop-up menu allows you to determine whether the current illustration is compatible with earlier versions of Illustrator as well as with other applications that support early formats. It includes the following options:

- **Adobe Illustrator 3**. Choose this option to save the illustration as a standard Illustrator 3.0 file. Such a file may *not* be opened in previous versions of Illustrator.

- **Adobe Illustrator 88**. Choose this option to save the illustration as an Illustrator 88 file. Such a file may be opened in Illustrator 88 and 3.0, but *not* in Illustrator 1.1.

- **Adobe Illustrator 1.1**. Choose this option to save the illustration as an Illustrator 1.1 file. Such a file may be opened in any version of Adobe Illustrator as well as in several other drawing applications such as Aldus FreeHand on the Mac, Corel Draw on the PC, and Adobe Illustrator on the PC.

Depending upon the complexity of the current illustration, choosing either "Adobe Illustrator 88" or "Adobe Illustrator 1.1" may result in some loss of information. Techniques such as tile patterns, masking, and placing EPS graphics are incompatible with the Illustrator 1.1 format; compound paths and area or path text blocks are not supported by Illustrator 88. In the Illustrator 1.1 format, objects painted with patterns will become filled or stroked with 100% black. Though the form of a clipping path or a compound path will remain intact, its purpose will be ignored; objects will not be masked, nor will they create holes. If an illustration contains a placed EPS image, that image will not appear when the file is opened in Illustrator 1.1. If an illustration contains text objects, they will be converted to point text blocks with fewer than 256 characters when saved in the Illustrator 88 format.

 When saving an illustration in either Illustrator 1.1 or 88 format, be sure that you have previously saved it in the Illustrator 3.0 format to avoid the permanent loss of information.

Saving illustrations
with placed EPS graphics

If the current illustration that you are saving as an EPS file contains one or more EPS images that have been imported with the PLACE ART... command, be sure to select the "Include Placed Images" check box in the SAVE ILLUSTRATION dialog box. This option directs Illustrator to include a PostScript description of all imported EPS graphics as part of the saved illustration file.

Note that selecting the "Include Placed Images" option does not free Illustrator from requiring access to the original EPS file when you open the illustration at some later point in time. However, it does ensure that an EPS illustration that contains EPS graphics will preview and print correctly from within another application, such as a page-composition or presentation program. If this option is *not* selected when saving an EPS illustration, any placed EPS graphics will appear on-screen but will not print successfully.

Converting drawings into illustrations

Included with Adobe Illustrator 3.0 is an updated version of the DrawOver utility, which allows you to convert a MacDraw PICT document to the Adobe Illustrator 1.1 format.

Shortly after you launch DrawOver by double-clicking its icon at the Finder level, the PLEASE OPEN PICT dialog box will appear. This dialog asks you to select a MacDraw document that has been saved in the PICT format. (MacDraw files that are not saved in the PICT format cannot be converted using DrawOver.) After you select and open a file, the PREVIEW dialog box appears, displaying the contents of the MacDraw PICT file. This dialog box permits you to confirm your selection before proceeding with the conversion. If you click the CANCEL button, you will be returned to the OPEN PICT dialog. If you click on OK or press RETURN, another dialog will ask you to determine and name the destination for the converted illustration.

Although most elements are retained, some portions of a MacDraw PICT graphic will be lost in the conversion process. For example, bit-mapped portions of a MacDraw document, including imported MacPaint documents and patterned lines and fills, do not convert properly. Also, color is not supported by DrawOver.

Printing
Your
Illustrations

Illustrator describes every text block and graphic object in an illustration as a combination of mathematically defined points and segments. This pure-math model allows Illustrator to translate the illustration to various hardware devices, regardless of device resolution. On a day-to-day basis, the primary display device is your monitor. However, finished illustrations are best displayed on a page printed from a high-resolution output device. In this chapter, we discuss the printing of Illustrator 3.0 files, including black-and-white standard prints, color composite prints, and color separations.

Printing from Illustrator

You may print black-and-white, gray scale, and color composites (using a color laser printer) directly from inside the Illustrator application. To create color separations for four-color process printing, you must use the Adobe Separator utility, as discussed in *Printing from Separator* later in this chapter.

Printing from Adobe Illustrator is a four-step process:

1. Use the Chooser desk accessory to select the LaserWriter driver.

2. Choose the PAGE SETUP... command from the FILE menu to determine the size of the printed page.

3. Position the page-size boundary in the drawing area.

4. Choose the PRINT... command from the FILE menu (⌘-P) to print the current illustration to the selected output device.

Each of these steps is described in detail in the following sections.

Choosing the PostScript printer

Illustrator prints high-resolution artwork only to PostScript-compatible output devices. Although you may print an illustration to a non-Post-Script printer, such as an ImageWriter or LaserWriter SC, it will print as a low-resolution bitmap, exactly as it appears on screen. For any but the most rudimentary proofing purposes, such a print is useless.

 Judging by Adobe's previous record, it is highly doubtful Illustrator will ever print to non-PostScript printers. If you use an ImageWriter or other QuickDraw-language output device on a regular basis, you may want to consider a different drawing program, such as MacDraw, Canvas, or Aldus FreeHand, all of which perform beautifully with non-PostScript devices. A better solution for those who can afford it is to purchase a PostScript-compatible printer, which are among the best and most widely supported output devices available.

To select a PostScript-compatible printer, choose the CHOOSER from the list of desk accessories under the APPLE menu. The Chooser desk accessory will appear, as shown in Figure 15.01. One or more *printer drivers* display on the left side of the window. Printer drivers help the current application translate the contents of a printed file to a specific variety of output device. Click on the icon labeled "LaserWriter," which is the driver for all PostScript-compatible printers. This allows you to prepare your illustration to be printed to a PostScript printer even if no such printer is currently hooked up to your Mac. If your computer is networked to one or more PostScript devices, select the desired printer from the "Select a LaserWriter" list on the right-hand side of the Chooser window. Then click the close box to return to the Illustrator desktop.

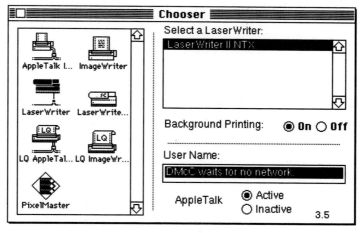

Figure 15.01: Use the Chooser desk accessory to select the LaserWriter printer driver.

Setting up the page

The next step is to define the size of the page on which your illustration will be printed. Choose the PAGE SETUP... command from the FILE menu to display the LASERWRITER PAGE SETUP dialog box shown in Figure 15.02. We first discussed this dialog box in the *Adjusting the page size* section of Chapter 3, where we used it to set the page size for a new document. We will now take a more complete look at this dialog box.

The most important options presented in this dialog box are the "Paper" radio buttons, which control the size of the printed page. Apple's LASERWRITER PAGE SETUP dialog box 5.2 or later offers five page sizes: "US Letter," "US Legal," "A4 Letter," "B5 Letter," and "Tabloid." If you use a version of the LaserWriter driver earlier than version 5.2, your LASERWRITER PAGE SETUP dialog will not offer the "Tabloid" option. Contact your Apple dealer for an upgrade to System 6.0.4, which contains both versions 5.2 and 6.0 of the LaserWriter driver and LaserPrep files.

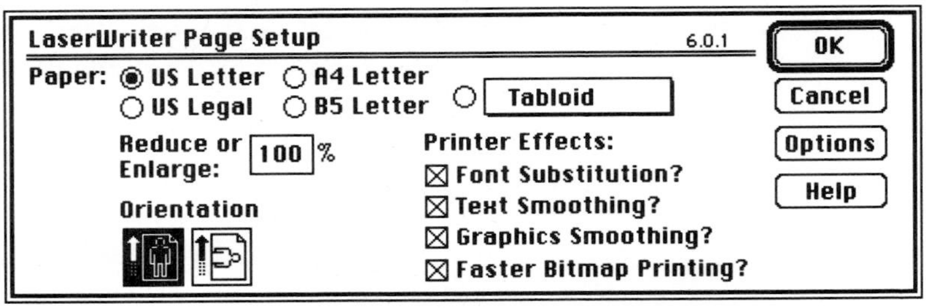

Figure 15.02: Use the LaserWriter Page Setup dialog box to determine page size and orientation. The LaserWriter driver version number is displayed to the left of the OK button.

As we discussed in Chapter 3, the selected page size also determines the current *margin size*, displayed within the page-size boundary in the drawing area. The margin size specifies the *imageable area* of a page; that is, the amount of the page on which objects may be printed. For example, a "US Letter" page measures 8½ inches by 11 inches, but only 7.68 inches by 10.16 inches is imageable. Objects that fall in the remaining margin will not print on Apple LaserWriters or most other PostScript-compatible laser printers. (High-resolution printers, such as the Linotronic family of imagesetters, will print the entire page size, regardless of the margin size.) You may enlarge the margin size by selecting the "Larger Print Area" option in the LASERWRITER OPTIONS dialog box, as described later in this section.

The LASERWRITER PAGE SETUP dialog box also allows you to set a reduction or enlargement to alter the size of your document. On the Apple LaserWriter, reductions may be as small as 25% and enlargements as large as 400%. If you enter a value in the "Reduce or Enlarge" option box that is beyond the capability of your printer, an alert box will warn you as soon as you click the OK button or press RETURN.

The "Orientation" icons are the next options. As in other Macintosh software, you may specify whether your page is upright (the portrait setting) or on its side (the landscape setting). Changing the orientation setting in this dialog box will also change the orientation of the page size in the drawing area. Text blocks and graphic objects will *not* be repositioned or rotated to match the new orientation.

Four "Printer Effects" options are available, all of which are ignored when printing from Adobe Illustrator.

The OPTIONS button brings up the LASERWRITER OPTIONS dialog box shown in Figure 15.03. The check boxes in this dialog can be very useful in adjusting the appearance of a printed illustration. The sample page on the left-hand side of the dialog box demonstrates the effect of the selected options. The dog represents the image on the page and the dotted line represents the margin size.

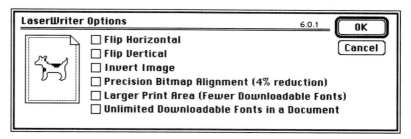

Figure 15.03: The LaserWriter Options dialog box allows you to adjust the appearance of an illustration on the printed page.

The options in the LASERWRITER OPTIONS dialog box work as follows:

- **Flip Horizontal**. Select this option to flip the objects in an illustration horizontally on the printed page. When printing film negatives, deselect "Flip Horizontal" to specify *emulsion up*; select the option to specify *emulsion down*. The creation of film negatives is discussed more thoroughly later in this chapter.

- **Flip Vertical**. Select this option to flip the objects in an illustration vertically on the printed page. You may also use this option to determine the emulsion side of a film negative. However, if you select *both* "Flip Horizontal" and "Flip Vertical," you will nullify the effect (emulsion up).

- **Invert Image**. Select this option to change all blacks to white and all whites to black. For example, black becomes white, 40% black becomes 60% black, 20% black becomes 80% black. This option prints a *negative* of the current illustration and is used primarily when printing to film on high-resolution Linotronic or Compugraphic imagesetters.

- **Precision Bitmap Alignment** (**4% reduction**). This option reduces 72-dot-per-inch MacPaint images to 96% of their current size, making them compatible with the resolution of a 300-dot-per-inch laser printer. Since bitmapped MacPaint images may be used only as non-printing tracing templates in Illustrator, this option is useless when printing an illustration.

- **Larger Print Area** (**Fewer Downloadable Fonts**). This option allows you to enlarge the imageable area of an illustration when printing to a laser printer. The margin size displayed in the drawing area will become larger when this option is selected. The standard and enlarged imageable areas for each page size are listed below. (All above imageable area measurements are notated in picas and points. For example, *60p9* means 60 picas and 9 points.)

Page size			Imageable area		Larger image area	
NAME	WIDTH	HEIGHT	WIDTH	HEIGHT	WIDTH	HEIGHT
US Letter	8.5″	11″	60p9	46p0	64p8	48p0
US Legal	8.5″	14″	75p0	40p4	81p6	48p0
Tabloid	11″	17″	99p0	63p6	99p0	63p6
A4 Letter	210mm	297mm	66p0	44p9	66p5	46p6
B5 Letter	176mm	250mm	58p6	38p9	58p6	38p9

- **Unlimited Downloadable Fonts in a Document**. When selected, this option forces a change in the PostScript commands that define your illustration. Normally, documents may contain only as many fonts as will fit into printer memory at once, but this option allows downloadable fonts to swap in and out of printer memory. Although this option may be selected to avoid printer out-of-memory errors, Adobe warns against using it, since it may cause printing complications of its own.

Adjusting the page size

The appearance of the page size in the drawing area is determined by the selected "Artwork board" radio button in the PREFERENCES dialog box (introduced in the *Setting preferences* section of Chapter 3). The options include the following:

- **Single full page**. Select this radio button to display a single page size and margin size.

- **Tile full pages**. Select this radio button to display as many whole pages as will fit in the drawing area. At most, two letter-sized pages may fit side by side.

- **Tile imageable areas**. Select this radio button to subdivide the drawing area into multiple partial margin sizes, called *tiles*.

After selecting one of these options, use the page tool to position the page size in relation to the objects in your illustration. If you selected the "Tile imageable areas" option, the page number of each tile is listed in the lower left corner of the tile, so that, in the LASERWRITER PRINT dialog box, you can specify particular pages, containing some or all of your illustration, to print.

For more information about using "Artwork board" options and the page tool, refer to the sections *Moving the page size in the drawing area* and *Creating a two-page layout* in Chapter 3.

Printing pages

To initiate the printing process, choose the PRINT... command from the FILE menu (⌘-P). The standard LASERWRITER PRINT dialog box will display, as shown in Figure 15.04. Enter the number of copies you want to print in the "Copies" option box. Then select a range of pages using the "Pages" options. By default, the "All" radio button is selected. If the drawing area displays a single page size, only that page will be printed. If the drawing area displays multiple pages or tiles, Illustrator will print all pages that contain type or graphic objects. To define a specific range of pages or tiles to be printed, enter the page numbers in the "From" and "To" option boxes. These numbers should correspond to the page numbers displayed in the lower left corners of pages in the drawing area.

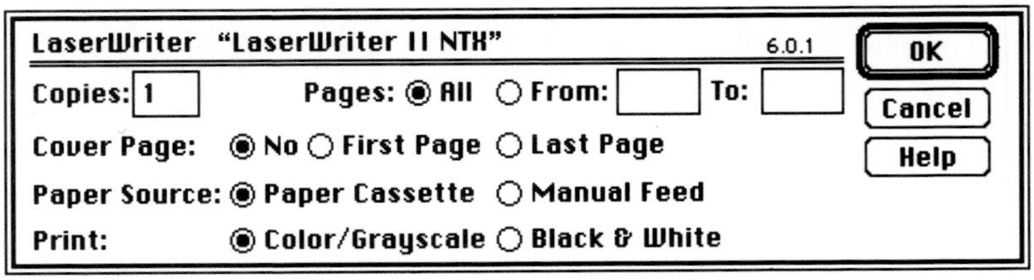

```
┌─────────────────────────────────────────────────────────────────┐
│ LaserWriter "LaserWriter II NTH"            6.0.1    ┌──────────┐ │
│                                                      │    OK    │ │
│ Copies: 1        Pages: ⦿ All  ○ From:      To:      └──────────┘ │
│                                                      ┌──────────┐ │
│ Cover Page:   ⦿ No ○ First Page  ○ Last Page         │  Cancel  │ │
│                                                      └──────────┘ │
│ Paper Source: ⦿ Paper Cassette  ○ Manual Feed        ┌──────────┐ │
│                                                      │   Help   │ │
│ Print:        ⦿ Color/Grayscale ○ Black & White      └──────────┘ │
└─────────────────────────────────────────────────────────────────┘
```

Figure 15.04: The LaserWriter Print dialog box allows you
to print a composite of an illustration to a PostScript-
compatible output device.

The "Cover Page" options allow you to print an extra page that lists
the user name, application, document name, date, time, and printer for
the current job. This page may precede or follow the illustration pages.

If you want to print your illustration on a letterhead or other special
piece of paper, select "Manual Feed" from the "Paper Source" options.
Your laser printer will display a manual feed light directing you to insert
the special paper. The "Paper Source" options are ignored when printing
to a color laser printer or to an imagesetter or other film-based output
device.

If you are using LaserWriter driver 6.0 (included in the Apple Color
folder of the Macintosh Printing Tools disk for System 6.0.4 and later),
two "Print" radio buttons appear at the bottom of the LASERWRITER PRINT
dialog box: "Color/Grayscale" and "Black & White." These options affect the printing of PICT images only and are ignored when printing
PostScript or Encapsulated PostScript illustrations.

Click the OK button or press RETURN to initiate the printing process.
If the current illustration contains color and your output device is not capable of printing colors, gray values will be used to represent colors, as on
a black-and-white television. Color documents output on color printers
will produce *color composites,* which are prints that contain all colors used
in the current illustration. To create color separations of illustrations that
include color, use the Adobe Separator program as described in the *Printing from Separator* section, later in this chapter.

Special printing considerations

Every print job is not the same. Although the process itself is straightforward, your illustration may require special treatment not addressed by the PRINT... command. Alternatively, your illustration may seem fine, but complications may occur that prevent the printing process from completing successfully. In any of these cases, the following sections may be of some assistance. They explain how to: 1) print oversized artwork, 2) create crop marks, 3) avoid "limitcheck" errors, and 4) solve "out of memory" errors.

Printing oversized documents

By virtue of the LASERWRITER PAGE SETUP dialog box, Illustrator provides access to various common page sizes. But many artists require custom page sizes that Illustrator cannot accommodate. And even if it could, most laser printers are set up to print letter-sized pages only. So how do you proof oversized artwork using a typical laser printer, and how do you print the final artwork from an imagesetter?

To proof your artwork, select the "US Letter" option in the LASER-WRITER PAGE SETUP dialog box, then select "Tile imageable areas" from the "Artwork board" options in the PREFERENCES dialog box. Your illustration will be sectioned onto separate tiles as indicated by the dotted lines in the drawing area. If these breaks are not at the most opportune locations in terms of easily reassembling your artwork, use the page tool to manually reposition the dotted lines. Then print your document one page at a time, manually repositioning the tile for each page before each print, as demonstrated in Figure 15.05 on the next page.

To print the finished illustration, use the Adobe Separator utility, which can take full advantage of the larger printable areas found on certain PostScript output devices, including Linotronic and Compugraphic imagesetters. Separator ignores tile locations, instead allowing you to specify a *bounding box* to define the custom size of your imageable area. (See the *Printing from Separator* section later in this chapter for complete information.)

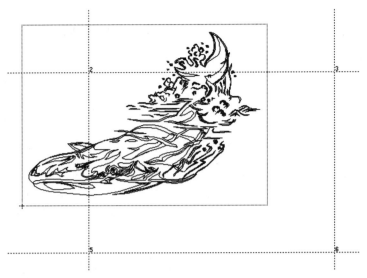

Figure 15.05: Using the page tool to reposition the tiles with respect to an oversized illustration.

Creating crop marks

Illustrator 3.0 provides new commands for creating *crop marks*, which are used to indicate the boundaries of an illustration. When printing to an Linotronic 100 imagesetter, for example, all illustrations are printed on pages 12 inches wide, regardless of their actual size. When you go to have the illustration commercially reproduced, the printer will want to know the dimensions of the final page size and how the illustration should be positioned on the page. Crop marks specify the boundaries of the reproduced page. Using properly positioned crop marks will prevent miscommunication with your commercial printer as well as help to avoid additional expense during the commercial printing phase.

To create crop marks, draw a box with the rectangle tool that represents the size of the paper onto which the final illustration will be reproduced. While the rectangle remains selected, choose the SET CROPMARKS command from the ARRANGE menu. The rectangle will be converted into crop marks, as shown in Figure 15.06. Notice that the marks are positioned outside the boundary, preventing them from appearing on the final, reproduced page.

Arrange	
Transform Again	**⌘D**
Group	**⌘G**
Ungroup	**⌘U**
Join...	**⌘J**
Average...	**⌘L**
Lock	**⌘1**
Unlock All	**⌘2**
Hide	**⌘3**
Show All	**⌘4**
Make Guide	**⌘5**
Release All Guides	**⌘6**
Set Cropmarks	
Release Cropmarks	

If no object is selected and a single page is displayed in the drawing area (as per the "Single full page" option in the PREFERENCES dialog box), choose SET CROPMARKS to create crop marks to match the current page size.

Only one set of crop marks may exist for the current illustration. When you choose SET CROPMARKS, you delete any previous crop marks while creating new ones.

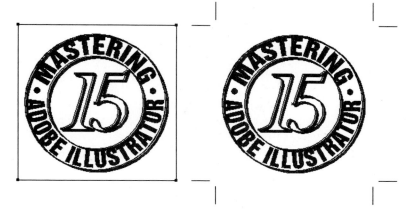

Figure 15.06: After drawing a rectangle to specify the size of the trimmed illustration (left), choose the Set Cropmarks command to convert the rectangle to crop marks (right).

Crop marks can also be useful for defining the boundaries of an EPS illustration that you intend to import into a page-layout or presentation program. In Aldus PageMaker, for example, you might import an illustration with crop marks, and then use the crop tool to trim the illustration to the proper size.

You may also export EPS illustrations with crop marks in order to combine multiple illustrations with multiple sets of crop marks on a single page. This saves imagesetting costs and provides any number of required crop marks for paste-up purposes.

To delete the crop marks from an illustration, choose the RELEASE CROPMARKS command from the ARRANGE menu. The crop marks will be converted back to a rectangle.

Splitting long paths

You may encounter several errors when printing an illustration. One of the most common is the "limitcheck" error, which results from a limitation in your printer's PostScript interpreter. If the number of points in the mathematical representation of a path exceeds this limitation, the illustration will not print successfully.

Unfortunately, the "points" used in this mathematical representation are not the points you used to define the object. Instead, they are calculated by the PostScript interpreter during the printing process. When presented with a curve, the PostScript interpreter has to plot hundreds of tiny straight lines to create the most accurate possible rendering. So rather than drawing a perfect curve, your printer creates a many-sided polygon whose exact number of sides in determined by a device-dependent variable known as *flatness*. The default flatness value for the Apple Laser-Writer is 1.0 device pixel, or ⅟₃₀₀ inch. This means the center of any tiny side of the polygon rendering may be at most ⅟₃₀₀ inch from the farthest X,Y-coordinate of the actual mathematical curve, as demonstrated by Figure 15.07.

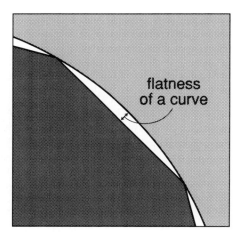

Figure 15.07: The flatness of a curve determines the greatest distance between any one of the tiny straight lines used to represent the curve and its true mathematical description.

Each tiny line in the polygon rendering is joined at a "point." If the number of "points" exceeds your printer's built-in "path" limit, an alert box will display, warning you that the printer has encountered a limit-check error, and the print job will be canceled. The "path" limit for the original LaserWriter was 1500, seemingly enough straight lines to imitate any curve. But every once in a while, you may create a curve that proves too much for the printer. For example, a standard signature contains several complex loops that might tax the limitations of the most advanced output device.

There are two ways to avoid limitcheck errors. The first and most preferred method is to select the "Split long paths on Save/Print" check box in the PREFERENCES dialog box. Then enter the resolution for the *final* output device in the "Output resolution" option box at the bottom of the dialog. The next time you save or print the current illustration, Illustrator will automatically break up every path that it considers to be at risk into several smaller paths. The integrity of your illustration will not be affected.

Unfortunately, changing any options in the PREFERENCES dialog box will affect future illustrations unless you deselect the "Split long paths on Save/Print" option before opening another file. Also, there is no way to automatically reassemble paths that have been split. They must be joined back together manually if and when you decide to make alterations to the illustration. And finally, Illustrator's automated path-splitting feature only accounts for the complexity of a path. It does not account for whether a path is filled or stroked with a complex tile pattern, which is the most likely cause of a "limitcheck" error.

If the automatic splitting technique does not solve your printing problem, you may use the "Flatness" value in the PAINT dialog box. Select the path that you think to be the culprit. Keep in mind that paths filled or stroked with tile patterns are the most likely candidates. Then choose the STYLE... command from the PAINT menu (⌘-I) and enter a value between 0 and 100 in the "Flatness" option box. This value will increase the distance that a straight line may vary from the mathematical curve, as shown in Figure 15.07, thus reducing the risk of limitcheck errors. However, the affected path will also appear less smooth. Use the "Flatness" option only as a last resort.

Printing pattern tiles

As described in the previous section, tile patterns may cause limitcheck errors. But more often, they will cause "out of memory" errors, especially if several patterns are used in a single illustration. To accelerate the printing process, Illustrator downloads tiles to your printer's memory, much as if they were non-resident fonts. In this way, the printer may access tile definitions repeatedly throughout the creation of an illustration. However, if the current illustration contains too many tile patterns, or a single tile is too complex, the printer's memory may become full, in which case the print operation will be cancelled and an alert box will warn you that an out-of-memory error has occurred.

Out-of-memory errors are less common in high-resolution output devices, such as imagesetters, because these machines tend to include updated PostScript interpreters and have increased memory capacity. Therefore, you will most often encounter an out-of-memory error when proofing an illustration to an old-model LaserWriter or other low-memory device. Try any one of these techniques to remedy the problem:

- Change all typefaces in the current illustration to Times, Helvetica, or some other printer-resident font. In this way, Illustrator will not have to download both patterns and printer fonts.

- Print objects painted with dissimilar tile patterns in separate illustrations. Then use traditional paste-up techniques to combine the pages into a composite proof.

- Deselect the "Preview and print patterns" option in the PREFERENCES dialog box. All patterned fills and strokes will print as gray. This technique allows you to proof all portions of your illustration except the patterns themselves.

When you print the final illustration to an imagesetter, it will probably print successfully because of the imagesetter's increased memory capacity. If the illustration still encounters an out-of-memory error, you will have to delete some patterns or resort to traditional paste-up techniques, as suggested in the second item of the list above.

Most service bureaus charge extra for printing complex documents that tie up their imagesetters for long periods of time. Tile patterns almost always complicate an illustration and slow down printing time. Therefore, use masks and compound paths instead of patterns whenever possible.

Printing from Separator

The Adobe Separator is a utility application that creates and outputs *color separations* from files created with Illustrator 3.0. The process of creating color separations results in a separate printed page, either on paper or film, for each of the four process colors and for each custom color used in the document. Each page displays only those objects, or portions of objects, that contain the specified color.

Before discussing the Adobe Separator any further, it must be made clear that the relative ease of use of this software belies the complexity of the process that it facilitates. Creating color separations to be used in four-color printing is an exacting and demanding undertaking. It requires specific knowledge of the four-color printing process, the press on which documents will be reproduced, and the imagesetter on which the separation positives or negatives will be output. This does not mean that you cannot successfully create and use separations from Adobe Illustrator and the Adobe Separator, but we strongly advise that you work very closely with your commercial printer, and be sure that the service bureau or print department that will be outputting your separations understands your requirements exactly.

Starting Separator

Prior to using Adobe Separator, you must install the Separator application and the PPD folder to your hard disk, as described in the installation procedure in Appendix A. Once installed, double-click the Separator icon at the Finder level to launch the application.

The PLEASE OPEN ADOBE ILLUSTRATOR OR (EPSF) FILE dialog box will appear, requesting that you select a PostScript-language file, as shown in Figure 15.08 on the next page. Locate the file you wish to separate in the scrolling list, and either double-click on the file name or select the file and click the OPEN button. Separator allows you to open not only Illustrator files, but also compatible Encapsulated PostScript files created in other applications. If the file name that you select is not compatible with the Separator application, a dialog box will notify you, and the file will not be opened. If the file you select is compatible, but not capable of being printed with the Separator application, the file will open but you will be alerted that you will not be able to print separations. This may occur when opening PostScript files that have been improperly modified in a word processor.

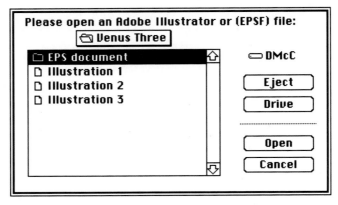

Figure 15.08: The Please open Adobe Illustrator or (EPSF) file dialog box allows you to select the illustration or Encapsulated PostScript document that you want to print.

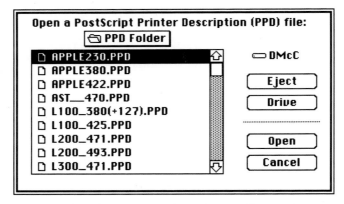

Figure 15.09: The Open PostScript Printer Description (PPD) file dialog box allows you to select the PPD file corresponding to the intended output device.

After selecting a file to be separated, the OPEN POSTSCRIPT PRINTER DESCRIPTION (PPD) FILE dialog box appears, as shown in Figure 15.09, asking you to select the *PostScript printer description* (PPD) file that corresponds to the intended output device. You will find the PPD files included with Adobe Illustrator 3.0 inside a PPD folder, which may reside in the folder containing the Illustrator application or in the System folder. Each PPD file is named for the printer model it describes. Some PPD files have numbers following the printer name, indicating the specific version of the PostScript ROM chips that the printer may contain. It is important to use the correct PPD file for your output device in order for the Adobe Separator to work properly. If you do not have a PPD file corresponding to your printer ROM, contact Adobe Systems or the printer manufacturer for information on obtaining the correct PPD file.

To avoid searching through the long list of PPD files over and over every time you use Separator, copy the PPD files you use regularly to a new folder. At the Finder level, choose the NEW FOLDER command from the FILE menu (⌘-N), name the folder something like *My PPDs*, and OPTION-drag the specific PPD files that you wish to copy from the original PPD folder to the new PPD folder. (Pressing OPTION copies the files rather than simply relocating them.)

Locate the desired PPD file in the scrolling list, and either double-click on the file name or select the file and click the OPEN button. Following this, the SETUP window will appear, as shown in Figure 15.10.

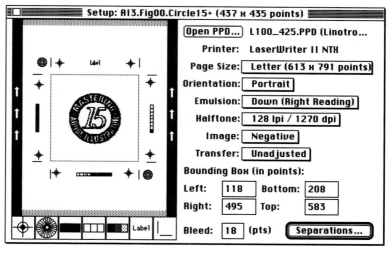

Figure 15.10: The Setup window displays after successfully launching Adobe Separator.

Setting Separator options

The SETUP window is divided into two parts: the *separation preview* on the left side of the window and a series of separation options along the right-hand side. The separation preview allows you to determine the *margin notes* that print with each separation, as described in the *Margin notes* section at the end of this chapter. The tile bar lists the name of the open Illustrator or EPS file. To open a different file, click the close box (or choose CLOSE from the FILE menu, ⌘-W) to first close the current window. Then choose the OPEN... command from the FILE menu (⌘-O) to display the PLEASE OPEN ADOBE ILLUSTRATOR OR (EPSF) FILE dialog box displayed in Figure 15.08, and select a different illustration. Adobe Separator allows only one open window at a time.

The upper right corner of the SETUP window contains an OPEN PPD... button, which allows you to change the selected PPD file. The current selection is listed to the right of the button. Click the button to redisplay the OPEN POSTSCRIPT PRINTER DESCRIPTION (PPD) FILE dialog box, shown in Figure 15.09, and select a different PPD file.

In the SETUP window, the current printer is listed below the OPEN PPD... button. You may select a different printer using the Chooser desk accessory, as described in the *Choosing the PostScript printer* section earlier in this chapter.

Beneath the current printer are a series of pop-up menu options, all of which are described in the following sections:

Page size

Based on information contained in the selected PPD file, the "Page Size" pop-up menu lists the page sizes available for your output device. Next to the common name of each page size is the imageable area of the page, measured in points. The area required for the margin notes, which Separator prints on each page, have not been subtracted, so the actual usable area is somewhat smaller than the displayed imageable area. Select a page size that is large enough to contain both illustration and margin notes, the latter of which consume about four picas all around.

If the selected printer allows custom page sizes to be defined, you may choose the "Other..." option to display the PAGE SIZE dialog box, shown in Figure 15.11. The default values for the "Width" and "Height" options are the dimensions of the smallest page that will contain the current illustration. The "Offset" option allows you to add additional space between your illustration and the right edge of the paper. If the "Offset" option is left at 0, the custom page will be centered in the width of the paper or film used by the current output device.

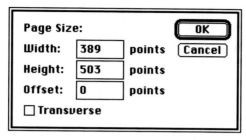

Figure 15.11: The Page Size dialog box allows you to specify a custom page size.

The "Transverse" option controls the position of your custom page relative to the paper or film on which it will be printed. This is most commonly used when printing on imagesetters which use long rolls of paper or film. The default positioning for any page on a PostScript printer places the long edge of the page parallel to the long edge of the paper. In most cases this is correct, but when printing to an imagesetter you can usually reduce paper or film waste by setting pages *transverse*, that is, with their short edges parallel to the long edge of the paper.

Orientation

Unlike the "Transverse" option, which controls the position of the page on the printer's paper, the "Orientation" option controls the position of an illustration on the page, just like the "Orientation" option offered in the LASERWRITER PAGE SETUP dialog box. By default, all Separator documents are output with the "Portrait" option selected, even if the "Landscape" option was selected in the LASERWRITER PAGE SETUP dialog box when the document was created and saved in Illustrator 3.0.

Selecting the "Landscape" option in the "Orientation" pop-up menu will rotate the illustration 90°. The Separator will perform this rotation regardless of whether the rotated image correctly fits on the paper, so be careful when altering this option.

Emulsion

The "Emulsion" option, like the "Flip Vertical" option in the LASERWRITER OPTIONS dialog box (shown in Figure 15.03), controls how the document is printed relative to the emulsion on photosensitive paper or film. The names given to the options, "Up" and "Down," refer to the sides of the paper or film on which the emulsion is laid. When printing film negatives, you will probably want to select "Down" from the pop-up menu, when printing on paper, the "Up" is usually the correct setting.

Halftone

The "Halftone" option is used to control the *resolution* (the number of pixels printed in a linear inch) and *screen frequency* (the number of *halftone cells* in a linear inch) of the output device. Halftone cells are the dots used to represent gray values and tints. Resolution is measured in *dots per inch*, or dpi, with "dots" being device pixels. Frequency is measured in *lines per inch*, or lpi. For example, the default resolution for an Apple LaserWriter is 300 dpi; the default screen frequency is 60 lpi.

Since a setting of 60 lpi assigns 60 halftone cells to every linear inch, every halftone cell printed on a 300-dpi laser printer measure five pixels wide by five pixels tall ($300 \div 60 = 5$), for a total of 25 pixels per cell. If all pixels in a cell are turned off, the cell appears white; all pixels turned on produces black; any number between 0 and 25 produces a shade of gray. A unique tint can be created by turning on each of 0 through 25 pixels, for a total of 26 gray values.

Therefore, when choosing a "Halftone" option, consider how your change affects the number of gray values printable by the current output device. Raising the resolution increases the number of gray values by providing more pixels. However, raising the frequency value decreases the number of gray values because it decreases the size of each halftone cell, and therefore the number of pixels per cell.

Image

Like the "Invert" option in the LASERWRITER OPTIONS dialog box, the "Image" option controls whether the document is printed as a positive or a negative image. If printing to paper, the default "Positive" is usually the correct setting. However, when printing to film, "Negative" will probably be the preferred setting. Be sure to confirm your selection with your commercial printer.

Transfer

The "Transfer" pop-up menu allows you to temporarily adjust the *transfer function* for the current output device and is specifically applicable to film output. The transfer function determines the *density* of various tints; that is, their lightness or darkness. If tints tend toward high density, your output will appear too dark when printing film positives and too light when printing film negatives. If tints tend toward low density, your output will appear too light when printing film positives and too dark when printing film negatives.

By default, the "Unadjusted" option is selected. This option instructs Separator to rely on its default density settings. Unless you are specifically instructed to do so by a commercial printing house, or you are skilled in the use of an *optical densitometer* (a typically hand-held device that measures reflected light), *do not* change the "Transfer" option. However, if you know what you're doing, you may choose the "Adjust tints..." option, which displays the UNADJUSTED TINT DENSITIES dialog box shown in Figure 15.12. This dialog box allows you to adjust the density settings for 10% incremental tints of the four process colors (cyan, magenta, yellow, and black) as well as a sample custom color. The values inside each cell may vary between 0.000 and 3.000. Each value represents the densitometer reading for that tint. Densitometer readings may be taken from the *gray bar* included on each separation produced by Separator (see *Margin notes* at the end of this chapter for more information).

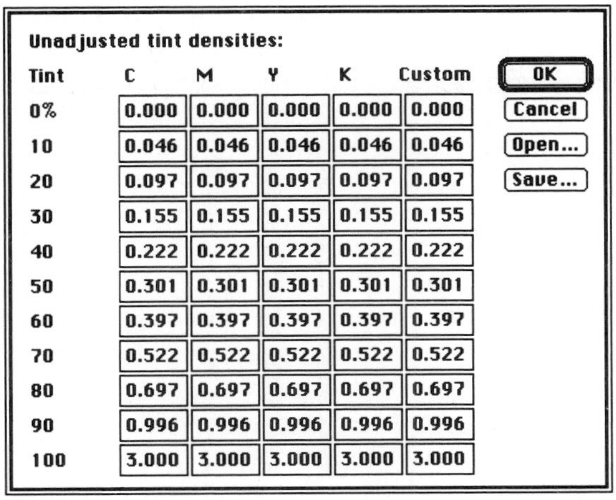

Unadjusted tint densities:

Tint	C	M	Y	K	Custom
0%	0.000	0.000	0.000	0.000	0.000
10	0.046	0.046	0.046	0.046	0.046
20	0.097	0.097	0.097	0.097	0.097
30	0.155	0.155	0.155	0.155	0.155
40	0.222	0.222	0.222	0.222	0.222
50	0.301	0.301	0.301	0.301	0.301
60	0.397	0.397	0.397	0.397	0.397
70	0.522	0.522	0.522	0.522	0.522
80	0.697	0.697	0.697	0.697	0.697
90	0.996	0.996	0.996	0.996	0.996
100	3.000	3.000	3.000	3.000	3.000

OK · Cancel · Open... · Save...

Figure 15.12: The Unadjusted tint densities dialog box allows you to adjust the density settings for the current output device. The large difference between 90% and 100% is typical.

Restoring pop-up menu settings

Choose the U_SE D_EFAULT S_ETTINGS command from the S_ETTINGS menu (⌘-T) to restore all pop-up menus in the S_ETUP window to their original settings.

Bounding box

The "Bounding Box" options allow you to adjust the size of the area Separator allots to the current illustration. The default values represent the smallest *bounding box* that may drawn around the illustration. Margin notes appear in the margins between the bounding box and the page size.

The values in the "Left," "Right," "Bottom," and "Top" option boxes represent the distance from the edge of the page size and the corresponding edge of the bounding box. Therefore, entering smaller values for any of these options will increase the size of the bounding box; entering larger values will shrink the bounding box.

You may also adjust the size of the bounding box by dragging directly on the dotted rectangle that represents the bounding box in the separation preview. Your cursor will change to a two-headed arrow, as shown in the first example of Figure 15.13. All margin notes will move with the bounding box. Or, if you prefer, you may drag the illustration to reposition it within the bounding box. In this case, your cursor will appear as a hand, as shown in the second example of the figure.

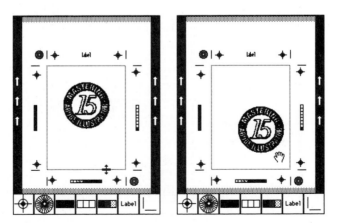

Figure 15.13: Dragging an edge of the bounding box in the separation preview (left) and moving the illustration (right).

Enter a value between 0 and 72 points for the "Bleed" option, which determines the distance between the bounding box and any margin note.

Choose the Use Default Bounding Box command from the Settings menu (⌘-B) to restore the original bounding box and bleed values, as well as the positioning of the illustration in the separation preview.

```
Settings
Use Default Marks          ⌘M
Use Default Settings       ⌘T
Use Default Bounding Box   #B
```

Margin notes

As we mentioned earlier, a variety of *margin notes* are included on each page output from Separator. Each separation includes the following:

- A *page label*, which lists the document name, separation color, line frequency, screen angle, and page number of the separation. This page label is printed both backward and forward, so it may be read either emulsion up or emulsion down.

- The right edge of each page includes a *progressive color bar*, and the left edge includes an *overprint bar*, which is a progressive color bar with process black overprinting all colors.

- Centered on the bottom of the page is a *gray bar* with 10% gradations. You may measure this bar with a densitometer to gauge density readings.

- A *star target* is placed in the upper left and lower right corners of the separation.

- In each corner of the page are both *crop marks*, used to determine the trim size, and *registration crosshairs*, used to help align separations.

Most, if not all, of these margin notes will be used by the commercial printer reproducing your illustration, so be sure that they are not removed when trimming excess paper or film from your printed separation.

Figure 15.14 on the following page shows how the margin notes appear in the separation preview. If you wish to adjust the placement of margin notes, you may do so by dragging them. Press the SHIFT key to constrain your drags. The new coordinates of the margin note will be listed at the top of the preview. You may add a margin note by dragging from one of the icons at the bottom of the preview. The margin note associated with each icon displays when you click on it at the top of the preview. To delete a margin note, drag the item off the window.

Figure 15.14: You may move, add, and delete margin notes in the separation preview.

Choose the Use Default Marks command from the Settings menu (⌘-M) to restore the original margin notes to their original positions in the separation preview.

 If you move, add, or delete a margin note inadvertently or incorrectly, Separator provides an Undo command under its Edit menu (⌘-Z) that allows you to undo the alteration.

Separation techniques

Once the basic parameters of the separations have been set using the options described above, it is time to actually select and print the separations. The number and type of separations that should be created for any document is dependent upon the color printing process that will be used to reproduce the document. There are two ways in which a specific color can be printed on a sheet of paper. Using the first method, *spot-color printing*, inks are pre-mixed to the desired color and then applied to the paper. Spot-color printing is usually used when only one or two colors (in addition to black) are used in an illustration. This printing method is neither exceedingly expensive nor very technically demanding. Spot-color printing allows for precise colors to be selected and applied with perfect color consistency.

In order for an illustration to be reproduced using the spot-color printing process, it must be separated by printing a page for each custom color of ink used in the illustration. Process colors should *not* be used in illustrations that will be printed using the spot-color process, because spot-color separations cannot be created from process colors.

In the alternative printing method, *four-color process printing*, cyan, magenta, yellow, and black ink are blended in specific percentages, to create a visual effect approximating a variety of desired colors. Four-color process printing is technically demanding and tends to be more expensive than spot-color printing. Many commercial print shops do not offer four-color printing services; however, by this process a virtually unlimited number of colors can be produced using only four colors of ink.

Documents that are to be reproduced using the four-color process printing method require four color separations, one for each of the component inks that will be printed. Every colored object in an illustration is broken down into its component color separations, which conform to the original definition of the process color in Illustrator 3.0. For example, Figure 15.15 contains four color separations followed by a monochrome composite print of the image. The square field behind the star in the image is filled with a process color that is defined as 100% cyan, 60% magenta, 0% yellow, and 10% black. It therefore outputs as solid on the cyan separation, a 60% tint on the magenta separation, transparent on the yellow separation, and a 10% tint on the black separation. When these colors are printed in these percentages, the placement of the halftoned dots will visually simulate a deep blue.

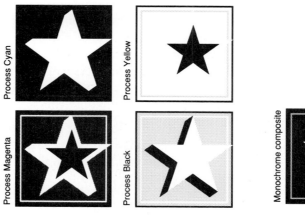

Figure 15.15: Four process-color separations (left) and a monochrome composite (right) of the same image.

It is possible in some cases to combine four-color process printing with spot-color printing. Although this process is more expensive, and is subject to the capabilities of your commercial printer, it provides the advantages of both four-color process (many colors with few inks) and spot colors (precise colors) in one printed piece. Many magazines, for example, are printed using four-color process colors for photos and spot color for advertisements.

In Chapter 11, *Coloring Fills and Strokes*, we discussed the two types of colors used in Illustrator 3.0—process colors and custom colors—and mentioned that, traditionally, process colors are applied to illustrations that will be reproduced using four-color process printing, and custom colors are applied to illustrations that will be reproduced using spot-color printing.

When an illustration is opened in the Adobe Separator, colors that were specified as process colors are automatically prepared for output as four-color separations, and custom colors are prepared for output as additional spot-color separations. It is possible, however, to *decompose* one or more custom colors back into their primary color components (as specified in the CUSTOM COLOR dialog box in Illustrator 3.0) so that they may be output as process-color separations. The following section describes how to decompose custom colors while creating separations.

Defining separations

To define the separations that you wish to print from Separator, click the SEPARATIONS… button in the lower right corner of the SETUP window or choose the SEPARATIONS… command from the FILE menu. The SEPARATION window shown in Figure 15.16 will display. This dialog allows you to change the label, select the process colors that you want to print, and select custom colors that you want to decompose.

Enter a new illustration name in the "Label" option box. This label will print on each separation name with the separation color and other margin notes. By default, the label is the file name under which the illustration is saved. Since file names tend to be rather cryptic, you may want to change the name to something more familiar that will help your commercial printer to keep track of your job.

```
╔═══════════════════════════════════════════════════╗
║ ▣▢▤▤▤▤  Separation: A13.Fig00.Circle15+  ▤▤▤▤ ║
╠═══════════════════════════════════════════════════╣
║  Label:  ┌─────────────────────────────────────┐  ║
║          │ A13.Fig00.Circle15+                 │  ║
║          └─────────────────────────────────────┘  ║
║                                                   ║
║  Process Colors:      Custom Colors:              ║
║                                                   ║
║  ⊠ Cyan          │  ┌─────────────────────┬──┐   ║
║  ⊠ Magenta       │  │ ☐ PANTONE 100 CU   │▲ │   ║
║  ⊠ Yellow        │  │ ☐ PANTONE 166 CU   │  │   ║
║  ⊠ Black         │  │ ☐ PANTONE 211 CU   │▓ │   ║
║                  │  │ ☐ PANTONE 287 CU   │▼ │   ║
║                  │  └─────────────────────┴──┘   ║
║                  │                                ║
║                  │  Selected (grayed out) custom  ║
║                  │  colors will be converted to   ║
║                  │  process colors.               ║
╚═══════════════════════════════════════════════════╝
```

Figure 15.16: The Separation window allows you to
specify the separations that you wish to print.

Select the process colors that you wish to print from the "Process
Colors" check boxes. If one or more process colors are not used in the
current illustration, they will be dimmed.

To decompose a custom color, click on its name in the scrolling
"Custom Colors" list. The color will appear dimmed to indicate that it is
selected. In Figure 15.16, Pantone colors 100 and 211 will be decomposed. Objects in the illustration that were filled or stroked with the custom color will now be included in the four-color process color
separations, just as if they had been defined as process colors. When
decomposing Pantone colors, be aware that because Pantone color standards are created with ink mixtures, the results obtained from four-color
process printing will vary from the Pantone standards.

To prevent a custom color from being decomposed, click on it again
so that it appears black rather than dimmed. In Figure 15.16, Pantone
colors 166 and 287 will not be decomposed.

To select a non-decomposed custom color that you wish to print,
click in its check box to select it. You may not select a decomposed custom color.

Click the close box to confirm your selections and return to the Setup
window. Or you may leave the Separation window open while choosing
commands from the File menu, as described in the next section.

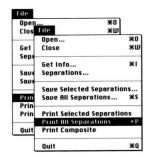

Printing separations

To print only those separations specified in the SEPARATION window, choose the PRINT SELECTED SEPARATIONS command from the FILE menu. A separation will be printed for every process color and every custom color whose check box is selected in the SEPARATION window.

To print all separations, regardless of whether they are selected in the SEPARATION window, choose the PRINT ALL SEPARATIONS command from the FILE menu (⌘-P). Only dimmed colors (process colors that do not exist in the current illustration and decomposed custom colors) will not receive their own separations.

Choose PRINT COMPOSITE from the FILE menu to print the entire document at once—including all process colors and custom colors. This creates a full-color composite on a color printer or a black-and-white composite on a monochrome printer. In either case the result is identical to that obtained by selecting the PRINT... command while inside the Illustrator 3.0 application.

Saving separations

It is also possible to print separations to disk as PostScript files, allowing for easy transport, storage, or modification. To save only those separations specified in the SEPARATION window, choose the SAVE SELECTED SEPARATIONS... command from the FILE menu. A separation will be saved to disk for every process color and every custom color whose check box is selected in the SEPARATION window.

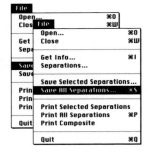

To save all separations, regardless of whether they are selected in the SEPARATION window, choose the SAVE ALL SEPARATIONS command from the FILE menu (⌘-S). Only dimmed colors (process colors that do not exist in the current illustration and decomposed custom colors) will not receive their own separation file.

Getting information

Choose the GET INFO... command from the FILE menu (⌘-I) to display the GET INFO window shown in Figure 15.17. This window contains information about the current illustration. As well as a general information field, the window displays a list of all fonts, tile patterns, and placed EPS documents included in the illustration.

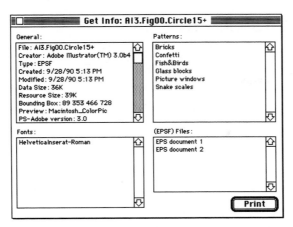

Figure 145.17: The Get Info window contains general information about the current illustrations, as well as lists of fonts, tile patterns, and placed EPS documents that the illustration contains.

Click the PRINT button or press RETURN to print the contents of the GET INFO window. Click the close box in the title bar to close the window.

Quitting Separator

When you have finished working in the Separator utility, choose the QUIT command from the FILE menu (⌘-Q). Control of your computer will be returned to the Macintosh Finder. Changes to the settings, margin notes, and bounding box are automatically saved with any illustration opened inside Adobe Separator.

Installing
Adobe
Illustrator

To use Adobe Illustrator, Adobe Separator, DrawOver, and the Adobe Type Manager, you must *install* these applications onto your Macintosh computer's hard drive. The process is simple, and you have to install each application only once, not every time you want to operate the program. If Illustrator and its related utilities are already installed, you may begin using it as described in Chapter 3, *A Brief Tour of Adobe Illustrator 3.0.*

Taking stock

The Adobe Illustrator 3.0 package includes four 800K disks, which contain the Illustrator application and all accessory files. Each disk and its contents are listed below:

- **Adobe Illustrator Program**. The Adobe Illustrator 3.0 Installer program, a ReadMe file, and TeachText.
- **Adobe Type Manager**. Adobe Type Manager 2.0, FontPorter utility, as well as screen fonts and printer fonts for Courier, Times, Helvetica, and Symbol.
- **Tutorial and Utilities**. Adobe Separator 3.0, DrawOver 2.0, and tutorial files.
- **Gallery**. Sample illustrations and graph designs.

Hardware requirements

Before beginning any installation procedure, it is important that your Macintosh hardware configuration is complete and compatible with Adobe Illustrator 3.0. The following equipment is required:

- A Macintosh Plus or later-model computer.
- 20 megabyte hard drive.
- 2 megabytes of RAM.
- Macintosh System version 6.0.3 or later.
- A PostScript-compatible printer (optional, but highly recommended).

Keep in mind that this is the minimal configuration. A larger hard drive and more RAM will certainly work as well or better. If your computer lacks a hard drive or sufficient RAM, you will need to upgrade your computer. Call your local computer dealer or discount house for more information. If your System Software is too old, you can obtain the newest System Software for a nominal fee from your Authorized Apple Dealer. If you do not own a PostScript printer, you can probably locate a service bureau in your area that will allow you to output your Illustrator files on their PostScript printers for a per-page charge.

The installation process

To use the Adobe Illustrator 3.0 Installer utility to install Illustrator onto your hard drive, power up your Macintosh as normal. If you use any anti-virus programs such as the Symantec Utilities' Shield Init or Symantec AntiVirus Macintosh (SAM) program, you may want to temporarily de-activate these, because the installation process will set them off. It is not required that you deactivate them, but it is a good idea.

Installing Illustrator

Insert the Adobe Illustrator 3.0 Program disk, and double-click on the Installer utility. A dialog box will display, asking you where you want to install the Illustrator 3.0 folder on your hard drive. After specifying a location and pressing RETURN, the *installation screen* will display, as shown in Figure A.01. The horizontal bar fills with gray to demonstrate how much of the installation process has been completed.

Figure A.01: The installation screen indicates how the installation process is progressing.

Throughout the installation process, you may be requested to exchange disks. Do so as prompted. After Illustrator 3.0 has been installed successfully, the installation program will quit and you will be returned to the Finder. A new folder called *Adobe Illustrator 3 folder* will exist at the location you specified on your hard drive. This folder will contain the Illustrator 3.0 application as well as the Pantone Colors file.

Installing Separator and DrawOver

Drag the Adobe Illustrator 3.0 Program disk to the Trash icon at the Finder level to eject the disk. Then insert the Tutorial and Utilities disk. Select both the Adobe Separator and DrawOver files by SHIFT-clicking or marqueeing. Then drag copy both files from the disk to the Adobe Illustrator 3 folder on your hard drive. After the files have copied successfully, drag the Tutorial and Utilities disk to the Trash icon.

Installing PPD files

Insert the Gallery disk, and double-click on the PPD Installer utility. A dialog box will display, asking you where on your hard drive you want to install the PPD folder containing the PostScript Printer Description files used by the Adobe Separator. After specifying a location and pressing return, another installation screen will display, similar to the one shown in Figure A.01. The horizontal bar fills with gray to demonstrate how close the installation process is to completing.

You may also copy the contents of the Gallery disk to the Adobe Illustrator 3 folder by double-clicking the Gallery Installer utility.

Installing Adobe Type Manager

The Illustrator 3.0 package includes Adobe Type Manager (ATM) 2.0, a utility that accurately displays PostScript fonts on your computer screen. The program reads the definition of the typeface provided by the printer font and generates high-resolution characters at any type size in most Macintosh programs.

To install the program, insert the Adobe Type Manager disk. The disk includes the following:

- One ATM control panel device (cdev), called simply *~ATM™*.
- Two ATM driver files, called *~ATM 68000* and *~ATM 68020/030*.
- Screen fonts for the Courier, Helvetica, Times, and Symbol font families, included in a *Bitmapped Fonts* folder.
- Printer fonts for the Courier, Helvetica, Times, and Symbol families.
- The Font Porter utility, which allows you to open screen fonts not loaded into your System file.

You must copy the ATM cdev and one of the ATM drivers to your System folder to install the Adobe Type Manager. If you are using a Macintosh Plus or older model Macintosh computer, a Macintosh SE, or a Macintosh Classic, select both ~ATM™ and ~ATM 68000 and drag-copy these files to the System folder on your hard drive. If you are using a Macintosh SE/30 or one of the Macintosh II series computers, copy the ~ATM™ and ~ATM 68020/030 files to the System folder of your hard drive.

The Adobe Type Manager requires both screen and printer versions of each font that you wish to use. The screen font must be loaded into the System file or attached to the System using a font utility such as Suitcase II or MasterJuggler.

Very likely, you already have installed all the screen fonts that you need. If you have not installed the Courier, Times, Helvetica, or System screen font, open the Bitmapped Fonts folder on the Adobe Type Manager disk and double-click on the screen font suitcase icon that you want to install. The Font/DA Mover window will display, as shown in Figure A.02. Click the Open... button on the right side of the window and locate and open your System file. Select the screen fonts that you want to copy from the scrolling list on the left and click the Copy button to copy them to the System.

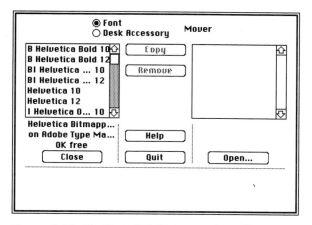

Figure A.02: The Font/DA Move window allows you to copy screen fonts to the System file.

To copy additional fonts to the System, click the left Close button, then click the Open... button and open another screen font suitcase in the Adobe Type Manager disk. When you have finished copying fonts, click the Quit button.

Select all printer fonts on the Adobe Type Manager disk (TimesRom, Helv, Couri, Symbo, and so on) and drag-copy them to the System folder. If you have attached one or more of these fonts using Suitcase II or MasterJuggler, copy the corresponding printer fonts to the same folder that contains your screen-font suitcases.

Now display the Macintosh Control Panel by choosing the CONTROL PANEL command from the APPLE menu. After the Control Panel window displays, scroll all the way to the bottom of the list of icons on the left-hand side of the window and select the ~ATM™ icon. A personalize dialog box will appear, requesting that you enter your name and organization. Type this information and click the OK button. The ATM window will appear, as shown in Figure A.03.

Figure A.03: The Adobe Type Manager control panel device allows you to allot memory for ATM.

The ATM window contains three options. Set them as follows:

- **ATM**. Select "On" to activate ATM; select "Off" to turn it off.

- **Font Cache**. Set the amount of memory that can be used by ATM on a regular basis. A large *font cache* (256K) improves ATM's performance, but takes away memory that could otherwise be used for applications. For best results, set this option to 128K if your computer has 2 megabytes of RAM, set it to 256K or higher if you have more than 4 megabytes of RAM.

- **Preserve**. Select the "Line Spacing" radio button to retain the line breaks and page breaks in documents that were previously opened without ATM. However, the tips of ascenders and descenders of some characters may appear chopped off when using this option. To avoid chopped characters, select the "Character shapes" option. You may have to reformat a few documents, but your printed type will look better.

After you set the ATM options as desired, click the Control Panel close box. An alert box will appear to warn you that you must restart your computer for your changes to take effect. Choose the RESTART command from the SPECIAL menu to restart your computer and load Adobe Type Manager.

You are now ready to begin using Adobe Illustrator 3.0 and its related utilities.

Index

Symbols

30% rule   228

A

A+ Mouse ADB   146
About Adobe Illustrator...
      command   33, 61
activating an endpoint   230
active path   157, 166
Actual Size command   41
actual view size   76
add-point tool   30, 231
additive primary model   399
Adobe Illustrator 1.1 option   522
Adobe Illustrator 3 option   522
Adobe Illustrator 88 option   522
Adobe Illustrator Program disk   556
Adobe Separator   539–553
Adobe Streamline   182–204
Adobe Type Manager   302, 558–561
   control panel window   560
   disk   556
Aldus FreeHand   98, 182, 186, 220,
      251, 390, 472, 516, 522, 526
Aldus PageMaker   34, 317, 535
Aldus Persuasion   475
alert boxes   18
Alignment command   44
alignment point   22, 262
all-or-nothing rule   227
alternate tools   19
Altsys Corporation   516
Apple Color Wheel dialog box   398,
      400
Apple Computer   270
Apple File Exchange   270
Apple menu   33

application RAM   61
arc   103, 140, 152
area chart   485
Area graph option   497
area text block   22, 264
area-graph tool   32, 485
area-type tool   23, 266
Arrange menu   37–39
arrow tool   20, 206
   slot   20
Artwork & Template
      command   40, 46, 79
Artwork board options   93
artwork display mode   40, 79, 123
Artwork Only command   40
artwork-&-template display
      mode   40, 79
ASCII format   270
ATM   558–561
Autotrace over gap
      option   93, 177–179
autotrace tool   24, 173–174
   dragging with   179
   extending a line   181
Average dialog box   38, 246, 251
Average... command   38, 251–257
   along a rotated axis   256
   applying   252–254
   before joining points   245
axis   113
Axis option   47

B

backspace key   48
banding   474
bar-graph tool   31, 479
   slot   31
baseline   23, 263

Q

QuarkXPress   34, 68, 193, 317
QuickDraw   82
QuicKeys   60
Quit command   35, 100

R

radio buttons   17
radius   92, 137
random access memory (RAM)   33
Rectangle dialog box   135
rectangle tool   25, 132
  slot   25
Redo command   35, 257
"Reduce or Enlarge" option boxes   86
reflect   113
Reflect across option   343, 436
Reflect dialog box   437
reflect tool   28, 433
  slot   28
reflect-dialog tool   28, 436
reflection axis   28, 433
reflection origin   433
reflowing a story   282–284
registration crosshairs   547
release   15
Release All Guides command   39, 420
Release Compound command   42, 364
Release Cropmarks command   39, 535
Release Text Wrap command   45, 322
Repeated option   509
Replace existing alert box   98
Reset Toolbox command   32, 46
reshaping   102
  area text paths   273–278
  by adding elements   230–234
  by converting points   237–241
  by deleting elements   234–237
  geometric paths   212–213
  path text paths   285–288
  segments   218–219, 225–229
resolution   93, 544
return key   48
Reverse image option   201
Reversed option   41, 331, 359
RGB color model   398

right cursor arrow key   48
Right option   44
Rotate angle option   343
Rotate dialog box   442
rotate tool   27, 437
  slot   27
rotate-dialog tool   28, 442
rotation origin   27
round cap   373
  option   378
round join   373
  option   380
rounded-rectangle tool   25, 136
RTF (Rich Text Format)   34, 270
ruler guides   39, 418
ruler origin   345, 416
  moving   417
Ruler units options   93
rulers   414–416

S

Same axis both sides option   500
Save All Separations command   552
Save As... command   34, 96
Save changes? dialog box   99
Save command   34, 96
Save converted images option   194
Save illustration dialog box   34, 96,
  187, 521
Save Selected Separations...
  command   552
Scale dialog box   431
Scale line weight option   91
Scale options   343
scale origin   27
scale tool   27, 424
  slot   27
scale-dialog tool   27, 431
scaling   110
scans   67
scatter chart   486
Scatter graph option   497
scatter-graph tool   32, 486
scissors tool   29, 248
  slot   29
screen frequency   332, 544
scroll arrows   70, 78

Also available from BUSINESS ONE IRWIN

Mastering Aldus® FreeHand™

Deke McClelland & Craig Danuloff
ISBN 1-55623-288-8   Order #32888

The PageMaker® Companion
Macintosh Version 4.0

Craig Danuloff & Deke McClelland
ISBN 1-55623-355-8   Order #33558

Painting on the Macintosh®

A Non-Artist's Guide to MacPaint®, SuperPaint™,
PixelPaint™, HyperCard®, and Many Others

Deke McClelland
ISBN 1-55623-265-9   Order #32659

Drawing on the Macintosh®

A Non-Artist's Guide to MacDraw®,
Illustrator®, FreeHand™, and Many Others

Deke McClelland
ISBN 1-55623-415-5   Order #34155

*Purchase these titles at your local bookseller or directly
from BUSINESS ONE IRWIN by calling 1-800-634-3966*